Regulation and Regulators after Global Financial Crises

AF762902

This book provides an original theoretically and empirically grounded analysis of regulatory enforcement activism in post-crisis periods and the ensuing regulatory interactions. It critically addresses the 'more regulation' enforcement agenda relating to financial misconduct in the aftermath of the 2008 financial crisis, showing how misconduct was constructed through the enforcement policies and practices of the powerful UK financial conduct regulator and its interactions with the subjects of enforcement proceedings and their legal representatives during a tumultuous time in the financial markets. Drawing from interviews with regulators, professional intermediaries, and markets participants; documentary analysis of enforcement decisions and speeches; and observations, the volume adopts an interdisciplinary approach grounded in social constructivist perspectives on compliance and deviance, regulation theory, and socio-legal research. Through a multi-dimensional analytical framework of regulatory enforcement activism that links shifts in regulatory policymaking; experimentations with legal powers in information-gathering, legal and extra-legal penalties, and individual accountability; and the use of enforcement tools in micro-level interactions, the book documents a more interventionist and punitive post-crisis enforcement agenda. The findings challenge current thinking in the 'scandal and reform' literature. The work argues that despite the increased focus on enforcement, it is not necessarily the case that the power has tilted more towards the regulator. This fine-grained socio-legal enquiry makes innovative and timely theoretical contributions to our understanding of the limitations of regulatory activism and regulatory control, regulatory relationships, the governance of financial markets, and broader thinking on regulating corporations and the individuals within them. It will appeal to academics, researchers, regulators, and policymakers working in regulation across law, criminology, sociology, and politics.

Aleksandra Jordanoska is Senior Lecturer at the Dickson Poon School of Law, King's College, London.

Regulation and Regulators after Global Financial Crises

Enforcement and Adaptation

Aleksandra Jordanoska

Routledge
Taylor & Francis Group
LONDON AND NEW YORK

First published 2025
by Routledge
4 Park Square, Milton Park, Abingdon, Oxon OX14 4RN

and by Routledge
605 Third Avenue, New York, NY 10158

Routledge is an imprint of the Taylor & Francis Group, an informa business

British Library Cataloguing-in-Publication Data
A catalogue record for this book is available from the British Library

ISBN: 978-1-138-47816-9 (hbk)
ISBN: 978-1-032-94426-5 (pbk)
ISBN: 978-1-351-06932-8 (ebk)

DOI: 10.4324/9781351069328

Typeset in Galliard
by Apex CoVantage, LLC

Contents

Abbreviations

APER	Approved Persons Regime
CASS	client assets
CFTC	Commodities and Futures Trading Commission
COBS	Conduct of Business Sourcebook
COCON	Code of Conduct for Staff Sourcebook
DEPP	Decisions Procedure and Penalties Manual
DoJ	Department of Justice
EFCD	Enforcement and Financial Crime Division
EG	Enforcement Guide
EURIBOR	Euro Interbank Offered Rate
FCA	Financial Conduct Authority
FIT	Fit and Proper Test for Employees and Senior Personnel
Forex	Foreign Exchange Market
FOS	Financial Services Ombudsman
FSA	Financial Services Authority
FSMA	Financial Services and Markets Act 2000
LIBOR	London Interbank Offered Rate
MAR	Market Abuse Regulation (Regulation (EU) No 596/2014)
PCBS	Parliamentary Commission on Banking Standards
POCA	Proceeds of Crime Act 2002
PPI	payment protection insurance
PRA	Prudential Regulation Authority
RDC	Regulatory Decisions Committee
SEC	Securities and Exchange Commission
SFO	Serious Fraud Office
SIF	significant influence function
SROs	self-regulatory organisations
STOR	suspicious transaction and order report
SYSC	senior management arrangements, systems, and controls
TSC	Treasury Select Committee

Figures

Tables

Tables of cases

Belize Alliance of Conservation Non-Governmental Organisations v Department of the Environment of Belize [2004] UKPC 6
Bilta (UK) Ltd v Royal Bank of Scotland Plc [2017] EWHC 3535.
Chaligne, Sejean, and Diallo v FSA [2012] UKUT B21 (TCC)
Digicel v Cable & Wireless LLC [2008] EWHC
Fieldglen [2009] EWHC 1939 (Ch), 30
Financial Conduct Authority (Appellant) v Macris (Respondent) [2017] UKSC 19
FSA v Westcott 2003 WL 22187694 (Ch D)
Hearts of Oak Assurance Co Ltd v A-G [1932] AC 392
In re Pergamom Press Ltd [1971] 1 Ch 388
K Ltd v NatWest [2006] 4 All ER 907
Legal & General Assurance Society Ltd v FSA [2005] UKFSM 11
Pottage v FSA FS/2010/33
Pottage v FSA FS/2010/33
R (Amro International SA) v FSA [2010] EWCA Civ 123
R (on the Application of AL) v. SFO [2018] EWHC 856 (Admin).
R (on the application of Prudential plc & anor) (appellants) v Special Commissioner of Income Tax & anor [2013] UKSC 1
R (on the application of Prudential plc & anor) (appellants) v Special Commissioner of Income Tax & anor [2013] UKSC 1
R (SFO) v Airbus SE (Statement of Facts)
R (SFO) v Guralp Systems Limited (Statement of Facts)
R v Anjam Ahmad [2010] (unreported)
R v Calvert [2010] (unreported)
R v McQuoid (Christopher) [2009] EWCA Crim 1301
R v Mustafa & others [2012] (unreported)
R v Rollins, R v McInerney [2010] UKSC 39
R v Sanders & others [2012] (unreported)
Re Barings plc (no. 5) [2000] 1 BCLC 523
Serious Fraud Office (SFO) v Eurasian Natural Resources Corp. Ltd [2018] EWCA Civ 2006 (5 September 2018)

Serious Fraud Office (SFO) v Eurasian Natural Resources Corporation Ltd [2017] EWHC 1017 (QB) (8 May 2017)
Sharma v FSA [2010] FS/2010/0008 (Upper Tax and Chancery Tribunal).
Stewart Owen Ford and Mark John Owen v the Financial Conduct Authority [2018] UKUT 0358 (TCC)
Three Rivers DC v Bank of England (Disclosure) (no. 4) [2004] UKHL 48 610, [10]
Three Rivers DC v Governor and Company of the Bank of England (no. 5) [2003]
Three Rivers District Council v Governor and Company of the Bank of England (no. 6) [2004], [102]
Three Rivers District Council v Governor and Company of the Bank of England (no. 5) [2003] QB 1556 ('Three Rivers (no. 5)

Tables of legislation

Statutes

Bank of England and Financial Services Act 2016
Consumer Rights Act 2015
Criminal Justice Act 1993 (Part V)
Enterprise Act 2002 (Part 8)
Financial Services and Markets Act 2000
Financial Services Act 2010
Financial Services Act 2012
Financial Services (Banking Reform) Act 2013
Police and Criminal Evidence Act 1984
Proceeds of Crime Act 2002

Statutory instruments

Money Laundering Regulations (MLRs) 2017 (As Amended in 2019)

EU directives and regulations

Directive 2014/65/EU of the European Parliament and of the Council of 15 May 2014 on markets in financial instruments and amending Directive 2002/92/EC and Directive 2011/61/EU (MiFID)
Market Abuse Regulation (Regulation (EU) No 596/2014

Acknowledgements

This book has been many years in the making and has benefited greatly from the assistance of numerous people. I would first like to acknowledge and immensely thank all the participants in the study, who I cannot name for ethical research reasons, for allowing me to gather a glimpse into their world.

I am especially grateful to Peter Alldridge and Kate Malleson for many insightful conversations, numerous comments on earlier drafts, and their unwavering support and encouragement over the years. I would like to particularly acknowledge the support by Kate, who has been an incredible mentor and role model, generously commenting on versions of the book and always making sure that I 'push through' with it. The research that forms the basis of the book benefited from feedback by Julia Black and Michael Levi, as well as from many conversations or comments on drafts by Julija Brsakoska-Bazerkoska, Fanny Froelich, Karin Kuhlemann, Nick Lord, Lavinia Maddaluno, Shavana Musa, Melissa Rorie, Judy Rifeser, Gabi Rusu, Reka Solymosi, Carla Teteris, Judith van Erp, Ana Alba Betancourt, Leonidas Cheliotis, Miso Dokmanovic, Lauren B. Edelman, Neil Gunningham, Fiona Haines, Biljana Jadrovska, Christine Parker, Filip Ristevski, Jodie Short, Laureen Snider, and James W. Williams. Any shortcomings of the text are, of course, solely my ownership. Special thank-you to Robin Calendar-Smith for 'infecting' me with the desire to know what happens in the confidential City regulators world, and to Bob Ferguson for facilitating some of that access.

The research at the heart of the book has received funding from Queen Mary, University of London, for which I am extremely grateful. Some of the work was written while I was a visiting PhD student at the Regulatory Institutions Network (RegNet) at the Australian National University; a visiting scholar at the Centre for the Study of Law and Society, University of California, Berkeley; and a visiting scholar at the Centre for Socio-Legal Studies, University of Oxford.

At Routledge, Alison Kirk and Anna Gallagher managed the manuscript submission with professionalism and immense patience and generosity, for which I am truly thankful.

My profound gratitude goes to my parents, Mito and Marija, for their constant encouragement and care from afar, and especially to my sister, Ele, for her admirable performance on the tedious task of tracing down the journal issue numbers of my references, amongst other caring support.

Finally, I cannot express how thankful I am to my family, my husband, Philip, and daughters, Kalina and Iskra. As well as showing great emotional support and love, Philip read the whole manuscript and provided sometimes devastating but always spot-on criticism. I thank Kalina for sustaining the writing of this book with her laughter and wonderful personality, and baby Iskra for bringing us joy during the final edits of the manuscript. This book owes much to their patience.

1 Introduction

This book investigates the enforcement of regulation relating to financial misconduct in the aftermath of the 2008 financial crisis. It examines how financial misconduct was constructed through the enforcement policies and practices of the UK financial regulator, and its interactions with the subjects of enforcement proceedings during a tumultuous time in the financial markets. It is, in essence, a book about the storm after the storm. More broadly, it is a socio-legal enquiry into the manipulations of the boundary between lawful and deviant activity through the administrative law process.

The effect of the financial crisis was to throw economies around the world into recession and to trigger an industry regulation meltdown. It put the industry and its participants on both sides of the regulatory relationship into the spotlight, with accusations that the 'regulators were asleep at the wheel' (Treasury Committee, 2012a: Q123), and of 'individuals with no principles' in the market (Sants, 2009a). By 2010, calls for 'more regulation' in the financial markets were widespread, prompting a sea change in the politics of regulation – a radical reform in response to the crisis conditions.

The reform process offers a 'laboratory for scholars' (Moschella & Tsingou, 2013) interested in regulation broadly and in the regulation of financial services specifically. This book investigates the 'more regulation' enforcement agenda launched in the aftermath of the crisis in the UK markets through a case study of the enforcement of financial regulation by the Financial Conduct Authority (FCA). The study draws on original and in-depth empirical research conducted between 2012 and 2018. It therefore provides a historical account of the patterns of regulatory change and interactions in the enforcement of financial regulation in the crisis aftermath – issues of intrinsic scholarly interest in their own right. Beyond this, the study also has crucial implications for our understanding of current and future regulatory relationships, the governance of financial markets, and broader thinking on regulation. Through investigating a particularly turbulent period of regulatory activism, the book makes innovative and timely theoretical contributions to complex debates over how to regulate markets, organisations, and individuals within them.

I use constructivist tools to consider some of the most important questions in regulation theory, such as regulatory dynamism, and the process of shaping

DOI: 10.4324/9781351069328-1

of (il)legitimate behaviour in the markets through enforcement practices. The book asks: What are the facets of regulatory enforcement dynamism in post-crisis periods? Have financial regulators moved towards a more activist or punitive agenda, and in what ways? What have been the responses by the subjects to enforcement actions and their representatives to post-crisis regulatory enforcement policies and practices? The book addresses how regulatory policies and interactions in the enforcement process restructure in the aftermath of crises, contributing towards constructing misconduct or (il)legal behaviour in finance.

This book offers a fuller and empirically grounded account of the nature of reform and dynamism in the regulatory process in the aftermath of crises, and the associated factors, actors, and resources employed by both regulators and regulated operators (regulatees). It focuses not directly on examining past regulatory failure, which is a common topic for research in the aftermath of significant scandals, but on examining the ways in which regulators reconceptualise their role, design ways to address perceived past failures, and the ways in which this shifts the boundaries of (il)legitimate behaviour in the markets. The study investigates the legal, organisational, and policy reactions; the changes in enforcement techniques and strategies and the reorientations in the philosophy that underlines the enforcement of financial regulation by national regulators; and the ensuing responses by the financial services industry. It presents a detailed picture of how various actors interact to affect the content of regulatory enforcement policies and practices, and the ways in which these interactions contribute towards constructing misconduct in finance. The book also engages with broader questions of the role of third-party stakeholders in the enforcement of the law, with a particular focus on the role of the legal profession.

The central argument of the book is that in the post-crisis period, the enforcement of financial regulation in the UK markets became more intrusive, intense, and punitive, evidenced by an aggressive regulation style and the expansion of a policy of 'credible deterrence', increased demands by the regulator for information, heightened control of corporate managers, and increased penalties for non-compliance. The response of regulated organisations and their legal representatives to the more interventionist regulatory agenda was to develop strategies of adaptation and resisting a deviant label in the guise of 'creative compliance', detection avoidance through detection facilitation, and constructing non-compliance, notably through the careful management of the self-reporting process, the negotiation of the wording of enforcement notices, and techniques for softening the liability of senior managers. Paradoxically, the effect of the more punitive approach was to promote strong cooperative relationships managed through regulatory conversations tightly controlled on both sides by regulatory lawyers. I argue that the negotiation and cooperation practices need to be understood in the context of a highly reputation-sensitive environment, in which the regulator and regulated benefited from a process of *mutual risk mitigation* through which credibility and trust were fostered on both sides. The regulatory game may have become more complicated and played out against changed regulatory conditions, yet not much changed in the power balance and the types of relationships between the same key players.

Regulatory games:[1] the social construction process

This book understands the law not as given but as shaped by, and emerging from, social interactions. It sees deviance not as static (as, for example, in positivist criminology) but as intrinsically connected to the social control apparatus of regulatory enforcement and it sees compliance as achieved through regulatory interactions. To this end, the research is rooted in, and merges perspectives from, social constructivist approaches to both compliance and deviance, regulation theory, and the socio-legal tradition of empirical research on 'law in action' and regulatory enforcement 'on the ground'. These theoretical perspectives enable also a 'grounded' theory approach towards discovering theoretical constructs from the data (Glaser & Straus, 1967).

Regulatory misconduct as an institutional product

Social constructivist perspectives, in the ways in which they have been separately used in the disciplines of regulation theory, deviance studies, and the sociology of finance, essentially talk about the same processes of attaching meanings to behaviour, relationships, objects, or fields. I draw on and develop these perspectives to argue that financial misconduct is a constructed business behaviour through regulatory enforcement policymaking and organisational practice and within regulatory interactions.

In the field of deviance studies, social constructivism has addressed the ways in which state categories and administrative systems construct crime and deviance as 'social problems' (Chambliss, 1964; Sumner, 2007; Muncie, 2011). Criminality and deviance must be understood as a dynamic *social construct* defined and modified through the *processes* of signified interactions between the individual and the audience that s/he is exposed to (Becker, 2008; Erikson, 1964; Lemert, 1951, 1972; Schur, 1971; Tannenbaum, 1951). The book adapts this view to the regulatory space, turning the gaze towards the 'institutions that lay claim' (Doyle et al., 2011) to regulatory misconduct. To paraphrase Ericson, Barry, and Doyle's tenets on the nature of crime, regulatory misconduct is an 'artefact of how a [regulatory] institution organizes to deal with it: [misconduct] is literally "made" through the risk management practices of the [regulatory] institution concerned' (2000: 535).

1 The reference to the 'regulatory game' does not mean that I employ a game theory approach, as in the rational choice analysis of public bureaucracy. It rather refers to the 'mouse and cat' game of interventions by regulators and of counterlearning and evasion responses by the regulated (Picciotto, 2007; Lodge & Wegrich, 2010).

The applicability of this view to organisational deviance has been emphasised by Ermann and Lundman (2002: 28), who argue that 'organizational actions are deviant only to the extent that they are perceived, reported, defined, accepted, and treated as deviant'. Therefore, whether an organisational action actually comes to be seen as deviant is dependent on official identification, determination, and enforcement processes and is fundamentally a matter of definition (Chambliss, 1964; Findlay, 2000; Ermann & Lundman, 2002: 27), since no deviance is intrinsically deviant. A complementary view is promoted by sociologists of financial markets, with suggestions that enforcement activities are directly involved in the drawing and redrawing of the very boundaries between illegitimate and legitimate activity on which 'finance' and 'markets' depend (Knorr-Cetina & Preda, 2005; Preda, 2009; Williams, 2012).

In the current study, it is the financial regulator which defines and treats organisational behaviour as deviant. Regulatory enforcement actions are still the dominant social control mechanism of corporate crime and other misconduct in the financial markets (Pontell & Geis, 2014; Pontell et al., 2014; Sutherland, 1983). Whether organisational actions become 'labelled and penalised as deviant depends on the power of the accusers to make their label stick' (Ermann & Lundman, 2002: 36). Did the power tilt more towards the regulators' side after the financial crisis, as the scandal and reform literature would suggest? How were these power relations deconstructed and reconstructed at the field level?

The book applies these arguments in conjunction with the regulatory literature on policymaking in organisations to examine the claims-making process of regulatory enforcement philosophies. One of the arguments of labelling theory is that at a macro-societal level, legal punishment also causes crime through the process of criminalisation (Taylor et al., 1973). A similar effect is achieved through drafting regulatory policies that designate certain business behaviour as misconduct that requires the expenditure of resources and regulatory attention in detecting, investigating, and sanctioning. Such processes can be most readily observed in periods of significant reforms and changes in policies. Chapter 2 examines this claims-making process in the crisis aftermath through changes in the FCA's enforcement policy towards a policy of 'credible deterrence.'

The social construction process and regulatory interactions

The book then extends social constructivist approaches by shifting the analysis from the macro-level of constructing social problems (organisational policy changes) to the micro-level processes of interactions between the regulator and the regulated (when regulators are acting upon the claimed social problem of financial misconduct and the need to enforce against it). This shift of levels is necessary to understand the construction of social problems and deviance, as the process does not finish with introducing organisational responses but also with implementing them in micro-level human interactions.

Enforcement activities take place in a complex web of interactions in which the meaning of regulation is shared, discussed, and contested. Within these 'regulatory conversations' (Black, 1997) or 'regulatory negotiations' (Reichman, 1992), the perceptions and understandings by both regulators and parties to enforcement provide the context in which law is understood and negotiated to meanings in practice (Black, 2002; Gilad, 2014; Lange, 1999). The ultimate product of these negotiations, interactions, and compromises among regulators, respondents, and various professional intermediaries constructs the meaning of compliance with the law (Edelman, 1992; Lange, 1999; Williams, 2012; Parker & Nielsen, 2009; Jordanoska & Lord, 2022; Picciotto, 2007; Reichman, 1992).

This means that in the claims-making process, the claims-making organisation and its staff are not the sole proprietors in structuring behaviour as misconduct. On the contrary, the micro-level interactions can be interconnected, multilateral, and communicational in the sense that both the organisation and the signified 'deviants' can and do participate in the process of construction and claim ownership of the same social problem. However, depending on the context, the participation of each of the parties to the process can vary, with some 'deviant' groups being able to participate and influence this process to a greater degree than others. The levels of influence depend on the relative power, resources, and extent of social embeddedness of the deviant: whilst alcoholics (Gusfield et al., 1984) and juvenile delinquents (Becker, 2008; Cohen, 1972) represent relatively disempowered groups, large financial institutions and their senior managers possess economic, legal, and human capital to participate actively in the process of avoiding their behaviour being constructed as 'deviant'. The organisational deviance-defining process is an 'exchange of claims and counterclaims' (Ermann & Lundman, 2002: 27) and of accusations of deviance (by prosecutors, media, or victims) and organisational responses with own assertions and version of events. For example, in her research on tax avoidance, McBarnet (1991: 323) found that the location of a transaction on the right (tax evasion) or wrong side (tax avoidance) depends on the labelling decision-making of those enforcing the law, but 'the boundaries can be stretched not just by regulators but also by the regulated'. To a varying degree, and depending on the political environment, powerful actors are able to influence this process, both to avoid being subjected to the societal reaction and to receive a more lenient treatment if this cannot be avoided.

The issue of who claims 'ownership' of a social problem, and how they claim it, is closely related to the question of constructing the financial misconduct that is revealed in the public domain and accessible to external audiences (other regulated subjects, social control agents, and the public at large). Publicity, public scrutiny, and political and media pressures represent a key consideration into the shaping of the meaning of the law for all stakeholders in the enforcement process. Regulators are deeply political entities (Hutter & Lloyd-Bostock, 2017; Short, 2021) and reputation-sensitive. In the sphere of regulation and litigation involving corporations and their principals, public outcomes and images are paramount to corporate reputation and thus fiercely debated and contested (Fisse & Braithwaite, 1983; Levi, 2006; Simpson, 2002). Within the regulatory interactions, frequently, the underlying process is one of managing stigma and working diligently to escape a deviant label (McBarnet, 1991; Ermann & Lundman, 2002).

This study draws on these perspectives to develop theoretical, socio-legal constructs on the enforcement of regulation. The realities of regulatory enforcement are the product of a joint enterprise in which there are power struggles at different points in the relationship and in which the power shifts between regulators and the regulated with differing dynamics. I argue that adaptation and resistance to deviant labels by the regulated can occur in regulatory enforcement through *mutual risk mitigation*, *detection avoidance through detection facilitation*, and *constructing non-compliance*. These processes do not exhaust all manners of organisational responses and interactions but emerge as pertinent from the empirical research. *Mutual risk mitigation* allows for cooperative regulatory interactions to be understood in the backdrop of a highly reputation-sensitive environment against which the regulator and regulated hedge risks to manage perceptions – each other's and from wider audiences. Regulators and regulated alike benefit from the process of mutual risk mitigation as it fosters credibility and trust on both sides of the relationship. The concept of *detection avoidance* was originally developed by Sanchirico (2006) to highlight that evidence is not only something that investigators uncover but also something that violators cover up. I expand upon this construct with the argument that, paradoxically, on occasion, avoiding detection can be facilitated by practices that enable detection. Through *constructing non-compliance*, the private sector attempts, with varying degrees of success, to construct the misconduct that ultimately reaches public consumption.

The role of legal intermediaries

The final contribution of this book is its engagement with the classic concerns of socio-legal scholarship regarding the involvement of legal actors in producing the 'life of the law'. It is critical to include a broader view of participants in the regulatory process rather than just the dichotomy of regulator–regulated, especially in the contentious regulatory process. Key stakeholders in the enforcement process in the financial markets are various types of professionals; prominent amongst these are lawyers (Black et al., 2007; McCahery & Picciotto, 1995; Snider, 2009; Williams, 2008, 2012; Clark et al., 2021).

Lawyers and lawyering play key roles in managing and creating ambiguity in the enforcement of legal provisions. Lawyers can be contributors to creative compliance, for example, with tax provisions (McBarnet, 1991) and through financial engineering, as seen in the financial crisis (McBarnet, 2010). The social interactions in the enforcement of financial regulation act as mechanisms by which normative and cognitive frameworks are formed both within and outside organisations, creating epistemic communities of legal experts whose ideas can exert a strong influence on behaviour within organisations, within markets, and on policymakers (Black, 2013: 427). This role extends to broader white-collar crime defence matters. Lawyers often perform an 'information-control' function by 'keeping information out of the forum of legal argument' (Mann, 1985: 16), or by controlling regulators' access to information for the benefit of the corporate case (Jordanoska, 2021).

The legal profession represents a crucial aspect of what Reichman (1992) has recognised as 'professional embeddedness' (also, Jordanoska, 2021). Professional embeddedness is a key part of the firm's regulatory authority, or 'the ability to assign legal significance to one's actions, to set the rules of the game . . . in regulatory negotiations' (Reichman, 1992: 256). This regulatory authority can be purchased by contracting the big law firms to take advantage of their authority and influence. The current study discusses the deployment of expert legal knowledge and the reliance on social and professional networks and professional authority to participate in the process of constructing (non) compliance. This is also how lawyers build professional authority through their ideological claims (Sarat & Felstiner, 1995; Shamir, 1995) of appropriate actions and through promoting the discourse of being indispensable for the regulatory relationship. This influence should be viewed within the professional trends of increasing specialisation of lawyers and sections of law firms into contentious regulatory matters and the fact that issues that might lead to litigation are outsourced to external law firms.

Regulatory enforcement as a multi-dimensional and interactionist construct

The book focuses on the enforcement of financial regulation by a state regulator, and for this purpose, it is suitable to employ the following operational definition of *financial regulation*:

1. The activity of using the law for the sustained and focused control and constraint of the activities of business
2. Performed by the state
3. Performed through a specialist regulatory agency
4. Performed with respect to regulating activities in financial markets that might run counter to what the legislature determines to be broader community values, and undertaken through promulgation of rules, accompanied by mechanisms for monitoring and enforcement of sanctions for their breaches

(Black, 2002: 35–45; Croall, 2003: 46; Grabosky & Braithwaite, 1986: 3; Hawkins & Hutter, 1993; Kagan, 1984: 61; Selznick, 1985: 363)

Financial regulation is a wide governance system covering diverse activities, such as banking, securities, insurance, mortgage provision, derivatives, investment and wealth management, and related fields. It includes frameworks on the soundness and financial health of financial institutions (prudential regulation) and on the conduct of business by financial institutions. The discussion in this book examines regulatory enforcement of conduct of business regulation: the rules on the sale and provision of financial products and services for the purpose of consumer and investor protection, the rules on the operation of trading markets and financial intermediaries for the purpose of market integrity and efficiency, and the rules on the prevention of financial crime by financial institutions.

Regulatory enforcement is the process of detecting a rule breach, investigating the facts of the rule breach, and imposing penalties on the rule-breaker, with the aim of seeking to gain compliance with regulation. This book advances a concept of regulatory enforcement that is multi-dimensional and interactionist in nature by connecting the agency-level regulatory enforcement style and the day-to-day processes in the enforcement of regulation. It draws from May and Burby's (1998; also May & Winter, 1999, 2000, 2011) arguments that regulatory enforcement operates against a combination of macro- and micro-levels of decision-making that seeks to bring about compliance with regulations: enforcement philosophy, strategy, and style (May & Burby, 1998; also, May & Winter, 1999, 2000, 2011). It further expands this framework by including the concept of regulatory conversations – critical at the frontline level of inspectors' behaviour.

The agency's enforcement philosophy is the most abstract level of decision-making (May & Burby, 1998), framing the contours of its strategy and style. I argue that the enforcement philosophy is shaped, formulated, and promulgated through the agency's enforcement policy. The policymaking process concerns decisions about the substantive direction to the legal mandate of a regulatory agency, how regulatory programmes are to be enforced, and how the discretion of regulatory officials is to be managed (Hawkins & Thomas, 1989a: vii; 1989b: 23). The understanding of the complex relationship between policy formation, implementation, and the enforcement of legal rules gives an insight into '*how* regulators actually regulate' (Hawkins & Thomas, 1989a: viii).

An agency's enforcement philosophy is formed along the continuum of negotiation, persuasion, and compliance approaches, or deterrence and punishment approaches (May & Burby, 1998). The debate on the assets and flaws of both is long-standing and has been extensively rehearsed (see Hawkins, 1990, 1991; Pearce & Tombs, 1990, 1991, McMullan & Perrier, 2002; Gray, 2006; Gunningham, 2010; Tombs & Whyte, 2013). Here, it is important to sketch these arguments briefly to be able to understand the nature of the pre- and post-crisis enforcement approach of the UK conduct of business financial regulator.

The compliance school views the regulated as 'political citizens', 'generally disposed to obey the law' (Kagan & Scholz, 1984: 75). In dealing with them, regulators must act as politicians to secure conformity with law. Amicable social relationships are valued, as they contribute to remedying harm, assisting with the discovery of future problems, and detecting future violators (Gunningham, 2010; Hawkins & Thomas, 1984). The techniques employed to persuade business to comply are heavily reliant upon 'privately practiced, low-visibility bargaining and bluffing' (Hawkins & Thomas, 1984: 14). As the compliance strategy focuses on achieving the broader aims of the legislation through correcting problems, not through punishment, the recourse to the formal legal process is a matter of last resort (Hawkins, 2002). Various empirical studies have showed that this negotiated justice system is the dominant enforcement style among regulatory agencies (e.g. Cranston, 1979; Hawkins, 2002; Kagan, 1984, 2000; Snider, 1993, though see Bardach & Kagan, 1982). However, also drawing from empirical evidence, severe criticisms have been levied on its usage. Authors have argued that relying on persuasion strategies underestimates the reality of imbalances of power between regulators and business. Relying on larger resources, knowledge, and expertise, industries can exert significant power over their environment, leading to regulatory capture (Pearce & Tombs, 1990, 1991; Tombs & Whyte, 2015). Regulatory capture is the 'result or process by which regulation, in law or application, is consistently or repeatedly directed away from the public interest and toward the interests of the regulated industry, by the intent and action of the industry itself' (Carpenter & Moss, 2013: 13). The significant resort to bargaining creates problems of control and accountability (Hawkins & Thomas, 1984).

The deterrence school views the causes and control of corporate crime as influenced by the social, economic, and political structures of capitalism (Gray, 2006; Snider, 1990). Regulatory offenders act as 'amoral calculators' (Kagan & Sholz, 1984: 67) who, motivated by instrumental incentives, break the law to maximise profits. The usage of swift, highly likely, and punitive sanctions would therefore act as powerful instrumental disincentives. In consequence, its proponents advocate a 'Regulator-as-Policeman-Strategy' (Kagan & Scholz, 1984), with punitive policing deemed as 'necessary, desirable and practicable' (Pearce & Tombs, 1990: 440). Several authors have suggested that the deterrence doctrine works well in the explanation of compliance with laws in the business sphere (Braithwaite & Geis, 1982; Hopkins, 1980; Snider, 1990; Tombs & Whyte, 2013). However, the empirical support is equivocal with inconsistent findings on the effect of formal sanctions and social disapproval as deterrents (see Braithwaite & Makkai, 1991; Gunningham et al., 2005; Haines, 1997; Makkai & Braithwaite, 1994; Paternoster & Simpson, 1996).

The agency's enforcement strategy, the second level of abstraction, is reflected in three sets of agency-level choices guided by the agency's philosophy: tools of enforcement (use of sanctions and incentives), priorities for enforcement (whom to target and what to inspect for), and the degree of effort in carrying out enforcement (the allocation and leveraging of resources) (May & Burby, 1998; May & Winter, 1999). Sparrow (2000) terms these as parts of the 'regulatory craft'. Some of these choices have been specifically examined in the context of the FCA's predecessor, the Financial Services

Authority (FSA), as an indicator of its 'regulatory intensity' through measuring the 'inputs' (resources in budget and staff) and 'outputs' (actions brought and sanctions imposed) (Coffee, 2007; Jackson, 2005, 2007). These quantitative studies on the pre-crisis FSA designate its enforcement philosophy as predominately compliance-oriented (Armour, 2008; Coffee, 2007), aligned with an overall 'light touch' approach to regulation. Chapter 2 examines the post-crisis changes in the financial regulator's enforcement philosophy towards a 'credible deterrence' enforcement policy, and the associated enforcement tools and priorities of enforcement.

The third, least-abstract level consists of the agency's in-the-field practices, such as the enforcement styles of individual inspectors (May & Burby, 1998; May & Winter, 2000). But this level should also be viewed as interactionist in nature, as it incorporates the day-to-day interactions of staff, regulatees, and intermediaries, including the adaptation and influence of regulatees' activities in steering enforcement. Chapters 3, 4, 5, and 6 examine these micro-level interactions at distinct points in the enforcement conveyor belt.

The financial crisis and the regulatory 'pendulum'

While it is recognised that a complex mix of political, economic, and market causes precipitated the 2008 financial crisis (Dorn, 2014; Davies, 2015; Ferran et al., 2012; Engelen et al., 2011; Lounsbury & Hirsch, 2010), deficient regulations and regulatory oversight represented a crucial contributing causal factor. Structurally and ideologically, the pre-crisis ethos of, and political pressures for, an extensive deregulation in finance and the reigning of the Chicago and Austrian schools of neoliberal economics notion of the free market (Lounsbury & Hirsch, 2010) produced and tolerated a market that was mostly left to its devices and where, accordingly, enforcement actions were rarely undertaken (Dorn, 2011). By way of example, the pre-crisis UK championed a 'light touch' regulation approach towards the financial markets, spurred by the drive to promote London as a global financial capital (Zimmerman, 2010). 'Light touch' regulation encapsulated a liberally regulated market with various incentives towards attracting capital and investment in finance. 'Light touch' regulation also permeated supervisory and enforcement matters, with a little appetite for an expansive control and inquisitiveness over financial institutions (Black, 2008, 2011; Coffee, 2007; Davies, 2015; Ford, 2008; Jackson, 2005; MacNeil, 2007; Tomasic, 2011).

Financial deregulation and weak or inadequate regulatory enforcement are structural causal factors for financial misfeasance, as well-documented by research on major financial debacles, such as the savings and loans scandals in the 1980s United States (Calavita & Pontell, 1990; Calavita et al., 1997). These were equally documented as structural causes to several levels of misbehaviour that preceded and contributed to the 2008 financial crisis: mortgage frauds, securities regulation breaches, and prudential regulation breaches (Barak, 2012; Carswell & Bachtel, 2009; Nguyen & Pontell, 2010;

Simpson, 2011; Shover & Grabosky, 2010; Will et al., 2013). Research by Carswell and Bachtel (2009) on mortgage fraud in the United States revealed that the lack of punitive enforcement created a sense among offenders that committing a mortgage fraud was a 'zero-risk' venture (also Braithwaite, 2010; Nguyen & Pontell, 2010). Deregulatory legislation was also accompanied by the acceptance of various practices of 'creative avoidance', 'gaming of the law', and 'legal engineering' by powerful financial institutions (Deakin, 2013; McBarnet, 2010) regarding securities and prudential regulation requirements.

The most damning indictments regarding financial regulators' failures over the pre-crisis events are that they simply relinquished their duties because they were captured by the industry (Fligstein & Goldstein, 2010). This is particularly with regard to the complex derivatives of the mortgage-based securities (MBS) market, where regulators enacted financial reforms that expanded the MBS market and allowed the largest banks to operate virtually without any controls (Lounsbury & Hirsch, 2010). The politics of deregulation also stymied regulators' preparedness to probe the industry, as regulators were often criticised by politicians for any perceived 'strong-arm' questioning of industry practices (Davies, 2015). This led to deference to banks' business strategies (Black, 2012, 2013) and few challenges of their organisational risk-taking and decision-making.

Additional criticisms were levied as to regulators' knowledge as a contributory supervisory failure to the crisis. Financial regulators operate against an informational asymmetry regarding the markets and corporations they supervise. The size of the industry, the rapid pace of market growth, innovation and complexity, and the growing scale of 'financial citizenship' challenge regulatory capacity to understand and make the regulated key proprietors of knowledge and expertise. The regulated community is too extensive to be thoroughly supervised, especially through close and ongoing supervisory relationships (Kingsford Smith, 2011), as suggested by the proponents of responsive regulation models (Ayres & Braithwaite, 1992). This is compounded by the growth of retail consumers, as these 'financial citizens' (Gray & Hamilton, 2006) are less capable of identifying misbehaviour and serving as a source of information and prevention. The relentless process of innovation often leaves regulators behind (Ford, 2017). Investment products are highly complex, based on mathematical formulas and speculative trading associated with gambling with future assumptions (MacKenzie, 2008; Esposito, 2011). New technologies continuously reshape the provision of financial services (Arner et al., 2017), disrupting the 'status quo' and known ways of operating in the markets. Breaches may be committed on the back of technically complex practices, of which supervisors may be unaware or lack the necessary IT skills to detect (Williams, 2009). For example, market manipulation may be committed through high-frequency trading (HFT) by programming complicated algorithms that beat 'ordinary' buy orders by a fraction of a second (Snider, 2013; Yadav, 2016), including through machine learning.

Regulatees are therefore the principal proprietors of information about the risks of products and market conduct practices. Regulatees are also often the key proprietors of technical expertise associated with the interpretation and analysis of this information (Ferran, 2004), especially if they are large firms (e.g. Arup, 2010) or financial industry groups (Pagliari & Young, 2014). The industry is an indispensable source of information for regulators, but this also pushes them to 'govern at a distance' in both time and space (Black, 2013) and in an uncertain environment.

The crisis laid bare the harmful consequences of limited regulatory knowledge. Regulators had an inadequate understanding of the level of complexity and interconnectedness of the retail and wholesale financial markets, as well as of the nature and risks behind the securitised subprime mortgage products (MacNeil & O'Brien, 2010; Levitin, 2014; Tett, 2010). Adequate information could not be gathered due to pre-existing problems in the calibration of the risk assessment framework, creating a myopia on where to look for problems (Black, 2013; Dorn, 2011). The inability and the lack of organisational capacity to gather appropriate information on the markets, the financial institutions, and their products, coupled in many circumstances with the overall trend of downsizing in regulatory resources, led to significant informational asymmetries between the two sides of the regulatory relationship. Black (2013) has suggested that this imbalance led to the regulators not so much being captured as being 'conned and cowed', but that is not the full story. Operating within the 'light touch' regulation approach, the pre-crisis FSA supervisors also failed to request adequate information on institutional practices and business models in the prudential sphere (Turner, 2009), though empowered with extensive information-gathering powers.

In the aftermath of crises, past regulatory failures commonly come to the fore. Decision-makers then commonly seek to reconceptualise their role and to design ways to address past shortcomings. Responses commonly entail swinging the 'regulatory pendulum' away from the industry-sympathetic and towards the pro-regulation peak in the regulatory cycle. Indeed, numerous studies have shown how agencies oscillate between pro-regulation and pro-industry dispositions, depending on current political appetites and agendas and political responses to crises (e.g. Bernstein, 1955; Boyer, 1989; Braithwaite, 2008; Haines, 2011b; Snider, 1990, 2009; Hutter & Lloyd-Bostock, 2017). For states and policymakers, post-crisis regulatory reform is continuously attractive as they 'demonstrate their sincerity in providing a sufficient response to tragedy and future threat' (Haines, 2011b: 6). Additionally, regulatory agencies are deeply political entities regarding their relationship with the environment in which they operate and in how they respond to heightened criticism after regulatory failures.

The crisis aftermath reactions and calls for re-regulation have led scholars to suggest that the regulatory pendulum in finance has also moved away from 'deregulation, self-regulation, and market discipline to a more assertive and interventionist role' (Moschella & Tsingou, 2013: 409) for regulators.

Set against these assumptions, the present study examines how the post-crisis period of dynamic changes led to a new organisational mandate and to shifts in regulators' attitudes towards enforcing regulation and securing compliance. It goes further than the standard focus on regulatory reform by looking not only into whether the power has tilted more towards the regulators' side but also equally into how post-crisis regulatory enforcement policies and practices have been intercepted by the subjects to enforcement and their representatives, and how the regulator–regulatees interactions have been deconstructed and reconstructed at the field level.

The Financial Conduct Authority

The focus of the empirical work presented in the book is the FSA/FCA, the most powerful regulatory agency in the UK (Macrory, 2006). This section describes the origins, structure, and powers of the FCA during the research period 2012–2018. It provides a targeted discussion on its risk-based and principles-based supervisory model and its supervisory and enforcement powers, which will be further explored in the subsequent chapters through their implementation in practice.

A brief organisational history

The FCA was originally established as the Financial Services Authority (FSA) under the Financial Services and Markets Act (FSMA).[2] Its establishment in 1997 was a prime example of state regulation penetrating a hereto self-regulated market with a grand entry (see further Ferran, 2003; FSA, 2000). FSMA gave the FSA a status of a 'super-regulator', both in terms of the breadth of its jurisdiction and in terms of its oversight powers. As the single regulator of the financial services industry, the FSA was entrusted with a broad remit to regulate, authorise, and supervise all providers of financial services in the UK (banks, insurance companies, investment and securities firms, mortgage providers, etc.) across prudential and conduct of business matters, and it also assumed responsibility as the UK Listing Authority (UKLA).

The financial crisis exposed the need for substantive overhaul of regulatory regimes, and in many jurisdictions, this meant strengthening of regulatory requirements (e.g. the US Frank–Dodd Act 2010). In the UK, this also meant organisational reshuffles, which led to the break-up of the FSA in April 2012 into two new bodies. These were entrusted with oversight of different aspects of financial regulation: the Prudential Regulation Authority (prudential and liquidity regulation of the largest and systemically important financial institutions) and the FCA (conduct of business regulation and prudential oversight

2 See on the predecessor SROs: Black (1997).

of less-systemically important institutions).[3] In addition, the FCA inherited many of the FSA's market functions (Ferran, 2011), all its enforcement powers, and importantly, its Enforcement and Financial Crime Division (EFCD), the organisational enforcement staff. Therefore, the research straddles the enforcement practices of both the FSA and the FCA. In the subsequent chapters, reference will be made to the FCA when discussing FCA enforcement practices, to both the FSA and FCA when discussing an organisational trend that stretches across the life of the two organisations, and to the FSA only when discussing historic developments of policies and use of powers.

Supervisory model: risk-based and principles-based regulation

Supervision of the financial markets is one of the FCA's main statutory responsibilities under Section 1L FSMA. The FCA is mandated with the single strategic objective of ensuring that the retail and wholesale markets under its supervision function well. Within this, it has further operational objectives: consumer protection, protecting the integrity of the UK financial system, and promoting effective competition in the interests of consumers.

The FCA's supervisory philosophy is risk-based and principles-based (Black, 2005; FCA, 2013, 2019; Ferran, 2011; Gray & Hamilton, 2006; MacNeil, 2010). Risk-based frameworks rely primarily on selectively targeting supervisory and enforcement resources based on an assessment of the degree of risk to their objectives by a regulated entity rather than on seeking to secure compliance with all rules by all firms (Black, 2004a, 2005; Black & Baldwin, 2010). The origins of risk-based supervision of the UK financial markets go back to the establishment of the FSA as the single regulator of all financial services. Due to the broad regulatory remit and the fact that the FSA was compiled of several predecessor authorities, each with a different set of objectives, techniques, and priorities (Black, 2004b: 20), the then FSA adopted a new and overarching risk-based approach to regulation and supervision (FSA, 2000). Risk-based regulation was also kept in the new PRA and FCA institutional regime. What changed, however, were the technical details of the risk assessment framework and the framework implementation attitudes along the lines of a more interventionist supervisor philosophy, detailed in Chapter 3.

Until the financial crisis, the UK was championed as the world's principles-based regulation (PBR) leader, with its regime dubbed as a competitive advantage to other financial markets (principally New York) (Baldwin et al., 2012; Ford, 2008). However, the credit crunch crisis brought to light the failures not only of rules-based regimes but also of PBR, with the FSA seeing 'its vaunted principles-based approach to regulation fall into as much reputational disrepute as that country's leading banks' (MacNeil & O'Brien,

3 With the Financial Services Act (FSA) 2012. See further, Hopper and Black (2010); Ferran (2011, 2012).

2010: 2). Despite the criticisms of the FSA's PBR failings, the new FCA retained a strong PBR commitment with a move towards 'more principles-based regulation' (FSA, 2008).

A formal PBR was achieved through the specific provision of the Principles for Business[4] in the Handbook, drafted as general statements of 'the fundamental obligations of firms under the regulatory system'.[5] The principles are 'applicable in new or unforeseen situations',[6] and despite the fact that some of the Handbook rules might further specify the implementation of a principle, these do not exhaust the reach of the principles themselves. The FCA can bring an enforcement action on the basis of a breach of a principle alone,[7] and the FSA started enforcing principles-only breaches before the crisis (Cole, 2006; Black, 2008). Therefore, they have the potential of a powerful enforcement tool, with one caveat: to establish liability for a principle breach, the FCA must show that the firm had been at fault in some way.[8]

The substantive facets of the FCA's principles-based regime are reflected in the requirements for firms to think through how to comply rather than being instructed in detail (Black et al., 2007; Black, 2008). The regulator provides the guidance, and the regulated have broader discretion as to how to implement the spirit of the principles through devising own systems and procedures. Connected to this is the use of management-based and meta-regulatory approaches (Coglianese & Lazer, 2003; Coglianese & Mendelson, 2010; Gilad, 2010; Parker, 2002) through the reliance on senior management to be engaged in the regulatory process and on achieving outcomes rather than processes of compliance. As firms are required to devise compliance systems, the primary role of the FCA becomes that of 'regulating at a distance', taking the necessary action to ensure that the organisations' systems and oversight mechanisms are working effectively (Coglianese & Mendelson, 2010; Parker, 2002).

4 Conducting business with integrity (Principle 1); conducting business with due skill, care, and diligence (Principle 2); conducting business with reasonable care, responsible control, and adequate risk management systems (the 'systems and controls' principle) (Principle 3); financial prudence (Principle 4); proper market conduct (Principle 5); due regard of customers' interests, and treating them fairly (the 'treating customers fairly' principle) (Principle 6); clear, fair, and not misleading communication with clients (Principle 7); fair management of conflicts of interest (Principle 8); suitability of advice and discretionary decisions (Principle 9); adequate protection for clients' assets (Principle 10); open and cooperative dealing with the FCA and reporting anything of which the regulator would reasonable require a notice (Principle 11). In 2023, consumer duty was added as Principle 12.

5 FCA Handbook Prin 1.1.2G.

6 FCA Handbook Prin 1.1.9G.

7 The principles do not give rise to actions for damages by a private person (FCA Handbook Prin 3.4.4R), and there can be no civil suits for redress on the basis of a principles-only enforcement action.

8 FCA Handbook Prin 1.1.7G.

Principles-based regulation also impacts enforcement work. The reliance on principles might ease enforcers' work in constructing evidence that a breach has occurred due to their less-prescriptive nature (Ford, 2008). However, principles may also hinder enforcement work, as frontline inspectors might prefer to rely on 'clear' breaches of detailed rules, thus eliminating opposition by business (Black et al., 2007; Haines, 2011b). Scholars have also argued that principles are more apt to avoid creative compliance, in which business actors formally comply with the wording but avoid the spirit of the law (Black et al., 2007; Ford, 2008; McBarnet, 1991).

Supervisory and enforcement powers

The FCA has extensive powers of gatekeeping the entry to the UK financial markets and to detect, investigate, and sanction financial misconduct. It acts as a gatekeeper through its licensing or authorisation regime – granting permissions to firms to carry out regulated financial activities. The FCA also vets and approves the appointment of individuals to the most senior decision-making roles in authorised financial firms.[9]

The regulator has vast information-gathering powers during both the supervisory process and formal investigations, with a significant potential to contribute to overcoming the information asymmetry inherently present in the regulatory process (Manning, 1989). The FCA supervisory tools of inspection rest on the powers to request information[10] and on information provided from the industry on a regular or incidental basis. The FCA can use the statutory information-gathering powers and the principles and rules that impose requirements to be open and cooperative with the regulator[11] during supervision and enforcement activities only against the regulated sector. The compulsory regular sources of information from the industry are regulatory returns (RMAR, annual compliance reports, and other regulatory reporting obligations) and transaction reporting.[12] Regulatees also need to submit suspicious transaction and order reports (STORs), which are mandatory requirements[13] on an authorised firm to inform the FCA where it suspects that market abuse may have occurred, either by itself, its clients, or a counterparty. Finally, there are requirements to report prescribed incidental matters[14] and a general obligation under Principle 11 to report anything of which the regulator would reasonably expect notice.

9 Section 59 FSMA.
10 Section 165 FSMA.
11 FCA Handbook Principle 11, APER 4 or Conduct Rule 3.
12 FCA Handbook SUP 17A.
13 Under Article 25 Directive 2014/65/EU of the European Parliament and of the Council of 15 May 2014 on markets in financial instruments and amending Directive 2002/92/EC and Directive 2011/61/EU (MiFiD) for all prescribed financial instruments.
14 FCA Handbook Chapter SUP 15.

Investigations concern the process of evidence construction (Shapiro, 1984), and the FCA has wide information-gathering powers in this respect:[15] document and information requests, interviews against a wider range of subjects,[16] and search and seizure powers.[17] The FCA can rely on third-party collection of relevant information by directly appointing or mandating a regulated firm to appoint a skilled person, with significant investigative powers, to compile a specified report.[18] The breadth of the investigative powers and the low thresholds in exercising them indicate that little can be done by targets to dissuade their exercise. These assumptions are challenged in Chapter 4.

The FCA is also a powerful regulator in terms of its administrative, civil, and criminal powers. The FCA disposes with extensive sanctioning powers that can be used in an enforcement pyramid manner (Ayres & Braithwaite, 1992), ranging from informal private warnings to potentially unlimited formal fines. The mildest action that the FCA enforcement could undertake is to issue a private warning, essentially a letter setting out the issue and concerns over the conduct but stating that no conclusive findings on whether a breach took place are made against the target.[19] Fines and public censures can be imposed on regulated firms for breaches of the principles and the Handbook rules and on regulated and unregulated firms for breaches of the market abuse regime.[20] Individuals can be fined or censured for being involved in the firm's misconduct (either knowingly or by failing to prevent the misconduct), for breaches of the approved persons regime (APER; only regulated individuals), or for breaches of the market conduct regime (everyone).[21] Fines and public censures are decided on the same considerations. The difference between the two is in the level of seriousness (fines are issued for more serious behaviour) and the punitive elements (public censures are solely public reprimands, whilst fines impose monetary costs).[22] The FCA may impose prohibition orders on

15 Investigations into non-compliance can be undertaken on the satisfaction of very low statutory thresholds: if it appears to the FCA that there is a good reason for doing so, or if it appears to the FCA that circumstances suggest that the specified misconduct had occurred. Sections 168(1), 168(2) FSMA.

16 The document and information requests and interviewing powers are supported by very low statutory thresholds for exercising them: (1) an objective standard: a reasonable belief that the information is relevant; (2) subjective standards: belief that the information is necessary and expedient, and the even lower subjective standard of a belief that the information is or may be relevant. Sections 169–170, 171(1)(a) and 171(2) FSMA.

17 The FCA cooperates with the police in search and seizure activities upon a warrant (Section 176 FSMA and Section 16 Police and Criminal Evidence Act 1984).

18 Section 166 FSMA.

19 FCA Enforcement Guide 7.15.

20 Sections 205–206 FSMA.

21 Sections 66, 66A and 206 FSMA.

22 The FCA's other administrative powers under FSMA are temporary suspensions of the permission to carry out regulated business (s. 206A(1b)), variation of permissions (s. 55J), and withdrawal of approvals (s. 63). It can apply for civil remedies and can criminally prosecute several offences under FSMA and under the Money Laundering Regulations (MLRs) 2017

individuals to ban them from the financial markets due to lack of integrity or incompetence.[23] It also has 'creative powers' to advertise enforcement actions, continuously extended through statutory changes (explored in detail in Chapter 5).

During the research period, the FCA's enforcement docket was quite varied. As in the study of the Securities and Exchange Commission (SEC) by Shapiro (1984) in the 1980s, the FCA's enforcement docket included offences by huge corporations and small businesses, by individuals and organisations, of long and short duration, of vast and narrow geographic scope, of witting and unwitting victims, and of no victims at all. Investigations could be undertaken into a range of regulatory contraventions and criminal offences. These could be divided into five general areas according to the nature of the harm. Retail cases focused on consumer protection and failures regarding offering services to consumers, such as mis-selling or consumer fraud. Client assets cases focused on failings regarding the proper segregation of client money from the firm's own funds. Wholesale markets cases focused on proper market conduct, including cases of 'mismarking' trading positions, issues with transactions reporting, benchmarks manipulation cases and other market manipulation, and insider dealing,[24] where the FCA is the lead prosecutor. Systems and controls cases reflected the FCA's crime prevention mandate and the meta-regulatory transmission (Jordanoska, 2018) of that mandate to firms by the rules requiring them to have systems and controls against the risk of being used for financial crime or regulatory contraventions. These cases focused on failings in the firm's control environment rather than on specific infractions. Finally, 'perimeter' cases involved persons providing unauthorised financial services, usually investment scams, such as boiler rooms or crypto investment scams.

Organisational structure

Of the FCA divisions, the supervisory and enforcement staff were most immediately involved in the enforcement process, though at different stages in the enforcement conveyor belt. Supervisory staff were primarily involved at the stage of detecting misconduct, whilst the enforcement division conducted formal investigations and imposed regulatory sanctions. At the time of research, the Enforcement and Financial Crime Division (EFCD) included the following divisions: Retail and Regulatory Intelligence Division (Retail 1 [large firms], 2 [medium firms], and 3 [smaller firms]); Wholesale, Unauthorised Business, and Intelligence (Wholesale 1 and 2); Financial Crime (Policy

(As Amended in 2019). After *R v Rollins, R v McInerney* [2010], it could potentially prosecute any offence as a private prosecutor.

23 Section 56 FSMA.

24 Section 52 Criminal Justice Act 1993 (Part V).

and Risk, Specialist Supervision, and FIN-NET); Market Oversight (Market Monitoring and the UK Listing Authority); Strategy and Delivery Division; and Legal Department. The book examines the activities and decision-making processes of these FSA/FCA organisational parts.

Within each division, case allocation was undertaken by the head of the division, who, at the end, also 'challenged' the evidentiary strength of the case and the proposed penalty. Investigations were conducted by a multidisciplinary team: lawyers, a paralegal and business support person, and in particularly challenging cases, a legal technical specialist or an e-discovery professional. The team was headed by a project manager, responsible for the day-to-day running of the case. Investigative practices represented part of a common enforcement culture with department-level standard approaches to the exercise of FSMA powers. Despite the industry or misconduct-type specialisation of different EFCD divisions, investigators followed similar procedures when using investigative powers. The joint enforcement culture was a product of several organisational factors. The EFCD had a highly hierarchical structure, with the director of enforcement a strong organisational leader and policy-maker.[25] Numerous interviews suggested that the director was seen as the 'face' of the FCA enforcement policy. Enforcement policies were transmitted and reaffirmed through monthly meetings of the director and the heads of the various enforcement divisions, at which both the docket and policies were discussed. Additionally, there was a common internal movement of enforcement staff across different misconduct areas. Staff specialised in, and acquired skills of, investigating different types of misconduct whilst sharing a common enforcement philosophy.

Research methodology

The data in this study is drawn from a larger empirical project on the enforcement of financial regulation in the UK markets 2012–2018 that used a combination of methods: a series of semi-structured interviews with regulators, professional intermediaries, and market participants; documentary analysis; and observations from public industry events (n = 12) and hearings at the Upper Tribunal (Tax and Chancery Chamber) (n = 2). Interviewing, archival, and observational methods complement each other as they provide an insight into the static and dynamic elements of enforcement work (Shapiro, 1984, also McCaffrey & Hart, 1998; van Erp, 2011a).

Data from semi-structured interviews form the crux of this research. In total, 61 in-depth, semi-structured interviews were conducted with 56 individuals in the period of late 2012–2015 and in 2017–2018. The pool of interviewees was assembled by purposive sampling and snowball sampling. The informants were selected on the basis that they were knowledgeable about

25 My own experience of negotiating access to staff through the director confirmed this.

financial regulation, willing to talk (not organisationally constrained against talking with 'outsiders'), and representative of a range of viewpoints, in line with the interactionist theoretical framework. This produced a diverse sample of informants: 25 current and former FCA enforcement staff (20 of these were currently working in private practice, so they were also interviewed regarding the legal advocacy employed on the defence side); 15 regulatory contentious lawyers involved in FCA proceedings; 7 managers or in-house compliance officers in sanctioned firms and 3 previously approved individuals; 6 'knowledgeable' informants, for example, industry consultants.[26] Most current and former FSA/FCA staff who were interviewed represented senior or experienced enforcement officials. Regulatory lawyers were interviewed as key intermediaries in the enforcement process in the financial markets (Black et al., 2007; Williams, 2012). The interview schedule was tailored to explore the key factors identified in the literature. The flexibility and reflexiveness of a semi-structured interview prompted discussion on a great variety of issues within the few prepared questions on the enforcement regime and regulatees' responses. All interviewees were guaranteed anonymity. The quotes in the book are represented under pseudonyms, indicating the profession of the respondent at the time of interview (e.g. Regulator; Lawyer [private practice]; LawyerFR [lawyer and former regulator]).

The documentary analysis consisted of coding of final notices ($N = 625$) and speeches ($N = 76$) for the period 2008–2017. Final notices are the public product of a formal FCA enforcement proceeding, setting out the breaches, penalties, and procedures through which these were imposed.[27] The notices were coded for categories of misconduct, violated regulations, types of regulatory interactions, and considerations in the penalty process. Speeches by senior FCA officials are regulatory tools that the FCA uses to convey their official policy (Black, 2005). The documentary analysis also included secondary data analysis of enforcement performance accounts (2004–2017) and analysis of legislative parliamentary debates, policy documents, and industry responses to consultation papers. The observations served to provide backdrop insights into the dynamics of regulatory enforcement and to offer a glimpse into the views of the legal 'practitioner communities' (Williams, 2012: 25) on enforcement policies channelled at industry events.

Organisation of the book

Chapter 2 analyses the regulatory ideas, factors, and actors that have driven the change of the FSA/FCA's enforcement policy towards a more aggressive

26 The 2017–2018 interviews included respondents and follow-ups from the first two categories only.

27 Required under s. 390 FSMA.

regulation style and the expansion of the agency's policy of 'credible deterrence'. It builds the argument that, in the post-crisis period, the enforcement of financial regulation became more intrusive, intense, and punitive, based on organisational and policy changes, associated regulatory ideas, and the formal outcomes of the regulator's decision-making. The analysis here contextualises the discussion in the rest of the book.

Chapter 3 examines the increased demands by the regulator for information and the focus on self-reporting by regulatees of their own non-compliance as evidence of the more intrusive and intense enforcement style. Yet the responses of the regulated sector were ones of adaptation through creative compliance, ***constructed non-compliance***, and ***detection avoidance through detection facilitation.*** I argue that the process of ***mutual risk mitigation*** accounts for the increased information requests and the types of responses and devices developed by financial institutions to information provision.

Chapters 4 and 5 explore enforcement against corporate targets. Chapter 4 depicts the context of formal investigations and the confidential settlements which remained to be largely cooperative despite the more punitive regulatory agenda. The processes of ***mutual risk mitigation*** and ***constructing non-compliance*** are further examined in Chapter 5, where the focus is on using reputation as a resource in the governance of financial markets. The chapter engages with movements towards an increased use of disclosure and reputational sanctions as an enforcement regulatory strategy, alongside rising financial penalties and the ensuing corporate responses to manage stigma within the discussions on settling enforcement outcomes.

Chapter 6 moves the focus to the post-crisis regulatory transformation towards a more interventionist and punitive engagement with corporate managers in financial institutions. The first line of enquiry examines the development of a stricter gatekeeping function during approving individuals to senior management roles. The second examines the enforcement strategies (and private industry responses) towards increased investigations and sanctioning of corporate managers.

Chapter 7 concludes by drawing together the main arguments and themes across the book, returning to the wider questions about the facets of regulatory activism in post-crisis periods, whether and how the financial regulator moved towards a more activist or punitive agenda, and how the regulatory interactions were restructured in the crisis aftermath. The chapter discusses the implications of the theoretical and empirical analysis in the book for the regulatory project more broadly, in particular, for the notions of 'more regulation', the limitations of regulatory enforcement activism in post-crisis periods, and the role of regulatory intermediaries and regulatory architectures. It also outlines future research proposals for achieving deeper engagement with the regulatory games played by both the regulator and the regulatees, and some implications for the policy agenda.

Bibliography

Armour J (2008) Enforcement Strategies in UK Corporate Governance: A Roadmap and Empirical Assessment. *ECGI – Law Working Paper No. 106/2008*. Available at: http://papers.ssrn.com/sol3/papers.cfm?abstract_id=1133542.

Arner DW, Barberis JN and Buckley RP (2017) FinTech, RegTech and the Reconceptualisation of Financial Regulation. *Journal of International Law and Business* 37(3):371–413.

Arup C (2010) The Global Financial Crisis: Learning from Regulatory and Governance Studies. *Law & Policy* 32: 363–381.

Ayres I and Braithwaite J (1992) *Responsive Regulation: Transcending the Deregulation Debate*. Oxford: Oxford University Press.

Baldwin R, Martin C and Martin L (2012) *Understanding Regulation: Theory, Strategy, and Practice*. Oxford: Oxford University Press.

Barak G (2012) *Theft of a Nation: Wall Street Looting and Federal Regulatory Colluding*. Lanham, MD: Rowman & Littlefield Publishers.

Bardach E and Kagan R (1982) *Going by the Book: The Problem of Regulatory Unreasonableness*. Philadelphia: Temple University Press.

Becker SH (2008) *Outsiders: Studies in the Sociology of Deviance (ED)*. New York: The Free Press.

Bernstein MH (1955) *Regulating Business by Independent Commission*. Princeton, NJ: Princeton University Press.

Black J (1997) *Rules and Regulators (Oxford Socio-Legal Studies)*. Oxford: Oxford University Press.

Black J (2002) Regulatory Conversations. *Journal of Law and Society* 29(1): 163–196.

Black J (2003) Enrolling Actors in Regulatory Processes: Examples from UK Financial Services Regulation. *Public Law* 47: 62–90.

Black J (2004a) Law and Regulation: The Case of Finance. In: Parker C, Scott C, Lacey N and Braithwaite J (eds) *Regulating Law*. Oxford: Oxford University Press, 33–59.

Black J (2004b) *The Development of Risk Based Regulation in Financial Services: Canada, the UK and Australia*. London, UK: ESRC Centre for the Analysis of Risk and Regulation, London School of Economics and Political Science.

Black J (2005) The Emergence of Risk-Based Regulation and the New Public Management in the UK. *Public Law* (Autumn): 512–549.

Black J (2008) Forms and Paradoxes of Principles-Based Regulation. *Capital Markets Law Journal* 3(4): 425–457.

Black J (2011) The Rise, Fall and Fate of Principles-Based Regulation. In: Kern A and Moloney N (eds) *Law Reform and Financial Markets (Elgar Financial Law Series)*. Cheltenham, UK: Edward Elgar Publishing, 3–34.

Black J (2012) Paradoxes and Failures: 'New Governance' Techniques and the Financial Crisis. *Modern Law Review* 75(6): 1037–1063.

Black J (2013) Reconceiving Financial Markets – From the Economic to the Social. *Journal of Corporate Law Studies* 13(2): 401–442.

Black J and Baldwin R (2010) Really Responsive Risk-Based Regulation. *Law and Policy* 32(2): 181–213.

Black J, Hopper M and Band C (2007) Making a Success of Principles-Based Regulation. *Law and Financial Markets Review* 1(3): 191–206.

Black WK (2005) *The Best Way to Rob a Bank Is to Own One: How Corporate Executives and Politicians Looted the S&L Industry*. Austin: University of Texas Press.

Boyer B (1989) The Federal Trade Commission and Consumer Protection Policy: A Postmortem Examination. In: Hawkins K and Thomas J (eds) *Making Policy in Regulatory Bureaucracies*. Pittsburgh: University of Pittsburgh, 93–132.

Braithwaite J (2008) *Regulatory Capitalism: How It Works, Ideas for Making It Work Better*. Northampton, MA: Edward Elgar Publishing.

Braithwaite J (2010) Diagnostics of White-Collar Crime Prevention. *Criminology & Public Policy* 9(3): 621–626.
Braithwaite J and Geis G (1982) On Theory and Action for Corporate Crime-Control. *Crime & Delinquency* 28(2): 292–314.
Braithwaite J and Makkai T (1991) Testing an Expected Utility Model of Corporate Deterrence. *Law & Society Review* 25(1): 7–40.
Calavita K and Pontell H (1990) 'Heads I Win, Tails You Lose': Deregulation, Crime and Crisis in the Savings and Loan Industry. *Crime and Delinquency* 36(3): 309–341.
Calavita K, Tillman R and Pontell HN (1997) The Savings and Loan Debacle, Financial Crime, and the State. *Annual Review of Sociology* 23: 19–38.
Carpenter D and Moss D (2013) *Preventing Regulatory Capture*. Cambridge: Cambridge University Press.
Carswell AT and Bachtel DC (2009) Mortgage Fraud: A Risk Factor Analysis of Affected Communities. *Crime, Law, and Social Change* 52: 347–364.
Chambliss W (1964) A Sociological Analysis of the Law of Vagrancy. *Social Problems* 12: 67–77.
Clark T, Moorhead R, Vaughan A and Brener A (2021) Agency Over Technocracy: How Lawyer Archetypes Infect Regulatory Approaches: The FCA Example. *Legal Ethics* 24(2): 91–110.
Coffee JC, Jr (2007) Law and the Market: The Impact of Enforcement. *University of Pennsylvania Law Review* 156(2): 229.
Coglianese C and Lazer D (2003) Management-Based Regulation: Prescribing Private Management to Achieve Public Goals. *Law & Society Review* 37(4): 691–730.
Coglianese C and Mendelson E (2010) Meta-Regulation and Self-Regulation. In: Baldwin R, Cave M and Lodge M (eds) *The Oxford Handbook of Regulation*. New York: Oxford University Press.
Cohen S (1972) *Folk Devils and Moral Panics*. London: MacGibbon & Kee.
Cole M (2006) *Enforcement: Priorities and Issues for 2006 (Speech)*. Available at: https://webarchive.nationalarchives.gov.uk/ukgwa/20121210232133/http://www.fsa.gov.uk/library/communication/speeches/2006/0411_mc.shtml.
Cranston R (1979) *Regulating Business: Law and Consumer Agencies*. Oxford: Centre for Socio-Legal Studies.
Croall H (2003) Combating Financial Crime: Regulatory Versus Crime Control Approaches. *Journal of Financial Crime* 11(1): 45–55.
Davies H (2015) *Can Financial Markets Be Controlled?* Cambridge and Malden, MA: Polity Press.
Deakin S (2013) The Legal Theory of Finance: Implications for Methodology and Empirical Research. *Journal of Comparative Economics* 41(2): 338–342.
Dorn N (2011) Reconstructing "Conflict of Interest" in Financial Markets: Private Management, Public Challenges, Future Prospects. *International Journal of Law, Crime and Justice* 39(3): 161–173.
Dorn N (2014) *Democracy and Diversity in Financial Market Regulation* (1st ed.). Routledge.
Doyle A, Chan J and Haggerty KD (2011) Transcending the Boundaries of Criminology: The Example of Richard Ericson. In: Bosworth M and Hoyle C (eds) *What is Criminology?* Oxford: Oxford University Press, 286–297.
Edelman LB (1992) Legal Ambiguity and Symbolic Structures: Organizational Mediation of Civil Rights Law. *American Journal of Sociology* 97(6): 1531–1576.
Engelen E, Ertürk I, Froud J, Johal S, Leaver A, Moran M, Nilsson A and Williams K (2011) *After the Great Complacence: Financial Crisis and the Politics of Reform*. Oxford: Oxford University Press.
Ericson R, Barry D and Doyle A (2000) The Moral Hazards of Neo-Liberalism: Lessons from the Private Insurance Industry. *Economy and Society* 29(4): 532–558.

Erikson KT (1964) Notes on the Sociology of Deviance. In: Becker H (ed) *The Other Side: Perspectives on Deviance*. New York: The Free Press, 9–21.
Ermann MD and Lundman RJ (2002) Introduction. In: Ermann MD and Lundman RJ (eds) *Corporate and Governmental Deviance: Problems of Organizational Behavior in Contemporary Society* (6th ed.). New York: Oxford University Press.
Esposito E (2011) *The Future of Futures. The Time of Money in Financing and Society*. Cheltenham: Edward Elgar.
FCA (2013) *The FCA's Approach to Advancing Its Objectives*. Available at: www.fca.org.uk/static/documents/fca-approach-advancing-objectives.pdf.
FCA (2019) *FCA Mission: Approach to Supervision*. Available at: www.fca.org.uk/publication/corporate/our-approach-supervision-final-report-feedback-statement.pdf.
Ferran E (2003) Examining the UK Experience in Adopting the Single Financial Regulator Model. *Brooklyn Journal of International Law* 28: 257–307.
Ferran E (2004) *Building an EU Securities Market*. Cambridge: Cambridge University Press.
Ferran E (2011) Break-up of the Financial Services Authority. *Oxford Journal of Legal Studies* 31(3): 455–480.
Ferran E (2012) The New Mandate for the Supervision of Financial Services Conduct. *Current Legal Problems* 65(1): 411–453.
Ferran E, Moloney N, Hill JG and Coffee JC, Jr (2012) *The Regulatory Aftermath of the Global Financial Crisis*. Cambridge University Press.
Findlay M (2000) *The Globalisation of Crime*. Cambridge: Cambridge University Press.
Fisse B and Braithwaite J (1983) *The Impact of Publicity on Corporate Offenders*. Albany, NY: State University of New York Press; Braithwaite, 1989.
Fligstein N and Goldstein A (2010) The Anatomy of the Mortgage Securitization Crisis. In: Lounsbury M and Hirsch PM (eds) *Markets on Trial: The Economic Sociology of the US Financial Crisis*. Bradford: Emerald Group Publishing Limited.
Ford CL (2008) New Governance, Compliance, and Principles-Based Securities Regulation. *American Business Law Journal* 45(1): 1–60.
Ford CL (2017) *Innovation and the State: Finance, Regulation, and Justice*. Cambridge: Cambridge University Press.
FSA (2000) *A New Regulator for the New Millennium*. Available at: https://webarchive.nationalarchives.gov.uk/ukgwa/20120904095921/http://www.fsa.gov.uk/library/publications_by_date/2000.
FSA (2008) *Business Plan 2008/09. Promoting Efficient, Orderly and Fair Markets Helping Retail Consumers Achieve a Fair Deal Improving Our Business Capability and Effectiveness*. Available at: https://webarchive.nationalarchives.gov.uk/ukgwa/20121115021202mp_/http://www.fsa.gov.uk/static/pubs/plan/pb2008_09.pdf.
Georgosouli A (2008) The Nature of the FSA Policy of Rule-Use: A Critical Overview. *Legal Studies* 28(1): 119–139.
Gilad S (2010) It Runs in the Family: Meta-Regulation and Its Siblings. *Regulation & Governance* 4(4): 485–506.
Gilad S (2014) Beyond Endogeneity: How Firms and Regulators Co-Construct the Meaning of Process-Oriented Regulation. *Law and Policy* 36(2): 134–164.
Glaser BG and Straus AL (1967) *The Discovery of Grounded Theory: Strategies for Qualitative Research*. Chicago, IL: Aldine Publishing Company.
Grabosky P and Braithwaite J (1986) *Of Manners Gentle: Enforcement Strategies of Australian Business Regulatory Agencies*. Melbourne: Oxford University Press.
Gray G (2006) The Regulation of Corporate Violations: Punishment, Compliance, and the Blurring of Responsibility. *British Journal of Criminology* 46(5): 875–892.
Gray J and Hamilton J (2006) *Implementing Financial Regulation*. Chichester: John Wiley & Sons Ltd.

Gunningham N (2010) Enforcement and Compliance Strategies. In: Baldwin R, Cave M and Lodge M (eds) *The Oxford Handbook of Regulation*. New York: Oxford University Press, 120–145.

Gunningham N, Thornton D and Kagan R (2005) Motivating Management: Corporate Compliance in Environmental Protection. *Law and Policy* 27(2): 289–316.

Gusfield JR, Rasmussen P and Kotarba JA (1984) The Social Control of Drinking-Driving: An Ethnographic Study of Bar Settings. *Law & Policy* 6(1): 45–66.

Haines F (1997) *Corporate Regulation: Beyond 'Punish or Persuade'*. Oxford: Clarendon Press.

Haines F (2011a) *The Paradox of Regulation: What Regulation Can Achieve and What It Cannot*. Cheltenham, UK: Edward Elgar Publishing.

Haines F (2011b) Facing the Compliance Challenge: Hercules, Houdini or the Charge of the Light Brigade. In: Parker C and Nielsen VL (eds) *Explaining Compliance: Business Responses to Regulation*. Cheltenham, UK: Edward Elgar Publishing, 287–304.

Hawkins K (1990) Compliance Strategy, Prosecution Policy and Aunt Sally: A Comment on Pearce and Tombs. *British Journal of Criminology* 30(4): 444–467.

Hawkins K (1991) Enforcing Regulation: More of the Same from Pearce and Tombs. *British Journal of Criminology* 31(4): 427–430.

Hawkins K (2002) *Law as Last Resort: Prosecution Decision-Making in a Regulatory Agency*. Oxford: Oxford University Press.

Hawkins K and Hutter BM (1993) The Response of Business to Social Regulation in England and Wales: An Enforcement Perspective. *Law & Policy* 15(3): 199–217.

Hawkins K and Thomas JM (1984) The Enforcement Process in Regulatory Bureaucracies. In: Hawkins K and Thomas J (eds) *Enforcing Regulation*. Boston: Kluwer-Nijhoff, 3–22.

Hawkins K and Thomas JM (1989a) Preface. In: Hawkins K and Thomas J (eds) *Making Policy in Regulatory Bureaucracies*. Pittsburgh: University of Pittsburgh, vii–viii.

Hawkins K and Thomas JM (1989b) Making Policy in Regulatory Bureaucracies. In: Hawkins K and Thomas J (eds) *Making Policy in Regulatory Bureaucracies*. Pittsburgh: University of Pittsburgh, 3–25.

Hopkins A (1980) Controlling Corporate Deviance. *Criminology* 18(2): 198–214.

Hopper M and Black J (2010) *Breaking Up Is Hard to Do: The Future of UK Financial Regulation?* London: Herbert Smith LLP and London School of Economics and Political Science.

Hutter BM and Lloyd-Bostock S (2017) *Regulatory Crises*. Cambridge University Press.

Jackson HE (2005) An American Perspective on the U.K. Financial Services Authority: Politics, Goals, & Regulatory Intensity. *Harvard Law School John M. Olin Center for Law, Economics and Business Discussion Paper Series. Paper No. 522*. Available at: www.law.harvard.edu/programs/corp_gov/papers/Jackson_522.pdf.

Jackson HE (2007) Variation in the Intensity of Financial Regulation: Preliminary Evidence and Potential Implications. *John M. Olin Working Paper No. 521*. Available at: http://papers.ssrn.com/sol3/papers.cfm?abstract_id=839250.

Jordanoska A (2018) The Dark Side of Finance: Policing Corruption through Regulatory Means. In: Campbell L and Lord N (eds) *Corruption in Commercial Enterprise: Law, Theory and Practice*. Abingdon: Routledge, 163–181.

Jordanoska A (2021) Regulatory Enforcement Against Organizational Insiders: Interactions in the Pursuit of Individual Accountability. *Regulation & Governance* 15: 298–316.

Jordanoska A and Lord N (2020) Scripting the Mechanics of the Benchmark Manipulation Corporate Scandals: The 'Guardian' Paradox. *European Journal of Criminology* 17(1): 9–30.

Jordanoska A and Lord N (2022) Mixing and Combining Research Strategies and Methods to Understand Compliance. In: Rorie M and van Rooij B (eds) *Measuring Compliance: Assessing Corporate Crime and Misconduct Prevention*. Cambridge: Cambridge University Press, 241–263.

Kagan R (1984) On Regulatory Inspectorates and the Police. In: Hawkins K and Thomas J (eds) *Enforcing Regulation*. Boston: Kluwer-Nijhoff, 37–64.

Kagan R (2000) How Much Do National Styles of Law Matter? In: Kagan RA and Axelrad L (eds) *Regulatory Encounters: Multinational Corporations and American Adversarial Legalism*. Berkeley: University of California Press, 1–30.

Kagan R and Scholz T (1984) The 'Criminology of the Corporation' and Regulatory Enforcement Strategies. In: Hawkins K and Thomas J (eds) *Enforcing Regulation*. Boston: Kluwer-Nijhoff, 67–95.

Kingsford Smith DA (2011) A Harder Nut to Crack? Responsive Regulation in the Financial Services Sector. *University of British Columbia Law Review* 44: 695–742.

Knorr-Cetina K and Preda A (2005) Introduction. In: Knorr-Cetina K and Preda A (eds) *The Sociology of Financial Markets*. Oxford: Oxford University Press, 1–16.

Lange B (1999) Compliance Construction in the Context of Environmental Regulation. *Social & Legal Studies* 8(4): 549–567.

Lemert EM (1951) *Social Pathology: A Systematic Approach to the Theory of Sociophatic Behavior*. New York: McGraw-Hill Book Company, Inc.

Lemert EM (1972) *Human Deviance, Social Problems, and Social Control*. NJ: Prentice-Hall, Inc.

Levi M (2006) The Media Construction of Financial White-Collar Crimes. *British Journal of Criminology* 46(6): 1037–1057.

Levitin AJ (2014) The Politics of Financial Regulation and the Regulation of Financial Politics: A Review Essay. *Harvard Law Review* 127(7):1991–2068.

Lodge M and Wegrich K (2010) Letter to the Editor of Public Administration Review in Response to a Recent Symposium on Financial Regulatory Reform. *Public Administration Review* 70(2): 336–341.

Lounsbury M and Hirsch PM (2010) *Markets on Trial: The Economic Sociology of the U.S. Financial Crisis*. Bingley, UK: Emerald Group Publishing.

MacKenzie D (2008) *An Engine, Not a Camera: How Financial Models Shape Markets. By Donald MacKenzie*. Cambridge, MA: MIT Press.

MacNeil I (2007) The Evolution of Regulatory Enforcement Action in the UK Capital Markets: A Case of 'Less is More'? *Capital Markets Law Journal* 2(4): 345–369.

MacNeil I (2010) Risk Control Strategies: An Assessment in the Context of the Credit Crisis. In: MacNeil I and O'Brien J (eds) *The Future of Financial Regulation*. Oxford: Hart Publishing, 141–159.

MacNeil I and O'Brien J (2010) Introduction. In: MacNeil IG and O'Brien (eds) *The Future of Financial Regulation*. Oxford: Hart Publishing, 1–22.

Macrory R (2006) *Regulatory Justice: Making Sanctions Effective*. Better Regulation Executive.

Makkai T and Braithwaite J (1994) The Dialectics of Corporate Deterrence. *Journal of Research in Crime and Delinquency* 31: 347–373.

Mann K (1985) *Defending White Collar Crime: A Portrait of Attorneys at Work*. New Haven, CT: Yale University Press.

Manning KP (1989) The Limits of Knowledge: A Note on the Role of Information in the Regulation of Complex Systems with Special Reference to Nuclear Power Generation. In: Hawkins K and Thomas J (eds) *Regulatory Policy-Making*. Pittsburgh: University of Pittsburgh Press, 49–87.

May PJ and Burby RJ (1998) Making Sense Out of Regulatory Enforcement. *Law & Policy* 20(2): 157–182.

May PJ and Winter S (1999) Regulatory Enforcement and Compliance: Examining Danish Agro-Environmental Policy. *Journal of Policy Analysis and Management* 18(4): 625–651.

May PJ and Winter S (2000) Reconsidering Styles of Regulatory Enforcement: Patterns in Danish Agro-Environmental Inspection. *Law & Policy* 22(2): 143–173.

May PJ and Winter S (2011) Regulatory Enforcement Styles and Compliance. In: Parker C and Nielsen VL (eds) *Explaining Compliance: Business Responses to Regulation*. Cheltenham, UK: Edward Elgar Publishing, 222–244.

McBarnet D (1991) Whiter than White Collar Crime: Tax, Fraud Insurance and the Management of Stigma. *British Journal of Sociology* 42(3): 323–344.

McBarnet D (2010) Financial Engineering or Legal Engineering? Legal Work, Legal Integrity and the Banking Crisis. In: MacNeil I and O'Brien J (eds) *The Future of Financial Regulation*. Oxford: Hart Publishing, 67–82.

McBarnet D and Whelan C (1991) The Elusive Spirit of the Law: Formalism and the Struggle for Legal Control. *Modern Law Review* 54(6): 848–873.

McCaffrey DP and Hart DW (1998) *Wall Street Polices Itself: How Securities Firms Manage the Legal Hazards of Competitive Pressures* (1st ed.). New York: Oxford University Press.

McCahery J and Picciotto S (1995) Creative Lawyering and the Dynamics of Business Regulation. In: Dezalay Y and Sugarman D (eds) *Professional Competition and Professional Power: Lawyers, Accountants and the Social Construction of Markets*. London: Routledge, 238–274.

McMullan JL and Perrier DC (2002) Lobster Poaching and the Ironies of Law Enforcement. *Law & Society Review* 36(4): 679–717.

Moschella M and Tsingou E (2013) Regulating Finance after the Crisis: Unveiling the Different Dynamics of the Regulatory Process. *Regulation & Governance* 7(4): 407–416.

Muncie J (2011) Labelling, Social Reaction and Social Constructionism. In: McLaughlin TNE (ed) *SAGE Handbook of Criminological Theory*. London: SAGE Publications, 139–152.

Nguyen TH and Pontell HP (2010) Mortgage Origination Fraud and the Global Economic Crisis. *Crime and Public Policy* 9(3): 591–612.

Pagliari S and Young KL (2014) Leveraged Interests: Financial Industry Power and the Role of Private Sector Coalitions. *Review of International Political Economy* 21(3): 575–610.

Parker C (2002) *The Open Corporation*. Cambridge: Cambridge University Press.

Parker C and Nielsen V (2009) The Challenge of Empirical Research on Business Compliance in Regulatory Capitalism. *Annual Review of Law and Social Science* 5: 45–70.

Paternoster R and Simpson SS (1996) Sanction Threats and Appeals to Morality: Testing a Rational Choice Model of Corporate Crime. *Law and Society Review* 30(3): 549–583.

Pearce F and Tombs S (1990) Ideology, Hegemony and Empiricism: Compliance Theories and Regulation. *British Journal of Criminology* 30(4): 432–443.

Pearce F and Tombs S (1991) Policing Corporate "Skid Rows": A Reply to Keith Hawkins. *British Journal of Criminology* 31(4): 415–426.

Picciotto S (2007) Constructing Compliance: Game-Playing, Tax Law and the Regulatory State. *Law and Policy* 29(1): 11–30.

Pontell HN, Black WK and Geis G (2014) Too Big to Fail, Too Powerful to Jail? On the Absence of Criminal Prosecutions after the 2008 Financial Meltdown. *Crime, Law and Social Change* 61(1): 1–13.

Pontell HN and Geis G (2014) The Trajectory of White-Collar Crime Following the Great Economic Meltdown. *Journal of Contemporary Criminal Justice* 30(1): 70–82.

Preda A (2009) *Framing Finance*. Chicago: The University of Chicago.

Reichman N (1992) Moving Backstage: Uncovering the Role of Compliance Practices in Shaping Regulatory Policy. In: Schlegel K and Weisburd D (eds) *White-Collar Crime Reconsidered*. Boston, MA: Northeastern University Press, 244–268.

Sanchirico CW (2006) Detection Avoidance. *New York University Law Review* 81: 1331–1399.

Sants H (2009a) *Delivering Intensive Supervision and Credible Deterrence (Speech)*. Available at: www.fsa.gov.uk/library/communication/speeches/2009/0312_hs.shtml.

Sarat A and Felstiner WF (1995) *Divorce Lawyers and Their Clients: Power and Meaning in the Legal Process*. New York: Oxford University Press.

Schur EM (1971) *Labeling Deviant Behavior*. New York: Harper & Row Publishers.

Selznick P (1985) Focusing Organizational Research on Regulation. In: Noll R (ed) *Regulatory Policy and Social Sciences*. Berkley: University of California, 363.

Shamir R (1995) *Managing Legal Uncertainty: Elite Lawyers in the New Deal*. Durham, NC: Duke University Press.

Shapiro S (1984) *Wayward Capitalists: Target of the Securities Exchange Commission*. New Haven: Yale University Press.

Short JL (2021) The Politics of Regulatory Enforcement and Compliance: Theorizing and Operationalizing Political Influences. *Regulation & Governance* 15: 653–685.

Shover N and Grabosky P (eds) (2010) The Global Economy, Economic Crisis, and White-Collar Crime (Special Issue). *Criminology and Public Policy* (3): 429–654.

Simpson S (2002) *Corporate Crime, Law, and Social Control*. New York: Cambridge University Press.

Simpson S (2011) Making Sense of White-Collar Crime: Theory and Research. *The Ohio State Journal of Criminal Law* 8(2): 481–502.

Snider L (1990) Cooperative Models and Corporate Crime: Panacea or Cop Out? *Crime & Delinquency* 36(3): 373–390.

Snider L (1993) *Bad Business: Corporate Crime in Canada*. Scarborough, ON: Nelson.

Snider L (2009) Accommodating Power: The 'Common Sense' of Regulators. *Social & Legal Studies* 18(2): 179.

Snider L (2013) The Technological Advantages of Stock Market Traders. In: Will S, Handelman S and Brotherton DC (eds) *How They Got Away with It: White Collar Criminals and the Financial Meltdown*. New York: Columbia University Press, 151–170.

Sparrow M (2000) *The Regulatory Craft: Controlling Risks, Solving Problems, and Managing Compliance*. Washington, DC: The Brookings Institute.

Sumner C (2007) The Social Nature of Crime and Deviance. In: Sumner C and Chambliss WJ (eds) *The Blackwell Companion to Criminology. Blackwell Companions to Sociology*. Malden: Blackwell Publishing, 3–31.

Sutherland EH (1983) *White-Collar Crime: Uncut Version (Foreword by Donald R. Cressey)*. New York: Holt, Rinehart and Winston.

Tannenbaum F (1951) *Crime and the Community*. New York: Columbia University Press.

Taylor I, Walton P and Young J (1973) *The New Criminology: For a Social Theory of Deviance*. London: Routledge and Kegan Paul.

Tett G (2010) Silos and Silences: Why so Few People Spotted the Problems in Complex Credit and What that Implies for the Future. *Banque de France, Financial Stability Review* (14): 121–129. Available at: https://publications.banque-france.fr/sites/default/files/medias/documents/financial-stability-review-14_2010-07.pdf.

Tomasic R (2011) The Financial Crisis and the Haphazard Pursuit of Financial Crime. *Journal of Financial Crime* 18(1): 7–31.

Tombs S and Whyte D (2013) The Myths and Realities of Deterrence in Workplace Safety Regulation. *British Journal of Criminology* 53(5): 746–763.

Tombs S and Whyte D (2015) *The Corporate Criminal: Why Corporations Must Be Abolished*. Abingdon: Routledge.

Treasury Committee (2012a) *Banking Crisis (Vol. I: Oral Evidence, HC 144-I)*. London: The Stationery Office.

Turner A (2009) *The Turner Review: A Regulatory Response to the Global Banking Crisis.* Availableat:https://webarchive.nationalarchives.gov.uk/ukgwa/20090320232953/http:/www.fsa.gov.uk/pubs/other/turner_review.pdf.

van Erp JG (2011a) Naming without Shaming: The Publication of Sanctions in the Dutch Financial Market. *Regulation & Governance* 5(3): 287–308.

Will S, Handelman S and Brotherton DC (eds) (2013) *How They Got Away with It: White Collar Criminals and the Financial Meltdown.* New York: Columbia University Press.

Williams JW (2008) Out of Place and Out of Line: Positioning the Police in the Regulation of Financial Markets. *Law & Policy* 30(3): 306–335.

Williams JW (2009) Envisioning Financial Disorder: Financial Surveillance and the Securities Industry. *Economy and Society* 38(3): 460–491.

Williams JW (2012) *Policing the Markets: Inside the Black Box of Securities Enforcement.* New York: Routledge.

Yadav Y (2016) Insider Trading and Market Structure. *UCLA Law Review* 63: 968.

Zimmerman H (2010) Varieties of Global Financial Governance? British and German Approaches to Financial Market Regulation. In: Helleiner E, Pagliari S and Zimmermann H (eds) *Global Finance in Crisis: The Politics of International Regulatory Change.* New York: Routledge, 121–136.

Cases

R v Rollins, R v McInerney [2010] UKSC 39.

2 The more punitive turn in regulatory enforcement

The effect of the crisis was to turn the spotlight on the financial services industry and participants on both sides of the regulatory relationship with extensive accusations of regulatory failures and of market malpractices. The reform in the enforcement of financial regulation was marked by a rapid movement towards a policy of 'credible deterrence'. Before we can address how regulatory dynamism in enforcement reconstructs the regulatory game, instigating modes of adaptation and resistance by the industry, it is necessary to establish the backdrop or 'momentum' of the regulatory shifts and their effects. In this chapter, I build the argument that in the post-crisis period, the enforcement of financial regulation by the UK national regulator became more intrusive, intense, and punitive, leading to redrafting of the boundaries of acceptable behaviour in finance.

The chapter chronicles these shifts and the regulatory ideas, factors, and actors that underpinned them, uncovering a social constructivist process that designated financial misconduct as a social problem. It demonstrates the claims-making process through which the financial regulator used rhetorical devices to persuade others that financial misconduct was a putative problem, proposing 'credible deterrence' as a response. The chapter also examines how the post-crisis 'credible deterrence' policy shifts were reflected in the regulator's use of formal enforcement powers and in its enforcement priorities. The analysis draws on officials' speeches, secondary analysis of statistical data on enforcement performances, and interview data. The empirical insights into the FCA's overall enforcement style and agency-level choices contribute to understanding two interconnected issues: the methods, extent, and consequences of regulatory activism in a post-crisis period (Moschella & Tsingou, 2013) and the extent of more punitive approaches with matching resources on the ground.

Chronicle of an enforcement strategy: from 'light touch' to 'credible deterrence'

As the FSA/FCA's formal enforcement policy, 'credible deterrence' was the set of decisions on the substantive direction to the agency's legal mandate

DOI: 10.4324/9781351069328-2

(Hawkins & Thomas, 1989: vii) of enforcing FSMA and the Handbook. 'Credible deterrence' designated a more punitive and aggressive enforcement policy and style to which the FSA/FCA shifted after a period of more selective use of enforcement powers during its 'light touch' regulation years (Black, 2008, 2011; Moloney, 2010; Tomasic, 2011; Wilson & Wilson, 2014).

The 'light touch' regulator

Historically, the control of the UK financial markets was described through the term 'light touch' regulation. The FSA was viewed as a 'light touch' regulator also in supervisory and enforcement matters, hesitant to undertake a scrutinising enforcement approach though vested with considerable enforcement powers (Coffee, 2007; Ford, 2008; Jackson, 2005; MacNeil, 2007). Instead of enforcement, agency officials conveyed that it significantly used 'supervision and on-going relationships with authorised firms as its front line means of regulation' (Cole, 2006b). The FSA's enforcement style, therefore, represented a typical example of compliance or 'advise and persuade' regulatory enforcement, as it relied heavily on dissemination of information, informal regulatory interactions, and persuasion of the regulatees to comply. As in a typical compliance regulatory model (Frank, 1984; Reiss, 1984), the relationship between the regulatory agency and the regulated was close, personal, and ongoing. Resorting to the formal legal process was considered to taint such relationships because 'it was an indication that the supervisor failed. If it happened on my watch, it must be my problem' (LawyerFR02):

> There used be a joke about cases being dragged out of Supervision because supervision people were much more keen on retaining the relationship with the firms they regulate and were reluctant to refer their firms to enforcement.
>
> (LawyerFR01)

Such adverse attitudes towards formal enforcement actions, however, were prevalent across the organisation as a whole, not only within its supervision departments. A senior former supervisor reflected on the enforcement division's apprehensiveness in the sense that 'you refer the case to Enforcement, and then you wait and wait – nothing for ages! Then you go and deal with the case through supervisory tools' (LawyerFR18). Therefore, the goal of the FSA as a whole was to secure compliance without resorting to formal powers that could lead to detecting, processing, and penalising violators.

Even as late as 2006, key senior officials – John Tiner (2006), the then CEO, and Margaret Cole (2006b), the then director of enforcement – stated that the agency was '*not* an enforcement-led regulator' (emphasis added): 'enforcement is one of a range of tools available to deal with non-compliant behaviour but it is not the most widely used. It is used selectively and strategically' (Cole, 2006b). In the post-crisis Turner review (2009: 86), then-Chairman

Adair Turner tried to distance the organisation from the 'light touch' regulator image, claiming that 'this was always somewhat of a caricature, and a term which the FSA never itself used'. However, a key speech by Cole (2006b) indicates that 'light touch' was indeed the regulatory philosophy of the time, with claims that it helped London 'in becoming the world's leading centre for mobile capital'.

Empirical research on the pre-crisis FSA's investigative and sanctioning patterns supports this informal enforcement position. Analysis of enforcement data as displayed in the FSA's annual reports shows that in the pre-crisis period, the authority had a smaller enforcement docket (see Figure 2.2), while the majority of cases were closed without the use of a formal enforcement power (see Figure 2.3). Based on an analysis of FSA's enforcement interventions in corporate governance, Armour (2008: 20) found that the FSA preferred 'where possible to maintain an informal approach, exhibiting commonalities with its self-regulatory predecessors'. The FSA's 'relative distaste for enforcement' (Coffee, 2007) was particularly prominent when compared to the enforcement intensity of its US counterpart, the Securities and Exchange Commission. The FSA dedicated three times less of the SEC's budget to enforcement expenditures, had a much smaller enforcement portfolio, and had a significantly smaller amount of regulatory fines (Coffee, 2007).

Completing the compliance-oriented enforcement philosophy, particularly in comparison to the SEC, is the fact that the FSA had not undertaken a criminal prosecution for market manipulation or market abuse offences up until 2006. In 2006, the FSA undertook its first criminal (and only successful) prosecution for the market manipulation offence.[1] However, the first criminal prosecution for insider dealing, the offence for which the FSA was the designated prosecutor, was undertaken as late as 2009.

The more punitive enforcement strategy: credible deterrence

'Credible deterrence' marked a shift in the FSA's enforcement style towards a more intensive regulatory approach and a stronger focus on using the formal legal process of enforcement as a regulatory tool. The policy was based on the premise that compliance in the financial services industry can be achieved through making the negative consequences of non-compliance a realistic outcome. It was encapsulated in the regulator's readiness, willingness, and ability to 'do enough cases of the right sort to get the right outcomes, to get the message out to firms and individuals that they will suffer meaningful consequences if they fail to raise their game and improve standards of behaviour' (Cole, 2008a).

Aside from an enforcement outlook implemented by the organisation's enforcement division, 'credible deterrence' also meant a more intrusive

1 Section 397 FSMA, now abolished.

supervision and risk mitigation, mostly conducted by other parts of the organisation (FSA, 2008). However, 'credible deterrence' remained principally an enforcement regulatory policy. Analysis of the speeches shows that, when discussed, 'credible deterrence' is mainly connected to the use of enforcement tools and strategies, with statements such as '[W]e recognise that Enforcement activity is right at the forefront of the drive to achieve credible deterrence' (FSA, 2008) and '[T]he Enforcement and Financial Crime Division (EFCD) takes the lead for the FSA in pursuing the strategy of credible deterrence' (Cole, 2009a). Therefore, over time, 'credible deterrence' perhaps became a principal 'ownership' of the EFCD.

The analysis of officials' speeches and interview data shows that there are two important points in the timeline of the development of 'credible deterrence' as an enforcement philosophy.

The origins of 'credible deterrence' (2006–2007)

These were connected to the need for insider dealing criminal prosecutions and higher civil penalties for market abuse. Discussed as 'effective deterrence' (Cole, 2006a), this encompassed fixing penalties at a level 'sufficient to deter potential wrongdoers' and imposing 'significant penalties' in the area of wholesale market misconduct. As early as 2006, and later in 2007, speeches by Cole mention the agency's consideration of using criminal powers to tackle insider dealing. These indications of a stronger enforcement approach emerged even before 'credible deterrence' was officially introduced as a term. However, the empirical data show that the statements were not yet matched with correspondent enforcement actions 'on the ground'.

The introduction and establishment of 'credible deterrence' as an enforcement policy (2007–2008)

'Credible deterrence' was first used as a term in 2007 in two speeches by the then-CEO Hector Sants (2007a, 2007b). The strategy was further elaborated and promoted as the new 'face' of enforcement through key speeches by Sants (2008) and Cole (2008b). The FSA's 2008/2009 business plan (FSA, 2008) first introduced 'credible deterrence' formally as the agency's regulatory philosophy in enforcement. In the first half of 2008, 'credible deterrence' appeared in other speeches relating to supervisory matters (e.g. on small firms [Titcomb, 2008] and mortgages [Fischel, 2008]), thus repeatedly introducing the concept and informing the industry that the regulator had adopted a new enforcement approach.

With the height of the financial crisis, 'credible deterrence' was established as the official enforcement policy across all areas of financial misconduct and was connected to intensive supervision and risk mitigation. Though 'credible deterrence' may have been originally envisaged to legitimise the FSA's focus on bringing criminal prosecutions in insider dealing and a heightened response to market abuse, after 2008, it had a spillover effect to other non-compliance areas. 'Credible deterrence' was advocated in officials' speeches as the appropriate response for the range of non-compliance that the FSA/FCA has the jurisdiction to govern: retail misconduct (consumer protection, mortgages, mis-selling), wholesale misconduct (market abuse/insider dealing, mismarking, LIBOR), financial crime systems and controls issues, and other targets (senior management, client assets, unauthorised business). These different misconduct types feature more frequently in officials' speeches at specific points in time. For example, mortgages top the 'credible deterrence' agenda in 2009 due to the objective of tackling self-certified mortgages mis-selling, whilst LIBOR populates the bulk of 'credible deterrence' statements on the wholesale markets across 2012–2013.

'Credible deterrence' statements and justifications: the claims-making process and enforcement policies

Case studies of regulatory agencies show that turbulences and shifts are commonplace in regulatory policymaking (Boyer, 1989; Snider, 2009; Haines, 2011a). These shifts also involve a process of claims-making along the lines suggested by social constructivism scholars (Malloy, 2010; Gusfield, 1981, 1989; Gusfield et al., 1984). The 'credible deterrence' policy was developed and promoted to claim 'ownership' of a putative social problem: financial misconduct and regulatory non-compliance in the financial markets.

Social constructivists state that the creation of a problem is conducted in two connected stages: claims-making and institutionalisation (Malloy, 2010; Sarbin & Kitsuse, 1994). Claims-making is a rhetorical undertaking consisting of persuading others that a particular condition is a social problem through defining its existence, nature, and scope (Malloy, 2010). Institutionalisation is 'the process by which government responds to a generally accepted social problem through policy' (Malloy, 2010: 272). Through the claims-making process, claims-makers not only identify the nature and the scope of a social problem but also propose responses to tackle it. This is the process through which institutions and other claims-makers establish 'ownership' of the problem or the control over the discourse about the existence, causes of, and remedies for the problem (Gusfield, 1981: 10–13). According to Gusfield (1981, 1989: 433), to 'own' a problem is

> to claim recognition of a problem and to have information and ideas about it given a high degree of attention and credibility, to the exclusion of others. To 'own' a social problem is to possess the authority to name that condition a 'problem' and to suggest what might be done about it.

The adoption of, or making changes to, a particular enforcement policy entails a process of claims-making: appropriating a particular social problem that the institution claims ownership of or abandoning the problem to the purview of other social control organisations. This appropriation may occur as a result of reactive bureaucratic behaviour to avoid regulatory blame and accusations of regulatory failures (Hood, 2006), due to threats to the existence of the bureaucracy (Chambliss & Seidman, 1971), or because of proactive 'moral crusades' (Becker, 2008) against deviant populations undertaken by the agency and individuals within it.

'Credible deterrence' was created to address the problem of non-improving standards of behaviour in the financial markets and the argument that the markets are still not clean, fair, and orderly and that retail customers do not get a fair deal. The designation of such behaviour as a putative problem also meant that the FSA started claiming 'ownership' of it and the viable solutions: it should be addressed by adopting a 'credible deterrence' enforcement outlook. In officials' speeches, the strategy was commonly connected to the need to 'change behaviour' towards consumer protection and towards guarding against abuse in the markets (Cole, 2008a).

In the claims-making process, the regulator used the three components of claims-making suggested by Best (1987): grounds, warrants, and conclusions. The following section dissects these rhetorical devices within the construction process.

Grounds and warrants

Grounds are statements that provide the basic 'facts' regarding a particular problem. *Facts* are themselves socially constructed, and they might include definitions, examples, or case studies and estimates of the incidence, growth, or range of the problem (Best, 1987: 102–108; Malloy, 2010). *Warrants* are statements which justify drawing conclusions from the grounds, bridging the gap between the identified problem and the need to act (Best, 1987). The reinforcement of the 'credible deterrence' strategy was embedded in two propositions that officials used to ground and define the putative problem (commonly used jointly): the ***unresponsiveness proposition*** and the ***lost trust in the markets proposition***, used in connection to warrants that justified the need to change the extent of using enforcement as a regulatory tool.

The ***unresponsiveness proposition*** asserts that, despite previous messages, warnings, or actions, non-compliance and poor industry standards have not changed. This was a frequent ground for justifying the introduction of a more punitive approach across market areas. 'Credible deterrence' interventions were needed as earlier regulatory messages (e.g. thematic reviews, 'Dear CEO' letters, or previous enforcement) had not resulted in improved behaviour. For example:

> [O]ne of the core problems we have in the PPI market is that firms have not listened to our repeated warnings about the need to improve sales standards.
>
> (Waters, 2009)

> [W]e have continued to put out clear messages, both on the wholesale and retail side. But we are not yet convinced that we are seeing better behaviour across the board.
>
> (Cole, 2008a)

> The focus will be on cases where they see 'evidence that standards are not improving despite clear messages to industry'.
>
> (FSA, 2008)

The *unresponsiveness proposition* was further supported by estimates of the incidence, growth, or range of financial misconduct. This is another type of claims-making *grounds*. Estimates of non-compliance were used across the retail and wholesale markets, thus promoting the need of 'credible deterrence' interventions on various types of misconduct, for example, anti–money laundering systems and controls (McDermott, 2011), senior management culpability, and market abuse (Treasury Committee, 2008: Ev 16): 'we would certainly expect 10% movement without there being any misuse of inside information. That brings the overall figure down to below 20%. We still think that figure is too high'.

The *unresponsiveness proposition* warrants escalating the regulatory intervention, taking a 'more robust approach to regulatory action' (Waters, 2009), and moving 'to increase penalties' (Sants, 2008). This approach of employing more punitive sanctions in industries where the standards of behaviour have not improved is an iteration of escalating up the enforcement pyramid suggested by proponents of responsive regulation models (Ayres & Braithwaite, 1992). The gameplay is now between the regulator and the industry, or different parts of it. Previous regulatory messages (either supervisory or enforcement actions) in an area of misconduct were considered a significant aggravating factor when calculating a financial penalty. This constructs as misconduct behaviour that might have occurred due to ignorance (which is not excused, as firms need to be alert to regulatory messages) and due to outright recalcitrance (which needs to be penalised more harshly).

Lost trust in the markets is the second proposition used to define the putative problem. Various speeches refer to a 'crisis of confidence' in different industry sectors as a ground that warranted heightened interventions to restore trust. For example, on:

Treating customers fairly: 'rebuilding confidence will not be a simple task' (Pain, 2010).

The mortgage market: 'this new approach aims to restore confidence in the system, rebuild trust and deliver the right outcomes for consumers and society as a whole' (Titcomb, 2010).

Senior management: 'This financial crisis has demonstrated that we can no longer rely on senior management judgements. In future, therefore, we will seek to make judgements on the judgements of senior management and

> take action if, in our view, those actions will lead to risks to our statutory objectives' (Sants, 2009c, 2009d).

Unsurprisingly, banking was constructed as the industry with the highest losses in trust, hence the frequent calls for more 'credible deterrence' interventionist approaches in retail banking services and banks' compliance systems. After the LIBOR scandal, calls for 'credible deterrence' interventions because of *lost trust* also spread to the wholesale markets. This is an important 'credible deterrence' development. Mis-selling in the retail markets was already subjected to increased scrutiny, earlier interventions, and sanctioning (e.g. payment protection insurance [PPI] mis-selling; see Gilad [2011]). LIBOR meant that similar approaches should be applied also to the wholesale markets rather than the long-standing approach of *caveat emptor* by sophisticated investors (Lawton, 2013):

> LIBOR-rigging, money-laundering and sanctions-busting have filled the pages of Britain's newspapers . . . an industry suffering a crisis of public confidence as a result of the financial crisis itself, as well as of mis-selling to retail and small business customers, has sunk further in the public eye. There has been 'a collapse of trust in bankers'. There is a real problem here that needs to be fixed.
>
> (McDermott, 2012)

The promotion of the *lost trust in the markets proposition* as a ground for 'credible deterrence' interventions implies that the FSA/FCA was responsive to the public and political backlash to corporate crime in the financial services (Braithwaite, 2010). However, the proposition that heightened interventions can restore the trust is also a vehicle for a market legitimation thesis that the financial markets can function in an orderly fashion despite the scandals and malpractices and criticisms of their inherent corruptibility (Barak, 2012; Snider, 1990; Zingales, 2015). Financial regulation and regulators often provide legitimacy to the existence of the market through the notion that what is needed is a reform, either of the rules or of regulatory practices, but not a more substantive overhaul or abolishment of the current complex and profit-driven market, based on uncertain information (Snider, 1990, 2013).

Conclusions: the instrumental aspects of 'credible deterrence'

Conclusions are statements that represent calls for action to alleviate or eradicate the social problem (Best, 1987). Hannigan (2006: 65, cited in Malloy, 2010: 282) states that, in many cases, conclusions will take the form of 'new social control policies by existing bureaucratic institutions'. Conclusions populate the most prominent part of the regulator's policy documents and speeches. These also represent the main tenets of the 'credible deterrence' approach as a social control policy in response to the putative problem of financial misconduct. With their introduction, the claims-making process is complete, and financial misconduct has been marked as a social problem that requires an adequate response in the guise of the 'credible deterrence' regulatory policy: 'if we get credible deterrence right we'll be well on our way to reforming actual behaviour' (Cole, 2008a).

The suggestions on the types of interventions needed to treat the social problem entail elements of true deterrence approaches. They are shaped around the three costs of offending suggested in rational choice and deterrence theories of corporate crime (Cornish & Clarke, 1986; Simpson et al., 2002): celerity (likely discovery), certainty (likely sanction), and severity (punitiveness) of the sanction. These are some examples of the crucial and repetitive messages organised around deterrence categories:

Celerity: 'Critical is to achieve a belief among practitioners that those who deliberately seek to evade their responsibilities have a strong likelihood of being caught' (Sants, 2008).

Certainty: 'We are more committed than ever to showing firms and individuals that they must play by the rules; because if they don't, robust sanctions are a matter of course' (McDermott, 2013b).

Severity: 'We need to be visible in the market place sending tough messages about wrongful behaviour and imposing sanctions . . . which are severe enough to have deterrent effect' (Cole, 2008b).

The costs of misconduct and the deterrent enforcement outlook were commonly showcased in officials' speeches through emphasising the increase in enforcement actions' statistics (e.g. 'We investigated XX firms', 'We prohibited XX individuals', 'We imposed a total of XX in fines'), the increase in enforcement resources (money, staff expertise, and technology), the changed staff culture (e.g. 'a far more confident, intelligent and sophisticated enforcement practice' [Wheatley, 2013]), and the willingness to fight enforcement cases at the Regulatory Decisions Committee (RDC) (an internal appeal organ within the FCA), the Tribunal, and the Court of Appeal. These statements were aimed at sending a strong message of the regulator's willingness and organisational ability to litigate and continue with a contentious process that costs significant resources (time and money). The adversarial tones further strengthened the regulator's 'credible deterrence' agenda and commitment.

Credible deterrence factors

Regulatory processes, policies, and innovations are influenced by different political, economic, organisational, and technological factors. The shifts in the FSA/FCA's enforcement style offer a real-time 'laboratory' to examine the factors involved in changes in enforcement strategies. At a first glance, and according to the scandal and reform literature (Braithwaite, 2008), the shifts that occurred around 2008 might be attributed solely to external factors: the financial crisis and the ensuing political pressures on the FSA. However, a deeper analysis of the factors surrounding 'credible deterrence' reveals that the tougher stance was promoted and subsequently sustained by a combination of internal and external factors. The roots of 'credible deterrence' were formulated just before the financial crisis, but with regard to market abuse only. The policy was not yet matched with any enforcement agency choices 'on the ground'. Post-crisis, it gained legitimacy and was expanded across the range of misconduct over which the FCA has jurisdiction.

This analysis supports the usefulness of connecting organisational factors (such as internal moral entrepreneurs, staff skills, and occupational cultures) with external factors of regulatory change (political and public activism). The internal organisational shifts towards creating a more risk-taking and litigious enforcement culture were aided post-crisis by external pressures from various political and public accountability mechanisms. This political climate enabled (and pushed) the FCA to move more firmly towards the deterrence end of the regulatory styles continuum, increasing the role of its response in attaching deviance labels to business behaviour.

Internal factors

The relevant internal factors for the shifts in the FSA's enforcement strategy are staff-connected: the appointment of enforcement-minded key officials and staff composition changes.

Senior regulatory officials as factors of change: moral entrepreneurs

Senior officials play a significant role in both the supervisory style and the enforcement outlook of a regulatory agency. Support from senior management and board members is especially relevant for developing a tougher enforcement stance so that the agency does not fall into a 'supervisory and enforcement paradox' (Black, 2008) due to the industry's opposition. In the context of the FSA, senior regulators were, for example, responsible for the regulatory innovations connected to the adoption of the FSA's principles-based (Black, 1997) and risk-based regulation (Black, 2004). There is therefore an organisational tradition of allowing key senior individuals to have a prominent place in the FSA/FCA's regulatory changes.

The key individual at the onset of the FSA's tougher enforcement stance was Margaret Cole, appointed in 2005 as the head of the EFCD. However, the role of senior officials in the 'credible deterrence' regulatory policymaking is not limited to her only. More senior FSA figures and board members also promoted or embraced various aspects of the strategy. For example, Sir Hector Sants (2009a), who took over as CEO at the height of the financial crisis, has a crucial role for the more intrusive supervisions: 'my intention was to radically change the supervision practices of the FSA. I set out to ensure the FSA is seen as a regulator which delivers "intensive supervision" and "credible deterrence"'. Further, Sants's (2009a) comment in a speech that 'people should be very frightened of the FSA' was often quoted by the interviewees as one of the key 'credible deterrence' messages and the more punitive enforcement outlook. In the new FCA, Martin Wheatley, then CEO, was credited with the record fines imposed for the LIBOR and Forex scandals and associated with a tough stance against financial institutions, including for his famous 2012 comment at the Association of British Insurers conference on conduct regulation that: '[T]he key difference between the future and now, and forgive me for being scary in my use of analogy, is we are being given the power to shoot first and ask questions later' (reported in Holt, 2012). Finally, the FSA was a highly hierarchical organisation, and the radical change in its enforcement approach would not have been possible without the internal support of the FSA's most senior regulator, its chairman, and at the time of the 'credible deterrence' promotion, this was Sir Adair Turner.

However, these officials have a more limited role in crafting 'credible deterrence' statements through public speeches in comparison to the head of the enforcement division. Numerous interviews confirmed that the director is seen as the 'face' of the FCA enforcement policy, and Ms Cole's role in reshaping the FSA's organisational culture and enforcement appetite was acknowledged by all interviewees: 'now, enforcement is a real, formidable part of its armoury. Margaret Cole did away with the prohibition of using enforcement' (LawyerFR01).

Margaret Cole's role in the 'credible deterrence' policymaking and promotion was both internal and external to the organisation. Internally, her involvement was crucial with respect to changing the organisational culture on two levels. First, this consisted of changes in the staff composition and skills (analysed later). Second, the staff changes were accompanied by remodelling the organisational attitudes towards what types of cases should be pursued (e.g. more complex or difficult cases) and what levels of penalty were appropriate. As reported by some interviewees, Margaret Cole's role was key in introducing certain policy changes, such as the 2010 significantly revised penalty policy that made the size of the fine calculable as a percentage of the level of the harm by the misconduct. Despite her private sector background, which might indicate a more industry-sympathetic approach (Gormley, 1979; Makkai & Braithwaite, 1992), she appeared determined to improve the insider dealing enforcement track record and to instil a matching organisational culture. With the height of the financial crisis, this enforcement attitude expanded to financial misconduct in general. Externally, Margaret Cole became the public face of the new FSA enforcement policy as she promoted its facets through numerous speeches and press releases on completed cases. This role has been maintained by her successors, and in this respect, speeches by key officials continue to be an important mechanism for transmitting regulatory messages in the enforcement sphere. A subsequent head of enforcement, Mr Mark Steward, has, for example, become associated with key messages on targeting individual liability (Steward, 2017a, 2017b).

The roles of Margaret Cole and, subsequently, of Martin Wheatley can be considered as ones of 'moral entrepreneurs' (Becker, 2008), both in terms of a rule creator and a rule enforcer. A *rule creator* is a moral crusader or a reformist who is on a mission to change current rules as there is some 'evil' which profoundly disturbs her (Becker, 2008: 147–148). The creation of new rules creates new classes of outsiders, in this case, corporations and senior individuals engaged in financial misconduct. Their behaviour is signified as deviant. Unlike the typical moral reformism oriented towards the vulnerable and less favourably situated, the crusade of these officials targeted corporations and individuals with superior positions and power in society. With the establishment of an organisation that will enforce the new set of rules, the crusade is institutionalised (Becker, 2008: 155). In this case, there was an existing organisation, though its culture and personnel were reshaped to accommodate the new rules.

Moral entrepreneurs are invariably rarer in white-collar crime and often consist of legislators or prosecutors reacting to public scandals. Other such examples have included the role of David Green, SFO director, in the LIBOR prosecutions, or Judge Jed Rakoff, federal judge in the Southern District of New York, famous for his strong stance on white-collar offenders (see also Katz, 1979; Levi, 2009; O'Brien, 2005). However, there is some criticism that the motives of moral entrepreneurs in white-collar crime are inspired not by moral outrage but from gaining some career advantage from pursuing white-collar offenders or from the need to 'reinforce confidence in established institutions' and the legitimacy of the system itself (Friedrichs, 2011: 17). The actions by high-ranking FCA enforcement officials can be seen as supporting a broader financial markets legitimation thesis. Also, the 'revolving door' phenomenon is a common occurrence in the UK financial markets, with enforcement officials moving to high-paid industry positions. Finally, moral entrepreneurialism and crusades on powerful institutions are vulnerable not only to private industry incentives but also to private industry pressures. This is evidenced in the fate of Martin Wheatley, who resigned in the summer of 2015 after a vote of 'no confidence' by then-Chancellor George Osborne. Reportedly, his 'confrontational style' approach towards the City and record bank fines attracted private industry complaints by banks and insurers with political decision-makers that ultimately led to the end of his career as UK regulator (Fortado et al., 2015; Inman, 2015). The ability of the industry to influence the choice of favourable regulatory officials, diminished with the crisis onset, had started picking up strength again.

Staff composition

The recruitment of Margaret Cole was accompanied by top-to-bottom changes in the internal composition of the enforcement staff. Her vision of a tougher stance towards market abuse and insider dealing needed suitable human resources for implementation. Insiders reported that this was done through two modes: firing and hiring practices.

First, a strategy was put in place to weed out the staff considered unsuitable for implementing the new regulatory policy. Present staff was 'made to reapply for their jobs' (LawyerFR15) and reassessed based on their compatibility with the desired ideology and technical skills. The staff deemed unsuitable were employees with entrenched views of the compliance-oriented, accommodating, and negotiating approaches. Whilst such views may have been acceptable for the supervisory side of the organisation, the enforcement side sought to create a new organisational image, distinct from the previous accommodative styles. Ultimately, this meant dispensing with staff members who did not have a significant litigation or investigative experience or had not been exposed to litigious and contentious practices due to their training and organisational career:

> All the sort of Bank of England staff, or previous Securities and Investment Board[2] staff who plodded their way through various iterations of the organisation, most of those went fairly shortly after she came.
>
> (LawyerFR15)

In practice, this meant that a significant contingent of enforcement staff was relocated to other parts of the organisation or left the organisation altogether.

Second, a strategy of hiring was deployed that would filter in suitable staff. Quantitatively, 'credible deterrence' meant an overall increase in the number of enforcement staff. This is commonly considered an indicator of higher regulatory intensity (Coffee, 2007), in accordance with the more punitive enforcement strategy. Figure 2.1 shows the movement of staff over a timeline that spans the pre-crisis and post-crisis periods.[3]

The quantitative indicators on the participation of enforcement staff in total staff show a steady percentage in the years 2004–2008 and 2009–2011, with around 9 per cent of total staff working in enforcement matters (here, the year 2007/2008 is of the least regulatory intensity). However, the percentage of participation should be viewed in context of the rise in total FSA/FCA staff, with a significant spike from 2009 onwards. This means more enforcement staff in relative numbers. Furthermore, enforcement staff numbers significantly rose after 2011, with a participation of around 11 per cent in the total staff. The movement continued after the FSA abolishment (2013/2014), where in a significantly lower number of total FCA staff, enforcement staff participates with between 17 and 20 per cent of total staff (an average of 18 per cent).

Qualitatively, the 'credible deterrence' policymaking and policy implementation were accompanied by hiring staff with adequate skills and expertise. Both the interviewee data and the analysis of speeches show this movement.

2 A self-regulatory organisation, predecessor of the FSA.

3 The numbers were calculated based on information in the FSA/FCA annual plans and annual reports.

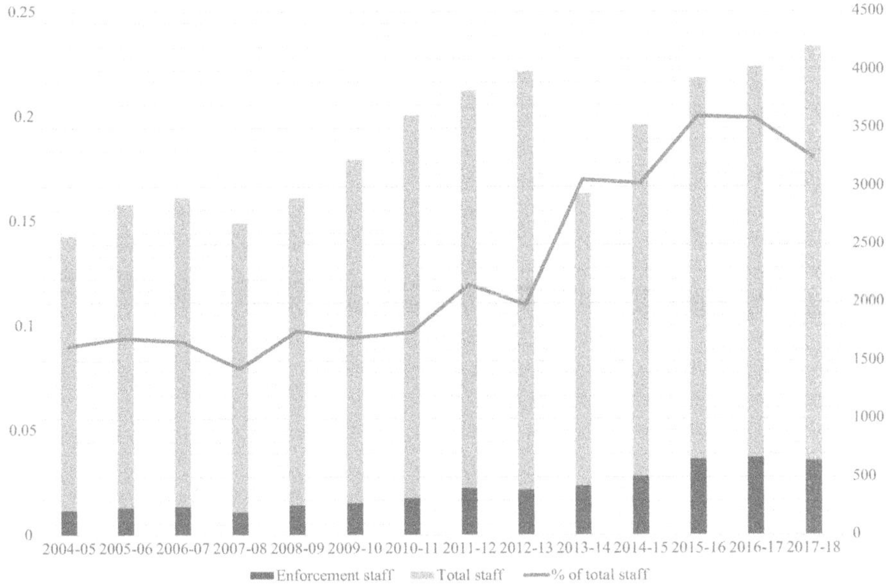

Figure 2.1 Enforcement staff.

The new regime required and cherished enforcement staff with different values and skills, most notably with litigation background and a progressive and dynamic enforcement outlook. This signifies a process of 'lawyering up' the organisation. The changing staff ideologies were reflected in the hiring of 'progressive, more experienced litigators' [LawyerFR15] and staff that were 'more focused, more hard-working, getting better headlines, visual successes' [LawyerFR06].

The activist pro-litigation beliefs of many of the new enforcement staff influenced both the establishment of an enforcement culture focusing on real outcomes and changing behaviours, and the retaining of a perception 'that there were no payoffs for cooperation – matter of moral right' (Boyer, 1989: 122). An informant reported that a significant role in these shifts was played by the increased hiring of criminal lawyers to strengthen the insider dealing prosecution skills of the organisation. For example, a notable hiring was the appointment of David Kirk, former head of the Crown Prosecution Service, as the chief criminal counsel of the FSA. The litigation experience of this group led also to discovering 'new' enforcement powers in the Financial Services and Markets Act that could be used in the civil or regulatory context and, ultimately, to 'pushing the boundaries of what the law allowed them to do' (LawyerFR6).

The staff composition promoted and reproduced 'credible deterrence' also through the fact that private legal counsel, more specifically, barristers from top chambers, was instructed by the FCA to offer advice in contentious cases.

Barristers were commonly retained for advising and litigation at the RDC, before the Tribunal, or in the FCA's criminal prosecution cases. Retention of outside lawyers occurred mostly in complex cases or cases that concern high-profile individuals, but also occasionally in smaller cases of dishonest individuals or unauthorised business. The ability to retain outside counsel for exercising a public function comes from the characteristics of the UK legal system where private barristers' chambers can be retained by public authorities for litigation, even in criminal cases. For example, this has been the practice in cases of complex fraud pursued by the Crown Prosecution Service[4] or the SFO. In the United States, such practice is less common and not currently exercised by the SEC. Other financial agencies, however, have retained private counsel in civil suits against directors and managers of failed banks (Federal Deposit Insurance Corporation) and major banks for losses they suffered on toxic collateralised debt obligations (Federal Housing Finance Agency) (Coffee, 2013).

The practice of retaining top private counsel has important procedural implications for implementing deterrence-oriented enforcement policies in view of limited regulatory resources and in markets that are constructed through complex legal provisions. For example, Coffee (2013) has proposed that the SEC should hire private legal counsel to reorient itself towards achieving deterrence after the crisis, as they already have 'trial experience, "star" quality, and ability to staff "mega"-sized cases'. Also, they might be more motivated to win if fees are made dependent on the success of the case or on penalty percentage. For these reasons, economically, the retention of private counsel reduces the need for budget increases to hire top litigants on a full-time basis 'while holding out a large carrot' (Coffee, 2013). Such tactics would counteract the significant legal resources employed by large financial institutions which, as the empirical research in this study found, are commonly used from the outset of what might amount to a contentious regulatory process. Outside law firms were contacted for advice as soon as a problem emerged, fairly early after the internal discovery of potential misconduct and before the FCA was notified of the issue.

However, the hiring of private counsel adds to the problem of agency capture in the control of financial markets. One source of capture is the well-known 'revolving door' phenomenon, which indicates movements of personnel between the regulated industry and the regulatory agency (Edelman, 1964; Gormley, 1979; Rex, 2020). These movements have been indicated as a source of agency capture in that industry practitioners appointed as senior regulatory officials might bring sympathetic-to-the-market views into the organisation or might be more lenient on the industry (Dal Bò, 2006; however, see Makkai & Braithwaite, 1992). However, as seen in the example of Margaret Cole, who came from private practice, this argument does not always withstand empirical scrutiny. Also, arguments of agency capture

4 On the selection conditions, see Crown Prosecution Service (2023).

due to personnel movements have been developed mostly in US regulatory scholarship, where senior regulators are appointed by Congress and, in that respect, the appointment of pro-market figures may be more representative of the main political views (party) in power rather than of internal organisational politics (Gormley, 1979). The circumstances surrounding the resignation of Martin Wheatley as the FCA CEO indicate that such political influences are also, on occasion, a UK practice.

The retention of barristers in contentious cases is very similar to the 'revolving door' practices. These chambers were able to acquire up-to-date knowledge of the regulator's current investigative tactics, internal enforcement considerations, and litigation strategies. This exacerbates the problem of 'repeat players' (Galanter, 1974), as the small legal profession market already meant that professional knowledge travelled fast within this circle. An insider, previously employed as a regulator, noted that lawyers in this area frequently held conferences, at which they exchanged experiences of cases and tactics on how to 'beat the common enemy'. In that sense, though the expert knowledge and extensive experience of private counsel may aid the regulator in undertaking 'mega' cases and achieving 'credible deterrence' objectives, the outlined problems of knowledge and experiences transfer argue for a more cautious and discriminating approach towards their instruction as counsel in contentious matters. However, such 'mega' cases or litigation in court by the FCA are not frequent undertakings. This might mean that the instructed barristers had access to only a section of the FCA's litigation experience, similarly to the prosecution barristers instructed in SFO criminal prosecutions.

Finally, in the UK markets, the movement of personnel between sectors may contribute towards agency capture in another, more subtle way. In the area of enforcement, 60 per cent of the lawyers interviewed had, at a certain point, worked in the FSA/FCA's enforcement team. After telling a senior regulator that my next interviewees would be defence lawyers, they remarked: 'They all used to work here anyway'. Defence lawyers considered this background a significant aid to their career and desirability to be employed as counsel, and the fact that they were employed by major City law firms speaks in favour of this. This background also contributed towards establishing good lines of communication, as regulators who had moved to the private sector frequently maintained professional or even personal relationships with their former colleagues. The situation aided 'repeat players' relationships, in which the same elite group of lawyers, law firms, and barristers represented regulatees in contentious matters. Unlike in criminal justice cases, where barristers appear interchangeably for the Crown and for different defendants in each case, here the pool of defendants was smaller and potentially repetitive in the case of big market players.

External factors

Political environments and agendas largely influence regulatory agencies' pro-regulation or pro-industry dispositions (Bernstein, 1955; Boyer,

1989; Braithwaite, 2008; Haines, 2011b; Snider, 1990, 2009; Hutter & Lloyd-Bostock, 2017). Agencies' contentious relationships with their political environment and stakeholders also transpire in how they respond to heightened criticism after regulatory failures. The following external factors sustained the 'credible deterrence' shifts already instigated in the FSA's enforcement style: the financial crisis and associated political and public pressures, and the role of formal oversight bodies. The two factors are connected but, for purposes of presentation, are examined separately.

The role of the financial crisis

The FSA suffered severe political criticisms for its pre-crisis prudential supervision of the banking industry (HM Treasury, 2009, see also Engelen et al., 2011; Ferran, 2011; Froud et al., 2012; Gray & Akseli, 2011; Hutter & Lloyd-Bostock, 2017). The criticisms concerned supervisory failings along the lines of a 'process-induced myopia' (Black, 2004) in the sense that the authority's risk-based framework blinded regulatory officials to risks not anticipated by the designers of the framework (see the fact-finding in the Turner Review [Turner, 2009]), incompetence (Engelen et al., 2011), and deference to banks' business strategies, leading to 'indulgent regulation' (Black, 2012). The ensuing UK banking failures put the FSA under an enhanced political pressure to reconfigure its mode of both regulation and enforcement and also, ultimately, led to its organisational death (see HM Treasury, 2010, 2011a, 2011b).

Responding to these criticisms but also fighting for its survival, the FSA adopted more adversarial tones in the guise of a more intrusive supervisory style (Turner, 2009; FSA, 2011). In the enforcement area, the political climate after the financial crisis legitimised and affirmed 'credible deterrence' as the dominant organisational enforcement voice. What started out as an initiative oriented towards increasing the FSA's use of the market abuse regime and criminal prosecutions for insider dealing was broadened to apply to all regulatory enforcement:

> [Before] there was much more of an emphasis on supervising firms well and having a more mature relationship. Since the financial crisis, the FSA realised that it was only getting bad headlines and one way of getting good headlines is showing that they were a tough enforcer. Very visibly, Hector Sants embraced the enforcement vision and said, 'You should be afraid of us, we will take aggressive action'.
>
> (LawyerFR06)

In the period of prudential stability scandals and financial markets volatility, the project of more punitive enforcement in market abuse, already underway, became complementary to the demands for a more intrusive supervisory approach. Therefore, the events surrounding the crisis and the subsequent legitimation of 'credible deterrence' as the overall enforcement philosophy show that the internal and external factors that shape regulatory policymaking are deeply intertwined and influence each other. The 2008 business plan (FSA, 2008) stated that, in the 'credible deterrence' philosophy, the newly introduced effective supervision and risk mitigation programmes accompany the increasing enforcement. However, these elements were not only companions to more punitive enforcement but also one of the bases to legitimise 'credible deterrence' across the board of financial services. If supervision was required to be more intrusive, demands for a more aggressive approach in overall enforcement could be more easily justified.

Though prompted by the crisis, such an outlook was maintained after the financial crisis during a period of fully publicised 'credible deterrence' agenda. Speeches by enforcement officials, aimed at the industry, continuously emphasised 'credible deterrence' as the established enforcement voice of the organisation, and this was confirmed in my interview with senior enforcement staff: '"Credible deterrence" is here to stay. We will still be devising our enforcement strategy around what we think we need to do in order to achieve "credible deterrence"' (Regulator02).

The gradual sunsetting of the 'credible deterrence' policy name and some of the discourse started from around 2017, marking a ten-year period of its implementation. The last incidents of 'credible deterrence' being mentioned were in the FCA's business plan of 2016/2017 and across speeches in 2016. The forewords of then-Chairman John Griffith-Jones, the 2017/2018 business plan, and the 2016/2017 annual report, published in April and July 2017, respectively, moved to the phrase 'constructive deterrence' to note 'preventative regulation' (FCA, 2017a, 2017b). However, even without the specific mention of 'credible deterrence', the policy approach on rules enforcement still used the familiar discourse of deterrence objectives: '[O]ur enforcement work supports our objectives by making it clear there are real and meaningful consequences for firms and individuals who don't follow the rules' (FCA, 2017a: 83, 2017b: 57). This language was fully edited out from the following year's business plan and annual report, published in March and July 2018, respectively, denoting the end of referring to 'deterrence' in the two key FCA organisational publications.

Accountability mechanisms

The second external factor suggested as influential in the 'credible deterrence' policymaking are the formal oversight bodies to which the FCA is *ex post* accountable, with the most important influence by the Treasury Select Committee (TSC) and the *ad hoc* Parliamentary Commission on Banking Standards (PCBS).[5]

The TSC and the PCBS exerted influence over the formation and sustainability of the FSA/FCA enforcement strategy through a proactive and critical

5 Interestingly, judicial review played a very limited role, unlike, for example, in the context of the consumer protection policymaking in the United States. See Boyer (1989).

stance toward the agency's enforcement priorities and through subjecting its senior officials to scrutiny and pressures to undertake enforcement actions against certain categories of targets. In the period of the 'credible deterrence' formation, its expansion over the rest of the FSA enforcement work as well as, subsequently, the TSC sent important signals suggesting that more aggressive enforcement was desirable or adequate. For example, the TSC committee demanded a strong response in tackling market abuse in 2008 when Callum McCarthy (then chairman), Hector Sants, and Margaret Cole appeared to give evidence and were questioned on their approach (Treasury Committee, 2008: Ev 17–18).

Similar pressures were exerted by the PCBS, specifically through the hearings on the collapse of HBOS bank, the LIBOR-rigging manipulation by Barclays, and the role of senior management in both banking scandals. Tracey McDermott, then head of enforcement, was particularly subjected to political pressures by PCBS members with accusations that the FSA 'had been subject to regulatory capture' and was 'subservient to the interests of [the banking] industry' (Parliamentary Commission on Banking Standards, 2013: Q3002) because of the few actions against the most senior executives at large banks.

Both the analysis of agency documents and the interview data suggest that the TSC and PCBS hearings and information requests represented an influential political factor. Enforcement staff were 'very sensitive' to such public criticism and demands for regulatory actions:

> [The TSC] have become very active as part of the process of accountability. Every few months, senior FCA people used to have to go and give a regular report, be grilled on it. They used to be very scared. It is that kind of political pressure coming back down the chain.
>
> (Lawyer05)

The Treasury Select Committee, therefore, appears to be a more effective accountability mechanism than suggested by earlier commentators (e.g. Lastra & Shams, 2001), at least in reviewing enforcement matters. The TSC also wielded significant influence in determining the organisational blame of the FSA for the crisis events (Hall, 2009; Hutter & Lloyd-Bostock, 2017). The two bodies also appeared as drivers behind enforcement actions in certain areas, or behind tougher (or additional) enforcement approaches. The TSC recommendations, for example, have asked particularly for the FSA 'to give high priority to its investigations into other banks' (Treasury Committee, 2012: 105), thus having a direct impact on its enforcement priorities and docket. The hearings procedure was also perceived as an additional enforcement mechanism in terms of the adverse publicity of calling senior management of investigated firms to publicly displayed account:[6]

6 Notable examples are Bob Diamond, CEO, Barclays; Fred Goodwin, CEO, RBS.

> If a public issue has gone wrong, now you have the TSC. Let's have these people here, let's have them explain themselves. The TSC can't fine anyone, but having people in front of the TV screen introduces a whole new dynamic to the regulatory enforcement relationship. We have that at the same time that the FSA is doing an investigation.
>
> (LawyerFR01)

The TSC had the power to subject both 'bankers and regulators' to 'degradation rituals' (Levi, 2011). The fears expressed by regulatees' representatives that the TSC was 'going to be the most powerful regulator in terms of reputation' (LawyerFR01) show both the body's importance in influencing the agency's enforcement policy and priorities and that concerns over negative publicity and public disapproval were high on the corporate agenda.

The FSA/FCA's enforcement strategy was therefore highly sensitive and responsive to political and public scrutiny, and these audiences emerged as important *de jure* and *de facto* FCA accountability mechanisms. The public image sensitivity and the need 'for external expectations management' (Regulator02) were one of the crucial factors for the shifts in the FCA's enforcement outlook and priorities towards becoming more pre-emptive and punitive: 'Everybody is expecting the FCA to fix any perceived problems with the current structure. That could be that we would take more and more enforcement actions, that we will use more and more powers' (Regulator02).

Finally, the fact that these shifts happened in a period of significant political and public backlash against the banking industry and, by extension, against financial institutions of any kind made it easier for the FSA/FCA to extend the tougher enforcement policy whilst, at the same time, avoiding what Parker (2006) terms a 'compliance trap'. A 'compliance trap' occurs 'when regulators are actively seeking to improve business compliance, and commitment to compliance, through their enforcement activity' (Parker, 2006: 593), but without an external political support for such activity. She argues that a tougher enforcement policy may be contested by regulatees if there is no political support for the moral seriousness of the enforced law. In the aftermath of the crisis, there was no such conflict, and the regulator had leeway to adopt a tougher enforcement approach. The political demands gave justification and legitimacy to the FCA's enforcement actions and sent a message to the industry that the regulator has political backing.

'Credible deterrence' through regulatory tools and priorities

'Credible deterrence' was not only an empty policy statement but was also matched on the ground. Analysis of quantitative data from enforcement statistics, coupled with qualitative data from interviews, shows that 'credible deterrence' was translated into key agency-level choices (May & Winter, 2000) and responses to the putative problem of financial misconduct: enforcement tools (formal powers used) and priorities (whom to target and what to inspect for).

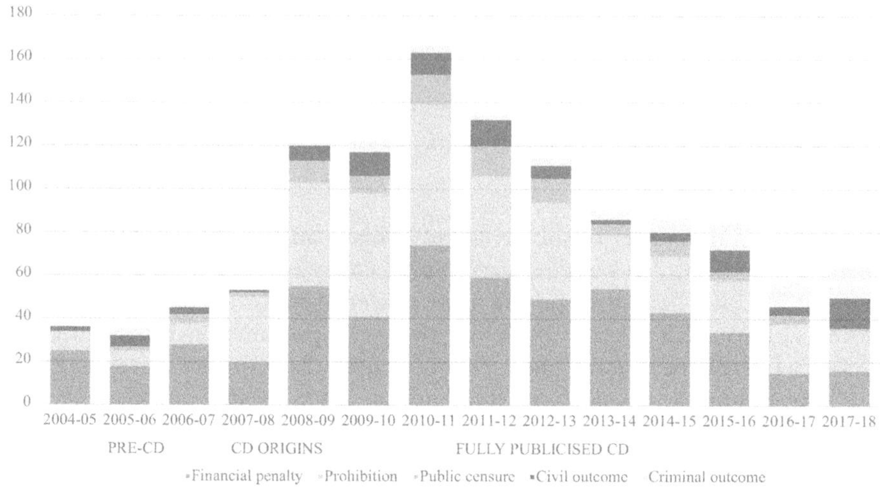

Figure 2.2 Use of formal enforcement powers in the financial years 2004–2005 to 2017–2018.

Enforcement tools

A key 'credible deterrence' message was the emphasis on 'using enforcement as a tool to change behaviour in the markets' (e.g. FSA, 2008; Cole, 2009a) amongst other standard tools, such as policy, authorisation, and more intensive supervision. Figure 2.2 shows the movements in the use of formal enforcement powers in the agency's enforcement docket in the period 2004/2005–2017/2018 based on the annual enforcement reports published by the FSA/FCA.[7] The period is divided into pre–'credible deterrence', 'credible deterrence' origins, and fully publicised 'credible deterrence' to showcase the shifts in the use of enforcement tools.

The data show that there is a significant spike in aggregate enforcement activity in the financial year 2008/2009 – the year of the 'credible deterrence' promotion. The growth continued in 2009/2010, and in 2010/2011, which tops the FSA's enforcement activity of all time. After this year, formal enforcement outcomes move downwards, and the gradual decline continues after 2011. The final counts may indicate that 'credible deterrence' slowly began to

7 The figure does not include: (1) Cancellations of the authorisation for regulated firms. The regulator used this power mostly for technical administrative issues than for serious criminogenic corporate culture. The cancellations commonly concerned small businesses that had ceased trading or no longer wished to provide financial services. In only 2 per cent of cases, the cancellation occurred due to the prohibition of a senior manager for impropriety, and even in these cases, the manager was the sole human resource of the firm. (2) Redress/restitution orders for 2016–2018 (four in total) and suspension orders for 2014–2018 (seven in total). I excluded these data to make the presentation more manageable.

dissipate after the momentum gained immediately after the crisis. However, a closer look at the types of misconduct in the cases and the powers used paints a different picture, indicating significant changes in the *tools of enforcement* towards more deterrence-oriented outcomes. This concerns the use of criminal prosecutions for insider dealing, the higher proportion of formal in comparison to informal enforcement outcomes, and the size of financial penalties. The agenda instigated shifts from the pre-crisis predominately confidential and informal dispute resolution to a greater use of enforcement tools. Other *tools* that further indicate the more punitive outlook, such as the increased requests for information, the presence of enforcement staff during supervisory matters, the use of Section 166 skilled person reports, and publicising enforcement outcomes, are examined later in context of their importance for the agency's detection, investigation, and sanctioning activities.

Criminal prosecutions for insider dealing

As raised earlier, 'credible deterrence' initially emerged with the key focus of strengthening the FSA's objective of preventing market abuse through criminal prosecutions for insider dealing. The focus on criminal prosecutions was also frequently emphasised in the interviews, where, on occasion, 'credible deterrence' was specifically associated with the use of this power. 'Credible deterrence' was precipitated by perceptions that the FSA was underperforming in terms of deterrence against insider dealing as it pursued its statutory objective of tackling insider dealing (as a financial crime of special interest to the regulator) solely through the civil regime of market abuse.[8] The lack of criminal prosecutions represented a basis for considerable criticism of the regulator (see Barnes, 2011; Coffee, 2007; Rider, 2008), as this was in stark contrast to the US position, where insider trading prosecutions had a long-standing history:

> It was in 2007–2008 when the first insider dealing prosecutions were inspired by having US discussions, and they were claiming that we had a weak system, with no prosecutions for insider dealing, basically saying that the market wasn't clean.
>
> (LawyerFR11)

Views on the insufficient deterrent potential of civil fines started to form also internally, largely as a consequence of a prominent case, *Jabre*.[9] Mr Jabre, a wealthy hedge fund trader, was fined £750,000 in 2006 for market abuse (at that time, a record penalty imposed on an individual). Then he moved to Switzerland and opened two new hedge funds (costing £1 m and £2 m). The lack

8 Abolished Section 118 FSMA. The first fine came in 2004: Robert Middlemiss FN10/02/04.
9 Jabre FN01/08/06.

of meaningful adverse consequences in this case had a significant impact on the FSA: '[I]n part, that drove the point about having more criminal prosecutions: the ultimate deterrence is putting people in prison, white-collar people' (LawyerFR01).

In 2007, the FSA started 'telegraphing [their] increased appetite for criminal prosecutions' (Cole, 2009c). Under 'credible deterrence', the FSA pursued and won its first insider dealing prosecution in 2009 (*R v McQuoid* (Christopher) [2009]). Criminal prosecutions have now become an integral part of the regulator's enforcement strategy, and as of 31 December 2023, the FSA/FCA has undertaken 50 prosecutions, securing 36 convictions; two cases are ongoing trial, and in two, the FCA has requested re-trial after a hung jury verdict. This indicates a considerable success rate for the regulator, with views that the FCA represents a sophisticated prosecutor (Jordanoska, 2017). The FCA has been continuously developing its criminal powers with innovations in their usage. For example, in *R v Calvert* [2010], Bertie Hatcher was only fined for market abuse in exchange for providing information on Mr Calvert, while in *R v Anjam Ahmad* [2010], the FSA entered into a Serious and Organised Crime Prosecutions Act 2005 cooperation agreement (see further Clarke, 2013). Finally, since *McQuoid*, a relatively simple case that did not involve financial services professionals, subsequent prosecutions demonstrate a commitment to pursue more complex and technologically sophisticated cases and cases involving senior City practitioners:[10] '[T]he FCA wouldn't bother now with such small-time cases as the first ones brought in 2009. The appetite and the experience have now been established' (LawyerFR15).

The proportion of formal in comparison to informal enforcement outcomes

A further change in the *tools* during the 'credible deterrence' agenda period, at least regarding cases ultimately referred for enforcement investigation, was the increased inclination towards closing the case by using a formal power rather than through supervisory means. Figure 2.3 displays the numbers on cases closed with and without the use of a formal enforcement power, cases closed with private warnings which represent regulatory reprimands which are not made public, and the total number of cases.[11]

Until 2006/2007, there was a significant prevalence or an almost-equal number of cases resolved without the use of an enforcement power, either

10 See *R v Mustafa & others* [2012], *R v Sanders & others* [2012], and Operation Tabernula (FCA, 2014).

11 There are two calculating discrepancies. First, in 2007–2010, the numbers on the use/no use of formal powers are in sum larger than the number on closed cases, as multiple outcomes arose from one case (e.g. against individual/firm, multiple defendants). This means that, in some closed cases, there might have been a formal outcome against the firm and no such outcome against investigated individuals. Second, there were no data available for private warnings in 2009/2010.

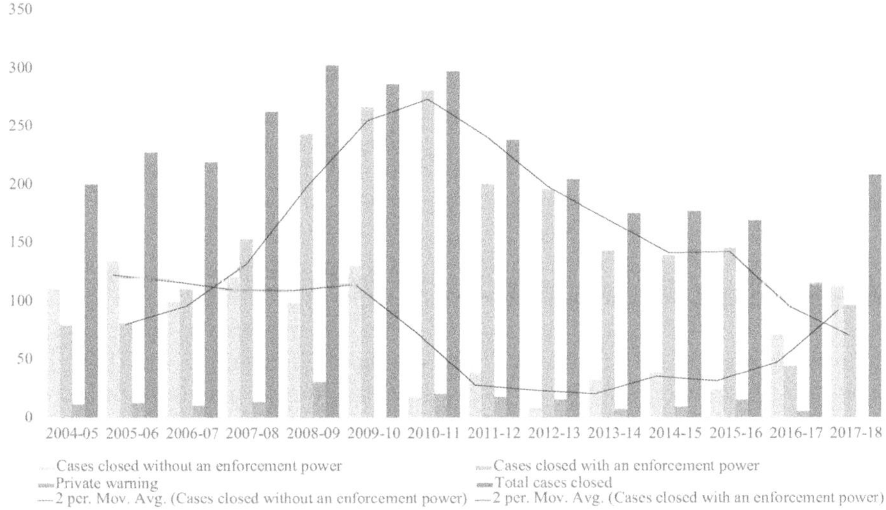

Figure 2.3 Cases closed with different outcomes.

through the case being discontinued or through a referral back to the supervision department. In the latter case, the detected misconduct was left to be resolved through supervisory or informal means (negotiation, education, or guidance) (Hawkins, 1984) rather than through invoking formal sanctions. These data echo accounts by former and current regulators that historically enforcement had been apprehensive.

The subsequent years show an overwhelming dominance of formal resolution of enforcement cases, especially in the period 2010–2016. This movement indicates that, at least regarding cases ultimately referred for an enforcement investigation, the regulator was more inclined towards invoking a formal or a deterrence response rather than a compliance response through supervisory means. These movements represent an important indicator of the 'credible deterrence' agenda. Though the total number of closed cases had started to decline, significantly more cases were resolved using sanctions. This achieves general deterrence since actions that result in formal sanctions have a wider industry visibility (May & Winter, 1999).

The movements in the treatment of misconduct could also be attributed to other organisational and discretionary factors. For example, it may be the case that, in the initial years, the informal resolution of cases was more of a result of the lack of expertise or experience by the enforcement division rather than a lack of will. However, as argued earlier, the 'credible deterrence' changes in staff indicated equipping the organisation not only with relevant human resources but also a new organisational will for a more 'robust' enforcement approach. Furthermore, the change in numbers might mean that the enforcement staff had become better over the years in selecting the cases and opening formal investigations that could realistically have a successful formal outcome. A former high-level enforcement official recounted that during their tenure at the FCA enforcement in the post-crisis period, 'the view was pragmatic: cases were opened, and investigations were carried out with good prospect of success. To get public outcomes' (LawyerFR20). Whilst this may have been the case regarding some referrals, Chapter 3, which discusses the case selection process, provides some evidence on the resolve of enforcement staff to also purse difficult and complex cases.

Under the leadership of Mark Steward, this 'pragmatic' approach towards opening formal investigations started to shift in 2017 towards a 'diagnostic' one (Steward, 2017c). The function of investigations was re-conceptualised as enabling the FCA to understand when serious misconduct may have happened and what to do about it. In practice, this meant a significant increase in the number of opened investigations and the processing of more suspected misconduct through formal investigative powers. The official numbers published in FCA annual reports show that while in the periods 2007–2008 and 2015–2016, the number of opened investigations was, on average, 103 (with outliers in 2012–2013 of 63, and in 2008–2009 of 165), that number more than doubled to 282 and 302 opened investigations in 2016–2017 and 2017–2018, respectively. The changed enforcement vision was prompted by the publication of the Green Report in 2015 that criticised the FSA's thinking around taking enforcement actions against senior managers at the bailed-out HBOS bank in 2009. The implications of the Green Report upon the Authority's enforcement against individuals are further discussed in Chapter 6, but it is important to highlight here that this review had a spillover effect upon the considerations of opening investigations across all targets. Additional reasons for the growth of formal investigations were connected to the FCA's 'broadening [its] shoulders' (Steward, 2017c) in investigating capital markets disclosure problems and the extended reporting imposed by MAR, leading to richer information on potential market abuse.

The rise in formal investigations reflects the gradual build-up of an enforcement ethos that is less apprehensive. Investigations are premised on invoking the formal legal powers of the contentious enforcement process, wresting away the dispute over whether non-compliance has happened from informal supervisory interactions. These also have specific deterrence effects, as investigated targets may suffer from ruptures in the relationship with the regulator and business costs to engage with the investigative demands. There might be an adverse effect, however, between the increasing number of investigations and the capacity of staff to conclude these in a timely fashion and publicise successful outcomes. Investigations were costly and demanded significant staff time and resources. Despite the rise in enforcement staff numbers discussed earlier, these already represented limited resources in view of the investigations load intensification: '[T]he FCA has never had enough resources to be able to carry out all these investigations. There are no extra resources. They'd need to hire more people, though the budget hasn't changed much'

(LawyerFR20). The resources constraints may explain the dip in public enforcement outcomes in the 2016–2018 financial years (Figure 2.2). The discrepancy between the enforcement vision and enforcement resources underscores the difficult balancing exercise confronting public regulators in choosing the tools of enforcement amidst considerations of furthering the public interest (including through deterrence), accountability, and the reality of limited means.

Record-breaking penalties as a key trait of 'credible deterrence'

Rising financial penalties, along the lines of the *unresponsiveness* of the industry proposition, represent one of the most important 'credible deterrence' agenda consequences. The acquired ability to push perceived limits on the size of the penalty represents one of the agenda's long-lasting legacies. Figure 2.4 shows that fines began to increase after 2008–2009 and then rose dramatically in the period 2012–2016.

The numbers in the 2012–2017 financial years are significantly higher even after subtracting the considerable penalties awarded for the LIBOR (see further, Jordanoska & Lord, 2020) and Forex-rigging scandals.

Record-breaking fines are a key indicator of the FCA's post-crisis more deterrence-oriented approach. Sanctions and, indirectly, the level of coerciveness of an agency's enforcement style vary not only regarding the frequency with which they are imposed but also with respect to their severity (May & Winter, 1999). The internal organisational resolve to increase the penalties as part of the 'credible deterrence' agenda resulted in redrafting the sentencing policy through the introduction of a complicated five-step procedure (with a great number of details) in 2010. This process seems to have been driven by two main considerations: first, to base the penalty decision principally on a concept of *harm* (i.e. the firm's revenue from a particular product line or

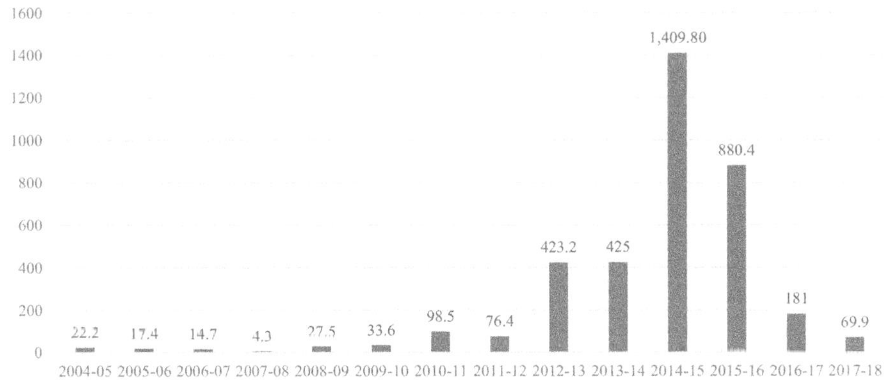

Figure 2.4 Value of fines (£m).

business[12] or the individual's income during the period of the misconduct) and, second, to show a more systematic, coherent, and transparent approach to the penalty decision-making (FSA, 2010; interview data).

Basing the harm on revenue or income was influenced partly by the FSA's perceptions that they had failed to achieve general and specific deterrence regarding wealthy practitioners in market abuse cases. *Jabre*,[13] again, was a case that had a large impact on the FSA in this regard. The enforcement team perceived this case as a failure to achieve deterrence ('How is fining someone that can pay with a cheque and carry out their business in the same way as usual going to deter anyone?' [LawyerFR01]). *Jabre* raised questions on how to make the effects of the penalties real. The solution was found in basing the fine on revenue or income. The desire to impose larger fines also warranted a more transparent or 'more scientific method' of calculating them. As regulatory scholars (e.g. Baldwin et al., 1998) have argued elsewhere, more formalistic and legalistic styles of regulation (of which more frequent and more severe sanctions might be an element) are also accompanied by greater transparency.

In practice, however, the complicated framework did not make the regulator's decision-making any more predictable in terms of what factors were taken into consideration and how they were graded as more/less serious to arrive at a specific amount. Regulatees and their legal representatives commonly complained of this lack of a predictable decision-making framework. Whilst coding the final notices, I also realised that certain factors were highlighted as important in some cases and not in others, though the same factors were also present on the facts. For example, in some cases, there was a particular emphasis on the fact that the breach was not committed deliberately or recklessly as a mitigating factor. In other cases, on a similar set of facts, this was not highlighted, though the misconduct was also not committed deliberately or recklessly.

There seem to be three main reasons behind this disparity in the sentencing factors across similar cases, coming from both sides of the regulatory relationship and frequently operating at the same time: the targets' influence during the settlement discussions, organisational differences across enforcement teams, and the regulator's focus on *just outcomes.* Some aggravating/mitigating factors might be excluded/included based on what the targets and their representatives were able to negotiate to be edited in or edited out during the settlement discussions (considered further in Chapter 5). On the regulator's side, different investigation teams might start from different premises on how the penalty should be justified, and this led to disparities in the final notices.

Finally, the disparity might arise from the fact that, as pointed out by interviewees across the board, a much more important consideration in arriving at a penalty number was the sense of a *just outcome*, crafted around considerations of *just deserts* and deterrence (see, for example, Braithwaite & Geis,

12 FCA Decisions Procedure and Penalties Manual 6.5A.2(1).
13 FN01/08/06.

1982; Schlegel, 1990; von Hirsch, 1993), rather than the predetermined framework. The practice was more akin to arriving first at a sufficiently high or *just number*, which should then be distributed and calculated around the five steps rather than meticulously following the five steps that will then produce a *number*. The 'right' or sufficiently high number took precedence over the calculated number, bringing into question the utility of the detailed guidance. As explained by a former head of enforcement who was involved in the drafting of the Enforcement Guide:

> You can have all of these considerations, seriousness, intentional impact on the market. But the key is: What is the starting point? That is still very subjective. The FCA may just say, 'This is such a serious case that there are these other earlier cases, but actually, that was under the old fining regime. Now we've said fines are going to be bigger. This is a case where there are massive systemic failings, so we actually need to set a really high fine as a starting point.' Also, if it's a novel situation, a case that they've never had regulatory action in before, then you look at all these factors and you think 'It's got to be half a million pounds to start with'.
>
> (LawyerFR07)

On occasion, therefore, regulators 'creatively comply' with their own precise guidance on the penalty calculations. The supposedly 'more scientific method' of calculating penalties appears in practice to be more an *art* than a *science*:

> At the end of the day, it always comes down to a judgement call. The judgement call is usually about whether there is credible deterrence and whether the number looks big enough. All those 15, 16 factors are things that you can keep throwing at the regulators, trying to make your point that they're being unreasonable and they're not sticking with their own guidance. But at the end of the day, it's a judgement call.
>
> (LawyerFR18)

The more resolute shift towards claiming ownership of misconduct in the markets is also evidenced in the difference in the corporate crime that attracted significant penalties. In the years before 'credible deterrence', the aggregate penalty figure was significantly affected by an outlier – a single market abuse case (e.g. Shell in 2004/2005,[14] Citigroup in 2005/2006,[15] and Deutsche Bank in 2006/2007).[16] In subsequent years, not only has the agency fined corporations for a range of misconduct, but also, other types of corporate crime

14 FN24/08/04.
15 FN28/06/05.
16 FN10/04/06.

Table 2.1 Highest corporate fines for different types of misconduct

Date	*Firm*	*Fine (£)*	*Issue*
2015	Barclays Bank Plc	284.432 m	Forex manipulation
2015	Deutsche Bank	226.8 m	LIBOR manipulation and failure to be open and cooperative
2021	Credit Suisse	147.2 m	Financial crime prevention failings as to bribery risks
2013	JPMorgan Chase	137 m	Mismarking and failure to be open and cooperative (the 'London Whale' case)
2015	The Bank of NY Mellon London Branch	126 m	Client assets failings
2015	Lloyd's Banking Group	117.4 m	Treating customers fairly
2017	Deutsche Bank AG	163 m	Culture/governance and AML financial crime prevention failings
2020	Goldman Sachs International	97 m	Risk management and financial crime prevention failings
2021	Lloyds Bank General Insurance	90.7 m	Misleading communications with customers
2019	Bank of Scotland	45 m	Failure to be open and cooperative with the FCA

than market abuse have attracted (much) higher penalties. Table 2.1 shows the highest corporate fines for a range of complex corporate misconduct.

These movements show the FSA/FCA's determination to use more severe sanctions to tackle a variety of misconduct, thus constructing it as a serious misbehaviour. This was, for example, the process of constructing the LIBOR-rigging as especially serious misconduct, reflected in, at that time, record fine imposed on Barclays:

> We believe that it was appropriate . . . This was the most significant penalty we have imposed. It was almost twice the highest penalty we have imposed in the past. That reflected our view that this was the *worst* misconduct.
>
> (Tracey McDermott at the Parliamentary Commission on Banking Standards, 2013: para. 196; emphasis added)

Therefore, the nine-figure fines imposed for the rigging of LIBOR and (particularly) Forex rates construct this misconduct as significantly *worse*. For example, the highest penalty of £227 m for the rigging of LIBOR was imposed on Deutsche Bank (this includes manipulating the EURIBOR rate and Principle 11 breaches),[17] and the highest penalty of £284 million for the rigging of

17 The rest of the sanctioned firms for LIBOR include UBS (£160 million), Rabobank (£105 million), RBS (£87 million), Barclays (£59 million), Lloyds (£50 million), ICAP (£14 million), and Martin Brokers (£630,000).

Forex was imposed on Barclays.[18] The record-breaking fines also represent a key legacy of the 'credible deterrence' years. As Table 2.1 shows, in the more recent years, when 'credible deterrence' has disappeared as an enforcement policy and from officials' speeches, the regulator still imposed significant fines, including nine-figure penalties. There is an attained ownership for the enforcement staff over high-figure penalties as a starting point for other types of serious misconduct which has not been walked back:

> The record fines were spearheaded by the LIBOR/FX misconduct. This led to an inflation of expectations, a £5 million penalty would today be considered meagre. The record fines then spread to other breaches.
>
> (Lawyer14)

Published penalties enable social control agencies to also rely on the reputational sanctions associated with their imposition. Heavier fines and penalising well-known firms cause more reputational damage as these are more newsworthy and attract more publicity (Feinberg & Round, 2005; van Erp, 2010). The governance of reputation and the use of adverse publicity as an additional weapon in the FCA's enforcement armour are discussed in Chapter 5.

Priorities of enforcement

The more intrusive regulatory responses to misconduct in finance were importantly translated into changes in the agency's *priorities* of enforcement and into considerations of *whom* to target and for *what* to inspect. Though different enforcement targets were more in focus at different times, the FCA had a general organisational emphasis on having a 'broad church of cases' within the enforcement docket, covering the range of industries, types of offenders, and misconduct under its jurisdiction. This diversity appeared to be a general enforcement priority:

> We take a very broad church of cases, cases against individuals, small firms, large firms, different types of misconduct. It is an important part of our strategy that we cover the ground like that. Even if we decide that taking action against individuals or clients assets cases are our priorities, we can't do just that. Somehow, we have got to find the resources and the means to cover all of the territory.
>
> (Regulator02)

Yet the additional 'credible deterrence' priorities concerned tackling the root causes of misconduct, actions against culpable individuals for organisational non-compliance, and the more complex cases. 'Credible deterrence' meant that the regulators perceived their new mandate as one of tackling the 'root

18 The rest of the sanctioned firms for Forex include UBS (£233 million), Citibank (£225 million), JPMorgan Chase (£222 million), RBS (£217 million), and HSBC (£216 million).

causes of non-compliance' rather than the earlier focus on 'just the symptoms' of non-compliant internal systems and controls (Cole, 2011; McDermott, 2013a). This approach was in line with the early intervention discourse of the more intrusive supervision:

> We will still be taking the kinds of cases that we are taking now, but we will also be taking some different kinds, cases where we don't wait for something really bad to happen but we will go in and say, 'There is a risk that something really bad is going to happen, and we want you to change'. Some of the work that we are doing now is already on that path. Incentive structures, for example.
>
> (Regulator01)

There was a shift in the regulators' theories of deviance (Hawkins, 2002), reflected in taking more cases that tackled the root causes of misconduct (e.g. incentives structures, flawed business models, or culture in banking), rather than only the manifestations of those roots (e.g. mis-selling or benchmark rigging). Post-crisis political pressure for changes in the risk-based framework calibrations also meant that the *risks* that the regulator was managing were extended beyond the visible manifestations of misconduct. This supports the notion that regulators' interventions in the markets are a key factor in drawing and redrawing the meaning of non-compliance with regulation: here, an expansion from misalignment of organisational systems with the rules to a deeper and more preventative reach into organisational and industry traits conducive to misconduct. The discussion in Chapter 3 shows that this was also embraced in detecting misconduct through proactive enforcement, representing an additional risk assessment layer to the already-existing risk-based framework.

The post-crisis emphasis on senior management responsibility also conveys changes in the regulatory perceptions of the causes of corporate crime in the financial markets (or, again, the underlying 'theories of deviance'). The complexity of finance at the market level is compounded by the complexity of the institutions that populate it at the organisational level (hence the 'too-big-to-fail' challenge in financial regulation). Global financial institutions have complex governance structures, and proving individual liability is difficult (Jordanoska, 2021). Compared to corporate liability for misconduct, it is difficult to establish the hierarchy of decision-making and the level of culpability of senior management or answering the proverbial question 'Where does the buck stop?' (Coffee, 1981; Fisse & Braithwaite, 1993; Katz, 1979). Chapter 6 documents the post-crisis movement towards devising ways to establish individual responsibility. This is an important indicator of the FCA's determination, as cases against individuals are more resource-intensive, more contested, and with more uncertain outcomes.

Finally, Table 2.1 shows that the FSA/FCA had undertaken enforcement actions against some of the biggest market players, the systemically important banks and other large financial institutions, and for complex misconduct, such as the LIBOR and Forex trading scandals. The willingness to refer a 'household' name for an enforcement action and to undertake cases of such scale reflected the implementation of the 'credible deterrence' enforcement policy through the agency's priorities of enforcement. The regulator was not risk-averse, and it did not focus only on technical cases and the marginal and moribund market participants (a common criticism of regulatory agencies and the white-collar crime social control in general [Bardach & Kagan, 1982; Braithwaite, 1989; Croall, 2003; Tombs & Whyte, 2015] and of the enforcement of securities in particular [Eitle, 2000; Ewick, 1985; Hagan & Parker, 1985; Shapiro, 1985]). This contradicts extant comparative research into securities enforcement, which has claimed that one of the failings of enforcement, even in a post-crisis period, is the lack of charges in high-profile cases (Snider, 2009).

Conclusion

In the crisis aftermath, the FCA adopted a more intrusive, punitive, and deterrence-oriented enforcement approach through its 'credible deterrence' policy. This also involved a process of claims-making in which, based on the grounds of unresponsiveness and lost trust in the industry, the FCA proposed more deterrence-oriented enforcement as a conclusion. Speeches of senior enforcement officials, introducing and expanding upon the facets of 'credible deterrence', signified financial misconduct as a social problem that needs to be tackled through enforcement means. Through the process of proposing solutions to the unchanged behaviour in the financial markets, the FCA began to claim ownership of the problem of financial misconduct, and this also contributed to the 're-birth' of corporate crime in the financial markets.

The shifts in the FSA/FCA's regulatory policy in the crisis aftermath and the increasing punitiveness were not only at the discourse level but were also reflected in the agency-level enforcement choices. The financial crisis, therefore, had an impact on the financial regulator on both levels suggested by Dorn (2011): (1) shifts in the regulatory enforcement style along the dimension of soft/hard with the FSA/FCA adopting a harder style, and (2) shifts in regulatory perceptions of what is to be enforced, with the FSA/FCA defining and prioritising complex cases, cases concerning the root causes of deviance, and senior management responsibility 'as objects for control'. The prioritisation of such cases also supports the FSA/FCA's more punitive style, since these are more difficult to resource, investigate, and prove.

All these activities led to identifying more business behaviour as non-compliance (through the increased substantive caseload) or identifying it as more serious non-compliance (increased amount of fines and associated reputational damages) by agency claims. The following chapters trace how the claims-making process of identifying and attaching a deviant label developed in the micro-level interactions of detection, reporting, investigations, and treatment of misconduct. They also introduce the regulatees' counter-claims and responses for actively resisting or managing the deviant label. The analysis presented here indicates that the FSA/FCA were in control of their enforcement agenda. Chapters 3–6 problematise this argument by uncovering the concessions, resistances, and adaptations to the FSA/FCA more punitive regulatory dynamism.

Bibliography

Armour J (2008) Enforcement Strategies in UK Corporate Governance: A Roadmap and Empirical Assessment. *ECGI – Law Working Paper No. 106/2008*. Available at: http://papers.ssrn.com/sol3/papers.cfm?abstract_id=1133542.

Ayres I and Braithwaite J (1992) *Responsive Regulation: Transcending the Deregulation Debate*. Oxford: Oxford University Press.

Baldwin R, Scott CD and Hood C (1998) *A Reader on Regulation*. Oxford: Oxford University Press.

Barak G (2012) *Theft of a Nation: Wall Street Looting and Federal Regulatory Colluding*. Lanham, MD: Rowman & Littlefield Publishers.

Bardach E and Kagan R (1982) *Going by the Book: The Problem of Regulatory Unreasonableness*. Philadelphia: Temple University Press.

Barnes P (2011) Insider Dealing and Market Abuse: The UK's Record on Enforcement. *International Journal of Law, Crime and Justice* 39(3): 174–189.

Becker SH (2008) *Outsiders: Studies in the Sociology of Deviance*. New York: The Free Press.

Bernstein MH (1955) *Regulating Business by Independent Commission*. Princeton, NJ: Princeton University Press.

Best J (1987) Rhetoric in Claims-Making: Constructing the Missing Children Problem. *Social Problems* 34(2): 101–121.

Black J (1997) *Rules and Regulators*. Oxford: Oxford University Press.

Black J (2002) Critical Reflections on Regulation. *Australian Journal of Legal Philosophy* 27(1): 1–35.

Black J (2004) Law and Regulation: The Case of Finance. In: Parker C, Scott C, Lacey N and Braithwaite J (eds) *Regulating Law*. Oxford: Oxford University Press, 33–59.

Black J (2008) Forms and Paradoxes of Principles-Based Regulation. *Capital Markets Law Journal* 3(4): 425–457.

Black J (2011) The Rise, Fall and Fate of Principles-Based Regulation. In: Kern A and Moloney N (eds) *Law Reform and Financial Markets (Elgar Financial Law Series)*. Cheltenham, UK: Edward Elgar Publishing, 3–34.

Black J (2012) Paradoxes and Failures: 'New Governance' Techniques and the Financial Crisis. *Modern Law Review* 75(6): 1037–1063.

Boyer B (1989) The Federal Trade Commission and Consumer Protection Policy: A Postmortem Examination. In: Hawkins K and Thomas J (eds) *Making Policy in Regulatory Bureaucracies*. Pittsburgh: University of Pittsburgh, 93–132.

Braithwaite J (1989) *Crime, Shame and Reintegration*. Cambridge: Cambridge University Press.

Braithwaite J (2008) *Regulatory Capitalism: How It Works, Ideas for Making It Work Better*. Northampton, MA: Edward Elgar Publishing.

Braithwaite J (2010) Diagnostics of White-Collar Crime Prevention. *Criminology & Public Policy* 9(3): 621–626.

Braithwaite J and Geis G (1982) On Theory and Action for Corporate Crime-Control. *Crime & Delinquency* 28(2): 292–314.

Chambliss W and Seidman R (1971) *Law, Order and Power*. Addison-Wesley Publications.

Clarke S (2013) *Insider Dealing: Law and Practice.* Oxford: Oxford University Press.

Coffee JC, Jr (1981) No Soul to Damn: No Body to Kick: An Unscandalized Inquiry into the Problem of Corporate Punishment. *Michigan Law Review* 79(3): 386–459.

Coffee JC, Jr (2007) Law and the Market: The Impact of Enforcement. *University of Pennsylvania Law Review* 156(2): 229.

Coffee JC, Jr (2013) *Missing in Action? A Closer Look at SEC Enforcement. What Happened? What Can Be Done?* [presentation] Centre for the Study of Business Ethics, Regulation and Crime, University of Maryland (08.11.2013).

Cole M (2006a) *Enforcement: Priorities and Issues for 2006 (Speech).* Available at: https://webarchive.nationalarchives.gov.uk/ukgwa/20121210232133/http://www.fsa.gov.uk/library/communication/speeches/2006/0411_mc.shtml.

Cole M (2006b) *The UK FSA: Nobody Does It Better? (Speech).* Available at: https://webarchive.nationalarchives.gov.uk/ukgwa/20121210232001/http://www.fsa.gov.uk/library/communication/speeches/2006/1017_mc.shtml.

Cole M (2008a) *How Enforcement Makes a Difference (Speech).* Available at: https://webarchive.nationalarchives.gov.uk/ukgwa/20121211011455/http://www.fsa.gov.uk/library/communication/speeches/2008/0618_mc.shtml.

Cole M (2008b) *Enforcing Financial Services Regulation: The UK FSA Perspective (Speech).* Available at: https://webarchive.nationalarchives.gov.uk/ukgwa/20121211011106/http://www.fsa.gov.uk/library/communication/speeches/2008/0404_mc.shtml.

Cole M (2009a) *Delivering Credible Deterrence (Speech).* Available at: https://webarchive.nationalarchives.gov.uk/ukgwa/20121210235327/http://www.fsa.gov.uk/library/communication/speeches/2009/0427_mc.shtml.

Cole M (2009b) *The FSA's Agenda for Fighting Financial Crime (Speech).* Available at: https://webarchive.nationalarchives.gov.uk/ukgwa/20121210235151/http://www.fsa.gov.uk/library/communication/speeches/2009/1119_mc.shtml.

Cole M (2009c) *Setting Out the FSA's Strategy and Approach to Fighting Fraud (Speech).* Available at: https://webarchive.nationalarchives.gov.uk/ukgwa/20121210234815/http://www.fsa.gov.uk/library/communication/speeches/2009/0910_mc.shtml.

Cole M (2011) *Financial Conduct Authority: A New Regulatory Approach (Speech).* Available at: https://webarchive.nationalarchives.gov.uk/ukgwa/20121211013103/http://www.fsa.gov.uk/library/communication/speeches/2011/0628_mc.shtml.

Cornish D and Clarke R (1986) Introduction. In: Cornish D and Clarke R (eds) *The Reasoning Criminal: Rational Choice Perspectives on Offending.* New York: Springer, 1–16.

Croall H (2003) Combating Financial Crime: Regulatory Versus Crime Control Approaches. *Journal of Financial Crime* 11(1): 45–55.

Crown Prosecution Service (2023) *Selection of Advocates.* Available at: www.gov.uk/advocate-panels.

Dal Bò E (2006) Regulatory Capture: A Review. *Oxford Review of Economic Policy* 22(2): 203–225.

Dorn N (2011) Reconstructing "Conflict of Interest" in Financial Markets: Private Management, Public Challenges, Future Prospects. *International Journal of Law, Crime and Justice* 39(3): 161–173.

Edelman M (1964) *The Symbolic Uses of Politics.* Urbana, IL: University of Illinois Press.

Eitle D (2000) Regulatory Justice: A Re-Examination of the Influence of Class Position on the Punishment of White-Collar Crime. *Justice Quarterly* 17(4): 809–839.

Engelen E, Ertürk I, Froud J, Johal S, Leaver A, Moran M, Nilsson A and Williams K (2011) *After the Great Complacence: Financial Crisis and the Politics of Reform.* Oxford: Oxford University Press.

Ewick P (1985) Redundant Regulation: Sanctioning Broker-Dealers. *Law & Policy* 7(4): 421.

FCA (2014) *Former Moore Capital Trader Pleads Guilty to Insider Dealing*. Available at: www.fca.org.uk/news/former-moore-capital-trader-pleads-guilty-to-insider-dealing.

FCA (2017a) *Annual Report and Accounts 2016/17 (for the Year Ended 31 March 2017) HC 149*. Available at: www.fca.org.uk/publication/annual-reports/annual-report-2016-17.pdf.

FCA (2017b) *FS17/1 Our Mission 2017 Feedback Statement*. Available at: https://webarchive.nationalarchives.gov.uk/ukgwa/20230902005300/https://www.fca.org.uk/publications/corporate-documents/our-mission.

Feinberg RM and Round DK (2005) Share-Price Responses to Antitrust Enforcement in Australia: Do Investors Care about Price-Fixing Cases? *Competition & Consumer Law Journal* 13(1): 23–39.

Ferran E (2011) Break-up of the Financial Services Authority. *Oxford Journal of Legal Studies* 31(3): 455–480.

Fischel J (2008) *Mortgages – An FSA Update (Speech)*. Available at: https://webarchive.nationalarchives.gov.uk/ukgwa/20121211010133/http://www.fsa.gov.uk/library/communication/speeches/2008/0515_jf.shtml.

Fisse B and Braithwaite J (1983) *The Impact of Publicity on Corporate Offenders*. Albany, NY: State University of New York Press.

Fisse B and Braithwaite J (1993) *Corporations, Crime and Accountability*. Cambridge: Cambridge University Press.

Ford CL (2008) New Governance, Compliance, and Principles-Based Securities Regulation. *American Business Law Journal* 45(1): 1–60.

Fortado L, Parker G, Arnold M and Binham C (2015) Martin Wheatley Resigns as Chief of Financial Conduct Authority. *Financial Times*. Available at: www.ft.com/cms/s/0/61f867fa-2c76-11e5-8613-e7aedbb7bdb7.html#axzz3itWuDjYH.

Frank N (1984) Policing Corporate Crime: A Typology of Enforcement Styles. *Justice Quarterly* 1(2): 235–251.

Friedrichs DO (2011) *Trusted Criminals: White Collar Crime in Contemporary Society* (5th ed.). Belmont: Wadsworth Publishing.

Froud J, Nilsson A, Moran M and Williams K (2012) Stories and Interests in Finance: Agendas of Governance before and after the Financial Crisis. *Governance* 25(1): 35–59.

FSA (2008) *Business Plan 2008/09. Promoting Efficient, Orderly and Fair Markets Helping Retail Consumers Achieve a Fair Deal Improving Our Business Capability and Effectiveness*. Available at: https://webarchive.nationalarchives.gov.uk/ukgwa/20110801164738/http://www.fsa.gov.uk/Pages/Library/corporate/Plan/bp2008.shtml.

FSA (2010) *PS11/3 Decision Procedure and Penalties Manual and Enforcement Guide Review*. Available at: www.fca.org.uk/publication/consultation/cp10_11.pdf.

FSA (2011) *The Failure of the Royal Bank of Scotland (FSA Board Report)*. Available at: www.fca.org.uk/publication/corporate/fsa-rbs.pdf.

Galanter M (1974) Why the "Haves" Come out Ahead: Speculations on the Limits of Legal Change. *Law & Society Review* 9(1): 95–160.

Gilad S (2011) Institutionalizing Fairness in Financial Markets: Mission Impossible? *Regulation & Governance* 5(3): 309–332.

Gormley WT, Jr (1979) A Test of the Revolving Door Hypothesis at the FCC. *American Journal of Political Science* 23(4): 665–683.

Gray J and Akseli O (2011) *Financial Regulation in Crisis: The Role of Law and the Failure of Northern Rock (Edward Elgar Financial Law Series)*. Cheltenham, UK: Edward Elgar Publishing.

Gusfield JR (1981) *The Culture of Public Problems: Drinking and Driving and the Symbolic Order*. Chicago: University of Chicago Press.

Gusfield JR (1989) Constructing the Ownership of Social Problems: Fun and Profit in the Welfare State. *Social Problems* 36(5): 431.

Gusfield JR, Rasmussen P and Kotarba JA (1984) The Social Control of Drinking-Driving: An Ethnographic Study of Bar Settings. *Law & Policy* 6(1): 45–66.

Hagan J and Parker P (1985) White-Collar Crime and Punishment: The Class Structure and Legal Sanctioning of Securities Violations. *American Sociological Review* 50(3): 302–316.

Haines F (2011a) *The Paradox of Regulation: What Regulation Can Achieve and What It Cannot.* Cheltenham, UK: Edward Elgar Publishing.

Haines F (2011b) Facing the Compliance Challenge: Hercules, Houdini or the Charge of the Light Brigade. In: Parker C and Nielsen VL (eds) *Explaining Compliance: Business Responses to Regulation.* Cheltenham, UK: Edward Elgar Publishing, 287–304.

Hall MJB (2009) The Sub-Prime Crisis, the Credit Crunch and Bank "Failure": An Assessment of the UK Authorities' Response. *Journal of Financial Regulation and Compliance* 17(4): 427–452.

Hawkins K (1984) *Environment and Enforcement: Regulation and the Social Definition of Pollution.* Oxford: Clarendon Press.

Hawkins K (2002) *Law as Last Resort: Prosecution Decision-Making in a Regulatory Agency.* Oxford: Oxford University Press.

Hawkins K and Thomas JM (1984) The Enforcement Process in Regulatory Bureaucracies. In: Hawkins K and Thomas J (eds) *Enforcing Regulation.* Boston: Kluwer-Nijhoff, 3–22.

Hawkins K and Thomas JM (1989) Preface. In: Hawkins K and Thomas J (eds) *Making Policy in Regulatory Bureaucracies.* Pittsburgh: University of Pittsburgh, vii–viii.

HM Treasury (2009) *Reforming Financial Markets (July 2009) CM 7667.* London: The Stationery Office.

HM Treasury (2010) *A New Approach to Financial Regulation: Judgement, Focus and Stability (July 2010) CM 7874.* London: The Stationery Office.

HM Treasury (2011a) *A New Approach to Financial Regulation: Building a Stronger System (February 2011) CM 8012.* London: The Stationery Office.

HM Treasury (2011b) *A New Approach to Financial Regulation: The Blueprint for Reform (June 2011) CM 8083.* London: The Stationery Office.

Holt N (2012) Martin Wheatley: FCA Will 'Shoot First and Ask Questions Later', *Money Marketing.* Available at: https://www.moneymarketing.co.uk/news/martin-wheatley-fca-will-shoot-first-and-ask-questions-later/.

Hood C (2006) A Historical Perspective on Transparency. In: Hood C and Heald DA (eds) *Transparency: The Key to Better Governance?* Oxford: British Academy and Oxford University Press.

Hutter BM and Lloyd-Bostock S (2017) *Regulatory Crises.* Cambridge University Press.

Inman P (2015) City Watchdog Chief Quits after George Osborne Vote of No Confidence. *The Guardian.* Available at: www.theguardian.com/business/2015/jul/17/city-watchdog-chief-quits-fca-george-osborne.

Jackson HE (2005) An American Perspective on the U.K. Financial Services Authority: Politics, Goals, & Regulatory Intensity. *Harvard Law School John M. Olin Center for Law, Economics and Business Discussion Paper Series. Paper 522.* Available at: www.law.harvard.edu/programs/corp_gov/papers/Jackson_522.pdf.

Jordanoska A (2017) Case Management in Complex Fraud Trials: Actors and Strategies in Achieving Procedural Efficiency. *International Journal of Law in Context* 13(3): 336–355.

Jordanoska A (2021) Regulatory Enforcement against Organizational Insiders: Interactions in the Pursuit of Individual Accountability. *Regulation & Governance* 15: 298–316.

Jordanoska A and Lord N (2020) Scripting the Mechanics of the Benchmark Manipulation Corporate Scandals: The 'Guardian' Paradox. *European Journal of Criminology* 17(1): 9–30.

Katz J (1979) Legality and Equality: Plea Bargaining in the Prosecution of White-Collar and Common Crimes. *Law & Society Review* 13(2): 431–459.
Lastra R and Shams H (2001) Public Accountability in the Financial Sector. In: Ferrán E and Goodhart C (eds) *Regulating Financial Services and Markets in the XXIst Century*. Oxford: Hart Publishing, 165–188.
Lawton D (2013) *Evolving the FCA's Approach to Markets Regulation (Speech)*. Available at: www.fca.org.uk/news/evolving-the-fca-approach-to-markets-regulation.
Levi M (2006) The Media Construction of Financial White-collar Crimes. *British Journal of Criminology* 46(6): 1037–1057.
Levi M (2009) Suite Revenge? The Shaping of Folk Devils and Moral Panics About White-Collar Crimes. *British Journal of Criminology* 49(1): 48–67.
Levi M (2011) Social Reactions to White-Collar Crimes and Their Relationship to Economic Crises. In: Deflem M (ed) *Economic Crisis and Crime (Sociology of Crime, Law and Deviance, Volume 16)*. Cambridge, MA: Emerald Group Publishing Limited, 87–105.
MacNeil I (2007) The Evolution of Regulatory Enforcement Action in the UK Capital Markets: A Case of 'Less is More'? *Capital Markets Law Journal* 2(4): 345–369.
Makkai T and Braithwaite J (1992) In and Out of the Revolving Door: Making Sense of Regulatory Capture. *Journal of Public Policy* 12(1): 61–78.
Malloy TF (2010) The Social Construction of Regulation: Lessons from the War Against Command and Control. *Buffalo Law Review* 58(2): 267–355.
May PJ and Winter S (1999) Regulatory Enforcement and Compliance: Examining Danish Agro-Environmental Policy. *Journal of Policy Analysis and Management* 18(4): 625–651.
May PJ and Winter S (2000) Reconsidering Styles of Regulatory Enforcement: Patterns in Danish Agro-Environmental Inspection. *Law & Policy* 22(2): 143–173.
McDermott T (2011) *Financial Crime from the FSA to the FCA (Speech)*. Available at: https://webarchive.nationalarchives.gov.uk/ukgwa/20121211012622/http://www.fsa.gov.uk/library/communication/speeches/2011/0622_tm.shtml.
McDermott T (2012) *Strengthening Defences: Tackling Financial Crime from the Regulator's Perspective (Speech)*. Available at: https://webarchive.nationalarchives.gov.uk/ukgwa/20121210045700/http://www.fsa.gov.uk/library/communication/speeches/2012/0926-tm.shtml.
McDermott T (2013a) *Financial Services Regulation and Enforcement: Recent Developments and Emerging Issues (Speech)*. Available at: www.fca.org.uk/news/speeches/financial-services-regulation-enforcement.
McDermott T (2013b) *Enforcement and Credible Deterrence in the FCA (Speech)*. Available at: www.fca.org.uk/news/speeches/enforcement-and-credible-deterrence-in-the-fca.
Moloney N (2010) Financial Services and Markets. In: Baldwin R, Cave M and Lodge M (eds) *The Oxford Handbook of Regulation*. New York: Oxford University Press, 120–145.
Moschella M and Tsingou E (2013) Regulating Finance after the Crisis: Unveiling the Different Dynamics of the Regulatory Process. *Regulation & Governance* 7(4): 407–416.
O'Brien J (2005) The Politics of Enforcement: Eliot Spitzer, State-Federal Relations, and the Redesign of Financial Regulation. *Publius* 35(3): 449–466.
Pain J (2010) *FSA's Approach to Intensive Supervision (Speech)*. Available at: https://webarchive.nationalarchives.gov.uk/ukgwa/20121211003950/http://www.fsa.gov.uk/library/communication/speeches/2010/0518_jp.shtml.
Parker C (2006) The "Compliance" Trap: The Moral Message in Regulatory Enforcement. *Law & Society Review* 40(3): 591–622.
Parliamentary Commission on Banking Standards (2013) *Changing Banking for Good: Report (Vol. I: Summary, and Conclusions and Recommendations, HL Paper 27-I HC 175-I)*.

Reiss AJ, Jr (1984) Selecting Strategies of Social Control Over Organziational Life. In: Hawkins K and Thomas J (eds) *Enforcing Regulation*. Boston: Kluwer-Nijhoff, 23–35.

Rex J (2020) Anatomy of Agency Capture: An Organizational Typology for Diagnosing and Remedying Capture. *Regulation & Governance* 14: 271–294.

Rider B (2008) Where Angels Fear! *Company Lawyer* 29(9): 257–258.

Sants H (2007a) *Hedge Funds – Lessons from the Recent Market Turmoil, a Supervisor's Perspective (Speech)*. Available at: https://webarchive.nationalarchives.gov.uk/ukgwa/20121210232001/http://www.fsa.gov.uk/library/communication/speeches/2006/1017_mc.shtml.

Sants H (2007b) *The FSA's Retail Agenda: Working with the Industry (Speech)*. Available at: https://webarchive.nationalarchives.gov.uk/ukgwa/20121211000932/http://www.fsa.gov.uk/library/communication/speeches/2007/1121_hs.shtml.

Sants H (2008) *Judgements on Judgements – Retail Firms and Principles-Based Regulation (Speech)*. Available at: https://webarchive.nationalarchives.gov.uk/ukgwa/20121211010802/http://www.fsa.gov.uk/library/communication/speeches/2008/0227_hs.shtml.

Sants H (2009a) *Delivering Intensive Supervision and Credible Deterrence (Speech)*. Available at: https://webarchive.nationalarchives.gov.uk/ukgwa/20121210234203/http://www.fsa.gov.uk/library/communication/speeches/2009/0312_hs.shtml.

Sants H (2009b) *CEO's Speech – FSA Annual Public Meeting (Speech)*. Available at: https://webarchive.nationalarchives.gov.uk/ukgwa/20121210235501/http://www.fsa.gov.uk/library/communication/speeches/2009/0723_hs.shtml.

Sants H (2009c) *The Regulator's Role in Judging Competence (Speech)*. Available at: https://webarchive.nationalarchives.gov.uk/ukgwa/20121210235425/http://www.fsa.gov.uk/library/communication/speeches/2009/0507_hs.shtml.

Sants H (2009d) *The Challenges Facing Bank Regulation (Speech)*. Available at: https://webarchive.nationalarchives.gov.uk/ukgwa/20121210235655/http://www.fsa.gov.uk/library/communication/speeches/2009/0514_hs.shtml.

Sants H (2009e) *Intensive Supervision: Delivering the Best Outcomes (Speech)*. Available at: https://webarchive.nationalarchives.gov.uk/ukgwa/20091203180100/http://www.fsa.gov.uk/pages/Library/Communication/Speeches/2009/1109_hs.shtml.

Sants H (2012) *Delivering 'Twin Peaks' within the FSA (Speech)*. Available at: https://webarchive.nationalarchives.gov.uk/ukgwa/20121210050646/http://www.fsa.gov.uk/library/communication/speeches/2012/0206-hs.shtml.

Sarbin TR and Kitsuse JI (1994) *Constructing the Social*. London: Sage Publications.

Schlegel K (1990) *Just Deserts for Corporate Criminals*. Boston: Northeastern University Press.

Shapiro SP (1985) The Road Not Taken: The Elusive Path to Criminal Prosecution for White-Collar Offenders. *Law & Society Review* 19(2): 179–217.

Simpson SS, Leeper-Piquero N and Paternoster R (2002) Rationality and Corporate Offending Decisions. In: Piquero AR and Tibbetts SG (eds) *Rational Choice and Criminal Behavior*. New York: Routledge, 25–39.

Snider L (1990) Cooperative Models and Corporate Crime: Panacea or Cop Out? *Crime & Delinquency* 36(3): 373–390.

Snider L (2009) Accommodating Power: The 'Common Sense' of Regulators. *Social & Legal Studies* 18(2): 179.

Snider L (2013) The Technological Advantages of Stock Market Traders. In: Will S, Handelman S and Brotherton DC (eds) *How They Got Away with It: White Collar Criminals and the Financial Meltdown*. New York: Columbia University Press, 151–170.

Steward M (2017a) *Practical Implications of US Law on EU Practice (Speech)*. Available at: www.fca.org.uk/news/speeches/practical-implications-us-law-eu-practice.

Steward M (2017b) *The Expanding Scope of Individual Accountability for Corporate Misconduct (Speech)*. Available at: https://www.fca.org.uk/news/speeches/expanding-scope-individual-accountability-corporate-misconduct.

Steward M (2017c) *A Better View (Speech)*. Available at: www.fca.org.uk/news/speeches/better-view.

Tiner J (2006) *Keynote Address – Enforcement Law Conference (Speech)*. Available at: https://webarchive.nationalarchives.gov.uk/ukgwa/20121210231514/http://www.fsa.gov.uk/library/communication/speeches/2006/0616_jt.shtml.

Titcomb L (2008) *Supervision of Small Firms (Speech)*. Available at: https://webarchive.nationalarchives.gov.uk/ukgwa/20121211011259/http://www.fsa.gov.uk/library/communication/speeches/2008/0305_lt.shtml.

Titcomb L (2010) *FSA Outlines Plans for Mortgage Market (Speech)*. Available at: https://webarchive.nationalarchives.gov.uk/ukgwa/20121211003508/http://www.fsa.gov.uk/library/communication/speeches/2010/0617_lt.shtml.

Tomasic R (2011) The Financial Crisis and the Haphazard Pursuit of Financial Crime. *Journal of Financial Crime* 18(1): 7–31.

Tombs S and Whyte D (2015) *The Corporate Criminal: Why Corporations must be Abolished*. Abingdon: Routledge.

Treasury Committee (2008) *Financial Stability and Transparency (Written and Oral Evidence, HC 536-i, ii and iii)*. London: The Stationary Office.

Treasury Committee (2012) *Second Report. Fixing LIBOR: Some Preliminary Findings (Vol. I: Oral Evidence, HC 481-II)*. London: The Stationery Office.

Turner A (2009) *The Turner Review: A Regulatory Response to the Global Banking Crisis*. Availableat:https://webarchive.nationalarchives.gov.uk/ukgwa/20090320232953/http:/www.fsa.gov.uk/pubs/other/turner_review.pdf.

van Erp J (2010) Regulatory Disclosure of Offending Companies in the Dutch Financial Market: Consumer Protection or Enforcement Publicity? *Law & Policy* 32(4): 407–433.

von Hirsch A (1993) *Censure and Sanctions*. Oxford: Oxford University Press.

Waters D (2009) *PPI and Competition Commission Remedies (Speech)*. Available at: https://webarchive.nationalarchives.gov.uk/ukgwa/20110801153024/http://www.fsa.gov.uk/pages/Library/Communication/Speeches/2009/0224_dw.shtml.

Wheatley M (2013) *The Changing Face of Financial Crime (Speech)*. Available at: www.fca.org.uk/news/speeches/the-changing-face-of-financial-crime.

Wilson G and Wilson S (2014) The FSA, "Credible Deterrence", and Criminal Enforcement – a "Haphazard Pursuit"? *Journal of Financial Crime* 21(1): 4–28.

Zingales L (2015) Does Finance Benefit Society? *Chicago Booth Research Paper No. 15-09*. Available at: https://ssrn.com/abstract=2585194.

Cases

R v Anjam Ahmad [2010] (unreported).

R v Calvert [2010] (unreported).

R v McQuoid (Christopher) [2009] EWCA Crim 1301.

R v Mustafa & others [2012] (unreported).

R v Sanders & others [2012] (unreported).

3 Detecting financial misconduct and the informational traffic

Mutual risk mitigation

Financial regulators inherently operate in an environment of informational asymmetry regarding the markets and corporations they supervise. Regulatory resources constraints and the complexities surrounding finance make regulatees the principal proprietors of information about the risks and hazards of products, market conduct practices, and non-compliant behaviour. Flawed regulatory knowledge, together with a lack of inquisitiveness and willingness to use discretionary powers to gather information, was a key contributing factor to the financial crisis (Black, 2013; MacNeil & O'Brien, 2010; Levitin, 2014; Tett, 2010; Turner, 2009).

This chapter documents the post-crisis shifts towards knowing more of the markets and deviant behaviour in them. It analyses the processes of gathering information in the crisis aftermath, the potential for detection of non-compliance that is embedded in the information traffic between the regulator and the regulated, and the recording of misconduct in the formal enforcement docket. Detection concerns how information on misconduct or compliance that falls short of the regulatory objectives first comes to the attention of regulators (Baldwin et al., 2012; Black, 2014), and how regulators decide what counts as information about compliance (Lange, 1999). This is the first step in the contentious regulatory relationship and the first point at which misconduct is constructed through confidential[1] micro-level regulatory interactions as regulators perceive business behaviour as problematic and potentially deviant.

Similarly to how the police detects crime (Reiss, 1983), the sources of detecting non-compliance by regulators can be divided into reactive and proactive (Almond, 2006; Hawkins, 1984, 2002; Hutter, 1986, 1997; Shapiro, 1984; Williams, 2009, 2012, 2013). *Proactive detection* occurs on the inspectors' own initiative to undertake on-site visits of regulated firms (Hutter, 1988, 1997). For the FCA, this includes supervisory activity of any kind:

1 Unless the FCA imposes a formal sanction, its enquiries, investigations, and use of information-gathering powers are protected with the statutory cloak of confidentiality of Section 348 FSMA.

DOI: 10.4324/9781351069328-3

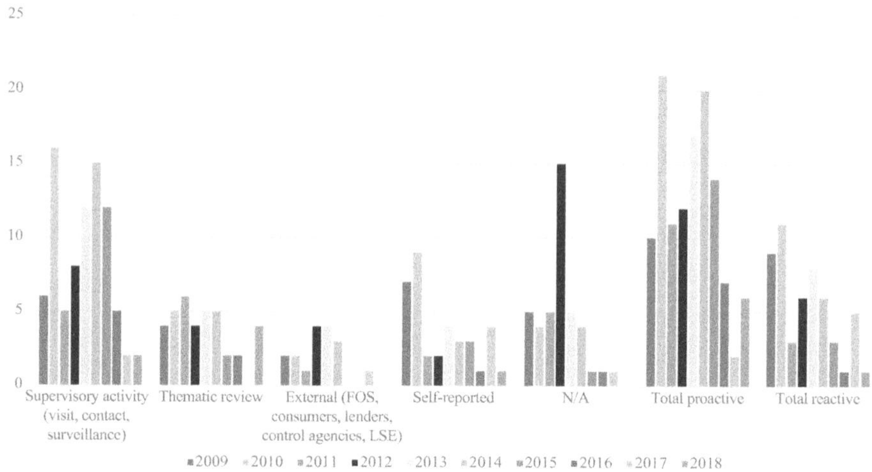

Figure 3.1 Detection sources.

visit, desk-based contact, and technological surveillance of the markets. ***Reactive detection*** occurs on sources that are external to the organisation. Following and adapting Shapiro's categorisation (1984), the reactive sources in the FCA context can be classified as five distinct groups: insiders or wrongdoers (self-reporting by regulatees); victims (complaints and, by extension, from the Financial Ombudsman Service [FOS]; see Gilad, 2008a, 2008b); other market participants, including whistle-blowers (see Wilson & Wilson, 2010); other organisations with some social control function (the Serious Fraud Office, the police, HMRC, etc.); and the press.

Figure 3.1 shows the distribution of the various routes through which corporate offending was detected as officially reported in FSA/FCA final notices (where this information was available) in the period 2009–2018. Proactive detection sources are clustered around supervisory activity (visit, contact, surveillance) and thematic reviews. Reactive detection sources are clustered around information provided by external actors (Financial Ombudsman Service or consumer complaints, lenders, social control agencies, the London Stock Exchange) and through self-reporting by the regulated.

The data show that proactive sources led to significantly more penalised misconduct than reactive ones, though the numbers should be approached with some caution because of the high number of notices with no detection information (19.2 per cent of the notices). This might indicate that most non-compliance was detected through agency initiative, involving 'officials going and seeking out offences' (Hutter, 1986: 114, 1997: Ch. 5). However, in the experience of the interviewees, the regulator learnt of most misconduct through self-reporting rather than through supervisory activities.

This chapter explores in detail the FCA detection sources, organised around supervisory activities, skilled persons reviews, self-reporting, and other external sources, and the complex relationship between the reactive and pro-active sources, notably supervisory information-gathering and self-reporting. Throughout, it identifies the trends supporting the movement towards proactive attitudes to using the considerable statutory and regulatory powers 'on the ground' to enquire, diagnose, and detect non-compliance. Informed by the interactionist and constructivist theoretical frameworks, I develop and employ the theoretical concept of ***mutual risk mitigation*** to account for the increased information requests and the types of responses and devices developed by financial institutions to information provision.

Regulatory use of information-gathering powers: the information-hungry regulator

As Figure 3.1 shows, supervisory activities (including thematic reviews) represented the most important FCA detection source, accounting for 69 per cent of all referrals. Supervisory activities operate along three internal dimensions: supervisory philosophy and framework, tools and techniques of inspection, and supervisor resources, such as staff numbers and skills. These are intertwined. For example, though the FCA's statutory tools of inspection (e.g. Section 165 FSMA on information requests) have remained fairly static, the ways and extent to which they were employed in practice depended on the agency's supervisory framework (e.g. through risk-based methods, such as themed work) and supervisors' attitudes (e.g. more or less interventionist). Resources affected both (e.g. lesser resources mean a lesser ability to inspect, thus a lesser ability for more interventionist attitudes).

Supervisory philosophy

After the crisis and the introduction of the intrusive supervision and risk mitigation policy approaches as 'credible deterrence' companions, the FSA adopted an intensive, direct, and judgement-oriented supervisory style (Sants, 2009b; Ferran, 2012). The judgement-led approach was meant to enable 'supervisors to identify and focus on the big risks to their statutory objectives; [and] make the right judgement as to the course of action to reduce the probability of risks to their statutory objectives' (Sants, 2012). A key component of the more pro-active style was a closer supervisory engagement with the corporate governance of financial firms, or closer engagement with firms' senior management (Ferran, 2011). The empirical data elicited some evidence that supervisory attitudes changed towards a more proactive supervisor. This entailed a willingness to undertake a more interventionist and 'aggressive' (a word frequently used by industry interviewees to describe the FCA's regulatory style [also, Sants, 2009a]) approach to detecting non-compliance evidenced through a judgement-based decision-making (including early intervention work) and an increased information appetite.

These shifts originated under the ARROW risk-based model and were then firmly cemented as the supervisory philosophy of the new FCA and its new risk model – the Firm Systematic Framework, events, and products supervision (FSF/E/P hereafter) (FSA, 2012a; FCA, 2013). In practice, regulators perceived their mandate of intrusive supervision as the need to make judgement-based decisions in line with the formal justifications provided for the introduction of the FSF/E/P framework (e.g. Sants, 2012). Judgement-based decision-making was closely aligned with the need to intervene early. This was interpreted in two ways: as acting to prevent the crystallisation of harm rather than to remedy an already-crystallised harm and as acting without being overly cautious regarding the required evidence and information on risks:

> The key part of the cultural change is around being more judgemental. We should be more prepared to make judgement-based decisions much earlier than we have in the past, taking the risk of making those decisions at an earlier stage, and perhaps with less evidence than we might have wanted in the past.
>
> (Regulator02)

As different types of detection approaches yield a different catch (Shapiro, 1984), judgement-based intervention also meant that a greater focus was placed on detecting and diagnosing the *root causes* of non-compliance (in terms of flawed business models, culture, product design, training, or rewards), rather than the earlier process-driven focus on detecting whether the firm's internal systems were compliant with regulation. The emphasis on tackling the perceived *root causes* of non-compliance drove the enforcement priorities and supervisors' attitudes on what they should be inspecting for. In some cases, where there was only a *risk* of crystallisation of harm, the focus on the *root causes* meant that detection was not solely about *actual* non-compliance but also about *potential* non-compliance. In other cases, however, the detected *root causes* of non-compliance were enforced as *actual* non-compliance:

> The cases [on incentives structures] are not because the incentive structures have led to loss to consumers. They are because we don't like the incentive structures because of the way they make salesmen behave, which could lead to loss to consumers.
>
> (Regulator01)

These attitudes support notions that there was a shift in the regulation of retail financial services from 'reactive regulation' to a deeper and more interventionist reach into the structural composition of the retail investment market, including its flawed incentives structure (Moloney, 2010: 439). A further example of proactive work on changing incentives structures were the new rules of the Retail Distribution Review (RDR), introduced in 2012, which amended disclosure rules on adviser charging and services, removed commission payments to advisers and platforms from product owners, and raised the minimum level of adviser qualification (FCA, 2014a). Such interventions, however, would only be effective if regulators dispose with adequate information to assess and make a judgement on where the root causes for non-compliance or the *risks* lie. Risk-based systems are even more so dependent on possessing quality information to feed into the risk assessment system (Baldwin & Black, 2008), and this is despite the lower threshold of information that regulators were apparently willing to accept as sufficient for acting.

Risk-based framework recalibrations: from firm-specific to thematic supervision

In technical terms, the new FSF/E/P risk-based framework marked a shift in supervisory emphasis from mostly firm-specific regulatory interactions to a broader canvass combining firm-specific supervision with enhanced sector and cross-sector analysis, the use of regulatory returns, thematic and combined firm-specific/thematic work, and a focus on the key drivers of risk (FCA, 2013). The Firm Systematic Framework (FSF) focused on preventative work through structured conduct assessment of firms, identifying and providing 'solutions for potential causes of poor conduct' (FCA, 2013: 18) that could result in risks to the FCA's statutory objectives: poor consumer outcomes, risks to market integrity, or barriers to effective competition. Firms were assigned to one of four categories, C1 to C4, based on their potential impact on FCA's objectives. The assessment moved from supervising firms only at specific times to continuous assessment only for the 'fixed portfolio' C1–C2 firms (banking and insurance groups with a very large number of retail customers or very large client assets and trading operations, firms across all sectors with a substantial number of retail customers, and/or large wholesale firms) through a nominated supervisor. C3 and C4 category firms (firms across all sectors with retail customers and/or a significant wholesale presence; smaller firms, including almost all intermediaries) were pooled into a 'flexible portfolio' firms supervised by a team of sector specialists. Close regulatory interactions of the responsive type were therefore available regarding the 'fixed', but not the 'flexible', portfolio firms. The events supervision pillar entailed rapid reactions to ongoing or developing events of potential or actual harm to consumers, market integrity, or competition (FCA, 2013). Finally, the issues and products pillar concerned thematic or cross-firm work, looking at 'issues which cut across a number of firms or sectors and where there is a risk of detriment to consumers' (FCA, 2013: 18). The pooling of firms into four categories and the fewer supervisors allocated to specific firms allowed a greater flexibility to address events risks and undertake more reviews on products and issues across sectors or markets (FSA, 2012a). It also relied on a greater outsourcing of inspection of remedial work, both to regulatees and to third parties, through expectations of follow-up by the firm instead of extensive follow-up work by supervisors, and a greater use of Section 166 or skilled persons reviews powers (FCA, 2013).

Thematic and combined firm-specific/thematic work took a prominent place. Thematic reviews are specialist risk-based inspection programmes organised not around assessing the potential level of risk posed by any one firm directly (Black, 2005) but around assessing the level of threat to the FCA's objectives posed by a theme that connects several firms within a sector or market (e.g. a product, governance, or conduct issue) (see FCA, 2013). This enables a more macro-level perspective of potential financial misconduct whilst efficiently managing resources around 'disaggregation-breaking down complex and overwhelming tasks into discrete, actionable projects' (Sparrow, 2000: 147). Consistent with the *broad church of cases* approach to enforcement priorities, thematic reviews were undertaken across the range of financial services, firm sizes, and conduct of business issues through on-site visits or through information-gathering from a chosen sample of firms.

Thematic reviews fared quite well as detection and enforcement docket sources. In the final notices sample, thematic reviews yielded 21 per cent of all referrals, and these included targets across the range and sizes of firms. That thematic reviews represented a crucial (and perhaps the dominant) detection source for the FCA was also confirmed in the joint interview with two senior enforcement staff, who indicated that most of their work in the retail sector was shaped by thematic work. For example, of the 50 firms visited regarding the advice quality of small mortgage brokers, 6 firms were referred to enforcement; of the 21 smaller banks visited to assess their AML and sanctions systems and controls, 2 banks were referred for enforcement (FCA, 2014b).

In addition, a cross-check analysis of the number of enforcement referrals, mentioned in a few thematic review reports and subsequent notices, shows that, in many cases, the thematic referrals resulted in a successful enforcement outcome. For example, the review of banks' management of high-money-laundering-risk situations (FSA, 2011) included a review of the AML systems of 27 banks, resulting in two referrals and considerations of further referrals (announced in 2011), with two banks sanctioned in 2012,[2] and two in 2013.[3] The referred cases were considered the 'worst' ones in the sample, hence the easiest to prove on the evidence. Yet the success rate was also connected to the fact that, though thematic reviews were chosen, designed, and undertaken by supervisors, enforcement staff were important stakeholders in the process. Their involvement was oriented toward providing input on how referrals from thematic reviews could stand scrutiny in a potential formal enforcement process regarding the evidentiary requirements:

> Supervision is inviting us in the planning of thematic reviews. If, for example, they're designing a methodology for reviewing sales of a product, that that methodology would stand scrutiny, it meets as evidence in an enforcement case. We can further advise on how to

2 Coutts & Company FN23/03/12 and Turkish Bank (UK) Ltd FN26/07/12.
3 EFG Private Bank FN28/03/13 and Guaranty Trust Bank UKFN 08/08/13.

> structure the thematic review to maximise prospects of an enforcement referral and an enforcement outcome.
>
> (Regulator01)

This quotation underscores the importance of thematic reviews as an enforcement tool. Thematic reviews were originally conceptualised as a supervisory tool, and their principal aim was not enforcement-led. Whilst the FSA was initially concerned that the industry does not perceive thematic work 'as being used by the FSA as a springboard to Enforcement' (Cole, 2007), an agency-level ethos developed of embracing thematic reviews as precursors to enforcement actions. Market participants and their advisers also recognised that the FCA worked on a 'fairly thematic basis' on perceived failures in the market, which inevitably resulted into 'taking a case and mak[ing] an example of somebody':

> It tends to be 'the flavour of the month' at any given time. You can get a pretty good idea from reading the annual business plan and Risk Outlook to see where their focus is, and the areas where they are currently working on. I am sure that if the FCA says 'We are taking a close look at conflicts of interests or asset managers', it means 'We got cases in the pipeline'.
>
> (Lawyer03)

For this reason, thematic reviews are similar to regulators' attempts to leverage general deterrence incentives by 'launching targeted enforcement initiatives that single out particular industries or activities for added scrutiny' (Short & Toffel, 2008: 53). In the UK markets, such efforts could have led to increased firms' expectations that their *theme* violations would be discovered, though it is uncertain whether this has led to motivating greater compliance. For example, in a follow-up thematic work on small banks' AML and sanctions systems, the FCA visited 21 banks, finding continuing weaknesses in most small banks' AML systems and controls (FCA, 2014b). This was despite the heightened regulatory focus on the *theme* of AML systems failings across the banking sector and the fact that the FCA had already visited some of the poor-performing banks during its previous thematic review.[4]

The 'information-hungry' regulator

In the crisis aftermath, the regulator adopted an increasingly growing appetite to receive information of various kinds, going well beyond the required regular submission of reports by firms. This was a crucial indicator of the more

4 This included Sonali Bank, which was investigated and fined in result of the follow-up thematic work. Sonali Bank UK Ltd FN12/10/16.

interventionist regulatory style. Supervisors' attitudes shifted towards a greater use of the statutory information-gathering powers to gain deeper insights into firms' governance structures, products, and services, and by extension, into industry practices. These attempts to overcome the informational imbalance (Manning, 1989) with the industry could lead to detecting both the root causes of non-compliance and non-compliance itself.

The changes in the risk-based framework towards sector supervision supported the growth in the information traffic. The supervision approach of the previous FSA relied on named supervisors and ongoing relationships with firms, containing the information exchange within narrower, firm-specific issues. The changes towards significantly less-firm-level-focused supervision and a greater emphasis on sector supervision supported and prompted greater and different types of information requests:

> There is no bespoke supervisory model, but there are sector-wide requests for data. This also means that the information that the FCA is requesting is less-specific. The FCA is now interested in collecting generic information across the sector. For example, in the investment banking market study, the FCA went and asked for the same information from all the firms in the sector that participated in the study.
>
> (LawyerFR20)

In practice, the growing appetite for information became one of the dominant traits of the more intrusive supervisory approach, and the FCA was described by one participant as an 'information-hungry regulator' that constantly wants more information:

> It's a real desire, 'give us information, we want to know, we'll decide if it's not very interesting, but tell us.' The supervision teams for the big banks, and the other financial institutions that we work for, are asking for more information to be divulged regularly. Firms are fully aware that the FCA wants more and more information, so a lot of clients are asking for advice around that difficult area.
>
> (Lawyer06)

Coupled with this were expectations of short turnover periods for providing the requested information, especially when non-compliance had been detected. The focus on demanding significant amounts of information aimed to prevent future informational imbalances and construct lack of record-keeping as deviance. This sent a message that firms should always be able to comply with tight deadline requests for information, that certain documents should always be kept, that record-keeping should be functioning flawlessly, and that documents and information should always be made easily accessible to the regulator – from whatever part of the organisation:

> The FCA has a rather high-minded expectation that you keep all this information, so you should just be able to produce it *like that*. The practicalities of how the financial institutions work mean that even if they are running completely compliant systems, it takes a bit of time to produce that or to find the right people to produce it, or to produce it in a way which is matched in the way the FCA wants to read it, rather than how it appears on their systems.
>
> (LawyerFR04; emphasis added)

The possible struggles, however, to provide information in short turnover periods are important, since compliant behaviour is not achieved solely by having a motivation to comply but also with having a capacity to comply (May, 2005; Nielsen & Parker, 2012; Winter & May, 2001). This encompasses awareness of the rules and how to comply with them (May, 2005: 322), but also available resources (economic, technical know-how, knowledge of the law, managerial capacity and oversight, etc.) (Nielsen & Parker, 2012; Parker & Nielsen, 2006; Winter & May, 2001). These capacity indicators vary across firms, with larger firms having more such resources (Gunningham et al., 2004; Parker & Nielsen, 2011). In practice, smaller firms especially struggled with the wide document requests.

The increased appetite for information and the lesser number of nominated supervisors within the FSF/E/P meant that more misconduct could be spotted through 'traditional reactive work' (Woodall, 2010) with desk-based tools of inspection rather than through visiting firms. However, for desk-based work to function as an effective detection mechanism, especially in the context of judgement-based regulation, obtaining knowledge is not enough. Two further conditions need to be met: supervisors need to be of sufficiently high quality (Lastra, 2013) to make adequate judgements based on that knowledge, and the knowledge itself also needs to be of sufficiently high quality. This chapter later problematises the (perceived) quality of supervisors, and of the knowledge, indicating that the desk-based system of detection could be impaired by both organisational regulatory factors and regulatees' influence.

Tools of inspection and constructing deviance

Supervisors did various types of work that generated referrals to enforcement, but these can be categorised into desk-based work and on-site visits to firms' premises. Desk-based work concerned requesting information and analysis of the requested information, regulatory returns, transaction reporting, information from reactive sources of detection (e.g. consumer complaints, or self-reporting), and broader internal considerations of 'risk alerts' (Pain, 2010). At the height of the financial crisis, such risk alert, for example, was triggered by the information on the endemic spread of dishonest mortgage brokers in the United States and the effects of their actions on the wider US financial system. This prompted UK regulators to analyse the spread of local mortgage brokers internally and to use complex algorithms to map the extent of the UK lending that could have been affected (interview data). This risk alert also prompted subsequent thematic reviews to detect mortgages misconduct and resulted into banning around 80 mortgage advisers.

Supervisors also conducted on-site visits of firms' premises, a crucial detection source. These were akin to regular inspections undertaken in other contexts (e.g. Hawkins, 2002; Hutter, 1997). Depending on the size of the business and the complexity of the issue, the visits lasted two to five days, with teams of two to six supervisors. The visits could be announced (including thematic work) and unannounced. Unannounced visits were the rarest form of inspection and were used only when there was an urgent need to disrupt deviant behaviour. In these cases, supervisors commonly interfered upon received consumer complaints, accusations by competitor organisations, or whistle-blowers.

During visits, supervisors undertook document reviews and interviews with employees. Document reviews included inspection of internal policies, communications, transactions, or organisational structures to detect flaws in the meta-regulatory governance, or to ascertain the responsibilities and hierarchy in the decision-making process. For small businesses without regular supervisory interactions, the visits and activities of poring through samples of files could be quite intimidating. Reviews also included sampling or inspecting a certain sample of documents or transactions (e.g. sales files, assessments of politically exposed persons' risk levels, etc.).[5] Due to resources constraints, in some cases, the sample was only 20 or 30 files. Sampling was a method of both detection and evidence-gathering. It was directly associated with statistics and the formulation of risks based on identifying patterns, hotspots, and deviations from the norm (Mazerolle & Ransley, 2005: 14). This meant that there was a certain threshold of acceptance, or an accepted 'norm' of non-compliant files. The firm was considered to be in breach if the sample had non-compliant files above the accepted deviance threshold. The margins of 'normal' deviance varied in terms of what the regulator would accept (1–2 per cent of non-compliant files; 'If we had found that only 1 or 2 per cent was a problem, I think we would have gotten away with it' [Lawyer02]), what it might accept with a 'bit of persuasion' (3–4 per cent), and what it will not accept (5 per cent and above). The 1–2 per cent margin could be dealt with through informal supervisory negotiations. The 3–4 per cent margin required more commitment on behalf of the firm in proposing remedial steps so that the detected non-compliance might be resolved informally. Finally, 'the rough rule of thumb is [that] 5 per cent of anything is viewed as significant' (Lawyer02). These numbers were not written down in official publications, yet

5 This inspection tool is similar to the process of sampling (e.g. of water, soil, etc.) in the enforcement of environmental regulation (Hawkins, 1984; Hutter, 1997).

they echoed across interviews. Deviance was constructed through what the regulators were prepared to acknowledge and record as deviance, in this case as a statistical deviance (see also Williams, 2013).

The risk-based assessments and visits should mean that the product of most routine supervisory visits was detection of non-compliance by the largest firms. However, this was not reflected in the officially penalised misconduct. The analysis of notices did not reveal that the largest firms were referred to enforcement more often because of a routine supervisory visit. The largest firms in the sample were commonly referred as a result of a thematic review, self-reporting, as a result of a spin-off of an investigation into one large institution on a common misconduct (e.g. LIBOR) or after analysing firms' transaction reporting to spot market abuse. For example, in several cases where large firms were fined for incorrect transaction reporting, the non-compliance was spotted by the Markets Oversight team. Supervisory visits to large firms could mean employing more negotiation or compliance-oriented approaches, provision of guidance and information, rather than more adversarial approaches. Large firms might still be able to keep close relational distance (Hutter, 2011) with their supervisors, enabling more negotiations based on trust. The importance of this relational distance was also evidenced in that medium-sized firms were most commonly referred based on supervisory visits and thematic reviews whilst only in a handful of cases were discovered through self-reporting. Small firms, the furthest in relational distance, were referred based on visits prompted by a reactive source (complaints, lender alerts) and from thematic reviews.

Supervisory inspections had a reinforcement relationship with motivating regulatees to comply and to self-report non-compliance. The data provided some evidence that announced visits had a specific deterrent effect as they increased self-reporting of own misconduct to the regulator:

> There could be an announcement of an ARROW visit. The internal compliance then undertakes an audit a month before the supervisors come. They might find something and then call us. We might do an internal investigation. . . . You self-report in advance so that the FCA doesn't discover this themselves.
>
> (Lawyer08)

This finding is in line with extant research that inspections encourage self-reporting and that compliance improves subsequent to inspections (Braithwaite & Makkai, 1991; Gunningham et al., 2005; Short & Toffel, 2008; Winter & May, 2001, though see Stretesky, 2006). Having a greater number of supervisors to conduct on-site visits instead of desk-based work would contribute to raising compliance. In practice, however, regulatees were frequently prepared for a supervisory visit by industry consultants or external lawyers. This raises the question of whether 'Potemkin villages' were created in view of the regulators' call (Gray, 2006): tidying up the business in view of inspection, but only in a cosmetic manner. Arguably, this could be difficult in terms of recreating the paperwork that often underpins financial services practices and is required at the time of a product sale or transaction completion; hence, there might be a lesser scope for building 'Potemkin villages' in finance.

Supervisory resources and the dynamics of stakeholder participation

The extent to which supervisory activities can lead to detecting misconduct is crucially shaped by the available human resources in terms of staff numbers and skills. Figure 2.1 shows that there was a constant increase in FSA/FCA staff, indicating also an increase in the agency's regulatory intensity (Jackson, 2005) and the ability to probe business. However, the rise in staff numbers should be viewed in context of the lesser number of nominated supervisors under FSF/E/P with a Janus-type effect on processing misconduct. A reduced number of supervisors indicated a lesser capacity for routine visits and information-gathering from specific firms, but in practice, it also meant that there were fewer opportunities for more sustained relationships to evolve between dedicated supervisors and regulatees. This increased relational distance might mean less opportunities for negotiating compliance based upon trust, but also less potential for allegations of 'capture' (Hutter, 2011: 311). The lesser number of relationships reduced the ability to influence the process of detection and enforcement referral, making it 'harder for firms to get leverage off a relationship with an individual supervisor' (LawyerFR03). This meant a lesser scope for supervisors to feel personal failure for regulatees' non-compliance and apprehensiveness to refer them to enforcement, as was occasionally the case in the past: '[I]t was a bit of a black mark against a supervisor to refer one of their firms to enforcement' (LawyerFR06). At the micro-level of regulatory interactions, this also contributed to the more punitive FCA enforcement style, since there could be more willingness to go to law, and formal sanctions could be more likely (Grabosky & Braithwaite, 1986; Hutter, 2011).

Regarding the quality of staff, opinions of supervisors' expertise and skills varied according to their organisational position. Enforcement staff was perceived as of mostly high quality across different hierarchical levels. The perceived differences in staff quality echoed internally within the FCA also as, according to a former enforcement member, '[a] lot of people in Enforcement are lawyers, so they would consider it a step down if they went to Supervision. It was considered less elite' (LawyerFR08). Junior supervisors, at the lower level of the hierarchy but with the most opportunities for direct interaction with supervisees, were commonly considered to lack the knowledge, the experience, or the authority to take decisive actions. This was especially problematic for the bracket of non-relationship managed firms, as 'the junior staff at the bottom of the food chain' were considered 'too scared and too inexperienced' or lacking an organisational 'clout' (Braithwaite & Murphy, 1993) to sanction a proposed remedy of spotted non-compliance:

> [In] any regulatory problem which involves a compromise between the regulator's view of the ideal outcome and the firm's view of the range of outcomes that they can produce in reality without going out of business, there needs to be a decision on what is the available compromise. It is very difficult to get a meeting with someone who is senior enough to actually take a decision to dispose of something.
>
> (LawyerFR18)

This made the regulatory conversations fraught with repetitive demands, either to remedy the problem according to the supervisor's view of the 'fix' or for further information. The latter approach falls below even the persuasive responses to non-compliance, located at the bottom of the enforcement pyramid. The situation could be overcome if a more senior supervisor became involved, and on occasion, being represented by a former FSA/FCA staff member accelerated this contact:

> What I tend to do is to phone up colleagues in the General Counsel Division and say, 'Can you please get a grip on this?' Sometimes a gentle push from the lawyers will do it, and sometimes, if I happen to know the head of [the] department in question, I will phone them up myself.
>
> (LawyerFR18)

The perceptions of the differential quality of FCA staff across organisational parts echo extant research showing that regulatees value inspectors who have experience and knowledge (May & Winter, 2011; May & Wood, 2003; Pautz, 2009). However, these perceptions are not promising for the feasibility and efficiency of judgement-based regulation. Judgement-based approaches require discretionary decision making by supervisors who have the adequate experience, skills, and authority to make judgements upon knowledge on non-compliance.

The advent of the regulator's more punitive agenda saw a shift towards a more frequent joint attendance of members of both organisational sides (supervisors and enforcers) during supervisory meetings or at the initial stages of a detected problem:

> Any discussion would also involve an enforcement person, or even at least supervision people will say we are discussing this issue with Enforcement. This is absolutely in the forefront of our minds when we advise our clients; even if they got a good relationship with their supervisor, the supervisors are under an edict to have an enforcement person behind them or with them.
>
> (LawyerFR01)

Such joint attendance has been suggested to mean efforts towards a more unified approach to misconduct by the organisation as a whole (Black, 2011).

This function was emphasised also in speeches: 'where once teams worked in baronies, we now place huge emphasis on the importance of the threads that run across and between divisions' (Wheatley, 2013). This unity was supported by a reverse process: supervisors were also known to attend enforcement meetings, though they formally did not represent part of the investigating team. This was due to a personal interest in the development of the case against their supervisee or a vested interest in cases of market watch.

However, joint attendance also sent a distinct message that in cases of rule violations, unlike in the earlier days, enforcement action was never too far from consideration. The threat of an official action was now present from the outset of regulatee–supervisor discussions, making the relationship more formal, legalistic, and 'juridified' (Habermas, 1987): 'enforcement has grown substantially and works very much hand in glove with supervision. Enforcement is never far from the problems, trying to manage the supervision–enforcement interface to get supervisors to bring cases to enforcement much earlier' (LawyerFR02). This created further erosions of the notion of an intimate, personalised, and close relationship between firms and supervisors. The increased presence of enforcement staff during supervisory matters represented a social or relational indicator of the FCA's overall more punitive enforcement strategy.

Despite the more legalistic supervisory relationship, supervisors were still keen to keep the communications informal and, as much as possible, de-lawyered. Firms abided by this, it seems, out of social motivations (May, 2005) – the need to be seen as good corporate citizens by supervisors as significant others:

> This client was called to a meeting with their supervisors; they knew there were some issues, so they asked whether they needed a lawyer present, to which the supervisors said, 'We're your supervisors. Why would you need a lawyer present? We're meant to have an open and cooperative dialogue.' So they went without their lawyers.
>
> (LawyerFR16)

The focus on de-lawyering the process meant that lawyers who specialised in contentious financial matters were 'invisible' during supervisory communications even though they were commonly retained either by non-contentious external counsel within the same law firm or by inside counsel to advise on detection issues. Here, they tended to be 'more behind the scenes 'cos it looks a bit aggressive to have an enforcement lawyer, a bit too defensive' (LawyerFR06).

However, on occasion, the focus on de-lawyering the process could threaten procedural justice for the party. Regulatees might not gather that they are being subjected to an adverse regulatory power, and the absence of lawyers in supervisory meetings could further mean that they do not have the recourse to the same legal protections as during the enforcement stage. For example, on one occasion, the senior managers of a firm were called to a supervisory meeting without their lawyers and had almost signed a document for varying their regulatory permissions without realising that this would mean effective cancellation of all the firms' activities. The cloak of informality when supervisors used statutory powers might affect regulatees' perceptions of the consistency, fairness, and legitimacy of the regulatory process (Tyler, 2003). For this reason, formalism (e.g. specific statements on the public powers that are being used by supervisors in seemingly informal communication) is necessary in some regulatory conversations in the complex and technical financial services industry, as this provides greater predictability (May & Wood, 2003).

Market surveillance

The market surveillance activities of the FCA yielded information on misconduct in the wholesale markets: market abuse/insider dealing, corporate finance activities, and market manipulation. Market abuse was processed by the FCA's Markets Oversight Division, whose activities, in many respects, resembled what supervisors of retail conduct did, a combination of reactive and proactive detection work. Proactive detection combined enlisting human and technological resources in conducting supervisory visits and employing an in-house surveillance proprietary technology (Spens, 2014). The surveillance visits focused mostly on spotting problems with firms' meta-regulatory controls of market abuse prevention and their use of post-trade surveillance systems and submissions of suspicious transactions (and orders) (STRs/STORs). Financial institutions have regulatory obligations to notify the FCA if they have a reasonable suspicion that an order or a transaction, including any cancellations or modifications, in any financial instrument could constitute market abuse (insider dealing or market manipulation) or attempted market abuse (under Article 16, Market Abuse Regulation).

Through technological surveillance and software, the markets team kept 'an eye on what is going on in the markets and is able to spot anomalous trading' (Regulator02). The in-house proprietary technology to detect suspicious behaviour in the marketplace was continuously upgraded to expand its capacities to ingest the large amounts of data on transactions and orders from regular corporate reporting as well as from incidental submissions of STRs/STORs and to analyse trading patterns. For example, the sophisticated Zen market data processor collated around 15 to 20 million transactions per day and could ingest the breadth of securities covered with the Market Abuse Regulations, held data for significant periods of time, and was 'subject to data enrichment with the use of reference and market data underpinning all ingested transactions' (Spens, 2014). The FCA also worked on internally developing further technological surveillance tools relying on big datasets not provided by regulated firms. For example, it developed its capacity to collect and aggregate order book data (data on electronic lists of buy-and-sell orders for securities or financial instruments) from all trading venues in cash markets using a cloud-based platform (Steward, 2017c). The mining of data has led to detecting certain complex practices, such as the gilt market manipulation,[6] as well as some of the more complex insider dealing cases (*R v Sanders*, interview data).

The ability of market data processors to function well depends on adequate informational input, so ensuring proper reporting of transactions and orders by regulated firms was a regulatory priority. Problematic transactions reporting featured significantly in the formal enforcement docket: in the sample, there were 14 enforcement actions for such non-compliance, and in the 'broad church of cases', this represents a significant number. The transactions reporting cases mostly resulted from proactive work by the markets staff (in one case, as a spin-off from analysing an individual market abuse case; in another case, as a combination of proactive detection of some breaches and the self-reporting of further breaches). This is in line with the importance of *themes* in shaping the FCA's formal enforcement docket and the emphasis on adequate informational traffic towards the regulator. Though the cases involved some of the largest market players (e.g. large investment banks),[7] they were nonetheless 'technical' cases, based on discrepancies in transactions reports.

Finally, the Markets Oversight Division conducted 'reactive' detection work through processing referrals by external sources (there was cooperation here with the London Stock Exchange) and, notably, through processing STRs/STORs. Figure 3.2, compiled based on the yearly STRs numbers published

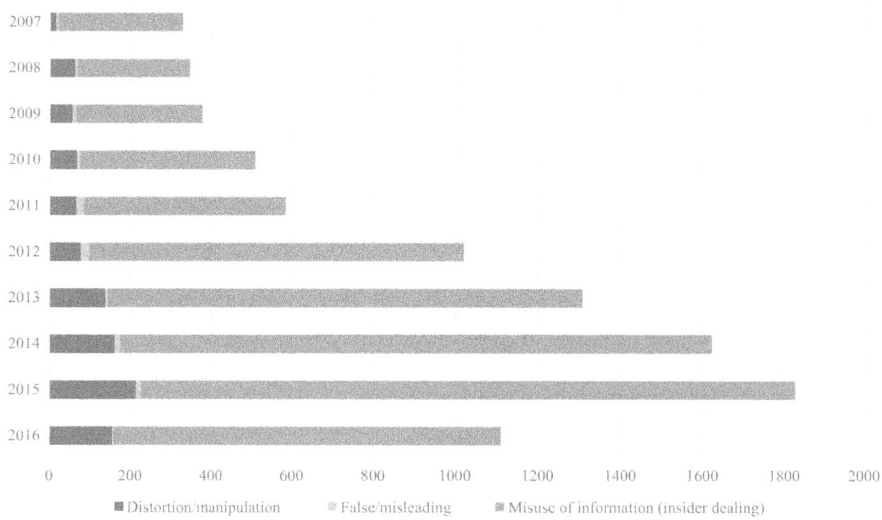

Figure 3.2 Suspicious transaction reports, January 2007–July 2016.

6 See Michael Coscia FN03/07/13.
7 See Merrill Lynch International FN22/04/2015 and FN18/10/17.

by the FCA, shows that since 2007 (when the FCA started publishing such information) to July 2016 (when the STRs regime was replaced by the STORs regime), the number of STRs rose significantly, first gradually until 2011, and then with a considerable spike.

This rise might imply a better understanding of the STR regime and the importance of compliance. The volume of reports to the FCA continued to increase exponentially with the start of the Market Abuse Regulations from July 2016, which extended the scope of the reporting regime to new markets, platforms, and conduct, capturing both suspicious transactions and suspicious orders (STORs). Already, the first full year of the STOR regime (July 2016–June 2017) saw a 129 per cent (from 1999 to 4572) increase on the correspondent 2015–2016 STR period, with a continuing upward trend. The expanding capability to collate and analyse transactions and other datasets through proactive work was coupled with an increase in reactive information from STRs/STORs, also increasing the potential to detect insider dealing/market abuse or market manipulation. As discussed in Chapter 2, this spike in reported suspicions of market misconduct contributed to the spike in the number of open formal investigations for 'diagnostic' purposes (Steward, 2017). However, market watch staff still operated within resources constraints, which meant that the suspicious transactions got 'reviewed on a value basis' (Regulator01) and the selection for further processing could depend on the amount that was involved.

There was a regular and close line of communication between markets and enforcement staff on a weekly basis, with enforcement staff giving 'real-time advice and trying to get evidence for legal challenges' (Regulator01). The enforcement staff was directly involved in designating anomalous trading as market manipulation that would require further processing. Even ST(O)Rs of value could be quickly dismissed due to legal or evidentiary challenges:

> There will be a large number of those files that come up every week; a very small percentage of those have a realistic prospect of the enforcement team proving that an offence has been committed. You might be able to spot statutory defences that the person may have, or evidential barriers.
>
> (Regulator01)

Staff constructed market abuse enforcement referrals on a cumulative basis. Often, spotted anomalies or suspicions over trading amounted to 'detected' misconduct only when additional evidentiary requirements and legal thresholds were satisfied:

> So whilst you might initially think market abuse has happened here, you have to be quite brave sometimes and say, 'We can spend another two months looking at this and it won't go anywhere, a complete waste of resources. Let's park it and see, for example, whether more comes

> through, whether there is other evidence by the same person, intelligence sources, and put it altogether and begin a case.'
>
> (Regulator01)

The very few incidents of anomalous trading that progressed through these barriers became enforcement referrals. This finding is akin to what Williams (2013) discovered in the Canadian markets: misconduct was also shaped around legal thresholds and more traditional detection work (such as assessments of the evidence strength) rather than relying solely on the technological surveillance information. What amounts to misconduct in the market abuse area, even in terms of detection, is marked not only by technological abilities but also by legal possibilities.

Skilled persons: third-party participation in information-gathering and detecting misconduct

The FCA can rely on third-party collection of relevant information by directly appointing or mandating a regulated firm to appoint a skilled person to compile a specified report under Section 166 FSMA.[8] The shifts towards a more interventionist supervisory style saw an increased outsourcing of enforcement functions to skilled persons to detect, collect information, and provide expert evidence on non-compliance.

The 166 reports served two important, necessarily intertwined enforcement functions: as an evidentiary and a detection source. The 166 reports were imposed for evidentiary purposes when regulators already suspected or had some evidence of potential misconduct but needed proof of its existence or extent. In these cases, misconduct had already been detected through proactive or reactive detection sources. The second enforcement function of 166 reports was that of misconduct detection: skilled persons not only ascertained the extent and nature of already-suspected misconduct; it was part of their remit to also uncover further, unsuspected breaches. These had to be reported to the FCA, as skilled persons were under an obligation to provide full reports on whatever area formed the scope of the report.

Skilled persons were appointed to an expert panel from large accounting firms, large consultancies, and large, even global, law firms. This was a networked approach in which the regulator was drawing on the special expertise of these professional services firms. The 166 reports allowed the FCA to save on resources since they were paid for by the firm. Yet the regulator's expectations were that the skilled person would act independently and effectively be 'the FCA's eyes and ears to lead that investigation' (Lawyer05). The reviews could be very expensive, long-running, disruptive, and intrusive exercises. The reports involved a meticulous information-gathering process by experts and contained a significant amount of facts to construct 'proof'. Although 166s

8 These will be referred to as '166 reports', or '166', as this was the popular terminology.

were mostly ordered by supervisors in the pre-enforcement stage (a 'supervisory 166', as referred to by interviewees), they served a valuable and expert evidentiary support for the formal enforcement case. In the following example, the 166 report results were used as evidence to support a formal enforcement action:

> This mis-selling case is the result of a thematic review that the FSA conducted last summer. The findings were poor, by the firm's own admission. We've been in a process of trying to see whether the findings from Supervision were justified across a wider population. The FSA took a small sample, and the firm has had a skilled person working with them to see whether the FSA findings are indicative of a wider problem. The skilled person has confirmed the FSA initial view that mis-selling is quite widespread.
>
> (LawyerFR03)

All interviewees commented on the increased frequency of imposing 166 reports, and that they had become 'business as usual'. An increased usage of 166 was specifically incorporated as an aspect of the FCA's FSF/E/P. Figure 3.3 displays the concentration of 166 reports imposed in the period April 2013–December 2015 across four key areas of business regulation (CASS, governance, COBS, and financial crime) and across firms with different risk levels (C1–C4).[9]

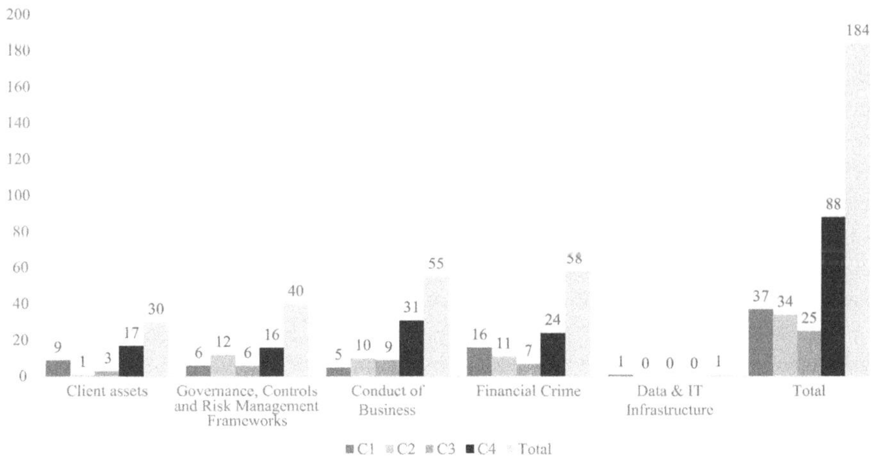

Figure 3.3 Skilled persons reports.

9 The FCA first published such information for quarter 1 in 2013, and last for quarter 3 in 2015. After this, the firms were divided into 'fixed' and 'flexible' portfolio categories.

The firms in the C4 bracket (smaller firms and independent financial advisers [IFAs]), assessed as the least risk threat and without a dedicated supervisor, were subjected to the highest number of 166 across all four areas. These firms were trusted the least to conduct their own reports or provide their own reviews on internals systems to the regulator. The firms with dedicated supervisors (C1 and C2) had a considerably lesser number of 166s. The second highest number of 166s were imposed against the C1 highest-risk-level firms in banking and insurance (indicated by their very large number of retail customers, client assets, or trading operations), with most of the reviews conducted into their financial crime prevention systems. Closely following were the 166s against C2 firms (firms with a substantial number of retail customers and/or large wholesale firms), in particular, into their governance and financial crime prevention frameworks.

The discrepancy between the number of reports imposed on the lowest- and highest-risk firms can be explained in several ways. The greater focus on the smallest firms was aligned with the thematic or sectoral supervision approach: certain governance problems could have been discovered regarding one institution, leading to imposing 166 on the whole range of firms in that industry or service provision. This led also to deviancy amplification (Cohen, 1972). Additionally, as C4 firms did not have a nominated supervisor but were supervised by a group of sectoral specialists, it could have been also easier and cheaper for the regulator to allocate the review to an external party. The highest-risk firms could have, conversely, more successfully drawn on their closer relational distance with their nominated supervisors to argue to be trusted to provide their own reviews instead. However, the population of 'fixed' portfolio firms was much smaller than the thousands of 'flexible' portfolio firms, so on aggregate, these numbers represent an indicator of the declining trust in financial institutions across the board. The growth of 166s in general can be connected to a growing distrust by the regulator in firms' own reports (La Porta et al., 1997) and to a lack of confidence that senior management could produce the information itself (either because management was perceived as incompetent or as not sufficiently disinterested or the FCA simply did not trust them).

Additionally, in practice, it had become very difficult for regulatees to dissuade the imposition of a 166 report. The interviewees could not recall a single recent instance in which they were able to dissuade the regulator and negotiate an alternative. In the past, this could have been done by the firms offering reports from their own internal investigations or by conducting 'shadow' skilled-person reviews where the firm carried out the review and then had it verified by an independent third party or where a review was conducted by that third party. In previous empirical research on the role of skilled persons in the FSA regime, Dewing and Russell (2005) found that supervisors would commonly be malleable to accepting 'shadow' reports instead of a formal 166. Both options allowed the firm to retain control over the review and construct the misconduct boundaries.

Regulators became significantly less open to such suggestions, especially if there was a perception of harm to consumers. In such circumstances, there was a significant focus on ascertaining the extent of the detriment, and a 166 report would not be prevented even by other proactive work by the firm and its management:

> We have a big retail fund manager where the quality of sales was poor. We set up a working party, chaired by the chief exec. We are sending reports into the FCA and proposing remedial action. But unfortunately, the results are bad, because the quality of advice to investors has been poor. Therefore, the FCA is not going to leave it to us to sort it out. The facts are too bad; the FCA has now appointed a Section 166 skilled person, which is very often the first step in a slippery slope to enforcement.
>
> (Lawyer03)

The outsourcing of enforcement functions to skilled persons further increased the flow of information and knowledge on the extent of misconduct toward the regulator. Their use supported the notions of an 'information-hungry' regulator, but also of one that was strapped for resources while aiming to implement a more interventionist and punitive agenda. The inability to retain control and influence over the review process frustrated a corporate response: 'if there's a skilled person, it feels very much like the odds are stacked against you' (Lawyer06). Lawyers had significantly less leverage when skilled persons were reviewing files or internal structures, and even less when they discovered a breach that needed to be reported to the regulator. The firm's control or ownership of the misconduct was relinquished to a third party, whose professional demands made it less malleable to influence, negotiations, or bargaining:

> In some cases, I think they feel very much that they are stepping into the shoes of the regulator. They see themselves in the regulator's cap and therefore not necessarily on the same wavelength as the firm that they're investigating.
>
> (Lawyer04)

Potentially contributing to this were the competitive practices that had developed due to the small number of firms appointed to the skilled person experts' panel. Previous experience in 166s was actively advertised; places on the panel were actively sought, and competitors who missed out on a place spoke with disdain about this (IndustryConsultant01). If one was appointed, this incentivised the production of detailed and complex reports ('[Y]ou've got to make the regulator love you so you can be appointed again' (LawyerFR18).

However, as with the retention of top private counsel in contentious enforcement proceedings, the appointment of City law firms to the expert panel exacerbated the problem of 'repeat players' (Galanter, 1974) in the financial markets. The same law firms were retained to defend targets in the enforcement process, enabling the retention of professional knowledge within a small circle. Though conflict-of-interest issues would prevent a law firm from acting as a skilled person for a current client, there were no such issues for other clients. This created opportunities for law firms to read their own 166 reviews as terms of reference, as 'certainly that would help us, give us good experience, will give us more insight into what the FCA is thinking and what its approach is' (Lawyer05). Regulatory intermediaries can also be subject to capture (Abbott et al., 2017), and the networks in the small world of professional services providers may prevent adequate regulatory oversight. Firms and their legal representatives still attempted to influence the process of reviewing, with one participant, representing large banks, commenting: '[T]he optimum is when you've got a good relationship with the skilled person. That depends on the skilled person being helpful, being open to a good line of communication' (Lawyer04). These issues warn of a more cautious use of skilled persons through a tighter control by the regulator of the reviewing process and the firm–reviewer interactions that develop within it.

Self-reporting

Self-reporting represents reporting by regulatees of their own harm-producing activities to an enforcement authority (Kaplow & Shavell, 1994). It is a civic source of information (Reiss, 1983) on legal violations that prompts an investigation by a regulatory agency. Self-reporting was an important detection source in the FCA regime, and in the sample, 21 per cent of the fined firms had disclosed their own wrongdoing.

Self-reporting through the regulatory requirements to disclose non-compliance

A growing number of laws targeting corporations require mandatory self-reporting of violations (Pfaff & Sanchirico, 2004; Stretesky, 2006; McAllister, 2012; Williams, 2013). These notifications enable social control agencies to keep an adequate record of the company's compliance sheet, even if the violations were successfully handled through corporate remedial actions or internal sanctioning. Mandatory self-reporting requirements reconcile the need for regulatory regimes to rely on corporations for self-policing, as suggested by enforced self-regulation, responsive regulation, meta-regulation, and other models of the 'regulatory orthodoxy' (Almond & Colover, 2012), and the recognition that corporations cannot be trusted to self-govern (Slapper & Tombs, 1999; Tombs & Whyte, 2013). They represent a legislative and societal indicator that corporations are not trusted to be motivated to self-report their violations unless specifically required or provided with incentives to do so.

The FCA self-reporting regime is an apt example of this trend. Self-reporting occurs due to Principle 11, which requires reporting anything of which the regulator would reasonably require a notice. These requirements, and the requirements to be open and cooperative with regulators (the other part of Principle 11) have not had as long a history in the UK financial services regulation as the other ten Handbook principles. The FSA incorporated Principle 11 from the earlier Principle 10 introduced by the 'New Settlement'. Unlike some of the other principles which codified and set at a standard level already-existing conduct rules, Principle 10, for the first time, posited requirements regarding relations with regulators. The regulator appeared 'in its own right for the first time' (Blair, 1991: 25–26). The introduction of cooperating and reporting obligations was an indicator of the growing centralisation of the regulatory structure.

The Principle 11 requirements are further specified, but not limited to, the notification obligations in Chapter SUP 15 of the Handbook. The mandatory notification rules can be divided into four sliding categories from being the most to the least precise on *what* should be reported and *when* an issue should be reported. The first category represents more detailed, prescriptive, or Type 1 ('bright line') (Black, 2008; Black et al., 2007; Braithwaite, 2002) reporting rules. These include requirements to report *any* breach of FSMA, FSMA secondary legislation, and other specified regulations.[10] These provisions cover reporting on violations by the firm and by a range of organisational insiders (directors, officers, employees, approved persons), reflecting the deep regulatory reach into corporate governance (Dewing & Russell, 2007; Gray & Hamilton, 2006). Of similar precision are the rules which require notification of any undertaking of criminal proceedings (a prosecution or a conviction for FSMA offences – both against the firm and organisational insiders, and any offence involving fraud or dishonesty against the firm only),[11] any action against the firm for damages,[12] and any disciplinary proceedings against the firm by any public and private bodies[13] (even outside the UK).[14] These notification requirements also mean disclosure of own regulatory misconduct. In many circumstances, the suspected criminal offence will also have the nature of a regulatory breach, and as criminal cases are notoriously difficult to bring, the FCA's response might ultimately be the only social control mechanism.

Less precise is the second category of notification rules that mandate disclosure of certain *significant* breaches (of a rule, including a Principle of Business by the firm, a Statement of a Principle, or conduct rules [COCON]

10 SUP 15.3.11(1) (b)-(ba), (d)-(i) FCA Handbook.
11 SUP 15.3.11(1) (c) and SUP 15.3.15(4) FCA Handbook.
12 SUP 15.3.15(2) FCA Handbook.
13 SUP 15.3.15(3) FCA Handbook.
14 See the Final Notice on Goldman Sachs International (FN09/09/10), in which the firm was penalised for not disclosing a Wells notice (a consideration of commencing an enforcement action), a subsequent enforcement complaint, and investigation by the SEC.

by individuals)[15] or *significant* events (discovered or suspected significant fraud against the firm or a customer, serious employee misconduct regarding financial services, significant accounting irregularities, significant civil proceedings claims).[16] The lesser precision comes from the fact that regulatees need to determine themselves that the breach/event was committed or suspected and that it is *significant*. There is no further guidance in the Handbook on how to interpret the mental threshold elements, nor has this been subject to judicial interpretation.[17] There is some guidance in the Handbook on the meaning of *significant* breach or matter.[18] However, this is also drafted in vague and broad terms, so the regulatees' interpretation is crucial for establishing whether a certain breach/matter is significant enough to be reported.

The third category of disclosure rules is somewhat even less precise. A firm must notify the FCA immediately it becomes aware, or has information which reasonably suggests, that the firm is failing to satisfy a threshold condition, a matter could have a significant adverse impact on the firm's reputation, a matter could affect the firm's ability to provide adequate customer services, resulting in serious customer detriment, or a firm-related matter could result in serious financial consequences to the UK financial system or to other firms.[19] It is open to interpretation whether and when these prescribed circumstances have occurred. The reporting of these issues may lead to the regulator acquiring information on related violations; for example, reporting on the firm's failure to satisfy the threshold conditions could reveal that a senior manager was disciplined in separate proceedings, questioning their 'fit and proper' status.

The final category of mandatory reporting is contained in the umbrella Principle 11 rule to report anything of which the regulator would *reasonably expect* notice. This encompasses all breaches and events not captured by the previous three categories. As a Type 2 rule (Black, 2008), it is the least precise, shifting the responsibility for interpreting the regulatory expectations

15 SUP 15.3.11(1)(a) and (aa) FCA Handbook. Under s. 64C FSMA firms also have obligations to report breaches of the conduct rules that had resulted in disciplinary action (formal written warning, suspension or dismissal, reduction or recovery of remuneration) against certified staff (annually) and senior managers (within seven business days).

16 SUP 15.3.17(1)-(5) and SUP 15.3.15(1) FCA Handbook.

17 Case law in other civil law areas has addressed the thresholds of suspicion regarding duties of banks to freeze assets when they suspect money laundering under Section 328(1) Proceeds of Crime Act (POCA) 2002. *K Ltd v NatWest* [2006] *states that* a person held a suspicion if s/he thought that there was a 'possibility, which is more than fanciful, that the relevant facts exist', with the further requirement that 'the suspicion so formed should be of a settled nature'. Suspicion is subjective, and there is no reasonableness requirement.

18 On *significant* breaches: potential financial losses to customers or the firm, frequency, implications for the firm's systems, and if there were delays in identifying or rectifying the breach (SUP 15.3.12G FCA Handbook). On *significant* matters (fraud, etc.): the size of any (potential) monetary loss, the risk of reputational loss, and whether the incident reflects weaknesses in the firm's systems and controls (SUP 15.3.18G FCA Handbook).

19 SUP 15.3.1(1)-(4) FCA Handbook.

predominately to the regulated. This exemplifies the responsibilisation of business (Parker & Nielsen, 2009) as it requires regulatees to employ internal resources to understand their regulatory obligations and interpret when an issue is a disclosable problem.

The notification timing is also not precisely defined since firms must notify the FCA *immediately* if they become aware of any of the breaches, events, and matters of regulatory impact,[20] or *immediately* if they have information which reasonably suggests that any of the regulatory breaches and matters of impact (may) have occurred or may occur in the foreseeable future.[21]

To summarise, the mandatory notification requirements have qualifications of 'bright line' rules in some respects, and of principles in others. The use of terms such as '*significant*' breach, '*immediately*' to be notified, and '*reasonable expectation*' renders these rules not fully formalistic (McBarnet & Whelan, 1991) or certain (Black, 1997). These terms are the juncture points at which regulatory conversations occur regarding the meaning and applicability (Black, 1998) of the notification requirements.

Interpreting the notification requirements: the role of lawyers

The interviews, both with lawyers and with representatives of (large) financial institutions, indicated that regulatees commonly understood the obligations of Principle 11 and the importance of the notifying requirements. However, they were also commonly uncertain whether an issue needed to be disclosed. Lawyers represented gatekeepers (Coffee, 2006) to this process since 'generally [clients] have got a good sense of whether or not there is an issue and they're looking for a second opinion as to whether or not we agree' (Lawyer04).

This need for a second opinion arose despite the FCA's guidance on the reporting requirements. In a principle-based regulatory framework, firms might constantly want to have further guidance (Black, 2008), and interpretative communities may not be easily formed (Black, 1997). For this reason, contentious financial practice lawyers were frequently consulted to adapt the notification rules' indeterminacy 'to the social transactions of their clients' (McCahery & Picciotto, 1995: 247). The self-policing requirements to interpret business behaviour along the lines of rule breach (need to disclose)/ rule abiding (nothing to disclose) contributed to the proliferation of a special advisory function by these lawyers, commonly consulted on where that line should be drawn.

Most of the lawyers whose work concerned predominately regulatory practice (as opposed to the ones whose work spanned the regulatory/criminal justice divide) had experience in advising clients on reporting obligations. The

20 SUP 15.3.15 FCA Handbook.
21 SUP 15.3.1 and SUP 15.3.11 (2) FCA Handbook.

workload on such issues varied across interviewees (e.g. one Magic Circle[22] lawyer estimated that reporting obligations made up around 20 per cent of their FCA-related practice). The pre-FCA involvement work for contentious regulatory lawyers consisted of 'regularly help[ing] people with problems that have been discovered within the business and the business needs to understand how to put them right, and how to notify . . . *how and whether* . . . to notify the FCA' (LawyerFR04; emphasis added). Other lawyers whose practice spanned wider regulatory/criminal justice areas did not report that they advised on notification obligations. However, they were frequently involved in conducting internal investigations upon self-discovered internal fraud or possible systems breaches – on many occasions, also before the involvement of the FCA. This work divide describes the differential role played by various practitioners. The initial advice on notifying the regulator was sought mostly from specialised regulatory lawyers. If the discovered problem concerned an issue that was either clearly criminal or on the boundary between the criminal/regulatory domains, specialist lawyers with criminal practice experience were sought for conducting internal investigations to ascertain what had happened and the possible criminal justice repercussions.

Contentious lawyers therefore represented important stakeholders in assessing whether a certain conduct had the quality of a disclosable *violation*. Thus, the notification process was 'juridified' (Habermas, 1987), with a growth in seeking professional legal advice. There were several reasons for the development of this practice. First, the financial regulatory area is complex, and professional advice could be decisive in understanding whether there was breach in the first place. Second, further guidance might be required anyway, as reporting 'immediately after becoming aware' and similar obligations are drafted as vague standards of behaviour. Third, a regulatory practice started to develop towards more detailed notification forms with questions on disclosing both the facts of the breach and the breach's legal basis (e.g. specific rule or principle). This was different to before, when it was important to 'make sure that the regulator has the facts of the problem. You don't go and tell them, "This is what we've seen has happened, and we've breached the following rules"' (LawyerFR06). Part of the legal interpretation, previously preserved for the regulator, had now shifted to regulatees: 'there are more forms that you have to submit if you are making a particular notification . . . [a]nd what you're putting your hands up to' (LawyerFR06). Fourth, there was the regulator's growing appetite for information, so firms might have felt more the obligation to provide it, but with less guidance on the circumstances in which this was necessary. Connected to this is a fifth reason: regulatees needed professional legal advice for not to be formally processed after self-reporting. This

22 A Magic Circle law firm is an informal term for what are generally considered the five leading law firms headquartered in the UK, and the four or five leading London-based commercial barristers' chambers.

reflected the growing perception that self-reporting was a necessary prerequisite to derail a case from formal enforcement, but also the *mutual risk mitigation* by firms and the regulator discussed later.

The involvement of contentious lawyers meant that the self-reporting process was carefully managed. It included numerous considerations, activities, and planning that ultimately contributed to crafting the meaning of the vague legal requirements in practice. These concerned two issues, considered jointly: (1) *what* to report and (2) *when* and *how* to report.

Constructing compliance with the notifying requirements: what to disclose, and the over-reporting paradox

The first consideration in observing the self-reporting requirements was *what* should be reported. This included various breaches and events, defined with different levels of precision. The involvement of lawyers was crucial in establishing the misconduct that the regulator should know of, especially in interpreting the meaning of a 'significant' breach of the rules and the 'reasonable expectation of notification' requirement.

Regulatees interpreted breaches as 'significant' around four main factors, similar to the Handbook guidance. The first consideration was whether the breach was *widespread*. 'Widespread' was measured in quantitative terms – for example, that 80 per cent of all customer services were flawed in some way. A second consideration was whether the breach was also *systemic* in terms of whether the widespread non-compliance occurred due to flawed internal control systems. A third consideration was whether the breach also crossed a certain threshold of separately measured *harm*. The fourth consideration, especially regarding notifying misconduct of individuals, was whether the breach was *intentional*.

The relationship between these 'seriousness' indicators was complex, as not all widespread, systemic, and even intentional breaches were disclosed by default, and this may require some involvement of harm. Widespread non-compliance did not automatically mean a 'serious' misconduct if it did not also satisfy the requirements of being 'systemic':

> In the retail space, there will routinely be record-keeping breaches, disclosure breaches. Bank staff don't get it right all the time; there are all sorts of slip-ups. Some of it might be intentional, some unintentional, but you wouldn't go around disclosing all of that; you would just sort of deal with it. [It's different] if you find a systemic rule breach, so that you know none of your customer-facing staff will have done X, and you know people haven't done it, 'cause they weren't monitored on it.
>
> (Lawyer06)

Furthermore, a 'systemic' misconduct could also not be disclosed if it did not cause harm: 'I'm supposed to give you my business card, and I don't. That may be a systemic problem, but it doesn't really cause any harm' (Lawyer06). Finally, lawyers often referred to the FCA's statutory objectives, for example, harm to consumers, to market integrity, and so on, to interpret whether any harm was caused and to assess the gravity of the non-compliance. The filtering process of what should be reported then took the following shape:

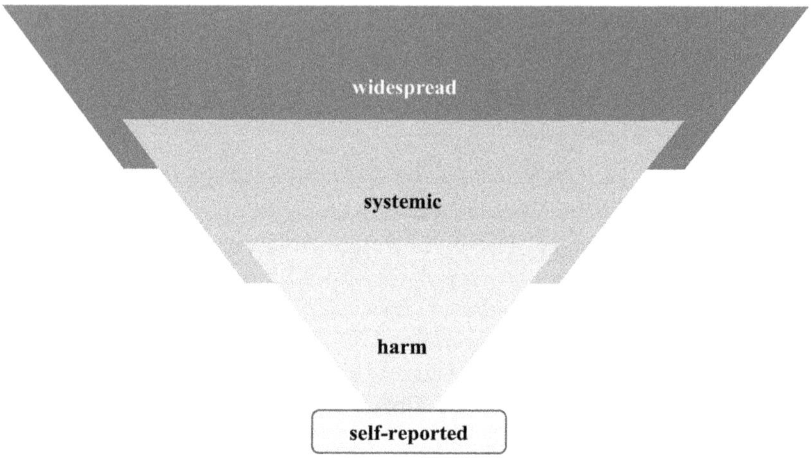

Figure 3.4 Filtering 'significant' breaches.

There was a common understanding between the parties over what was a 'serious' or 'significant' breach, and the same considerations were prominent throughout the whole enforcement process. Previous enforcement work and other regulatory messages had contributed to establishing a shared interpretative community (Black, 1997) over what business deviance was considered 'serious' across reporting, enforcement referrals, and sanctioning. That this was the case was suggested in the account of an interviewee lawyer who referred to the sanctioning factors and 'the gradation of severity of conduct there' (Lawyer12) to determine whether the breach was 'serious' enough to warrant reporting.

The 'reasonable expectation of notification' was interpreted more extensively in practice, leading to more occasions when information was disclosed. It appeared that after the financial crisis, the deployment of the 'credible deterrence' strategy, and the regulator's tougher enforcement stance, financial institutions took up a route of heightened and more extensive self-reporting, especially of incidents of suspected financial crime (employee fraud, AML breaches, insider dealing). There is no concrete statistical information on the number of notifications to be able to compare their extent before and after the 'credible deterrence' policy, but this was suggested as a rising trend in the interviewees' experience. That this was the case in the banking sector was supported by the claims of a senior manager in one of the largest UK banks.

The head of internal investigations stated that what 'is currently going on is what they call in the industry "defensive reporting". That is what they use when talking about reporting to the FCA' (FinancialInstitution01). A regulatory lawyer further commented that 'in the current climate, there are very few businesses who would consider to take a brave decision not to report to the FCA' (Lawyer08). This trend explains why very few examples were provided on nothing to disclose: the aforementioned widespread not giving of a business card and cases where suspicions of market abuse on a telephone transcript turned out to be a 'bad turn of phrase on a call or in an email . . . and nothing behind it' (Lawyer04).

The possibility of cautious approaches was raised as a concern in academic debates and practitioners' writings on the original installation of the FSA self-reporting regime (e.g. Long, 2006). After the crisis, it seems that the cautious approaches had developed into standard practice. Several interviewees echoed earlier writings by stating that the present mantra was 'if in doubt, disclose': 'certainly, there is clients' err on the side of caution now than they would have done seven, eight years ago. Since the crisis, I think people have become more attuned to reporting things to the regulator' (Lawyer04). Contentious lawyers also contributed to the extensive self-reporting since they provided advice based on both legal and extra-legal factors, such as their experience and professional interests. They encouraged a wider view of Principle 11 and notification: 'sometimes you decide, "Well, you don't have a duty to tell them under Principle 11, but we think you should tell them when you next have a meeting, to just make them aware"' (LawyerFR06).

The effect of this in practice was the creation of a paradox of over-reporting and 'over-compliance' with regulatory demands (Etienne, 2010; Gunningham et al., 2004; Short & Toffel, 2008). The over-reporting paradox means that, in complying with the self-reporting obligations, a more crucial consideration was not *what* to report (as it appeared that most incidents of non-compliance were reported in practice) but *how* and *how soon* after discovery to report the non-compliance.

Constructing compliance with the notification requirements: when and how to report, and establishing trust

The starting point for deciding *when* after discovery to report non-compliance is the regulatory requirement to make a notification 'immediately' after becoming aware, or after having information which 'reasonably suggests' any of the notifiable matters. An additional guidance was that the regulator expected discussion of relevant matters at an 'early stage', before the firm made any internal or external commitments.[23] However, there was no published time frame to satisfy these requirements, and this could allow for an extensive interpretation.

23 SUP 15.3.9G FCA Handbook.

Regulatees understood the importance of the timeliness of notifications, including self-reporting; in cases of an emerging problem, notifying the regulator was an immediate and crucial consideration. However, regulatees commonly constructed such compliance without contacting the regulator directly, but after taking advice from outside counsel on whether, when, and how to report. The involvement of lawyers meant that self-reporting did not occur 'immediately', though it seemed that the regulator considered this threshold to be satisfied even if the regulatee did not immediately phone up but consulted outside lawyers. This represented a shared understanding within the regulatory relationship. Therefore, the requirement of 'becoming aware' of a potential breach was satisfied not just when a potential problem was discovered but also when advice was received that there *was* such a problem.

The leeway to engage outside counsel and establish what happened was quite short, and its length depended on the type of the discovered breach. A lawyer with a previous extensive experience working at the FSA/FCA enforcement division categorised the notifications into two groups: ongoing notifications and emergency notifications, depending on the immediacy with which to notify the regulator. The first category concerned the Chapter 15 requirements discussed earlier, whereas the emergency notifications concerned the discovery of a major internal issue, such as, for example, a major internal fraud that threatened the life of the firm. This would represent an issue that the regulator would have wanted to know immediately about. The enforcement decision against Sonali Bank (UK) Ltd. (SBUK) for breaches of Principle 11 supports this, also giving some indication of what would be considered non-compliant with 'immediate' disclosure of a 'significant' adverse event. SBUK was fined for taking at least seven weeks to notify the FCA that it had become aware of a potentially significant internal fraud. SBUK had itself acknowledged in its notification that it considered the matter 'significant' in view of the amount of the fraud and the potential reputational risk and loss to SBUK.[24] The notification timescales regarding other disclosable issues were still short, and firms could not delay notifying the regulator without suffering adverse consequences from additional reprimand.

Timely notifications were important for an additional reason: they appeared to facilitate retaining 'ownership' over the misconduct. Lawyers often advised notifying the regulator as soon as feasible to gain trust and retain control over the fact-finding:

> You have a right to at least ascertain whether or not there is a regulatory issue, and the broad scale and nature of it. Once you've identified what an issue is, you're much better off telling them sooner and giving them good information, because there's a very big issue around *trust*. Ideally, what you're looking to do is to get the FCA to allow you to conduct

24 Sonali Bank (UK) Ltd. FN12/10/16.

> the investigation yourself, rather than them storm in and take it away from you.
>
> (LawyerFR02; emphasis added)

Trust was sought by being proactive before and during disclosure, and the process of *how* to report was carefully managed. This was 'hugely important, as you want to keep control over the case. If you just go and don't show you are investigating it yourself, or doing something, they will just take over the control' (LawyerFR08). In the period before notification, regulatees undertook various activities that could facilitate retaining 'control' over the case, claiming 'ownership' of the misconduct, and constructing its nature of financial misconduct, the level of its seriousness, and the proposed solutions. These concerned undertaking internal investigations[25] for fact-finding and, if a decision was made to report, compiling remedial plans.

Internal investigations and the organisational ascertaining of the facts commonly consisted of several activities, many of which mirrored what FCA enforcement investigators did themselves. They were undertaken by outside counsel to ascertain what and how solid the facts were, who could have them, if the breach concerned an individual and HR issues so that employment lawyers should also be called; if there was a whistle-blower, how certain it was that a regulatory breach had happened, and what the plausible explanations for (non-)compliance were. This included understanding how the organisation, its monitoring, and other compliance procedures operated; understanding whether there was any adverse impact by the misconduct on third parties or whether it had stayed internal; securing and reviewing relevant documents; securing access to, and interviewing, relevant individuals.

As some of this work was done before notifying the regulator, it could include tactics of weakening a potential formal enforcement outcome. Most notably, this concerned creating legally privileged documents protected from disclosure. The statute provides protection of both common-law legal professional privilege (LLP) categories: legal advice privilege (LAP) and litigation privilege (LP).[26] LAP covers 'communications between lawyers and their clients whereby legal advice is sought or given' (*Three Rivers DC v Bank of England (Disclosure) (No.4)* [2004], at 10) in a relevant legal context (both non-contentious and in litigation). LAP is constrained to the lawyer–client relationship (*Three Rivers DC v Governor and Company of the Bank of England (no 5)* [2003]; *R (on the application of Prudential plc & anor) (appellants) v Special Commissioner of Income Tax & anor* [2013]). Communications extending to third parties (e.g. other corporate managers or employees not expressly covered by the LAP, accountants, witnesses) can be potentially covered by

25 On the proliferation of internal investigations in view of the heightened scrutiny of corporations in the United States, see Duggin (2003) and Copeland (2017).

26 Section 413(2–3) FSMA.

litigation privilege. LP is given to documents created for the dominant purpose of an ongoing litigation or for one that is reasonably in prospect.[27] Depending on the defence strategy, both categories could offer protection from disclosing to the FCA documents from an internal investigation, such as notes from interviews with employees. Chapter 4 discusses this strategising in detail. The practice of creating legally privileged documents could mean that many documents were created during formal investigations, yet many of them could be edited and protected:

> You need to structure things appropriately so that the documentation that gets generated is protected by legal privilege, so people don't necessarily have to disclose it at the conclusion of the discussion.
>
> (Lawyer12)

> The thing is to bring your house in order beforehand. So to go to them and say that you have appointed internal investigators, and here you might want to do some things with privilege.
>
> (LawyerFR20)

Remedial plans were the second crucial activity undertaken to establish trust and 'retain control' (LawyerFR08) over the case pre-notifying the FCA. Whilst a notification was perceived as the minimum response, firms could be seen as even more trustworthy if they contacted the regulator with some kind of plan for 'fixing' the discovered non-compliance. The lawyers suggested that notifying the FCA without a contingency plan meant 'releasing the control of the case to Supervision,' as supervisors would then have to investigate it and suggest remedial steps on their own or transfer the case to enforcement immediately. Coming up with a plan that supervisors could go over quickly meant that regulatees retained 'ownership' of the problem and of proposing ways in which it should be resolved. The advice on the preferred route was therefore not to go to the regulator and say, 'We think this is a problem – how would you like us to deal with it?' but 'Here's how we're proposing to deal with it – is that okay?' (Lawyer04).

However, *when* to disclose after an issue had been discovered was not always easily managed in practice. There were still tensions between quick notification and appearing trustworthy on the one hand and knowing the facts and having an appropriate, albeit initial, remedial plan on the other:

> The tension and the question for the firm must be telling the FCA quickly enough to follow the rules and do what the FCA would want it to do, but also going to the FCA with enough information about

27 The litigation must be adversarial, not investigative, or inquisitorial, *Three Rivers District Council v Governor and Company of the Bank of England (No 6)* [2004], [102].

> what has gone wrong and how they plan to fix it, so that the FCA can understand the context. The advice will be more around how and when and how far they need to have developed their remedial or action plan when they talk to the FCA, and to make sure they're not breaching any of the notification obligations by not telling them early enough. It's not always a black-and-white issue.
>
> (LawyerFR04)

Despite these activities and attempts to 'appropriate' the response to the misconduct, some cases were not to be left to regulatees' devices, and the regulator could take an *interventionist* approach. This concerned instances where, at the moment of reporting, the non-compliance was already perceived to be too serious because of its scale (e.g. a significant internal fraud or consumer detriment) or because it fit within an ongoing thematic concern. In one instance, this concerned a notification of non-compliance with the transactions reporting requirements at a time when discrepancies in this area represented an enforcement focus. A more *interventionist* approach could also be taken when the FCA was not satisfied with the reporting process or the internal investigation. If the regulator perceived that senior management were not dealing properly with the issue and did not trust the process, there was a need to show 'visibility of how things are being done' (Lawyer08). There would be more questions on the terms and scope of reference of the investigation, reporting timescales, and what the output would look like. There could also be demands to see the underlying documents in the internal investigation and not just the prepared final report. For this reason, it was even more important to undertake measures to create legally privileged documents. The final situation of a more *interventionist* approach was when the firm's own investigation might damage the process by tipping off a wrongdoing individual (e.g. in cases involving criminal behaviour, market abuse, etc.).

Theorising self-reporting as a detection source: mutual risk mitigation or detection avoidance?

How self-reporting was implemented in practice raises questions about its worth as a detection source. This must be viewed in context of the reasons behind over-reporting, the process of *mutual risk mitigation*, and possible detection avoidance through detection facilitation.

The extent of self-reporting should be related to the perceptions of the FCA as an 'information-hungry regulator'. These perceptions seemed to arise from experiences of dealing with the regulator at the micro-level of interactions, since demands for self-reporting did not feature extensively (if at all) in speeches by officials across the organisation. At the micro-level, such perceptions were related to the more inquisitive supervisory relationship discussed earlier, but also to how Principle 11 breaches were treated in the enforcement context.

First, the FCA had brought a few 'signal cases' (Thornton et al., 2005) with significant penalties that carried the important regulatory and deterrence message that 'Principle 11 has teeth' (Lawyer06). Notable cases, for example, include a record £30 m fine against Prudential Plc for not notifying the FSA of its 2010 acquisition plans,[28] a joint enforcement action by the PRA and the FCA in censuring the Co-Operative Bank Plc for Principle 3 breaches and for not notifying the regulators of intended changes to two senior positions[29] and the Sonali Bank case discussed earlier. Failure to self-reporting also increased the ultimate fine, even if the firm was not pursued for breaching Principle 11. Principle 11 was therefore protected in a double manner: breaches of the notification requirements could either be treated as a standalone misconduct (as in the example of Prudential Inc.) or as an aggravated factor in the sentencing of another substantive misconduct (see, for example, the final notice for Pas).[30] The stream of cases underscored the weight the Authority attached to Principle 11 and the notification requirements as essential for its supervisory process:

> The FCA considers Principle 11 as one of the most important principles. They are a supervision-led regulator, so they'll say that to supervise and perform their function, they need to know what is going on, you need to tell them, they depend on you to tell them. This is why there have been enforcement actions in this area.
>
> (LawyerFR20)

Second, the regulated community seemed to perceive that there was a tangible risk that a charge for breaching Principle 11 reporting requirements might be added to existing charges. According to an experienced industry consultant, 'they will pile [a Principle 11 charge] up on top of the other charges and threaten you with it, increase the penalty because of it. If they can't get you for anything else, they can get you for Principle 11' (IndustryConsultant01). This possibility resembled the US criminal justice system in the prosecution of what Sanchirico (2006) terms 'process crimes' (crimes of perjury and obstruction of justice). According to Sanchirico (2006: 1392), prosecutors can, and reportedly do, pile obstruction and perjury charges onto primary activity indictments. When a suspect on some underlying violation is also suspected of obstructing justice, some of the costs of investigating and adjudicating the obstruction can be shared with prosecution of the primary violation.

Therefore, by enforcing Principle 11 reporting breaches, the FCA might have been able to avoid the regulatory costs of an unsuccessful investigation or get a greater return from a successful investigation and maintain a 'credible

28 FN27/03/13.

29 PRA FN10/08/15; FCA FN10/08/15. Both regulators considered that the misconduct merited a substantial financial penalty (the PRA proposed £121.86 million) had it not been for its significant impact on the bank's capital.

30 FN01/07/13.

deterrent' mechanism in its dealings with the regulated. Having in mind the breadth of the requirements, liability for reporting and cooperation violations could have been easier to establish. Though this should not be taken for granted, as costs might still be significant, even to pursue the Principle 11 charge, evidentiary standards in administrative proceedings are lower. The mere knowledge of the regulator that an incident occurred and that this had not been reported (a highly objective fact) would satisfy a Principle 11 reporting breach. The firm might still be able to attempt to contest whether an incident was something that the regulator would *reasonably* expect a notice of, but such contestation was unlikely in practice, and so far, it has not been a subject to judicial challenge and interpretation.

The regulatory message that 'Principle 11 has teeth' and the emphasis on compliance with the self-reporting obligations had not gone unnoticed by the industry, especially by large and medium-sized firms. The statements on defensive reporting lend some support to the argument that there were industry perceptions of at least a tangible risk of an enforcement action in case of non-disclosure. Elsewhere, the increased stringency of the anti–money laundering (AML) regimes has also been suggested as responsible for the significant increase in suspicious activity reports (SARs) across jurisdictions (Levi, 2007; Levi & Reuter, 2006; Reuter & Truman, 2004: 107–108; Law Commission, 2019). Therefore, tangible risks of non-reporting represent a crucial factor in the efficiency of any self-reporting system, since a violator has an incentive to self-report his harmful act if the authority proposes a reduced sanction that equals (or is slightly less than) the expected value of not reporting, which is the (full) stipulated sanction times the probability of apprehension and prosecution (Kaplow & Shavell, 1994; Malik, 1993).

What happened in practice can be conceptualised as ***mutual risk mitigation*** or ***mutual risk shifting***. By demanding more information and emphasising the importance of Principle 11, regulators hedged the *risk* of being seen as risk-averse, not asking enough questions, and not probing regulatees – one of the main criticisms of the pre-crisis FSA. For example, severe criticisms were levied on the FSA for failing to be more inquisitive of Northern Rock senior management, thus failing to prevent the bank's excessive risk-taking (Black, 2012; Gray & Akseli, 2011). The increase in information demands could be a strategy to avoid vulnerabilities in the design and operationalisation of the risk-based system: it could help avoid building the system on 'wrong indicators' and missing the right ones (Black, 2012: 1055). As risk-based systems are outward-looking (Black & Baldwin, 2010: 189), this strategy could also represent mitigation of risks to the regulator's reputation and accusations of 'fault' or 'laziness' in cases of regulatory failure. For the regulators, therefore, this represented a safety net in view of preserving their public image and giving the appearance of a regulator who is proactive, probing, and willing to intervene.

By providing more information, regulatees hedged the *risk* of ending up in enforcement, either for the original breach and/or for the Principle 11 breach.

(Over-)reporting served a function of shifting the responsibility for a regulatory failure back to the regulator. For regulatees, this also represented a safety net in view of preserving their standing with the regulator (a social motive for compliance), and also avoiding enforcement (a calculated motive for compliance). For both sides of the regulatory relationship, the reporting process and the mutual risk mitigation were a mechanism for managing perceptions – mutual and from wider audiences.

This process raises further questions as to the extent to which self-reporting, though a detection source, contributes to overall *detection avoidance*. Detection avoidance is a companion of creative compliance. It especially comes to the fore after large corporate scandals, such as Enron (McBarnet, 2006), the Madoff Ponzi scheme (Barak, 2012), and the corporate fallings associated with the financial crisis (Will et al., 2013). However, detection avoidance has not been studied much in the literature. As Sanchirico (2006: 1332–1333) points out:

> [O]ur theories of crime and regulation view evidence too much as something that investigators uncover, and not enough as something that violators cover up. Our theories of evidence and procedure focus too much on wrongdoing as the subject of evidence, and not enough on evidence as the object of wrongdoing.

In the FCA context, the question is whether the facilitation and promotion of detection through self-reporting achieved (in)advertent detection avoidance. This may be the case for two reasons: retaining 'ownership' of the case and creating reporting 'noise'.

The empirical data reveal that zealous compliance with Principle 11 also allowed greater ability to retain 'ownership' of the misconduct through carefully managing *when* and *how* to report and gaining the regulator's trust. If the firm reported the issue to the FCA and was trusted, which might mostly be the case with larger organisations, as suggested by the regulatory literature (Hawkins, 2002), the issue might be left to its management. Firms could continue with their internal investigations and organisational assertion of the facts. Though the regulator might review the remedial plans and be ascertained of the quality of the process, this also meant that the facts on the actual scope and nature of the misconduct were left under the control of corporations and their lawyers but out of the regulator's considerations and, ultimately, out of public insight. The internal fact-finding is a companion to the process of legal endogeneity, through which organisations construct the meaning of the law and compliance (Edelman, 1992; Edelman & Talesh, 2011; Edelman et al., 1999; Edelman, 2016: Ch. 2). It encompasses not only organisational construction of *compliance*, as originally suggested by Edelman (1992), but also organisational construction of *non-compliance*. Facilitating detection through self-reporting, therefore, enabled detection avoidance, since the firm might retain ownership of the fact-finding, propose its own 'counterclaims'

(Ermann & Lundman, 2002) on what happened, and not be subjected to further proactive detection. This also contributed to dealing with white-collar offences in private – a problem outlined by the literature on white-collar crime as contributing to decreasing specific deterrence of individuals and increasing the chances of re-offending (Clarke, 1990).

The identified existence of over-reporting was therefore a paradox in the sense that it would imply that business had developed a sense of legal (though not necessarily moral) obligation to notify the regulator of any regulatory breaches, however minor, and that firms were acting as 'corporate citizens' (Kagan & Scholz, 1984). However, the findings indicate that self-reporting might occur more so because of deterrence considerations or the firm acting as an 'amoral calculator', rather than due to a perceived sense of ethical binding, belief in the regulatory standards, or the established trust between the parties, as the principles-based regulatory model suggests (Black, 2008). In this sense, corporate responses can be also paradoxical and complicated, as detection through self-reporting was encouraged because of various risk calculations. If you disclose:

- You might claim 'ownership' of the case.
- You might avoid formal enforcement.
- You might not avoid formal enforcement but could control outcomes.
- You might not avoid formal enforcement but will receive a more favourable treatment: discounts for cooperation.

Even when not calculated, facilitating detection contributes towards detection avoidance, as it also creates reporting 'noise' (Dorn, 2012b), in which the regulator is notified of plenty – both significant and insignificant issues. Too much information without the desired quality or relevance might impair the regulator's ability to deploy limited enforcement resources accordingly (also Gunningham, 2010: 137). We already know from research on the AML reporting system that though there might be a rise in submitted SARs, enforcement upon them is comparatively rare (Gold & Levi, 1994; Levi, 2007; Law Commission, 2019). As the quality of SARs is variable (Reuter & Truman, 2004: 107), this increase could be reducing the effectiveness of the AML regime 'by lowering the signal-to-noise ratio' (Levi & Reuter, 2006: 341–342).

Reporting 'noise' limits the potential for regulatory learning on both sides of the relationship. Regulatory learning is crucial in a regime built around risk assessments requiring adequate insights by the regulator, and around principles requiring adequate understanding of regulatory expectations by regulatees. For example, the FSA's internal audit of the way it handled the investigation into Barclays's LIBOR-rigging showed 'a number of instances where the information received could have suggested that lowballing may have been occurring' (FSA, 2013: 5), of which 26 instances contained what the regulator described as 'direct' mentions of the activity. Half of these were supplied by Barclays in the period from summer 2007 to early 2009. This information did not trigger an investigation at that time (it was instigated only in 2010), and it may have given Barclays employees a perception of immunity, especially after the crisis onset. In this case, the lack of reaction did not happen because of reporting 'noise' but because of preoccupation with the prudential market turmoil (FSA, 2013), yet it is an apt example of how detection avoidance can occur if regulators are unfocused, despite the self-reporting.

These arguments point to the paradoxical side of regulatory enforcement and the unexpected effects of both principles-based regulation and the 'credible deterrence' strategy. They also emphasise the need to recognise that 'enforcement is a two-sided affair' (Sanchirico, 2006: 1361): issues of mutual risk mitigation, over-reporting, establishing trust, and detection avoidance might explain why self-reporting featured less prominently as a detection source in the formal enforcement docket, though it was encouraged, and it enabled significant informational traffic.

Other external referrals

The rest of the reactive detection sources show a variety of channels through which the regulator learnt of deviance: victims, market participants (including whistle-blowers), other control organisations, and the press. However, these featured less prominently across the interviews and in notices (10 per cent of all cases).

Victims (consumer complaints) rarely mobilised the FCA's control mechanism directly (outside its thematic work or other planned supervisory activities), and mostly in cases of small firms or unauthorised business, when enforcers acted on hotline tip-offs to disrupt pressure selling and 'boiler room' types of misconduct. Also, in only one case in the sample, the FCA reacted on redress concerns raised by the FOS. This is in line with Gilad's (2008a) findings on the FSA's reluctance to initiate enforcement upon FOS referrals. The FCA was more likely to react if complaints were received directly from consumers, rather than from the FOS (presumably because of the greater impact on its reputation for not acting), but also only if these exposed additional breaches, for example, failure in financial crime prevention or inadequate complaints handling.

Detection of non-compliant smaller firms frequently came also from other market participants, such as competitor firms 'who don't see why firm A should be allowed to do the business without being regulated' (LawyerFR18). Such 'city grasses' (Wilson & Wilson, 2010) could also trigger investigations into the integrity of individuals. Finally, whistle-blowers seemed to contribute to detecting mostly market abuse. Whistle-blowers could trigger formal investigations in these cases, as their information could identify the insiders or manipulators – a notoriously difficult *discovery* issue.

Referrals from other control organisations represented an even less-prominent detection source. In the rare instances in which formal action was taken, the information came mostly from other regulators (HMRC, the Pensions Regulator, or the London Stock Exchange), or from 'private' governance organisations (Ericson & Haggerty, 1997; Ericson et al., 2000, 2003), such as lenders in the mortgage industry (two cases). There were no accounts of when deviance was exposed by police agencies. In the multi-agency network tasked with policing financial crimes (Levi, 2010), the information on deviance run mostly *out* from rather than *into* the FCA.

Finally, although such information was less present in the notices analysis, informants reported that the media were a significantly more important reactive source, both in terms of spotting the development of new risks and in flashing out individual incidents of misconduct. The greater prominence of media as a detection source could be connected to the FCA's responsiveness to public criticism and reputational concerns.

Sifting through information on non-compliance: the referral process

There are many more leads to suspected violations and potential enforcement cases than regulators have human and financial resources to formally process, even where negotiations and persuasion are not a viable route or have broken down (Braithwaite, 1982; Clinard & Yeager, 1980). Like the police, regulators exercise much discretion over what is counted as non-compliance through their decisions about which misconduct to record, investigate, and sanction (Parker & Nielsen, 2009). The FCA enforcement division was 'very selective about what we take on, not because we are fussy, but [because] there are many more cases than we can ever resource' (Regulator01). The FCA attempted to clarify and make more transparent the discretionary enforcement processing through its enforcement referral criteria (ERC) guidance on the factors that it considered when opening a new enforcement investigation. Over the years, the ERC underwent different iterations towards being more detailed, including in response to recommendations made by the HM Treasury (2014). Yet the considerations remained broadly similar[31] and included several non-exhaustive factors: the likelihood of the action furthering the FCA's aims and statutory objectives, evidentiary strength and proportionality of a formal action (including the seriousness of the misconduct and resources needed), deterrence, justice, and prevention potential (including any widespread harm or senior individuals' involvement) (FCA, 2016). Though designed to frame the decision-making process within predictable factors, the ERC still left considerable space for staff discretion.

Enforcement referrals were discussed between enforcement staff and the supervisory team (including market watch staff) that first detected the misconduct around whether the detected deviance deserved to be recorded and investigated formally, left to be processed informally through supervisory means, or not processed at all. However, the value of this was limited, as even

31 On 24 April 2019, the enforcement referral criteria were renamed 'investigation opening criteria'.

after applying the criteria, there was still a far too great number of potential cases to be processed. Limited resources, therefore, led to a second set of considerations, internal to the organisation, over the types of cases that were either more attractive for the EFCD to pursue or that they felt obligated to do so: '[W]e have, *not* referral criteria, but we have other judgements that we will make underneath that, in a softer, more subdued, more subjective kind of way' (Regulator01; emphasis added by interviewee). These can be termed the best return on an enforcement investment, and the 'egregious' case. Similar considerations guide regulators in other jurisdictions (Shapiro, 1984; Williams, 2013: 552–553), and in other industries (Hawkins, 2002).

Enforcement returns were a principal consideration in accepting referrals. This concerned (risk-based) deliberations on *sending a message* (general deterrence and educational) and *themes.* Considerations of general deterrence, the construction of a 'signal' case (Thornton et al., 2005), and the need to send messages on unacceptable behaviour were quite prominent at the micro-level decision-making process on the enforcement docket. These decisions were governed by the typical 'efficiency-based balancing of expected gains and penalties' (Baldwin et al., 2012: 248). However, 'the enforcement mindset was not just about that particular firm, that particular breach' (LawyerFR07), but about broader audiences. Compliance officers were one of the main audience targets in this process, as they should convey these messages to senior management:

> One of the key financial crime risks for investment banks is that traders can mismark, they can make up a value of their books, they can book fictitious trades. Having a case with that kind of conduct, the value you might get from bringing it would be higher because you'd be punishing that firm and sending a strong message to that firm, but other compliance officers would actually learn from it. If a case has that potential, it's probably a more attractive proposition for us.
>
> (Regulator01)

These deliberations highlight the different ways in which marginality was considered in the UK financial markets. Other researchers (Coffee, 2013; Shapiro, 1985; Williams, 2013) have noted that financial regulators frequently tackle marginal or 'rogue' players, as this has several advantages: bad intent may be easier to show, there is less risk of jeopardising ongoing relationships as opposed to large, repeat players, and this inflates the success rate of regulatory enforcement actions. Marginality was also a consideration of UK financial regulators, but not in the same sense. The focus was on whether the behaviour or the sector in question was so marginal that bringing an enforcement action would have little return value:

> One of the questions I will have in my mind is, 'Is the behaviour that the firm is exhibiting very, very esoteric, very peculiar to that firm, is it the only firm in the market that is likely to exhibit that behaviour?'
>
> (Regulator01)

Where resources are scarce but there is a will for bringing enforcement actions, these actions will be undertaken to avoid marginal players, rather than to process them. The discussion of the enforcement tools in Chapter 2 supports this argument. Cases against firms often had protracted, complex, and resources-intensive investigations aimed mostly at non-marginal players and behaviour.

Closely connected to considerations of deterrence and *sending a message* was the issue of *themes*. There was less interest in pursuing a referred case if enforcement staff had a perception that a theme had already been exhausted and that existing public cases had sent the necessary deterrence messages: 'enforcement doesn't want it because maybe they think, "We've already got five mis-selling cases for investigation – we don't really need a sixth"' (LawyerFR07). This finding means that regulators operated within similar considerations as the 'last 10%' (Breyer, 1993) on the point where the costs of further enforcement were not justified by the gains. *Themes* considerations can also mean that some types of misconduct, previously dealt with only by persuasive and negotiation responses, might be escalated for formal processing if they had been prioritised as a theme. The prioritisation of themes provides a further explanation on the relatively high participation of thematic work as a detection source into the formal enforcement docket. Through a constructivist process, corporate crime was, at any given time, the segment of the market and market practices to which the regulator wanted to 'send a message' of disapproval:

> It depends on the nature and severity of the issue, on the political climate, and [on] the FCA's agenda. You might have a minor sanctions problem, but because sanctions are very high on the FCA's agenda, you end up going to enforcement because it continues to publicise the message that the FCA are not happy about the way firms approach sanctions.
>
> (LawyerFR03)

Even enforcement returns took second place if the misconduct in question was perceived as *'egregious'*. This word was used repeatedly by both current and former regulators ('just really bad'). On my question of whether a senior enforcement official could describe what 'egregious' meant, the first answer was structured around notions of victimisation and blameworthiness: 'crystallised risk to consumers. If there is a retail firm who, in quite a cruel, knowing way, ripped off socially vulnerable people, instinctively that kind of case is more of a "must do" type' (Regulator01). The formal processing of significant consumer detriment was in line with the ERC policy. Yet the 'instinctive' labelling of such cases as 'must do' types meant that FCA enforcers were also guided by 'equitable considerations' (Baldwin et al., 2012: 248) when deciding whether to investigate business behaviour and record it as deviance.

The second consideration of 'egregious' misconduct, however, was less visible and concerned cases with the potential to impair the FCA's public image. The need 'to be seen to be doing stuff' about a public problem was highly important on the scale of enforcement objectives, especially since the 'enforcement action ultimately is public' (Regulator02). This is unsurprising, bearing in mind the FSA's significant reputational damages for several regulatory failures and scandals, for example, the poor handling of the pre-crisis events, the criticisms for handling the crisis aftermath with almost no enforcement actions against senior managers involved in the banking failures, and the informal redress settlements with large banks for the mis-selling of interest rate hedging products (FSA, 2012b):

> Another characteristic of a [bad] case is, it is often known in the outside world that this has happened, so as a regulator, you have to be seen to be doing something about it; otherwise, your own credibility is shot.
>
> (Regulator01)

The discretionary considerations over the cases that should be formally enforced overlapped. Behaviour could be both egregious and such that its tackling would serve general deterrence purposes. However, if a case was 'egregious', this seemed to take precedence over its enforcement return value, so a case would be processed even if 'the conduct is esoteric, but it's just so bad' (Regulator01). This indicates that the FCA was willing, especially in the light of public humiliation, to tackle difficult cases, complex cases, and cases involving large market players. In addition, FCA enforcement could skip steps in the enforcement pyramid and opt for a more severe formal action immediately if there was a need to *send a message* or to tackle an *'egregious'* case. This finding shows that, in practice, the progression up the enforcement pyramid is not necessarily linear, as originally envisaged by Ayres and Braithwaite (1992). Normative considerations of enforcement priorities and harm, and organisational considerations of regulatory reputation, may take precedence over the pyramid's instrumental aspects.

The skipping of the pyramid steps and the less publicly visible enforcement referral considerations might provide an explanation for regulatees' perceptions that it was difficult to predict which cases would ultimately go to enforcement. Lawyers claimed that some of the cases which they perceived as 'very serious' and 'highly likely' to go to enforcement were ultimately not referred, and they had 'absolutely no idea why not' (LawyerFR03). Whilst there was a common shared understanding of what misconduct was 'serious', there was not always a common understanding over what serious misconduct would be formally processed. This uncertainty challenges the deterrence and effectiveness of enforcement policies if regulatees cannot predict when formal enforcement will happen.

Conclusion

Post-crisis, the more intrusive and intensive regulatory style consisted of shifts towards knowing more of the markets and deviant behaviour in them, as observed in three important trends. First, there was a shift in supervisory attitudes towards an increased use of the information-gathering legal powers to proactively request significant amounts of information in shorter timescales. The FCA turned into an 'information-hungry regulator' that constantly wanted more information. This could lead to more misconduct potentially being detected through supervisory desk-based work as a proactive detection source. Second, there was an increasing trend towards using third-party experts ('skilled persons'), such as accounting and law firms, as an enforcement evidence-gathering and detection mechanism. The third parties conducted diagnostic work of financial institutions' compliance programmes, with obligations to report any detected non-compliance. The ability to outsource enforcement functions to third parties paid by the firm provided necessary regulatory resources in view of the more interventionist attitudes. Third, there was a significant reliance on using Principle 11 in the Handbook as a self-reporting tool. The requirements under Principle 11 essentially impose mandatory self-reporting by regulatees of their own non-compliance. The image of an 'information-hungry regulator', supported further by enforcement activities on the back of breaching Principle 11, also led to an increase in the awareness and extent of self-reporting as a reactive detection source.

The increase in information exchanges was supported by an underlying process of *mutual risk mitigation*, in which regulators and the regulated mutually hedged risks to manage perceptions – each other's and that of wider audiences. The increase in the informational traffic enabled more potential for detecting misconduct, but regulatory judgements might be impaired by the staff level of experience and by the corporate responses that had developed to adapt to the more inquisitive agenda, such as the careful management of the self-reporting process, and detection facilitation to enable detection avoidance. These could also influence what detected misconduct was formally investigated, together with the discretionary enforcement priorities of returns, harms, and managing credibility and reputation.

Bibliography

Abbott KW, Levi-Faur D and Snidal D (2017) Theorizing Regulatory Intermediaries: The RIT Model. *The ANNALS of the American Academy of Political and Social Science* 670(1): 14–35.

Almond P (2006) An Inspector's-Eye View: The Prospective Enforcement of Work-Related Fatality Cases. *British Journal of Criminology* 46(5): 893–916.

Almond P and Colover S (2012) The Criminalization of Workplace Death. *British Journal of Criminology* 52: 997–1016.

Ayres I and Braithwaite J (1992) *Responsive Regulation: Transcending the Deregulation Debate*. Oxford: Oxford University Press.

Baldwin R and Black J (2008) Really Responsive Regulation. *Modern Law Review* 71(1): 59–94.

Baldwin R, Martin C and Martin L (2012) *Understanding Regulation: Theory, Strategy, and Practice*. Oxford: Oxford University Press.

Barak G (2012) *Theft of a Nation: Wall Street Looting and Federal Regulatory Colluding*. Lanham, MD: Rowman & Littlefield Publishers.

Black J (1997) *Rules and Regulators (Oxford Socio-Legal Studies)*. Oxford: Oxford University Press.

Black J (1998) Talking about Regulation. *Public Law*: 77–105.
Black J (2005) The Emergence of Risk-based Regulation and the New Public Management in the UK. *Public Law* (Autumn): 512–549.
Black J (2008) Forms and Paradoxes of Principles-Based Regulation. *Capital Markets Law Journal* 3(4): 425–457.
Black J (2011) The Rise, Fall and Fate of Principles-Based Regulation. In: Kern A and Moloney N (eds) *Law Reform and Financial Markets (Elgar Financial Law Series)*. Cheltenham, UK: Edward Elgar Publishing, 3–34.
Black J (2012) Paradoxes and Failures: 'New Governance' Techniques and the Financial Crisis. *Modern Law Review* 75(6): 1037–1063.
Black J (2013) Reconceiving Financial Markets – From the Economic to the Social. *Journal of Corporate Law Studies* 13(2): 401–442.
Black J (2014) Learning from Regulatory Disasters. *LSE Law, Society and Economy Working Papers 24/2014*. Available at: http://eprints.lse.ac.uk/60569/1/WPS2014-24_Black.pdf
Black J and Baldwin R (2010) Really Responsive Risk-Based Regulation. *Law and Policy* 32(2): 181–213.
Black J, Hopper M and Band C (2007) Making a Success of Principles-Based Regulation. *Law and Financial Markets Review* 1(3): 191–206.
Blair M (1991) *Financial Services: The New Core Rules*. London: Blackstone Press Ltd.
Braithwaite J (1982) Enforced Self-Regulation: A New Strategy for Corporate Crime Control. *Michigan Law Review* 80(7): 1466–1507.
Braithwaite J (2002) Rules and Principles: A Theory of Legal Certainty. *Australian Journal of Legal Philosophy* 27: 47–82.
Braithwaite J and Makkai T (1991) Testing an Expected Utility Model of Corporate Deterrence. *Law & Society Review* 25(1): 7–40.
Braithwaite J and Murphy J (1993) Clout and Internal Compliance Systems. *Corporate Conduct Quarterly* 2: 52–54.
Breyer S (1993) *Breaking the Vicious Circle: Toward Effective Risk Regulation*. Cambridge, MA: Harvard University Press.
Clarke M (1990) *Business Crime: Its Nature and Control*. Cambridge: Polity Press.
Clinard BM and Yeager CP (1980) *Corporate Crime*. New York: Free Press.
Coffee JC, Jr (2006) *Gatekeepers: The Professions and Corporate Governance*. Oxford: Oxford University Press.
Coffee JC, Jr (2013) *Missing in Action? A Closer Look at SEC Enforcement. What Happened? What Can Be Done?* [presentation] Centre for the Study of Business Ethics, Regulation and Crime, University of Maryland (08.11.2013).
Cohen S (1972) *Folk Devils and Moral Panics*. London: MacGibbon & Kee.
Cole M (2007) *Enforcement Briefing (Speech)*. Available at: https://webarchive.nationalarchives.gov.uk/ukgwa/20081231115518/http://www.fsa.gov.uk/pages/Library/Communication/Speeches/2007/0314_mc.shtml.
Copeland CB (2017) The Yates Memo: Looking for Individual Accountability in All the Wrong Places. *Iowa Law Review* 102: 1897–1927.
Dewing IP and Rusell PO (2005) *The Role of Auditors Reporting Accountants and Skilled Persons in UK Financial Services Supervision*. Edinburgh: Institute of Chartered Accountants of Scotland.
Dewing IP and Russell PO (2007) The Individualization of Corporate Governance: The Approved Persons' Regime for UK Financial Services Firms. *Accounting, Auditing & Accountability Journal* 21(7): 978–1000.
Dorn N (2012b) Knowing Markets: Would Less be More? *Economy and Society* 41(3): 316–334.
Duggin SH (2003) Internal Corporate Investigations: Legal Ethics, Professionalism and the Employee Interview. *Columbia Business Law Review* 859–964.
Edelman LB (1992) Legal Ambiguity and Symbolic Structures: Organizational Mediation of Civil Rights Law. *American Journal of Sociology* 97(6): 1531–1576.

Edelman LB (2016) *Working Law: Courts, Corporations, and Symbolic Civil Rights.* Chicago University Press.

Edelman LB and Talesh SA (2011) To Comply or Not to Comply-That Isn't the Question: How Organizations Construct the Meaning of Compliance. In: Parker C and Nielsen VL (eds) *Explaining Compliance: Business Responses to Regulation.* Cheltenham, UK: Edward Elgar Publishing, 103–122.

Edelman LB, Uggen C and Erlanger HS (1999) The Endogeneity of Legal Regulation: Grievance Procedures as Rational Myth. *American Journal of Sociology* 105(2): 406–454.

Ericson R, Barry D and Doyle A (2000) The Moral Hazards of Neo-Liberalism: Lessons from the Private Insurance Industry. *Economy and Society* 29(4): 532–558.

Ericson R, Doyle A and Barry D (2003) *Insurance as Governance.* Toronto: University of Toronto Press.

Ericson R and Haggerty KD (1997) *Policing the Risk Society.* Oxford: Clarendon Press.

Ermann MD and Lundman RJ (2002) Introduction. In: Ermann MD and Lundman RJ (eds) *Corporate and Governmental Deviance: Problems of Organizational Behavior in Contemporary Society* (6th ed.). New York: Oxford University Press.

Etienne J (2010) Self-Reporting Untoward Events to External Controllers: Accounting for Reporting Failure by a Top Tier Chemical Plant. *Discussion Paper No. 66, CARR.* Available at: https://eprints.lse.ac.uk/36546/1/Disspaper66.pdf.

FCA (2013) *The FCA's Approach to Advancing Its Objectives.* Available at: www.fca.org.uk/static/documents/fca-approach-advancing-objectives.pdf.

FCA (2014a) *Post-Implementation Review of the Retail Distribution Review – Phase 1.* Available at: www.fca.org.uk/publication/research/post-implementation-review-rdr-phase-1.pdf.

FCA (2014b) *How Small Banks Manage Money Laundering and Sanctions Risk: Update. TR14/16.* Available at: www.fca.org.uk/publication/thematic-reviews/tr14-16.pdf.

FCA (2016) *Referral Criteria.* Available at: https://webarchive.nationalarchives.gov.uk/ukgwa/20160907165637/https://www.fca.org.uk/about/enforcement/referral-criteria.

Ferran E (2011) Break-up of the Financial Services Authority. *Oxford Journal of Legal Studies* 31(3): 455–480.

Ferran E (2012) The New Mandate for the Supervision of Financial Services Conduct. *Current Legal Problems* 65(1): 411–453.

FSA (2011) *Banks' Management of High Money-Laundering Risk Situations: How Banks Deal with High-Risk Customers (Including Politically Exposed Persons), Correspondent Banking Relationships and Wire Transfers.* Available at: www.fca.org.uk/static/documents/fsa-aml-final-report.pdf.

FSA (2012a) *Journey to the FCA: To Make Financial Markets Work Well so Consumers Get a Fair Deal.* Available at: www.fca.org.uk/static/documents/fsa-journey-to-the-fca.pdf.

FSA (2012b) *FSA Agrees Settlement with Four Banks Over Interest Rate Hedging Products.* Available at: https://webarchive.nationalarchives.gov.uk/ukgwa/20121210053412/http://www.fsa.gov.uk/library/communication/pr/2012/071.shtml.

FSA (2013) *Internal Audit Report: A Review of the Extent of Awareness within the FSA of Inappropriate LIBOR Submissions: Management Response.* Available at: www.fca.org.uk/static/documents/fsa-ia-libor-management-response.pdf.

Galanter M (1974) Why the "Haves" Come out Ahead: Speculations on the Limits of Legal Change. *Law & Society Review* 9(1): 95–160.

Gilad S (2008a) Exchange without Capture: The UK Financial Ombudsman Service's Struggle for Accepted Domain. *Public Administration* 86(4): 907–924.

Gilad S (2008b) Accountability or Expectations Management: The Role of the Ombudsman in Financial Regulation. *Law & Policy* 30(2): 227–253.

Gold M and Levi M (1994) *Money-Laundering in the UK: An Appraisal of Suspicion-Based Reporting.* London: Police Foundation.

Grabosky P and Braithwaite J (1986) *Of Manners Gentle: Enforcement Strategies of Australian Business Regulatory Agencies*. Melbourne: Oxford University Press.
Gray G (2006) The Regulation of Corporate Violations: Punishment, Compliance, and the Blurring of Responsibility. *British Journal of Criminology* 46(5): 875–892.
Gray J and Akseli O (2011) *Financial Regulation in Crisis: The Role of Law and the Failure of Northern Rock (Edward Elgar Financial Law Series)*. Cheltenham, UK: Edward Elgar Publishing.
Gray J and Hamilton J (2006) *Implementing Financial Regulation*. Chichester: John Wiley & Sons Ltd.
Gunningham N (2010) Enforcement and Compliance Strategies. In: Baldwin R, Cave M and Lodge M (eds) *The Oxford Handbook of Regulation*. New York: Oxford University Press, 120–145.
Gunningham N, Kagan RA and Thornton D (2004) Social License and Environmental Protection: Why Businesses Go beyond Compliance. *Law & Social Inquiry* 29(2): 307–341.
Gunningham N, Thornton D and Kagan R (2005) Motivating Management: Corporate Compliance in Environmental Protection. *Law and Policy* 27(2): 289–316.
Habermas J (1987) *The Theory of Communicative Action (Vol. 2: Lifeworld and System: A Critique of Functionalist Reason)*. Boston, MA: Bacon Press.
Hawkins K (1984) *Environment and Enforcement: Regulation and the Social Definition of Pollution*. Oxford: Clarendon Press.
Hawkins K (2002) *Law as Last Resort: Prosecution Decision-Making in a Regulatory Agency*. Oxford: Oxford University Press.
HM Treasury (2014) *Review of Enforcement Decision-Making at the Financial Services Regulators: Final Report*. Available at: https://assets.publishing.service.gov.uk/media/5a7ecd2c40f0b62305b8344a/enforcement_review_response_final.pdf.
Hutter BM (1986) An Inspector Calls. *British Journal of Criminology* 26(2): 114–128.
Hutter BM (1988) *The Reasonable Arm of the Law? Law Enforcement Procedures of Environmental Health Officers (Oxford Socio-Legal Studies)*. Oxford: Clarendon Press.
Hutter BM (1997) *Compliance: Regulation and Environment: Oxford Socio-Legal Studies*. Oxford, UK: Oxford University Press.
Hutter BM (2011) Negotiating Social, Economic and Political Environments: Compliance with Regulation within and beyond the State. In: Parker C and Nielsen VL (eds) *Explaining Compliance: Business Responses to Regulation*. Cheltenham, UK: Edward Elgar Publishing, 305–321.
Jackson HE (2005) An American Perspective on the U.K. Financial Services Authority: Politics, Goals, & Regulatory Intensity. *Harvard Law School John M. Olin Center for Law, Economics and Business Discussion Paper Series. Paper 522*. Available at: www.law.harvard.edu/programs/corp_gov/papers/Jackson_522.pdf.
Kagan R and Scholz T (1984) The 'Criminology of the Corporation' and Regulatory Enforcement Strategies. In: Hawkins K and Thomas J (eds) *Enforcing Regulation*. Boston: Kluwer-Nijhoff, 67–95.
Kaplow L and Shavell S (1994) Optimal Law Enforcement with Self-Reporting of Behavior. *Journal of Political Economy* 102(3): 583–606.
La Porta R, Lopez-de-Silanes F, Shleifer A and Vishny RW (1997) Trust in Large Organizations. *American Economic Association Papers and Proceedings* 87(2): 333–338.
Lange B (1999) Compliance Construction in the Context of Environmental Regulation. *Social & Legal Studies* 8(4): 549–567.
Lastra RM (2013) Defining Forward-Looking, Judgement-Based Supervision. *Journal of Banking Regulation* 14(3–4): 221–227.
Law Commission (2019) *Anti-Money Laundering: The SARs Regime, Law Com. No. 384, HC 2098*. London: The Stationary Office.

Levi M (2007) Pecunia Non Olet? The Control of Money-Laundering Revisited. In: Bovenkerk F and Levi M (eds) *The Organized Crime Community: Essays in Honor of Alan A. Block. Studies in Organized Crime* (Vol. 6). New York: Springer.

Levi M (2010) Policing Financial Crimes. In: Pontell HN and Geis G (eds) *International Handbook of White-collar and Corporate Crime*. Dordrecht, The Netherlands: Kluwer Academic Plenum Publishers, 588–606.

Levi M and Reuter P (2006) Money Laundering. In: Tonry M (ed) *Crime and Justice: A Review of Research* (Vol. 34). Chicago: Chicago University Press, 289–375.

Levitin AJ (2014) The Politics of Financial Regulation and the Regulation of Financial Politics: A Review Essay. *Harvard Law Review* 127(7): 1991–2068.

Long A (2006) Investment Firms: Retail Market. In: Blair M and Walker G (eds) *Financial Services Law*. Oxford: Oxford University Press, 449–485.

MacNeil IG and O'Brien J (2010) Introduction. In: MacNeil IG and O'Brien (eds) *The Future of Financial Regulation*. Oxford: Hart Publishing, 1–22.

Malik AS (1993) Self-Reporting and the Design of Policies for Regulating Stochastic Pollution. *Journal of Environmental Economics and Management* 24(3): 241–257.

Manning KP (1989) The Limits of Knowledge: A Note on the Role of Information in the Regulation of Complex Systems with Special Reference to Nuclear Power Generation. In: Hawkins K and Thomas J (eds) *Regulatory Policy-Making*. Pittsburgh: University of Pittsburgh Press, 49–87.

May PJ (2005) Regulation and Compliance Motivations: Examining Different Approaches. *Public Administration Review* 65(1): 31–44.

May PJ and Winter SC (2011) Regulatory Enforcement Styles and Compliance. In: Parker C and Nielsen VL (eds) *Explaining Compliance: Business Responses to Regulation*. Cheltenham, UK: Edward Elgar Publishing, 222–244.

May PJ and Wood RS (2003) At the Regulatory Front Lines: Inspectors' Enforcement Styles and Regulatory Compliance. *Journal of Public Administration Research and Theory* 13(2): 117–139.

Mazerolle L and Ransley J (2005) *Third Party Policing*. Cambridge, UK: Cambridge University Press.

McAllister LK (2012) Regulation by Third-Party Verification. *Boston College Law Review* 53(1): 1–64.

McBarnet D (2006) After Enron Will 'Whiter Than White Collar Crime' Still Wash? *British Journal of Criminology* 46(6): 1091–1109.

McBarnet D and Whelan C (1991) The Elusive Spirit of the Law: Formalism and the Struggle for Legal Control. *Modern Law Review* 54(6): 848–873.

McCahery J and Picciotto S (1995) Creative Lawyering and the Dynamics of Business Regulation. In: Dezalay Y and Sugarman D (eds) *Professional Competition and Professional Power: Lawyers, Accountants and the Social Construction of Markets*. London: Routledge, 238–274.

Moloney N (2010) Financial Services and Markets. In: Baldwin R, Cave M and Lodge M (eds) *The Oxford Handbook of Regulation*. New York: Oxford University Press, 120–145.

Nielsen V and Parker C (2012) Mixed Motives: Economic, Social, and Normative Motivations in Business Compliance. *Law & Policy* 34(4): 428–462.

Pain J (2010) *FSA's Approach to Intensive Supervision (Speech)*. Available at: https://webarchive.nationalarchives.gov.uk/ukgwa/20121211003950/http://www.fsa.gov.uk/library/communication/speeches/2010/0518_jp.shtml.

Parker C and Nielsen V (2006) Do Businesses Take Compliance Systems Seriously? An Empirical Study of Implementation of Trade Practices Compliance Systems in Australia. *Melbourne University Law Review* 30(2): 441–494.

Parker C and Nielsen V (2009) The Challenge of Empirical Research on Business Compliance in Regulatory Capitalism. *Annual Review of Law and Social Science* 5: 45–70.

Parker C and Nielsen V (2011) Introduction: From Regulation to Compliance. In: Parker C and Nielsen VL (eds) *Explaining Compliance: Business Responses to Regulation*. Cheltenham, UK: Edward Elgar Publishing, 1–33.
Pautz MC (2009) Trust between Regulators and the Regulated: A Case Study of Environmental Inspectors and Facility Personnel in Virginia. *Politics and Policy* 37: 1047–1072.
Pfaff A and Sanchirico CW (2004) Big Field, Small Potatoes: An Empirical Assessment of EPA's Self-Audit Policy. *Journal of Policy Analysis and Management* 23(3): 415–432.
Reiss AJ, Jr (1983) The Policing of Organizational Life. In: Punch M (ed) *Control in the Police Organization*. Cambridge, MA: MIT Press.
Reuter P and Truman EM (2004) *Chasing Dirty Money. The Fight Against Money Laundering*. Washington, DC: Institute for International Economics.
Sanchirico CW (2006) Detection Avoidance. *New York University Law Review* 81: 1331.
Sants H (2009a) *CEO's Speech – FSA Annual Public Meeting (Speech)*. Available at: https://webarchive.nationalarchives.gov.uk/ukgwa/20121210235501/http://www.fsa.gov.uk/library/communication/speeches/2009/0723_hs.shtml.
Sants H (2009b) *The Regulator's Role in Judging Competence (Speech)*. Available at: https://webarchive.nationalarchives.gov.uk/ukgwa/20121210235501/http://www.fsa.gov.uk/library/communication/speeches/2009/0723_hs.shtml.
Sants H (2012) *Delivering 'Twin Peaks' within the FSA (Speech)*. Available at: https://webarchive.nationalarchives.gov.uk/ukgwa/20121210050646/http://www.fsa.gov.uk/library/communication/speeches/2012/0206-hs.shtml.
Shapiro SP (1984) *Wayward Capitalists: Target of the Securities Exchange Commission*. New Haven: Yale University Press.
Shapiro SP (1985) The Road Not Taken: The Elusive Path to Criminal Prosecution for White-Collar Offenders. *Law & Society Review* 19(2): 179–217.
Short JL and Toffel MW (2008) Coerced Confessions: Self-Policing in the Shadow of the Regulator. *Journal of Law, Economics, & Organization* 24(1): 45–71.
Slapper G and Tombs S (1990) *Corporate Crime*. Harlow: Longman.
Slapper G and Tombs S (1999) *Corporate Crime*. Harlow: Longman.
Sparrow M (2000) *The Regulatory Craft: Controlling Risks, Solving Problems, and Managing Compliance*. Washington, DC: The Brookings Institute.
Spens P (2014) *Surveillance: The FCA's Expectations and Toolkits*. Available at: www.fca.org.uk/news/surveillance-the-fcas-expectations-and-toolkits.
Steward M (2017) *A Better View (Speech)*. Available at: www.fca.org.uk/news/speeches/better-view.
Stretesky PB (2006) Corporate Self-Policing and the Environment. *Criminology* 44(3): 671–708.
Tett G (2010) Silos and Silences: Why So Few People Spotted the Problems in Complex Credit and What That Implies for the Future. *Banque de France, Financial Stability Review* (14): 121–129. Available at: https://publications.banque-france.fr/sites/default/files/medias/documents/financial-stability-review-14_2010-07.pdf.
Thornton D, Gunningham NA and Kagan RA (2005) General Deterrence and Corporate Environmental Behavior. *Law & Policy* 27(2): 262–288.
Tombs S and Whyte D (2013) The Myths and Realities of Deterrence in Workplace Safety Regulation. *British Journal of Criminology* 53(5): 746–763.
Turner A (2009) *The Turner Review: A Regulatory Response to the Global Banking Crisis*. Available at: https://webarchive.nationalarchives.gov.uk/ukgwa/20090320232953/http:/www.fsa.gov.uk/pubs/other/turner_review.pdf.
Tyler TR (2003) Procedural Justice, Legitimacy, and the Effective Rule of Law. *Crime and Justice – A Review of Research* 30: 431–505.

Wheatley M (2013) *The Changing Face of Financial Crime (Speech)*. Available at: www.fca.org.uk/news/speeches/the-changing-face-of-financial-crime.

Will S, Handelman S and Brotherton DC (eds) (2013) *How They Got Away with It: White Collar Criminals and the Financial Meltdown*. New York: Columbia University Press.

Williams JW (2009) Envisioning Financial Disorder: Financial Surveillance and the Securities Industry. *Economy and Society* 38(3): 460–491.

Williams JW (2012) *Policing the Markets: Inside the Black box of Securities Enforcement*. New York: Routledge.

Williams JW (2013) Regulatory Technologies, Risky Subjects, and Financial Boundaries: Governing 'Fraud' in the Financial Markets. *Accounting, Organizations and Society* 38(6): 544–558.

Wilson G and Wilson S (2010) Market Misconduct, the Financial Services Authority and Creating a System of "City Grasses": Blowing the Whistle on Whistle-Blowing. *Company Lawyer* 31(3): 67–80.

Winter SC and May PJ (2001) Motivation for Compliance with Environmental Regulations. *Journal of Policy Analysis and Management* 20: 675–698.

Woodall L (2010) *What Intensive Supervision Means for Small Firms (Speech)*. Available at: https://webarchive.nationalarchives.gov.uk/ukgwa/20121211003141/http://www.fsa.gov.uk/library/communication/speeches/2010/0309_lw.shtml.

Cases

K Ltd v NatWest [2006] 4 All ER 907.

R (on the Application of Prudential plc & anor) (appellants) v Special Commissioner of Income Tax & anor [2013] UKSC 1.

Three Rivers DC v Bank of England (Disclosure) (No. 4) [2004] UKHL 48 610.

Three Rivers DC v Governor and Company of the Bank of England (No. 5) [2003].

Three Rivers District Council v Governor and Company of the Bank of England (No. 6) [2004].

4 The cooperative context during the contentious enforcement procedure

Investigations and settlements

Chapter 4 is the first of two chapters dedicated to the social control of corporate targets within the post-crisis regulatory enforcement agenda. It examines the processes of, and regulatory interactions within, enforcement investigations, the regulator's use of evidence-gathering powers, and the claims, counter-claims, and adaptation that developed in the investigative setting. Investigations are concerned with evidence construction through formal investigative powers. The FCA's use of these powers depended not only on what was possible in law but also on the investigators' attitudes and capabilities in exercising the legal powers 'on the ground' and on how targets responded to the legal process of evidence construction, actively participating in the patterning of regulatory violations (Reichman, 1992). The chapter further examines the resolution of the enforcement action through the confidential world of corporate settlements, uncovering the motives behind settling on both sides of the regulatory relationship. Despite the record-breaking financial penalties for a range of corporate misconduct, as well as the rise in the number of formal investigations, the process of regulatory interactions during investigations and case settlement fostered strong cooperative relationships between the regulator and regulated organisations.

Investigations procedure and tactics over information control

The successful filtering of the detected misconduct through the enforcement referral criteria and the internal appointment of an investigating team[1] marked the start of the formal investigation procedure. The first communication sent by the investigating team was the Memorandum of Appointment of Investigators. The Memorandum performed two main functions: it notified the targets that a formal investigation was started (a more limited function in practice), and it set out the misconduct allegations. These functions were maintained throughout the enforcement process, as any significant changes in the investigation's scope, such as spin-offs or allegation changes (either adding

1 Sections 167(1) and 168(3), (5) FSMA.

DOI: 10.4324/9781351069328-4

new ones or dropping existing ones),[2] were communicated through various Memorandum versions. The alleged misconduct was constructed principally through the content of the Memorandum, giving indications to the targets of the current focus of the developing investigation. The Memorandum must have certain minimum elements required by statute,[3] and these were of different levels of precision and detail: the statutory basis and the reason for the start of the investigation. The vagueness of the prescriptive aspects of the principles-based regime was reflected in social practice as memoranda mostly conveyed the misconduct allegations as breaches of Type 2 rules or as breaches of the principles.

The regulatory lawyers had mixed experiences regarding how specific the Memorandum allegations were. Some contended that it outlined a relatively clear set of charges that would enable ascertaining the regulator's case. Others, however, reported that the allegations could be phrased in general terms: with a broad statement of the allegations and an indication of the principle that was breached, but without specific details on the facts considered or indication of specific Handbook rules. For the second group, the vagueness of the Memorandum represented one of the overarching challenges of the investigation:

> Getting the FCA to tell you what it is that they are really investigating, what the issues they're concerned about are can be difficult. They are obliged to give you a notice that specifies their concerns, but they tend to be at a quite high level. . . . They can be quite coy about the specifics.
> (Lawyer03)

A tactical measure to overcome this initial uncertainty was the organisation of scoping meetings, at which the party and enforcement investigators discussed the timescale and the content of the investigation. These were commonly attended by the investigators, the firm's senior management, or the individual under investigation, and their lawyers. Scoping meetings are not statutory instruments but arose from regulatory practice.[4] They were an opportunity for the investigators to introduce themselves and explain to senior management the process, scope, and time frames of the investigation and needed documents. For targets, scoping meetings were also the first opportunity to manage their appearance in front of the investigators. The advice was always to use them to 'set the tone of the investigation, make clear they want to cooperate, make a good impression' (LawyerFR07). Despite these familiarisation functions, like the Memorandum, scoping meetings did not always contribute

2 New memoranda were also issued for the appointment of new principal investigators, though this is not a statutory requirement. It was the FCA's practical approach to personalise the investigating team members to the party.

3 Section 170(4)(a)–(b) FSMA.

4 FCA Enforcement Guide 4.8.

to communicating to the target what the suspected breaches were. The conversations mostly concerned a high-level restatement of the investigation process (already familiar to lawyers), but enforcement members did not share a full investigation plan.

In practice, therefore, the misconduct was constructed quite broadly by the regulator for two reasons, which were not mutually exclusive and may also not be present in every case: informational disadvantage and tactical considerations. In some cases, the regulator did not yet have a clear picture of what misconduct had occurred, its extent, and what it was looking for. This was then reflected in the allegations being non-specific, and the evidence-gathering powers served a real function in overcoming this informational disadvantage (Manning, 1989). The vagueness could also be motivated by tactical considerations and the desire of enforcement staff to maintain a strategic advantage of spreading the investigation as widely as possible. Phrasing the boundaries of the investigation in high-level terms allowed staff to investigate a firm across the whole range of conduct in a business area, a product area, or sales channel, and across a range of different violations, 'until they find something that they like' (Lawyer06). This further enabled a maximum enforcement return from the case. Though at first glance this may appear as a type of 'fishing expedition', the low statutory investigation thresholds legally enable the FCA to phrase the written notice in such vague terms.[5] The threshold requires only a 'good reason' for the investigation, which gave an advantage to the enforcement staff but discouraged judicial challenges of the scope of the Memorandum, deemed a fully unfeasible and hopeless route (Lawyer06).

The vagueness of the charges introduced goal discrepancies between the parties as 'the dynamic is [that] the regulator wants to keep it fairly high-level. The firm wants more detail' (LawyerFR07). In the enforcement context of the Canadian securities market, Williams (2012: 153) found similar dynamic between regulators and targets and called it 'legal gamesmanship'. In the FCA regulatory game, frequent attempts were made by firms to engage with the investigators to obtain more information. Though these attempts were not always successful, they were nonetheless persistent. The surrounding uncertainties also made the involvement of contentious regulatory lawyers indispensable. In contrast to the backstage involvement before the enforcement referral, partly because of the supervisors' disapproving attitudes, the dynamics of formal investigations were shaped by the ***normalised*** and accepted presence of contentious lawyers as intermediaries. Their role was to assess, interpret, and predict the intentions of the regulator, or 'to understand your own case, but also to understand your opponent's case even better' (Lawyer06). Thus, they retained the position of key players and key providers of regulatory interpretations (Mann, 1985; McCahery & Picciotto, 1995; Schmidt, 2005). This is even though, in the UK markets, the services

5 On fishing expeditions, see *Belize Alliance of Conservation Non-Governmental Organisations v Department of the Environment of Belize* [2004].

of contentious lawyers are rarely used for more litigious or adversarial functions due to the very low number of judicial challenges. Therefore, in formal investigations, most interactions occurred between lawyers on both sides of the process speaking with a common language (Black et al., 2007). The tactics and attempts to take 'ownership' of the case were mostly played out between the same category of professionals who were mostly familiar with one another and 'repeatedly played' (Galanter, 1974) with or against one another.

Once investigations were underway, their scope frequently changed, as the use of formal powers was an important source of misconduct detection, often leading to investigation spin-offs. This was supported by the very low statutory investigation thresholds and the fact that changes in scope did not need to undergo the same demanding process of sifting as the initial enforcement referral. Once the case was 'owned' by the investigation team, investigators tended to pursue every possible avenue of enquiry and achieve the most optimal enforcement return. The agency's overall enforcement philosophy led to increased investigations into potentially culpable individuals in line with the 'credible deterrence' priorities, and these are discussed in Chapter 6. Other spin-offs included investigating similar breaches regarding additional products or business sectors or into any links between individual instances of misconduct and corporate systems' failures. Systems and controls failures spotted as a result of a thematic review or a supervisory visit could result in constructing facts (Lange, 2002) on an additional breach (e.g. market abuse or committed fraud by individuals). Equally, an investigation into a reported single misconduct (e.g. mis-selling, client assets protection, or communication with clients) would commonly result in an overarching systems and controls investigation. Discovery of systemic or widespread non-compliance elicited additional charges of flaws in the firm's governance structure, transforming the misconduct into also Principle 3 or systems and controls breach. High-profile examples are the two investigations into UBS's internal systems after the reported internal fraud of Kweku Adoboli[6] and the reported unauthorised trading of staff in the wealth management division.[7] Facts of new breaches could emerge from the investigation dynamic itself. These would be cases where the subject actively frustrated the investigation by falsifying records or statements (amounting to Principle 1 [integrity] breach or to declaring the individual 'not fit and proper'). The final notices showed that such situations occurred mostly regarding individuals, particularly small IFAs. As the initial allegations could transform, expand, or become limited, any initial certainty of the enforcement process for the targets was fragile. There was always a risk that the FCA would 'start investigating one thing and then turn over some world of stone and find something underneath that nobody thought about' (Lawyer03).

6 UBS FN25/11/12.
7 UBS FN05/08/09.

Constructing misconduct claims: the use of evidence-gathering powers

The conduct of the investigative process showcases an 'informational interdependence' (Hawkins & Hutter, 1993) between the parties. The FCA's investigative powers served a real function of overcoming the regulator's informational disadvantage regarding the misconduct extent. The FCA's *modus operandi* was to begin an investigation with document requests, a core investigative tactic, before interviewing individuals.

The 'information traffic' through document requests

Document requests represented a core investigative tactic. Documents served important purposes in the initial construction of the wrongdoing facts, or their proof: they could provide the 'smoking gun' (LawyerFR07) of the case, and ultimately, they would form the 'case theory'[8] on what might have happened. Documents were also used to trace the decision-making trail in organisations.

Document requests were commonly a massive exercise in terms of the documents volume and the time and resources spent on sifting through them. Variations of this were market abuse cases, where there might not be a readily available paper trail but where investigators analysed scores of transactions and telephone records to establish manipulative trading and an insider/trader connection. Investigators, much alike supervisors, frequently demanded an extensive range of documents since the legal test was interpreted to capture documents that were 'broadly within the scope of the investigation' (LawyerFR07). This still satisfied the 'reasonableness' requirement since, according to a former senior enforcement official involved in the drafting of the Enforcement Guide and internal enforcement policy manuals, significant consideration was given to align internal documents with statutory boundaries to counteract the legal risks of potential judicial reviews. In *Fieldglen* [2009], the Court of Appeal confirmed that most document requests by the FCA would be reasonable as it was the regulator which 'was in a position to know best the scope of its inquiries'. In practice, considerations of what would be a 'reasonable' document request concerned procedural justice issues, such as fairness and natural justice, influenced by practical considerations of time frames and firms' capability to comply. The FCA documents requests process was similar to the discovery regime in UK civil procedure. Discovery also is bounded by the standard of reasonableness, assessed against a range of factors, such as the number of documents, the complexity of the proceedings, and the ease, accessibility, and expense of retrieving documents.[9]

The FCA's appetite for information and the low legal thresholds for document requests explain why, in the UK financial markets, most of the document

8 This phrase was used by both lawyers and regulators to designate the views formed on the contested issue. On case theories in criminal justice, see Anderson et al. (2005).

9 See, for example, *Digicel v Cable & Wireless LLC* [2008].

'traffic' occurred upon the regulator's request. This is unlike what researchers have found on financial regulators in other jurisdictions, such as Canada (Snider, 2009), where investigated firms frequently swamped the regulator with papers and information, with cynical motives. Other researchers in the corporate crime literature have also pointed out the strategic use of corporate power and resources to send documents as a conscious strategy to clog and diminish the available enforcement resources (Punch, 1996). The traffic movements were also supported by targets-related reasons: (1) it was less of an effort to submit the documents than to vet them, (2) this removed the possibility of allegations of keeping anything back in breach of Principle 11, and (3) they did not judicially challenge the requests to prevent publicity and to preserve a good relationship with the regulator.

Presentations and constructing facts in the interview room

Next to document requests, interviewing individuals, either as representatives of targeted firms or as targets themselves, was the most important and frequently used evidence-gathering power. Interviews occurred commonly after most documents were gathered and examined. The gist of the interviewing was aimed at 'constructing proof' (Baldwin, 1993) that the legal elements of the violation had been satisfied, and testing the investigator's 'case theory' of what s/he believes happened.

There was a formality to the enforcement interview process, unlike the more informal regulatory conversations that occur during the supervision stage. FCA normally invited individuals to an interview through its compulsory statutory powers with the standard public law protections: fairness, transparency, and efficiency.[10] The specified use of formal enforcement powers alerted targets of possible adverse effects of attending the interview and answering questions. Sometimes the FCA invited suspects or possible suspects in market abuse investigations (possibly under caution) to a voluntary interview. In such a case, the interviewee does not have to answer, but if they do, those answers may be used against them in subsequent proceedings, including criminal or market abuse proceedings. Interviews took place at FCA premises and were always tape-recorded, contributing to the formality of the process. A final qualitative difference to supervisory conversations was that, again, the presence of contentious lawyers was *normalised*. The right to have a legal adviser present throughout was guaranteed, and even expected, by the investigators.

Across cases, the regulator followed a concentric approach towards the interviewees. In firms' investigations, these first included witnesses external to the organisation, then narrowed down to more junior firm employees, and then, the narrowest layer, top senior management. In investigations of individuals, the schedule was temporally similar, though with fewer layers of concentric circles: the broadest included witnesses, the narrowest one the target himself/

10 FCA Enforcement Guide 4.7.1.

herself. Lawyers followed the same schedule in pre-notification internal investigations, and this adds to the importance of 'securing employees' statements' (LawyerFR10) as means of protection from possible cross-examination by the investigators, or to create legally privileged documents.

Both sides of the enforcement process considered it crucial to be well prepared for the interview. Investigators received training in how to conduct interviews and therefore represented skilled interviewers. By comparison, only a minority of police officers could be regarded as skilled interviewers (Baldwin, 1993: 326). Lawyers prepared themselves and the targets for the questioning principally on the basis of a pre-disclosed 'interview bundle' with the documents on which the individual will be questioned. More vigilant lawyers prepared beyond this: whilst the FCA had sent a single documents bundle, the lawyer had prepared an extra, larger one. Preparing the client for the interview was a crucial part of the defence work with mock interviews, depending on the enforcement bundle size, sometimes over several days. Pre-interview preparations involved a process of structuring the facts so that the client's behaviour was seen as falling within legal boundaries (Mann, 1985). The preparations also involved 'impression management' (Levi, 1994): crafting a perception of the target as a 'more modest' individual. This was a psychological strategy employed by lawyers to counteract the economic status differences between well-off financial practitioners and public authority investigators. In regulatory interrogations, these were the social characteristics considered 'anti-normative and deserv[ing] condemnation' (McConville & Baldwin, 1982: 172):

> I've had some oligarch clients. . . . I say to them beforehand: 'Don't wear lots of jewellery, don't dress in a very ostentatious or rich sort of way. Do not turn up in a racing car. Don't start talking about your bonus.' You don't want to get on the wrong side of the regulator from that point of view.
>
> (LawyerFR07)

The 'case theory' on the nature of the individual's involvement and extent of culpability affected the level of the interviewing aggressiveness, so individuals could become nervous and struggle during the interview. The successful management of these situations depended on whether legal advisors were present, and here the disparities in individuals' resources to retain them came to the fore. For regulatory offenders who could not afford legal representation, the interview was a highly intimidating process, as part of the lawyer's job was to recognise struggles, interrupt the interview, and coach the target back to being questioned in an unnerving way.

Most targets with a legal representation adopted a cooperative (submissive) attitude, according to the typology suggested by Baldwin (1993: 332). Such a stance was advised by most lawyers, motivated by impression management ('How did we appear? Did we seem to be cooperative?'), and with a view to constructing an 'open and cooperative attitude' by the target that could be credited as a mitigating factor in sentencing. An exception to this were occasions where the target was an individual, as lawyers would adopt an overall more adversarial approach than the standard cooperation (Jordanoska, 2021). The boundaries of the overall cooperative approaches were, however, occasionally contested, with lawyers being instrumental in attempts to prevent the interaction going too far in either direction: too friendly or too aggressive. The tactics used by each side (in italics) as reported in interviews are displayed in Table 4.1 through a binary presentation. The model shows the process of

Table 4.1 Interview tactics

Investigators	*Targets/their lawyers*
Too friendly. To create an impression of a safe environment and elicit 'honest' answers, some investigators adopted an approach of being overly friendly and informal.	*These are not your friends.* Lawyers attempted to prevent the relationship from becoming 'too cooperative', by stepping in if it seemed that it was going in that direction: '[T]hey may try and be your friends, but they're definitely not your friend, so do not become over-matey' (LawyerFR07).
The same question, over and over. This is an interviewing technique in which investigators did not challenge the target's version of events but rather repeatedly asked the same question in various forms at different points. The aim was to catch the interviewee out and prove the investigator's 'case theory'.	*The question has been answered.* Lawyers intervened to protect the client from persistent questioning 'if the client has already answered the question fairly fully'. This prevented further imposition of the investigator's case theory on the allegation or factual circumstances.
Hypothetical scenarios. Investigators attempted to support their 'case theory' through floating a 'hypothesis' on the facts and getting the target to speculate: 'Sometimes investigators will have a prosecution mindset. If you could draw, without being unfair, the interviewee into that sort of mindset, if you can get something which isn't a fact exactly but supports your hypothesis, then that might be quite helpful to [them]' (LawyerFR07). The tactic was especially opportune when the target did not remember all of the factual details ('If you had done it, what would you have done?') or was asked to interpret others' documents ('Here's somebody else's diary, what do you think about that?').	*Don't speculate.* Amid the cooperative atmosphere, targets tried to be helpful despite a lacking memory on the facts. The lawyer's job was to try to prevent that by steering the client away from speculating or answering questions on facts and documents they could not remember or did not own ('It's not my diary, so I don't know').
The surprise evidence. Most of the questioning concerned documents in the previously disclosed interview bundle. On occasion, however, investigators could pull out new and surprise documents.	*Not a surprise anymore.* Lawyers managed the surprise evidence by not allowing questions on unseen documents and intermitting the meeting to prepare the client.

constructing the facts on the misconduct and the evidence on them, as well as how the flow of information was managed by lawyers.

These binary tactics support the notion of McConville et al. (1991: 56) that investigators (they refer to the police originally) 'have, at a most fundamental level, the ability to select facts, to reject facts, to not seek facts, to evaluate facts and to generate facts'. Here, facts are also 'not objective entities which exist independently of the social actors but are created by them' (McConville et al., 1991: 56). But facts were created (or recreated) by both categories of social actors, not just by the investigators. At all points, defence lawyers performed what Mann (1985, 1992) has described as their information-control function in the white-collar criminal case. Consequently, the differential ability of targets to steer and influence the enforcement case was most immediately connected to their resources and whether these can be employed to exert 'regulatory authority' (Reichman, 1992) by retaining high-level contentious regulatory lawyers (Jordanoska, 2021).

The cooperative context of enforcement investigations

The context and nature of the regulatory relations in formal investigations are crucial to understanding how the rules on evidence-gathering were shaped by the social reality of FCA investigations. Underlying these interactions is an exchange of claims and counterclaims that form the organisational deviance-defining process (Ermann & Lundman, 2002). Regulatees provide organisational responses with own assertions and versions of the events, 'work[ing] diligently to escape' (Ermann & Lundman, 2002: 31) or manage the deviant label in formal investigations.

The overall stance by targets was one of cooperation with the investigators' demands rather than resistance or adversarialism. As described by LawyerFR03: 'In nine out of ten cases, firms accept the *need* to provide a degree of cooperation. The firm's desire – and rightly so – is to provide a degree of assistance to the FCA' (emphasis added). The minority of regulatees that adopted an adversarial approach mostly concerned categories that did not have long-lasting relationships with the regulator: 'rogue' traders with dishonest intentions from the outset,[11] IFAs and mortgage intermediaries caught out in the changing regulatory requirements with the imposition of the FSA/FCA regime, and newcomers to the regime from other jurisdictions. As one lawyer at a global law firm described:

> [Cooperation] is very much a UK – perhaps a European – kind of mindset. But we deal with institutions from other countries, from Russia, or increasingly from the Near East, Kazakhstan. [There are] some smaller universal institutions that are much more aggressive; they don't have the same kind of ethos.
>
> (Lawyer05)

11 See, for example, *FSA v Westcott* [2003].

The overall cooperative stance means that evidence-gathering powers were mostly enforced without the regulator making explicit threats of compulsion or sanction in case of non-compliance, although an implicit threat of compulsory enforcement could be present. Also, though firms could challenge the regulator's decision to use investigative powers, either through adversarial responses to evidence requests or, ultimately, through judicial reviews, they rarely chose to do so. This is supported by both the empirical data collected for this study and the fact that there are only a handful of public cases in which investigative powers have been challenged. The low thresholds have been confirmed in case law, and the only ways of challenging them are either through showing that the investigators acted unfairly in conducting the investigation[12] or that they made their decision unreasonably.[13] There has been some modest case law where the FSA/FCA itself has applied for contempt of court[14] or undertaken a criminal prosecution for providing misleading information within the investigation.[15] However, these cases concern investigations involving individuals and mostly marginal players in the market.

Even though the 'credible deterrence' policy led to a more punitive regulator, the FCA's regulatory process was still not as adversarial as that by its much-feared US counterpart, the SEC. This is no surprise, as UK regulators have historically been considered to have a less-formal, less-transparent, and subject-to-less-accountability approach to regulation, as opposed to the formalised, relatively transparent, and legalistic US style, often involving lengthy decision cycles (Baldwin et al., 1998: 22, also Axelrad, 2000; Welles & Engel, 2000).[16] Therefore, the overall national regulatory style could be taken as an explanation for the cooperative and accommodative approaches within the enforcement proceedings.

However, this is only part of the picture: it does not explain what lies behind the motives of targets to be accommodating and to contribute to the less-legalistic, less-formalised, and less-public regulatory system. To understand the basis of these cooperative approaches and why they develop in contentious regulatory interactions, I refer to the extant literature on business motives for compliance with regulation in general: calculated, social, and normative motivations (Burby & Paterson, 1993; May, 2005; Nielsen & Parker, 2012; Winter & May, 2001). The interview data revealed similar reasons for the cooperative approaches and compliance with evidence-gathering requests by the regulator. In line with extant findings (May, 2005; Nielsen & Parker, 2012), the motives were also not mutually exclusive, and targets complied for more than one reason.

12 This is a general requirement upon all public investigators: *Hearts of Oak Assurance Co Ltd v A-G* [1932]; *In re Pergamom Press Ltd* [1971].
13 *R (Amro International SA) v FSA* [2010].
14 Section 177 FSMA. *FSA v Westcott* [2003].
15 Section 398 FSMA. See *Sharma V FSA* [2010].
16 This has also contributed to arguments on the exceptionalism of US adversarialism.

Calculated motivations

A principal reason for compliance with evidence requests was based on calculations that the benefits of compliance (legal and economic rewards) overweigh costs (legal risks). Deterrence-based calculations concern fears of attracting further legal charges and sanctions for breaching the Principle 11 requirement to be open and cooperative with the regulator. This necessarily vague requirement shaped the normative background against which the regulator exercised its investigative powers. The FCA's powers were coercive to the extent that failure to react accordingly might also form a breach of Principle 11 that, as for non-disclosure, the FCA can enforce as a separate misconduct, assess as an aggravating factor to the original misconduct, or find as an indicator of lack of integrity and a breach of Principle 1. There were considerable legal risks in deciding not to comply, especially in light of the already-discussed heightened importance attached to Principle 11. This was evidenced in the LIBOR fine against Deutsche Bank: the bank's failings were compounded by its repeated misleading of the FCA investigators. The record size of the penalty directly reflected how seriously the FCA viewed a failure to cooperate with its investigations (FCA, 2015). In the calculations of whether to abide by an evidence request and act honestly when abiding, the risk of further or aggravated penalties was calculated as costs that outweigh the benefits of non-compliance. This represented an important incentive for providing various types of assistance.

Aside from legal risks, calculations included two different incentives for complying with evidence requests: a legal incentive (penalty mitigation) and a business-economic consideration (benefits for concluding the enforcement case quickly or more quickly). Cooperation during the investigation represents a mitigating factor under the fine calculations of the FCA's sentencing policy.[17] An open and cooperative attitude within the investigation was frequently highlighted in final notices as a mitigating factor, and 78 per cent of the analysed final notices contained a statement to this effect. Final notices therefore strengthened the regulatory message of receiving benefits for cooperative behaviour.

The business-oriented incentive emerged from internal strategising over the costs of responding to investigation requests and the formal enforcement process in general. This is a classic utilitarian calculation (Simpson, 2002): business was interested in reducing the costs of work disruptions, intrusive communications with the regulator, the senior management time devoted to this end, and the additional costs of legal representation. FCA investigations could be very costly, lengthy, protracted, and highly intrusive for day-to-day business life. A regulatory lawyer estimated the costs of an investigation into a large firm in the range of millions of pounds: 'in the old days,[18] an FSA investigation would have cost as much as the fine at the end' (Lawyer06).

17 FCA Decisions Procedure and Penalties Manual DEPP 6.5A.3.

18 The reference to the 'old days' was to the pre–'credible deterrence' era, when fines were relatively modest in comparison to current penalties but still within the range of £1–10 million.

The common objectives of firms were therefore 'to get through the process as quickly and efficiently as possible and come out the other side with as little damage as possible' (LawyerFR03). Cooperation facilitated a cheaper conclusion since the investigation costs would be added to a potential fine, but also a better-controlled enforcement outcome, as will be argued in Chapter 5.

Social motivations

Regulatees comply with regulation so that they attract the approval or respect of a range of 'significant others' (Nielsen & Parker, 2012). As FCA investigations are confidential, the significant other here was mostly the regulator itself. Firms 'just cannot afford to have a bad relationship with the regulator' (Lawyer06). The exceptions to this might be the occasional investigation after media coverage (e.g. the LIBOR and Forex investigations) in which significant others may be the public, shareholders, or consumers. These, however, are invariably rarer occasions, and in most investigations, the concern of targets was to preserve a good relationship with the regulator.

Social motivations were shaped by both long-term and short-term considerations. In the long run, earning the approval and trust of the regulator was important, as most regulated subjects were not a 'rogue' or recalcitrant set up solely for criminal or misconduct purposes. The situation was, of course, different with respect to companies that may have been set up as a 'boiler room' scam or other types of 'phantom' businesses (see Levi, 2008). The use of regulatory means (e.g. warning letters or visits) or criminal prosecutions means closure of such businesses, so there was no fundamental interest in preserving an ongoing relationship with the FCA. Most targets, however, were firms or individuals that would continue to operate in the markets and to interact with the regulator (Ayres & Braithwaite, 1992; Nielsen & Parker, 2012). Though this would not necessarily include continuous interactions with the enforcement staff themselves, as they were involved only in contentious matters, a cooperative and compliant attitude would feature on the firm's general compliance history. Also, considering the internal movement toward a more integrated approach and a more consistent attendance of the two organisational parts throughout the whole regulatory process, information on the firm's attitude in a prior formal investigation could easily be fed into supervisors' knowledge and assessments of the firm's disposition. For this reason, firms often had long-term considerations when dealing with the regulator in a current matter, such as a formal investigation. If firms were perceived to be cooperative and engaged with the investigation, the current rupture or antagonism in the overall regulatory relationship might still be remedied:

> You don't gain anything from not cooperating. This isn't just like a one-off piece of litigation with a contractual counterparty that they are never gonna deal with again. This is like having an argument within your family: you still gotta live with these people afterwards.
>
> (LawyerFR02)

The short-term considerations that influenced the motivation to cooperate and gain the approval and trust specifically by the enforcement staff were of a tactical nature. Cooperation enabled the party to be trusted to present its case and was a defence strategy devised by legal representatives. This enabled the party to promote its 'case theory' through the defence tactics considered in the following, whilst adopting an accommodating attitude to the regulator's investigative demands. If one was deemed cooperative with the investigation, and thus trusted (not to be a 'rogue' or an adversary), it was also much easier to promote one's counterclaims and gradually attempt to take ownership of the case. The social motivation to comply might therefore not be genuinely held by the firms themselves but adopted after legal intermediaries' preparation or suggestions. It was therefore akin to a calculated motive to comply even though it was aimed at gaining the trust and positive perceptions of the regulator.

Normative motivations

The research did not reveal much support for normative motivations for complying with investigative requests because it 'was the right thing to do'. In fact, across interviewee categories, calculated and social motivations dominated the reasoning behind appearing cooperative. Normative motivations were indicated only in interviews with senior staff or heads of compliance from large firms. This finding differs from current research on businesspersons' motivations to comply (May, 2005; Nielsen & Parker, 2012; Winter & May, 2001) which found that most firms adopt either a social citizen or a good citizen approach. Both approaches see, to a different degree, the combination of normative and social motivations to comply, taking precedence over economic considerations.

Lawyers, however, might have an incentive to overplay the importance of social motivations and downplay normative motivations due to professional interests. Cooperation was in lawyers' interest, as it allowed them to maintain access to enforcement staff, be perceived as trustworthy in future interactions, and strengthen their position of 'repeat players'. Therefore, although the presence of contentious lawyers might indicate an adversarial stance, this professional group also promoted the cooperative context of formal enforcement investigations. Individuals in firms could even hold views that they should challenge the regulator and not feel motivated to provide cooperation. Part of the advisor's work was to reconcile the differing company voices and streamline them into (not always) genuinely held cooperative attitudes:

> Feelings can run very deep. You get a different range around the board table, where some people say, 'I don't care whether this is hurting the relationship or not. If they lessen the charge, I'll happily accept [that] maybe we didn't do that quite right, but this is very black and white, and

> it's a serious charge.' Then you get other people, the pragmatists: 'Life's too short, let's move on.' As the stakes get higher, those things become more and more challenging.
>
> (Lawyer06)

Downplaying normative motivations also justified lawyers' involvement in the careful management of the regulatee–regulator relationship. If regulatees were behaving cooperatively due to genuine beliefs in the regulatory enforcement regime, what would be the purpose of hiring contentious lawyers who would not be able to contribute much?

Responding to the regulator: counterclaims

The cooperative stances by regulatees contributed to successful outcomes not solely for investigators but also for the investigated. Within the cooperative channels of communication, regulatees employed various strategies to steer the enforcement case away from an adverse outcome. Some strategies were prevalent throughout the whole contentious regulatory relationship and could be employed to avoid an enforcement referral, discontinue a formal investigation, or achieve a better penalty outcome. Other strategies were employed only at, or were more important at, some of the enforcement stages: for example, the detection avoidance through detection facilitation in self-reporting, discussed in Chapter 3, and settlement tactics in fining, which will be discussed in Chapter 5. The counterclaims strategies during the enforcement investigation consisted of meta-regulatory responses focusing on internal business and compliance behaviour and legal responses of challenging the points of law and evidence. Some of these could also appear earlier in the process, but they culminated during the investigation.

Meta-regulatory approaches

Meta-regulatory strategies concerned showing the regulator that the firm's business was conducted in accordance with the regulatory objectives – hence, the internal compliance systems were not flawed ('getting to know the business') – and, if this was not applicable or successful, remedial work. Much of the defence work was ensuring that the regulator has a clear understanding of how the business of the firm operates and that the meta-regulatory process has been successful. 'Getting to know the business' was a method of engaging 'grey panthers' (Black, 2003) by the company to provide information sessions or presentations to regulatory staff on how the business worked, with the 'hope that they listen and that they learn' (Lawyer04). This was important, as whether a certain rule had been breached depended on the regulator's proper understanding of the nature of the behaviour and its acceptability. There was a particular need to communicate this if the target operated in a small, esoteric, or complicated market. In the UK financial meta-regulatory relationship, both supervisory and, later, enforcement staff were open to these attempts to be 'educated':

> They can have a scoping visit at the beginning of an investigation. The enforcement team comes and visits the firm specifically for that purpose to find out more about how the organisation works and who the relevant people might be. Let's say it was a mis-selling case: get them to walk through the sales process and understand how that works.
>
> (Lawyer04)

Here, the application of the rules on the firm's behaviour to ascertain whether it constituted 'mis-selling' was constructed through an active discussion between the parties, as required in a substantive principles-based regime (Black, 2008). This is a prime example of regulatory conversations in the enforcement area (Black, 1998). For this reason, in some circumstances, the 'informational interdependency' (Hawkins & Hutter, 1993) went beyond the provision of information and documents to assess whether a breach has occurred. It consisted of provision of information to assess how the rules/businesses operate in the first place and only then comparing those to regulatory expectations. Both the facts and the evidence of (non)violation (Lange, 2002) were constructed by an active engagement and participation of the two sides. There are therefore three steps to the functioning of meta-regulatory regimes: (1) regulatory demands to implement such systems, (2) the implementation itself, and (3) providing evidence to the regulator, when challenged, that adequate compliance systems have been implemented.

Remedial plans were a crucial response for steering the case away from enforcement, as 'how you deal with a problem once it's been identified, how quickly and genuinely the firm is willing to sort it out, is often the critical determinant of whether it goes into enforcement or not' (Lawyer03). It was already discussed that remedial work, however initial, was necessary when self-reporting non-compliance. Further down the line, remedial steps were still relevant either to attempt to discontinue the investigation ('a case can be put forward on "What else does enforcement achieve?"' [Lawyer05]) or to mitigate the fine if the firm had offered redress.

Remedial work consisted of (re)installing the broken internal compliance systems, compensating affected victims, and employing the 'private justice system' of the corporation (Parker, 2002). One of the important features of the operation of the UK meta-regulatory regime was the clear regulatory expectation that remedial plans are or will be immediately put in place. These demands increased with the more proactive regulatory style since, in the past, 'if a firm identified a problem, it may not have had any real motivation to resolve it' (LawyerFR03). The regulatory expectations were now that 'getting it right once something has gone wrong is taken as a minimum response' (LawyerFR03). There were also short periods given for securing compliance, and in line with the judgement-based regulation approach, this was an indicator of the lesser tolerance for management to remedy a spotted issue on their own pace.

Significant work went towards assembling remedial plans to enable the regulator to conduct post-fact reviews (Parker, 2002: 246) of the firm's compliance systems. Firms aimed to assure the regulator that their systems worked in practice, that they had proper risk management measures, and that the company had the 'leadership, staff, systems and procedures' to meet its regulatory obligations (Gunningham, 2011: 130). This was done through showing 'the willingness and desire to put it right, quickly' (LawyerFR03); showing appropriate focus, seriousness, and time by senior management; and investing appropriate resources towards remediation. Remedial work was also undertaken to show that the internal compliance management systems were not implemented partially and half-heartedly for the purposes of external impression management (Parker & Gilad, 2011: 171) or 'window dressing' (Krawiec, 2003). For example, in cases involving systems breaches, firms aimed to show the FCA that 'whatever happened was a one-off and couldn't have been avoided; the systems and controls were not at fault' (Lawyer11). These arguments were used to negotiate with the regulator that the firm was achieving also desirable regulatory outcomes, not solely processes, by having compliant internal systems.

In line with true meta-regulatory assessments of internal corporate programmes, key factors for accepting the viability of the remedial work were the attitude, commitment, and competence of senior management. As top management commitment was crucial in responding to regulatory demands in the first place (McCaffrey & Hart, 1998; Parker, 2002: 57–60; Parker & Gilad, 2011), their posture was a crucial consideration when deciding how to proceed with the case. Senior management attitudes were important at two interrelated levels: how management dealt with the detected non-compliance, and how it dealt with the regulator during the contentious process. As discussed earlier, being seen as open and cooperative was crucial, and in fixing the problem, this also meant taking supervisors and their remedial proposals or demands 'seriously; otherwise, it might be a fast train to enforcement' (LawyerFR13). The assessment of the seriousness of senior management involved considerations of whether they were dedicating sufficient resources and time to fixing the non-compliance and dealing with regulators. These assessments were necessary for the regulator to confidently 'regulate at a distance' and have trust in the firm to have appropriate oversight mechanisms in place (Coglianese & Mendelson, 2010; Gilad, 2010; Parker, 2002). Finally, remedial work also included dealing with culpable individuals through the 'private justice of internal management systems' (Clarke, 1990; Parker, 2002: 246), examined in Chapter 6.

The activities of (re)installing the broken systems were varied and ranged from significant interventions and enhanced monitoring, such as voluntarily varying the regulatory permissions until the systems were deemed effective (e.g. so to not enter into new business relationships without prior approval from an independent skilled person); heavy investments into improving the internal systems (e.g. increasing compliance resources by hiring additional staff or external consultants); conducting past business reviews; moving away from certain lines of business (assessed as too risky for the firm's current resources); diagnostic work around whether consumers suffered any loss, the number of affected customers, and the extent of the loss (sales files reviews, customer contact exercises); etc.

In retail-type cases, this also involved compiling a compensation scheme and providing redress. Having in mind the FCA's consumer-oriented outlook (FCA, 2013a, 2016, 2017), compensation was a crucial expectation in the remedial process.[19] Arguably, the FCA's expectations that compensation would be paid out meant that the same effects (compensation for damages) were achieved even if an enforcement action was brought on the basis of the principles alone (commonly Principle 6). In this respect, the rule that the principles do not give rise to actions for damages[20] was, in practice, circumvented by insisting on consumer redress. This was frequently an expensive exercise for large market players with a significant number of consumers, to the extent that it could dwarf any enforcement fines. For example, the enforcement fines imposed for the PPI mis-selling scandal pale in comparison to the extent of the redress scheme – the largest scheme yet in the history of the UK financial markets. As of December 2019, banks had paid £38.3 billion in redress (FCA, 2021), with the Lloyds Banking Group itself paying out nearly £22 billion (BBC, 2020).

The notices showed that it was not irrelevant whether the steps were undertaken on the firm's own initiative or on the demand of regulatory agencies (the FCA, the Financial Ombudsman, or others). For example, in the case of Catalyst Inc.,[21] the FSA used its own initiative powers to vary the firm's Part IV permission so that the firm would cease promoting highly risky bonds. The fact that Catalyst refused to voluntarily vary its permission and continued to promote the bonds until the Authority used its own power was indicated as a serious aggravating factor, as this implied a significant rupture in the regulatory relationship.

Legal approaches

Legal approaches concerned defence work around the evidence-gathering process and around disputing the elements of the misconduct: creating and waiving legal privilege, compiling 'own evidence' or additional work, legal

19 The FCA also has significant legislation-based, consumer-related powers under FSMA (restitution orders and consumer redress schemes) and under general consumer law in the Consumer Rights Act 2015 and the Enterprise Act 2002 (Part 8).

20 FCA Handbook PRIN 3.4.4R.

21 FN30/09/13.

advocacy, contextualising documents, and challenging the reasonableness of evidence-gathering requests. Here the lawyers' 'information-control function' (Mann, 1985, 1992) came to full potential.

The shifting balance in power: legal privilege

Chapter 3 showed that legal professional privilege (LPP) represented an immediate and poignant consideration in internal investigations leading up to, or in result of, self reporting. This was an important mechanism for taking 'ownership' of the case towards influencing the construction of the misconduct. This section fleshes out the dynamics of creating privileged documents and of waiving privilege – strategies transpiring across detection and formal investigations. The strategies commonly focused on the documents created during internal investigations, such as witness statements, interview notes (from witnesses or potential suspects), or communications with accounting firms. These documents are not covered by legal advice privilege (LAP) since they are commonly not created in a lawyer–client interaction and concern fact-finding rather than legal advice (*Three Rivers District Council v Governor and Company of the Bank of England (No 5)* [2003]).

The documents may instead be subject to litigation privilege (LP) if created for the dominant purpose of adversarial proceedings, either ongoing or in 'reasonable contemplation'. Litigation privilege extends to communications with third parties, such as witness interview notes with (ex-)employees taken by external lawyers, reports generated by external forensic accountants, or presentations by external lawyers for the purpose of advising and receiving instructions from the firm's internal team (*Serious Fraud Office (SFO) v Eurasian Natural Resources Corp. Ltd (ENRC)* [2018]). Whether communications will attract litigation privilege and whether a company is investigating internally for the dominant purpose of contemplation of litigation still remain highly factual questions. Internal investigations started after the FCA has commenced formally investigating could attract litigation privilege, given 'the seriousness of the allegations . . . and the potential consequences' (*Tesco Stores Limited & ors v Office of Fair Trading* [2012]). Even some threatening communications by regulatory agencies could form the basis for arguing that litigation was reasonably in contemplation (*Bilta (UK) Ltd v Royal Bank of Scotland Plc* [2017]). However, *ENRC* confirmed that 'not all concerns raised by law enforcement authorities or all processes (including self-reporting processes) should be regarded as crossing the threshold required for a reasonable contemplation of litigation' (Higgins, 2019: 152). Thus, it cannot be always assumed that litigation privilege would cover documents created for self-reporting purposes before the FCA even has any knowledge of the matter.

The interviewed lawyers spoke also with uncertainty regarding this issue. One lawyer claimed that when investigating a potentially disclosable rule breach, privilege 'in contemplation of litigation' would be created around the legal advice and the material used to give advice on whether there was a rule breach and whether it should be disclosed (LawyerFR18). For documents where a sole or dominant purpose of litigation could not be claimed, the advice was that (external) lawyers should be involved as soon as possible to ensure that communications generated during the investigation can attract LAP in case an LP claim fails. One tactic to do so was to produce a lawyer's advice note with what was said in the interview, its legal implications, or what should be done, rather than minutes. Verbatim records of interviews would not be privileged, but a detailed lawyer's analysis of the communication and the areas where the risks lie would be:

> The interviewer could write: 'I interviewed someone this morning. I'm writing a letter to tell you what happened. He said this . . .' And then have a verbatim record of what he said. 'And I think the steps you should take as a result of this interview are . . .' If the regulator or someone in litigation is saying, 'I want copies of these meeting notes', you'd say, 'We didn't produce standalone memoranda of those meetings. We did report to our client on the implications of those meetings, but they are in letters between us and our client'. Quite difficult to challenge that.
>
> (LawyerFR06)

Though such letters would contain a combination of fact-finding and legal advice, the view was that they would be privileged in their entirety rather than to have the portions of legal advice redacted. Another creative, though less certain, tactic, aimed at overcoming challenges to memorise complex discussions, was to go into the interview 'with a laptop with a letter that you've already got the template as a letter to the client, and then you start recording this communication in that meeting. Whether that works or not, who knows!' (LawyerFR06). These 'creative' responses were also suggested as potentially able to overcome the effects of the High Court ruling in *Serious Fraud Office v Eurasian Natural Resources Corporation Ltd* [2017] that significantly limited the reach of litigation privilege before it was overturned by the Court of Appeal.

Further strategising arose where external lawyers had been instructed by senior management. Fact-finding through interviews with managers whose actions could be vicariously attributed to the firm to construct the firm's liability would not be protected by legal advice privilege. Yet there were blurred boundaries on the nature of those communications, as they could be differentially labelled as 'interviews' (not protected) or 'meetings' (protected):

> One person's interview is another person's meeting. . . . When you first get instructed on a case or a matter, you go to a meeting with someone; they tell you information, you ask them questions. You don't call that an interview; you call it a meeting. Sometimes we produce notes: we don't refer to it as an interview; we refer to it as a meeting. In both cases, as lawyers, you're gathering facts to enable you to advise.
>
> (LawyerFR06)

These documents and the ensuing investigative reports may obscure or distort the extent of managerial involvement and responsibility for the suspected misconduct. As a key 'corporatisation' strategy of controlling the flow of information, this also aids the firm's case. Senior individuals and firms can claim a joint defence that the manager took 'reasonable steps' and that the firm had compliant systems and controls (SYSC), including properly executed senior management responsibilities (Jordanoska, 2021: 305, 310).

In the regulatory game (Picciotto, 2007), regulators were aware of these information control tactics (e.g. see speech by Symington, 2015), and that internal investigations meant relinquishing control to the target. There was a cautious approach towards the quality of the produced evidence, and it could be subjected to further scrutiny:

> Law firms probably know of our resource constraints, so one of the tactics they employ is to minimise our resource spend by offering to conduct the investigation for us, thereby wresting control over it from us to them. The result would probably provide an enforcement outcome; it might be quite helpful, but it is quite carefully controlled and managed by the law firm.
>
> (Regulator01)

Regulators would not take a favourable stance to claims that all the internal investigation products were privileged or when the investigation was intentionally structured to be fully privileged. This would be considered 'non-cooperative' (LawyerFR20) and as 'gaming the system' (Symington, 2015). The power balance also shifted when a firm proposed to conduct an internal investigation after the regulator had already perceived non-compliance:

> If you get a law firm in, what you can't do is conduct [an] internal investigation and then seek to protect the whole thing by legal professional privilege, 'cause otherwise, what's the point? The FCA want to know at the start of that process that you are going to waive privilege on the report and any transcripts of evidence from investigative interviews. I think it does come down to trust and knowing that the firm is going to tell the FCA what it is that [it] is going to find. It's about ensuring that the FCA trust that you are independent, rigorous, and good enough to identify what the problem is.
>
> (LawyerFR02)

To maintain some kind of 'quality control' (Regulator02) over the internal investigations process, regulators attempted to scope it if undertaken after notifying the regulator, or to ask for both the final reports and the underlying documents. The targets' strategic adaptation was to balance between being responsive to regulatory expectations of cooperation and information flow but still maintaining information control. Some of the strategies around creating legal advice privileged (LAP) documents were also used to adapt to the increased regulatory expectations of information provision: 'People try to get around that. You could do an interview without taking any notes . . . then produce a note of advice. Or you could brief orally the FCA on the investigation' (LawyerFR20).

The balancing act also included careful considerations around waiving legal privilege over documents or information. Waiving privilege occurred as a conscious strategy by the defence counsel, rather than in result of a potential abuse of power. Privilege could be waived to aid the party's case. Firms might also have to agree to waiving privilege on some or all underlying documents in conjunction with the final report if they were to be trusted to conduct the investigation themselves. What is more important for issues of procedural justice, occasionally, legal privilege, both over documents and of internal investigations' reports, could be waived for reasons of being seen as very cooperative and getting 'maximum credit for cooperation' (LawyerFR07). These micro-level considerations contributed to the overarching informal and cooperative UK administrative justice system.

Decisions on waiving privilege would often be made in advance of the creation of the document. The documents could be generated with a view to cooperate with the FCA while retaining strategic information control over the presentation of the content: '[Y]ou need to form a view as to whether you decide to waive privilege. I say that you should be naturally wary of waiving privilege, and then you must be sensible as to how we write it up' (LawyerFR20). Lawyers could produce a record in the knowledge that it might get disclosed and so 'write it in a way that is less definite, more protective' (LawyerFR06). Finally, lawyers could attempt to negotiate waiving the privilege on a limited basis, especially if there were additional concerns that third parties, such as cross-border enforcement agencies or class action litigants, might get access to the investigations report or documents (Symington, 2015).

How legal privilege was used, then, in conducting internal investigations prior to notifying the FCA might lead to protecting the underlying documents that the regulator will then be prevented from receiving. Interviewees echoed that enforcement teams respected the boundaries of legal privilege and were acting reasonably regarding such documents (LawyerFR10). Though regulators might still ask for those to be disclosed, proper oppositions of legal privilege were accepted. Additionally, documents might be carefully structured to provide limited or favourable insight. Ultimately, these practices had the effect that many documents were handed in, yet many of them had been edited and protected.

These findings underscore extant concerns in the literature on the use of privilege as an extension of corporate power and to shield corporate responsibility (Braithwaite, 2002; Williams, 2008). Some have even argued that legal advice privilege should not be extended to corporate actors (Higgins, 2008, 2010; Loughrey, 2005, 2014). It is a corporate weapon that transcends different types of justice systems: Mann (1985) and Williams (2008) have found similar practices by lawyers in criminal investigations. The requirements of claiming privilege also strengthened the involvement and influence of the same relatively small group of contentious legal practitioners. Case law also supports this involvement: *R (on the application of Prudential plc & anor) (appellants) v Special Commissioner of Income Tax & anor* [2013] warns to use lawyers to facilitate the creation of litigation privilege documents.

The findings also show how internal investigations reduce regulators' scrutinising capacity. Regulators have limited enforcement resources compared to corporate pockets, reducing their ability to undertake own investigations in every circumstance (Jordanoska, 2021). Investigative operations into large-scale misconduct may be impossible without, at least an initial, fact-finding being undertaken by the firm (Steward, 2017). For example, the FCA was able to conclude the FX manipulation investigations, revealing complex corporate misconduct and attracting record-breaking penalties, relatively quickly as it relied on internal investigations and reports generated by external lawyers (LawyerFR20; Symington, 2015). Limited resources sustain the need to rely on internal investigations reports as a source of evidence despite the full regulatory understanding of their carefully crafted nature.

Additional work or compiling 'own evidence'

Amongst the proactive stances taken by legal advisers to shift or stop the investigation was to undertake extra efforts and compile 'own' evidence either that the breach did not happen or, if it did, that this did not create any harm or risk of harm. Depending on the misconduct, these activities included providing reports from internal investigations and from consumer-contacting exercises. In the retail area, the additional work was commonly around disputing consumer detriment and included, for example, undertaking own sample review of files comparable to the regulator's and contacting consumers to obtain their inadvertent support for the party's case:

> We had an alleged mis-selling case. The FCA said, 'We got concerns about these [files]'. My client instructed one of the Big Four accountancy firms to oversee a process of customer contact where they contacted each of these customers to re-check whether or not they have been mis-sold. In the vast majority of the cases, they ascertained that, in fact, there was no mis-selling.
>
> (LawyerFR02)

The ability to show the enforcement staff that consumers did not suffer losses, or to show that consumers would not have made different decisions without selling omissions, was considered quite a powerful message. This could be used to argue that the case should be dropped as 'it's a technical breach, but no one suffered' (Lawyer06).

Legal advocacy: representations and the 'grey' areas you can talk about

Subjects of enforcement proceedings and their legal representatives frequently put forward legal advocacy representations to refute the allegations on both the prescriptive and descriptive aspects of the behaviour. It was important to be proactive, not allowing the FCA to 'get a "case theory"' (LawyerFR02). Depending on the legal team's tactic, (extensive) written representations could be submitted at any point during the investigation: 'in three cases recently, a tactical decision was taken to put in a very, very full response to the FCA, meeting them with hundreds of pages of your own' (LawyerFR17). However, there were also attempts to promote the defence's case and make representations through using the professional relationships discussed in Chapter 2. There were attempts to 'deliberately create' opportunities to present the case:

> I know these enforcement people quite well. I know the head of enforcement well. I know all their senior management team, a number of the junior people. Some of them used to work in this firm. I was in a different firm before, and some of them used to work there. They used to be my associates. So there are a lot of personal relationships there as well, and we can use those. There's nothing to stop us ever from picking up the phone and having a chat with these people at the appropriate time.
>
> (Lawyer05)

The representations often concerned the meaning of language and whether the legal requirements for finding misconduct had been satisfied. They also concerned fact construction (Lange, 2002) and whether the enforcement team had the 'right' facts:

> I can seek to persuade them that they have misinterpreted the data or looked at the wrong data, they misread the files, or they are wrong on their interpretation of the rules: 'The file says this, that is correct, but COBS 1, 2, 3, 4, 5 says that, or MiFID means that you are misinterpreting COBS'. If the FCA says you have put the wrong money in that client's account, I can say that is not a client account in the first place, or you have misinterpreted the cash flows.
>
> (Lawyer03)

Important advocacy work was undertaken to muddle the decision-making channels and limit the responsibility of senior managers. The senior management *priority of enforcement* also affected legal practice: a lawyer commented that, whilst in the past their Magic Circle law firm dealt predominately with corporations, now its high-end services were increasingly sought after by senior managers (LawyerFR01). The increased workload of Magic Circle law firms in representing individuals meant that wealthier managers, next to their powerful companies, were also able to rely on greater 'professional embeddedness' (Reichman, 1992; Jordanoska, 2021). In practice, this meant that 'they will be able to seal the damage and call a battalion of lawyers to fight for them' (LawyerFR11). The odds of 'winning' through disputing individual responsibility were greater here also because, in these institutions, the senior management was rather removed from the trading or sales floors. In contrast, legal advocacy was significantly more impaired on small and medium-sized institutions, where 'you can easily find who should have been on the watch' (LawyerFR11).

Whilst investigators were open to processing representations over questions of law or fact, they were less conducive to accepting explanations that the behaviour was in line with industry practice, especially where regulators were seeking to change it. Even less acceptable were arguments that the misconduct was in line with 'the client's' or 'the company's' interests – suggested in the literature as a common defence for corporate crime (Conklin, 1977). Such a line of argument was also, on occasion, attempted in the FCA context (mostly as a tactic by defending barristers) to show lack of malevolence on behalf of the investigated individual or to represent him/her in a better light. These arguments were rejected as 'not reasonable', thus not acceptable. As a lawyer explained: 'If there has been a regulatory breach, then probably either it is not truly in the client's interests or it may be in your client's interests but not in the interests of other market participants' (Lawyer12). The rejection of this argument was a consequence of different objectives: the regulator's expectations of proper business conduct and the firms' interest in profits and market share (Black, 2005: 545–546; Georgosouli, 2008).

However, legal advocacy may be more difficult in a PBR (see also Black et al., 2007), as 'what are the right judgements to draw from a particular set of facts is the big issue when you have regulation and enforcement based on principles and not the hard letter of the law' (Lawyer06). This also created the problem of enforcing 'retrospective regulation' (term used by the informants) or 'regulatory creep' (Black, 2008). An oft-cited example was the PPI selling practices. Once problematic issues arose from the fact that these were sold to unsuitable consumers, the FSA moved to enforce the selling practices as misconduct under the umbrella standards of Principle 6. Such an approach created frustration and insecurity for regulated firms as, depending on the public pressures on the regulator or consumer interests, the previously accepted industry standards might not validate the misconduct. Therefore, principles-based regulation did not necessarily allow space for organisations to contest and negotiate the meaning of compliance as claimed by some commentators (Edelman & Talesh, 2011; Hutter, 2011). In contrast, principles-based regulation might limit the extent to which corporate legal resources can be used to challenge the enforcers' case and exert 'regulatory authority' (Reichman, 1992). It may not always be the case that enforcers 'prefer precise rules because they are much easier and clearer to enforce and legally act on in terms of standards of proof' (Hutter, 2011: 307):

> [Principles-based regulation] hasn't been without its challenges; trying to allege a breach of principle is more difficult because it is more

> subjective than alleging a breach of a narrow rule. In terms of getting messages across and covering a broad range of misconduct, then the principles-led enforcement has been useful. Pressure selling is always the example I think of to prove that principles have a purpose that might not be covered otherwise. To capture that misconduct and to change behaviour, you need principles-based regulation; there aren't any rules that say don't pressure-sell.
>
> (Regulator02)

This reinforces the usefulness of principle-based regulation in capturing unanticipated harmful areas of business behaviour. Principles also allowed to dig deeper into industry practices and challenge the *root causes of deviance*, in accordance with the 'credible deterrence' priorities of enforcement.

Responses over documents: contextualisation and reasonableness

As a proactive defence strategy, contextualising documents developed as a response to the extensive document request exercises. It was an attempt to steer the regulator's analysis of the documents into a more favourable outlook. It was not enough simply to photocopy the documents but also to highlight the 'positive things' or put in context the 'negative things' in them (LawyerFR02). This also included the discussed waiving of legal privilege.

Questioning the *reasonableness* of document, information, and interview requests was one of the few ways to challenge the regulator within the overarching cooperative style of interactions. For firms, the feasibility of responding to these requests depended on several factors: the organisational structure of the business (e.g. size and reporting lines), legal drafting (broadly drafted requests could ask for documents that may not exist in the required format or at all 'because they're sort of guessing what it is that the firm might have that's relevant' [Lawyer04]),[22] and importantly, time frames (as often documents were required in very short turnaround periods). The meaning and limits of a *reasonable* document request were shaped in regulatory negotiations through lawyers as intermediaries. This defence work concerned challenging the requests in view of the FCA regulatory objectives (e.g., proportionality or efficiency). The negotiations were aimed at establishing a sensible timetable in cases of large firms or establishing the extent and substance of documents, next to timetabling, in cases of smaller firms commonly without dedicated compliance officers for communicating with the regulator.

These discussions rarely developed into an adversarial response, leading to judicial reviews. Even concerns of *reasonableness* were mainly discussed and

22 It is arguable whether this might amount to a 'fishing expedition'. The legal threshold is very low, and it requires only that the documents are of a specified nature; hence, the regulator has significant leeway.

resolved informally rather than through the formal justice systems of the courts. Akin to the dynamics in the supervisory relationship, in practice, former FSA/FCA staff could retain certain 'clout' (Braithwaite & Murphy, 1993) in dealing with their former colleagues in discussions over the *reasonableness* of regulatory demands:

> You can usually have some sort of sensible discussion with them. Obviously, from my background, I knew quite a lot of the team at the FCA who used to work for me. If you have the credibility, you can have a little bit of pushback saying 'The client just can't provide this within the time period, this is a huge request, so let's try and be reasonable here' sort of thing.
>
> (LawyerFR07)

The 'revolving door' (Dal Bò, 2006) and 'repeat players' (Galanter, 1974) phenomena contributed to establishing good lines of communication with the regulator and to appearing more 'credible' in the negotiations over the *reasonableness* of the regulator's requests. This again emphasises the important role played by contentious regulatory lawyers in the enforcement of financial regulation, and the (in)ability to pay for them contributed to uneven outcomes for the small and big market players.

The investigation nears the end: dropped and penalised misconduct

The issuing of a preliminary investigation report (PIR) and, in later years, an accompanying preliminary findings letter marked the successful conclusion of an investigation. These contained the misconduct allegations, the legal basis, and the evidentiary support. After the *Legal & General Assurance Society Ltd v FSA* [2005] case and the subsequent Strachan Review (FSA, 2005), PIRs were issued after an internal review by the Legal Department. This was a process of scrutinising whether the evidence met the allegations, and was described as not unlike what the Crown Prosecution Service does (LawyerFR09). PIRs tended to be detailed and thorough, and on occasion, contained allegations that were not fully anticipated by the targets. The PIR ultimately contained the regulator's construction of the behaviour as misconduct, and this was fully revealed only at the end of the formal investigation.

Unsuccessful investigations were dropped with a variable frequency. The average percentage of dropped investigations (no formal power used) for the financial years 2008–2009 through to 2017–2018 was 27 per cent, with the lowest in 2012–2013 (3.92 per cent) and 2010–2011 (5.72 per cent, the smallest number of drops having in mind the high overall caseload). Unsurprisingly, the highest percentages of dropped investigations were in 2016–2017 (62 per cent) and 2017–2018 (54 per cent), and this corresponds to the significant spike in opened investigations (282 and 302, respectively) under Mark Steward's 'diagnostic investigations' approach. Without these outliers, the average percentage of closed cases until 2015–2016 was 19.5 per cent. The relatively high success rate in bringing an enforcement outcome might be explained by various reasons, some of which have already been mentioned: higher quality of human resources in skilled investigators (themselves lawyers), selection bias toward cases with higher chances of success (e.g. 'the worst firms' detected in thematic reviews), and perceptions that, if investigations have been taking place for a number of years with a lot of invested resources, investigators may be more reluctant to discontinue the investigation without a public outcome of some kind. For this reason, the strategies employed by targets to steer and claim 'ownership' of the misconduct could be much more successful pre-enforcement referral rather than in a formal investigation.

Cases were discontinued because of legal (evidentiary) and economic (resources) reasons. Investigations could be dropped for legal reasons, such as lack of supporting evidence (very common in establishing individual culpability), the inability to satisfy the elements of the legal violation (the most common in market abuse cases), or due to ultimately accepting the targets' responses examined earlier. Resources and efficiency were the more pragmatic reasons for discontinuing an investigation. The investigation team could take the view that it was no longer worth expending resources to achieve a successful outcome. However, similarly to the assessment of enforcement referrals, feeding into considerations of costs and efficiency were not simply the economics of gain/loss but, again, equity, policy, and reputation considerations – this time over a *priority case* and *themes*.

Occasionally, *priority cases* could overtake and monopolise the enforcement resources allocation. When this happened, other, less detrimental or less publicly exposed cases could be completely shelved or left to the investigator to 'deal with it in my own time' (LawyerFR08). Some interviewees suggested that such a *priority case* happened with the focus on the LIBOR-rigging scandal as a highly publicly exposed issue. The resources diverted to LIBOR may have resulted in some of their cases being dropped around that time.

To a more limited extent, *themes* also formed the basis of economic considerations for discontinuing a case, and this was similar to the decision-making in (not) accepting an enforcement referral in the first place. A strategic decision could be made to divert resources and drop cases if the enforcement staff thought that they no longer had the same 'credible deterrence' value as at the beginning of the referral process. This enabled parties to 'play' the regulator's focus on 'credible deterrence' considerations. A defence strategy, employed especially by large firms, was to persuade the regulator that 'this isn't the big case you were looking for' (Lawyer06). The strategy indicates that the transmission of 'credible deterrence' messages and their 'signalling effects' (Thornton et al., 2005) were intercepted by the industry. However, they were not internalised solely for general and specific deterrence purposes but also to dissuade an enforcement action once it was underway. Contentious lawyers especially listened carefully to these messages to input them into their defence tactics. These messages were not read only for educational purposes in preventing non-compliance in the first instance but also for educational purposes, to prevent non-compliance from being enforced in the second instance. Arguably, this was an unintended consequence (Grabosky, 1995) of the 'credible deterrence' regulatory strategy.

Cooperation during sanctioning: the confidential world of corporate settlements

The successful conclusion of a formal investigation initiated the process of imposing administrative sanctions, amongst which fines represented the bulk of the FCA's enforcement activity against substantive corporate misconduct. Chapter 2 argued that record-breaking financial penalties represent a key trait of the 'credible deterrence' policy. It also established that the FSA/FCA had imposed fines against some of the largest market players for a range of complex corporate misconduct.

Despite the rising penalties, data from final notices and from interviews show that the culture of settling rather than challenging the penalty was pervasive in the FCA enforcement process. About 93 per cent of the firms in the sample resolved the case through the non-contested executive settlements procedure, with a stable figure of settlements across the years of the 'credible deterrence' agenda. This contrasted with the more common stance of resistance and adversarialism adopted by investigated individuals. Individuals more commonly fought and contested the enforcement case, either internally within the FCA (the RDC procedure) or further at the Tribunal or the Court of Appeal (Jordanoska, 2021). This finding resonates with insights on the preference of corporations to resolve criminal justice actions through settlements and negotiated justice (Campbell, 2019; Garrett, 2014; Hock & Dávid Barret, 2022; King & Lord, 2018; Lord, 2023).

Executive settlements were available when the targets did not contest the imposition of the penalty, with discounts on the size of the penalty if early conclusion of the case was reached. Initially, the settlements procedure was staged with 30 per cent discount given at stage 1, 20 per cent at stage 2, and 10 per cent at stage 3. With changes introduced in 2016, there is only 30 per cent for settling early and no discount for allowing the period for settlement discussions to lapse.[23] If the targets challenged the penalty, the decision-making process was contentious, and any discounts were lost. The first remedy is challenging the case at the Regulatory Decisions Committee (RDC), the FCA's own second-tier mechanism, which still maintained the case confidential. The RDC is considered a separate decision-making body from the enforcement part of the organisation, and its function is to provide an independent and

23 The changes were made in response to the review of enforcement decision-making by the HM Treasury (2014). FCA Decisions Procedure and Penalties Manual 6.7.3G.

'quasi-judicial' review[24] of the enforcement case. The second remedy is challenging the case at the Upper Tax and Chancery Tribunal. This is when the case becomes compulsorily public through the publication of the decision notice. Only a minority of cases against corporate targets were resolved via challenging the regulator at the RDC (12 firms) or at the Tribunal (6 firms).

The FCA settlement process much resembled the US criminal justice (see Bibas, 2004; Stuntz, 2004) or the UK magistrates court settlements (Baldwin, 1985) in the sense that the process is concluded with an admission of 'guilt' by the targets. This is especially the case when the FCA alleges breaches of the principles, where it must show that the target was at fault. The most important aspect in which the FCA settlements differ from both criminal justice and the SEC administrative settlements is the fact that they are reached wholly internally within the organisation, without judicial scrutiny or possibility of judicial review. Even if the settlement discussions fall apart, the Tribunal always hears the case *de novo*,[25] so any discussions would have been undertaken on a 'without prejudice' basis.

Both sides of the regulatory relationship supported the resolution of the enforcement case through a settlement. For the regulator, issues of effective administration of justice, earlier consumer redress,[26] and cost savings of further contested proceedings contributed towards settling being the overwhelmingly preferred approach. Settlements enabled the regulator to achieve 'outcomes quicker, which means that we can then devote resource to other areas that are coming up. It saves an awful lot of time, and if you are saving time, you are saving money as well' (Regulator02). Contested cases were significantly more costly and resource-intensive as they attracted significant costs in enforcement staff time and in legal fees for external counsel whilst also being an uncertain remedy. Settlements were the desirable outcome, as they also meant having an 'earlier result out in the public domain' (LawyerFR07). The executive settlements process was therefore guided by regulatory considerations of efficiency and quicker publicity of outcomes.

Firms were interested in settling rather than contesting the enforcement case for various motives, both calculated and social (May, 2005). The social motive was the need to have a 'continuing relationship with the regulator' (LawyerFR04). The calculated motives involved considerations of saving business, legal, and reputational costs. Firms settled as they were keen to pay the fine and move on with business. The risks to challenging a case were similar to the uncertainties and potential costs about which regulators were also concerned. The RDC and Tribunal procedures cost management time and legal advice money. There was also the risk that the Tribunal could impose a more

24 Though the FCA is keen to emphasise that the RDC 'is not a Tribunal' (FCA Decisions Procedure and Penalties Manual 3.2.11).

25 Section 135(5) FSMA.

26 FCA Decisions Procedure and Penalties Manual 6.7.1.

severe penalty than that originally suggested by the FCA.[27] In addition, a new Tribunal discussion of the case could expose the firm to greater reputational damages, as the publicity could not be controlled.[28] As the next chapter argues, firms had the greatest ability to control negative publicity during the settlement discussions, when certain aspects of the case could still be edited out from final publication. Such control was lost in the appeal procedures. For this reason, there were 'risks rather than rewards of challenging decisions' (Lawyer07), whereas the settlement provided certain, albeit unwanted, closure.

A more clandestine calculated motive was connected to perceptions that settling and paying the fine early might prevent the FCA from further investigations and possibly discovering new or more serious breaches. One lawyer argued that, 'quite often, a firm will settle because it is worried that the regulator might unearth something worse' (Lawyer03). Admitting wrongdoing to prevent further detection might occur even if the target did not believe that they have committed the alleged misconduct. However, to avoid being penalised for a different or potentially more serious misconduct, firms were willing to admit committing the lesser charge. The same lawyer compared these incidents to admitting a speeding offence, despite not being convinced that you were speeding, to avoid the detection of a more serious offence, such as drinking and driving.

Therefore, in some cases, firms aimed to prompt the regulator towards early settlement discussions for reasons of ***detection avoidance***. This finding is important since, as discussed earlier, every deterrence intervention is based on, and can be successful due to, certainty of detection (Cornish & Clarke, 1986; Paternoster & Simpson, 1996; Tibbetts & Gibson, 2002). The regulator's deterrence focus could be undermined if there were perceptions in the markets that, through settling early, the 'skeletons in the closet' might remain hidden. The investigators, however, seemed to be aware of this desire to steer the case towards early settlement.[29] The interviewees acknowledged that FCA investigations were mostly concluded when the regulator had investigated all avenues that it wanted to investigate and only then would move towards proposing a fine. In this sense, the targets' focus on settling early as an attempt to steer the case and the regulator's focus on protracting the case as long as deemed necessary to establish the facts were also part of the 'legal gamesman ship' (Williams, 2012) in regulatory enforcement.

27 The Tribunal is not bound by the FCA's submission on the level of the fine. See *Chaligne, Sejean and Diallo v FSA* [2012], where the Tribunal increased the fine on Mr Sejean for market abuse from £550,000 to £650,000.

28 To minimise publicity damages, wealthy regulatory offenders hire PR firms in a bid to manage the Tribunal process media coverage (observation, Upper Tribunal [Tax and Chancery] hearing, 2013).

29 FCA Enforcement Guide 5.2 specifically stated that 'the FCA will only engage in [settlement] discussions once it has a sufficient understanding of the nature and gravity of the suspected misconduct or issue to make a reasonable assessment of the appropriate outcome'.

Both calculated and social motives reveal the active role played by subjects to enforcement in shaping the final outcomes of the process. The level of cooperation provided by firms reflected pragmatic considerations to achieve short- and long-term advantages. This manoeuvring strategy shows that cooperative and 'good' relationships with the regulator were not necessarily the 'right' relationships. On the one hand, firms might provide cooperation which is more than necessary, and this brings into question issues of procedural justice (Tyler, 2003). On the other hand, the regulator may also lose some inquisitiveness in the process, and this brings into question the issue of just outcomes.

Conclusion: cooperation and considerations of credibility and trust

This chapter highlights that despite the rhetoric and indicators of a more punitive and interventionist approach in the post-crisis period, FCA investigations and case resolution commonly operated in a cooperative rather than adversarial context.

FCA investigators made extensive use of formal investigation powers in practice, and this was aided by legal (low investigation powers' thresholds), organisational (level of staff experience), and relational factors (the cooperative ways in which targets responded). Though the regulator relied on the statutory provisions when using investigative powers, there was rarely an invocation of penalties for not abiding by them or judicial challenges. The provision of documents was an especially massive investigation exercise that posed special challenges for targets and contributed to significant information 'traffic' towards the regulator. The extensive document requests reflect the notions of an 'information-hungry regulator' examined in the previous chapter, but also the initial lack of knowledge on the alleged misconduct. The investigation subsequently developed into mutual requests for information and withholding of information on both sides of the relationship. At the beginning of the process, investigators kept the focus of the investigation fairly general, withholding information on the specifics, whilst targets attempted to gain more information on the regulator's 'case theory' on the basis of the evidentiary requests (what was the *actual* misconduct that the regulator was interested in but not yet disclosing?). Further down the line, the use of evidence-gathering powers meant that investigators required detailed and extensive information, whilst targets attempted to manage this through providing 'own evidence,' using legal privilege, or contextualising documents.

The cooperative context allowed for various (meta-regulatory and legal) 'counterclaims' to be launched either to steer the case away from enforcement or for the formal investigation to be dropped. The extent and success of the responses depended not solely on the merits of the target's defence work but also on the extent of its 'professional embeddedness' and the ability to employ contentious regulatory lawyers as a resource. Lawyers facilitated the cooperative attitudes, managed the appearance of targets at interviews, prepared legal advocacy, strategised over claiming and waiving legal privilege, and channelled discussions of reasonableness, on occasion through ex-professional channels. The cooperative ethos culminated during the resolution of the enforcement action, as corporate cases were overwhelmingly resolved through confidential corporate settlements rather than challenged through the internal appeals process or judicial means.

That financial regulators operate in an environment of cooperation rather than adversarialism resonates with findings from other jurisdictions (e.g. Williams, 2012). This chapter pushes further our understanding of why cooperation happens within micro-level regulatory interactions by applying the literature on business motives to compliance with regulation in general. Across the enforcement process, the cooperative attitudes by targets involved multiple motives for compliance with formal powers: calculated, social, and normative (May, 2005). The mix of calculated (considerations of costs and incentives) and social motives appeared to be the most potent. The costs that discouraged being adversarial were legal (being penalised for not abiding by Principle 11 to be open and cooperative with the regulator, challenging the regulator in view of uncertain judicial outcomes) and business (losses in management time, legal advice, dealing with regulators). The incentives were also legal (discounts to the penalty for cooperation during the investigation, and from settlement) and business-oriented. The social motives encompassed preserving a good relationship and potentially short-term and long-term trust with the regulator in current and future interactions. In the short-term, being trusted might give the perception of the target as a partner rather than an adversary to the process and could lead to a more favourable outcome in the current case. The establishment of short-term trust could have several effects: firms could be allowed to undertake their own investigations upon self-reporting; targets could be allowed to contextualise the documents they provide, conduct additional work, and submit their own representations as to what happened; and being cooperative could enable benefits through the settlement process, discussed also in the next chapter. Being trusted in the current case could have long-term impacts on the regulatory relationship, as the trustworthiness in the current rupture might contribute to credibility in future enforcement cases and in the ongoing supervisory relationship in general. In these considerations, the argument of 'having an argument with your family' was the most potent. Such attitudes also affected how repeat players were perceived – despite being a regulatory recidivist, cooperative approaches might still lead to having a 'good dialogue' with the regulator.

Cooperative approaches were of interest also to regulators, as they made the enforcement process more efficient and less resource-intensive. Paradoxically, the interests of the two parties merged, labelling the contentious process as ultimately cooperative. However, there were side effects to the cooperative enforcement context. Chapter 3 showed how over-compliance with the self-reporting requirements could enable detection avoidance through detection facilitation. Relinquishing control over case ownership in internal investigations could hinder the regulator to gain insight into the full extent of the misconduct. Legal representatives could also employ tactics to align with the regulatory expectations of cooperation yet still maintain information control through strategic decisions around creating and waiving legal privilege over documents. Finally, if the process was finished quickly, the 'skeletons in the closet' might not be revealed, with the regulator losing some inquisitiveness in the process. These notions are explored further in the following chapter.

Some recognition of the limitations of settled cases began to emerge in regulatory policy and practice towards the end of the research period. These were spearheaded by a senior enforcement official, Mark Steward, the then head of the enforcement division, who was of the view that settlements had less value as precedents than contested cases so should be of less use (LawyerFR20). In March 2017, a new procedure called focused resolution agreement (FRA) was introduced in the Handbook, which allows to partially contest the proposed action. The FRA confirms an agreed position between the parties on some of the issues of a proposed enforcement action while allowing partial contestation, for example, of the penalty (while other facts are agreed), the breach (with agreed facts), or other narrower issues. The issues which remain in dispute are then heard at the Regulatory Decisions Committee. Contestation of only the penalty while there has been an agreement on the facts and liability still allows for the 30 per cent settlement discount. The first partially contested case was only published in December 2018, so this process, the motives behind it, and the role of discussions around the wording and of the misconduct in practice should be subject to future research.

Bibliography

Anderson T, Schum D and Twining W (2005) *Analysis of Evidence* (2nd ed.). Cambridge, UK: Cambridge University Press.

Axelrad L (2000) Investigation and Remediation of Contaminated Manufacturing Sites in the United States, the United Kingdom, and the Netherlands. In: Kagan RA and Axelrad L (eds) *Regulatory Encounters: Multinational Corporations and American Adversarial Legalism*. Berkeley: University of California Press, 96–121.

Ayres I and Braithwaite J (1992) *Responsive Regulation: Transcending the Deregulation Debate*. Oxford: Oxford University Press.

Baldwin J (1985) *Pre-Trial Justice: A Study of Case Settlements in Magistrates' Courts*. Oxford: Basil Blackwell Ltd.

Baldwin J (1993) Police Interview Techniques: Establishing Truth or Proof? *The British Journal of Criminology* 33(3): 325–352.

Baldwin R, Scott CD and Hood C (1998) *A Reader on Regulation*. Oxford: Oxford University Press.

BBC (2020) *Lloyds Pays £2.5bn to Deal with Final PPI Claims*. Available at: www.bbc.co.uk/news/business-51570395.

Bibas S (2004) Plea Bargaining Outside the Shadow of Trial. *Harvard Law Review* 117(8): 2469–2547.

Black J (1998) Talking about Regulation. *Public Law*: 77–105.

Black J (2003) Enrolling Actors in Regulatory Processes: Examples from UK Financial Services Regulation. *Public Law* 47: 62–90.
Black J (2005) The Emergence of Risk-Based Regulation and the New Public Management in the UK. *Public Law* (Autumn): 512–549.
Black J (2008) Forms and Paradoxes of Principles-Based Regulation. *Capital Markets Law Journal* 3(4): 425–457.
Black J, Hopper M and Band C (2007) Making a Success of Principles-Based Regulation. *Law and Financial Markets Review* 1(3): 191–206.
Braithwaite J (2002) Rules and Principles: A Theory of Legal Certainty. *Australian Journal of Legal Philosophy* 27: 47–82.
Braithwaite J and Murphy J (1993) Clout and Internal Compliance Systems. *Corporate Conduct Quarterly* 2: 52–54.
Burby RJ and Paterson RG (1993) Improving Compliance with State Environmental Regulations. *Journal of Policy Analysis and Management* 12(4): 753–772.
Campbell L (2019) Trying Corporations: Why Not Prosecute? *Current Issues in Criminal Justice* 31(2): 269–291.
Clarke M (1990) *Business Crime: Its Nature and Control.* Cambridge: Polity Press.
Coglianese C and Mendelson E (2010) Meta-Regulation and Self-Regulation. In: Baldwin R, Cave M and Lodge M (eds) *The Oxford Handbook of Regulation.* New York: Oxford University Press.
Conklin JE (1977) *Illegal but Not Criminal: Business Crime in America.* Englewood Cliffs, NJ: Prentice-Hall.
Cornish D and Clarke R (1986) Introduction. In: Cornish D and Clarke R (eds) *The Reasoning Criminal: Rational Choice Perspectives on Offending.* New York: Springer, 1–16.
Dal Bò E (2006) Regulatory Capture: A Review. *Oxford Review of Economic Policy* 22(2): 203–225.
Edelman LB and Talesh SA (2011) To Comply or Not to Comply-That Isn't the Question: How Organizations Construct the Meaning of Compliance. In: Parker C and Nielsen VL (eds) *Explaining Compliance: Business Responses to Regulation.* Cheltenham, UK: Edward Elgar Publishing, 103–122.
Ermann MD and Lundman RJ (2002) Introduction. In: Ermann MD and Lundman RJ (eds) *Corporate and Governmental Deviance: Problems of Organizational Behavior in Contemporary Society* (6th ed.). New York: Oxford University Press.
FCA (2013a) *The FCA's Approach to Advancing Its Objectives.* Available at: www.fca.org.uk/static/documents/fca-approach-advancing-objectives.pdf.
FCA (2013b) *The FCA's Response to the Parliamentary Commission on Banking Standards.* Available at: www.fca.org.uk/publication/corporate/pcbs-response.pdf.
FCA (2013c) *Enhancing Accountability within the Financial Services Sector, Banking Standards: Written Evidence from the Financial Conduct Authority.* Available at: https://publications.parliament.uk/pa/jt201314/jtselect/jtpcbs/27/27v_we76.htm.
FCA (2015) *Deutsche Bank Fined £227 Million by Financial Conduct Authority for LIBOR and EURIBOR Failings and for Misleading the Regulator.* Available at: www.fca.org.uk/news/deutsche-bank-fined-by-fca-for-libor-and-euribor-failings.
FCA (2016) *Our Future Mission.* Available at: https://webarchive.nationalarchives.gov.uk/ukgwa/20230902005300/https://www.fca.org.uk/publications/corporate-documents/our-mission.
FCA (2017) *FCA Mission: Our Future Approach to Consumers.* Available at: https://www.fca.org.uk/publication/corporate/our-future-approach-consumers.pdf.
FCA (2021) *Monthly PPI Refunds and Compensation.* Available at: www.fca.org.uk/data/monthly-ppi-refunds-and-compensation.
FSA (2005) *Financial Services Authority Enforcement Process Review Report and Recommendations.* Available at: https://webarchive.nationalarchives.gov.uk/ukgwa/

20110801173807mp_/http://www.fsa.gov.uk/pubs/other/enf_process_review_report.pdf.

Galanter M (1974) Why the "Haves" Come Out Ahead: Speculations on the Limits of Legal Change. *Law & Society Review* 9(1): 95–160.

Garrett BL (2014) *Too Big to Jail: How Prosecutors Compromise with Corporations.* Boston, MA: Harvard University Press.

Georgosouli A (2008) The Nature of the FSA Policy of Rule-Use: A Critical Overview. *Legal Studies* 28(1): 119–139.

Gilad S (2010) It Runs in the Family: Meta-Regulation and Its Siblings. *Regulation & Governance* 4(4): 485–506.

Grabosky PN (1995) Counterproductive Regulation. *International Journal of the Sociology of Law* 23: 347–369.

Gunningham N (2011) Strategizing Compliance and Enforcement: Responsive Regulation and Beyond. In: Parker C and Nielsen VL (eds) *Explaining Compliance: Business Responses to Regulation.* Cheltenham, UK: Edward Elgar Publishing, 199–221.

Hawkins K and Hutter BM (1993) The Response of Business to Social Regulation in England and Wales: An Enforcement Perspective. *Law & Policy* 15(3): 199–217.

Higgins A (2008) Corporate Abuse of Legal Professional Privilege. *Civil Justice Quarterly* 27(3): 377–406.

Higgins A (2010) Legal Advice Privilege and its Relevance to Corporations. *Modern Law Review* 73(3): 371–398.

Higgins A (2019) Too Much and Too Little Secrecy in the Law of Corporate Privilege. *Civil Justice Quarterly* 38(2): 145–167.

HM Treasury (2014) *Review of Enforcement Decision-Making at the Financial Services Regulators: Final Report.* Available at: https://assets.publishing.service.gov.uk/media/5a7ecd2c40f0b62305b8344a/enforcement_review_response_final.pdf.

Hock B and Dávid-Barret E (2022) The Compliance Game: Legal Endogeneity in Anti-Bribery Settlement Negotiations. *International Journal of Law, Crime and Justice* 71: 1–13.

Hutter BM (2011) Negotiating Social, Economic and Political Environments: Compliance with Regulation within and beyond the State. In: Parker C and Nielsen VL (eds) *Explaining Compliance: Business Responses to Regulation.* Cheltenham, UK: Edward Elgar Publishing, 305–321.

Jordanoska A (2021) Regulatory Enforcement against Organizational Insiders: Interactions in the Pursuit of Individual Accountability. *Regulation & Governance* 15: 298–316.

King C and Lord N (2018) *Negotiated Justice and Corporate.* London, UK: Palgrave Macmillan.

Krawiec KD (2003) Cosmetic Compliance and the Failure of Negotiated Governance. *Washington University Law Quarterly* 81(2): 487–544.

Lange B (2002) What Does Law Know? Prescribing and Describing the Social World in the Enforcement of Legal Rules. *International Journal of the Sociology of Law* 30(2): 131–150.

Levi M (1994) Masculinities and White-Collar Crime. In: Newburn T and Stanko EA (eds) *Just Boys Doing Business?* London: Routledge, 234–252.

Levi M (2008) *The Phantom Capitalists: The Organization and Control of Long-Firm Fraud* (revised ed.). Aldershot: Ashgate.

Lord N (2023) Prosecution Deferred, Prosecution Exempt: On the Interests of (In)Justice in the Non-Trial Resolution of Transnational Corporate Bribery. *The British Journal of Criminology* 63(4): 848–866.

Loughrey JM (2005) Legal Advice Privilege and the Corporate Client. *International Journal of Evidence and Proof* 9(3): 183–203.

Loughrey JM (2014) An Unsatisfactory Stalemate: R (on the Application of Prudential plc) v Special Commissioner of Income Tax. *International Journal of Evidence and Proof* 18(1): 65–77.

Mann K (1985) *Defending White Collar Crime: A Portrait of Attorneys at Work*. New Haven, CT: Yale University Press.
Mann K (1992) Procedure Rules and Information Control: Gaining Leverage Over White-Collar Crime. In: Schlegel K and Weisburd D (eds) *White-Collar Crime Reconsidered*. Boston: Northeastern University Press, 332–351.
Manning KP (1989) The Limits of Knowledge: A Note on the Role of Information in the Regulation of Complex Systems with Special Reference to Nuclear Power Generation. In: Hawkins K and Thomas J (eds) *Regulatory Policy-Making*. Pittsburgh: University of Pittsburgh Press, 49–87.
May PJ (2005) Regulation and Compliance Motivations: Examining Different Approaches. *Public Administration Review* 65(1): 31–44.
McCaffrey DP and Hart DW (1998) *Wall Street Polices Itself: How Securities Firms Manage the Legal Hazards of Competitive Pressures* (1st ed.). New York: Oxford University Press.
McCahery J and Picciotto S (1995) Creative Lawyering and the Dynamics of Business Regulation. In: Dezalay Y and Sugarman D (eds) *Professional Competition and Professional Power: Lawyers, Accountants and the Social Construction of Markets*. London: Routledge, 238–274.
McConville M and Baldwin J (1982) The Role of Interrogation in Crime Discovery and Conviction. *British Journal of Criminology* 22(1): 165–175.
McConville M, Sanders A and Leng R (1991) *The Case for the Prosecution*. London: Routledge.
Nielsen V and Parker C (2012) Mixed Motives: Economic, Social, and Normative Motivations in Business Compliance. *Law & Policy* 34(4): 428–462.
Parker C (2002) *The Open Corporation*. Cambridge: Cambridge University Press.
Parker C and Gilad S (2011) Internal Corporate Compliance Management Systems: Structure, Culture and Agency. In: Parker C and Nielsen VL (eds) *Explaining Compliance: Business Responses to Regulation*. Cheltenham, UK: Edward Elgar Publishing, 170–195.
Parker C and Nielsen V (2011) Introduction: From Regulation to Compliance. In: Parker C and Nielsen VL (eds) *Explaining Compliance: Business Responses to Regulation*. Cheltenham, UK: Edward Elgar Publishing, 1–33.
Paternoster R and Simpson SS (1996) Sanction Threats and Appeals to Morality: Testing a Rational Choice Model of Corporate Crime. *Law and Society Review* 30(3): 549–583.
Picciotto S (2007) Constructing Compliance: Game-Playing, Tax Law and the Regulatory State. *Law and Policy* 29(1): 11–30.
Punch M (1996) *Dirty Business: Exploring Corporate Misconduct. Analysis and Cases*. London: SAGE Publications.
Reichman N (1992) Moving Backstage: Uncovering the Role of Compliance Practices in Shaping Regulatory Policy. In: Schlegel K and Weisburd D (eds) *White-Collar Crime Reconsidered*. Boston, MA: Northeastern University Press, 244–268.
Schmidt PD (2005) *Lawyers and Regulation: The Politics of the Administrative Process*. New York: Cambridge University Press.
Simpson SS (2002) *Corporate Crime, Law, and Social Control*. New York: Cambridge University Press.
Snider L (2009) Accommodating Power: The 'Common Sense' of Regulators. *Social & Legal Studies* 18(2): 179.
Steward M (2017) *Practical Implications of US Law on EU Practice (Speech)*. Available at: www.fca.org.uk/news/speeches/practical-implications-us-law-eu-practice.
Stuntz WJ (2004) Plea Bargaining and Criminal Law's Disappearing Shadow. *Harvard Law Review* 117(8): 2548–2569.
Symington J (2015) *Internal Investigations by Firms (Speech)*. Available at: www.fca.org.uk/news/speeches/internal-investigations-firms.

Thornton D, Gunningham NA and Kagan RA (2005) General Deterrence and Corporate Environmental Behavior. *Law & Policy* 27(2): 262–288.

Tibbetts SG and Gibson CL (2002) Individual Propensities and Rational Decision-Making: Recent Findings and Promising Approaches. In: Piquero A and Tibbetts SG (eds) *Rational Choice and Criminal Behavior: Recent Research and Future Challenges*. New York: Routledge Press, 3–24.

Tyler TR (2003) Procedural Justice, Legitimacy, and the Effective Rule of Law. *Crime and Justice – A Review of Research* 30: 431–505.

Welles H and Engel K (2000) Siting Solid Waste Landfills: The Permit Process in California, Pennsylvania, the United Kingdom, and the Netherlands. In: Kagan RA and Axelrad L (eds) *Regulatory Encounters: Multinational Corporations and American Adversarial Legalism*. Berkeley: University of California Press, 122–172.

Williams JW (2008) Out of Place and Out of Line: Positioning the Police in the Regulation of Financial Markets. *Law & Policy* 30(3): 306–335.

Williams JW (2012) *Policing the Markets: Inside the Black box of Securities Enforcement*. New York: Routledge.

Winter SC and May PJ (2001) Motivation for Compliance with Environmental Regulations. *Journal of Policy Analysis and Management* 20: 675–698.

Cases

Belize Alliance of Conservation Non-Governmental Organisations v Department of the Environment of Belize [2004] UKPC 6.

Bilta (UK) Ltd v Royal Bank of Scotland Plc [2017] EWHC 3535.

Chaligne, Sejean and Diallo v FSA [2012] UKUT B21 (TCC).

Digicel v Cable & Wireless LLC [2008] EWHC.

Fieldglen [2009] EWHC 1939 (Ch), 30.

FSA v Westcott [2003] WL 22187694 (Ch D).

Hearts of Oak Assurance Co Ltd v A-G [1932] AC 392.

In re Pergamom Press Ltd [1971] 1 Ch 388.

Legal & General Assurance Society Ltd v FSA [2005] UKFSM 11.

R (Amro International SA) v FSA [2010] EWCA Civ 123.

R (on the Application of Prudential plc & anor) (appellants) v Special Commissioner of Income Tax & anor [2013] UKSC 1.

Serious Fraud Office (SFO) v Eurasian Natural Resources Corporation Ltd [2017] EWHC 1017 (QB) (08 May 2017).

Serious Fraud Office (SFO) v Eurasian Natural Resources Corporation Ltd [2018] EWCA Civ 2006 (05 September 2018).

Sharma v FSA [2010] FS/2010/0008 (Upper Tax and Chancery Tribunal).

Tesco Stores Limited & ors v Office of Fair Trading [2012] CAT 6.

Three Rivers District Council v Governor and Company of the Bank of England (No. 5) [2003] QB 1556 (Three Rivers (No. 5)).

5 Reputation as a resource in the governance of financial markets

Reputation and shame in the financial markets: an industry in disrepute

Reputation and finance have an intimate relationship. Financial markets cannot trade and develop without the presence of high levels of trust, confidence, and reputation in the market. Reputation and trust are so ingrained in financial transactions that bank clients consider that it is more important to trust their financial organisation than to receive the best value for their investment (Gillespie & Hurley, 2013; Nienaber et al., 2014). Investors are likely to come to a market that can be trusted as 'clean' from market abuse and market manipulation (Guiso et al., 2008; La Porta et al., 1998), and as cycles of scandals and crises have shown, the overall systemic health of a financial system depends on the level of trust in individual financial institutions.

The notions of confidence and trust in the industry are embedded in the organisational reputations on both sides of the regulatory relationship. Financial institutions with low levels of trust due to poor financial health and unfair dealings with consumers, and wholesale markets with high degrees of uncleanliness, disrepute both the industry and the regulatory system that monitors it. Organisational reputation, therefore, understood in its core meaning as a 'set of symbolic beliefs about an organization – its capacities, intentions, history, [and] mission' (Carpenter, 2010: 33) – is a key asset and commodity in finance. It performs multiple functions for both parties of the regulatory relationship. The positive reputation of regulatory bodies performs regulatory functions on its own; legitimises regulatory regimes, actions, and proposals (Hood, 2007, 2010); and confirms the accountability of regulators. Positive firm reputation instils trust in the organisation by regulators and contractual parties, and leads to better economic performance and better treatment by regulators.

Central to the performance of these functions is the notion that organisational reputation is a social construct – it is established in an interactionist process between the organisation and the audiences with some power over the organisation. Reputation is formed, assessed, and destroyed in the relationship between the viewed and the spectators – the audiences within the organisation's environment that have a vested interest into the functioning of that

DOI: 10.4324/9781351069328-5

organisation. The audiences of regulatory agencies are legislative and accountability bodies, the industry they regulate, the end users of the industry services or products, the media, and the public at large. The audiences of corporations are principally their stakeholders, ranging from shareholders, consumers, and contractual parties, as well as the regulators themselves. The management of reputation is guided by taking into consideration these audiences, and the feat has grown increasingly more complex with the advent of globalisation, technology, and the media. Building and maintaining high positive reputation in the financial markets has become a key concern and enterprise for both regulators and the regulated alike, as evidenced also by a growth in media and press departments in regulatory bodies and systems for measuring reputation in companies. For example, in 1998, 19 per cent of the surveyed companies had formal systems for measuring reputation, while in 2000 such systems were indicated by 42 per cent of respondents (Kitchen & Laurence, 2003).

Yet as outlined in Chapter 2, the industry was brought in a significant disrepute with the turmoil of the 2008 crisis, the collapse of the subprime mortgages market, the associated domino effect of failing universal banks, and the triggering of global austerity. The cascade nature of the global financial system is also mirrored in the close interface between the organisational reputations of financial institutions: as soon as Lehman Brothers filed for bankruptcy in 2008 (Arner, 2009), the event eroded the trust in the liquidity of universal banks worldwide. As the crisis unfolded and the involvement of various financial institutions and their regulators gradually became visible, publicised, and understood, the industry became closely watched, judged, and subjected to a growth of public resentment and distrust (see, for example, the Edelman Barometer findings; Edelman, 2013). In the UK, in 2010, one in five of the surveyed respondents said that they will never trust financial services again, whereas 72 per cent of the respondents had little or no trust in financial advisers (Chartered Insurance Institute, 2010, also Bennett & Kottasz, 2012). As reputations are relational, the mirrored view by the audiences painted the industry as 'stupid' (by an accountability audience, comment by Timothy Geithner, then US Treasury Secretary, cited in Myers [2012]), 'greedy' (by non-governmental organisations and media, statement by Transparency International [2012]), and 'irresponsible' (by political audiences, comment by Gordon Brown, then UK Prime Minister, cited in Porter & Winnett [2008]). The regulators, in turn, were painted as 'asleep at the wheel' (by accountability bodies, Treasury Committee [2012a]) and 'incompetent' (by the media). The tarnished images have been further blackened by scandals of mis-selling of financial products to retail consumers (such as the interest default swaps in the UK) and the benchmark-rigging scandals (Libor, Forex, and recently, ISDA-fix). The FSA suffered further criticisms for handling the crisis aftermath with almost no enforcement actions against senior managers involved in the banking failures (Parliamentary Commission on Banking Standards, 2013) and the informal redress settlements with large banks for the mis-selling of interest-rate hedging products (FSA, 2012).

This chapter unpacks how reputation as a commodity was used, pursued, and threatened in the enforcement of regulation in finance in the aftermath of the 2008 crisis. The first part discusses the strategies and rationales to manage the reputational risks arising in the enforcement context, from the angle of the regulator. The later sections analyse the corporate responses to the growth in the use of reputational sanctions and the management of stigma, specifically in the context of settling enforcement outcomes. Criminological and regulatory scholarship is expanded by conceptualising some of these corporate strategies, through deploying legal advocacy, to craft the description and regulation of their misconduct as *constructing non-compliance*. The final sections reconceptualise organisational reputation and the construction of image in finance as a two-sided affair: there is a simultaneous process of avoiding regulatory blame and of avoiding tarnished corporate reputations. I term this two-sided process *mutual risk mitigation*, calling into question how disclosure is used as a reputational sanction, and whether the associated shaming is adequate to achieve deterrence.

Management of reputational risks from the angle of the regulator

The political responses over the FSA pre-crisis failures in the governance of the industry (HM Treasury, 2010, 2011a, 2011b, 2016), examined in Chapter 2, led to certain legislative changes that enhanced its accountability and the transparency of its decision-making. The legislative changes brought in by the Financial Services Act (FSA) 2010 and the Financial Services Act (FSA) 2012 have enabled the Treasury, the FCA's principal accountability body, to conduct greater oversight of the financial regulator's decision-making. This consists of the imposition of new obligations upon the FCA to report to the Treasury of its own regulatory failures.[1] In the sphere of enforcement decision-making, transparency (and, by extension, accountability) was enhanced by legislative changes in the level of public disclosure that the agency can make in relation to specific enforcement actions and their targets.

The FCA makes public disclosures on the enforcement actions it has undertaken and/or completed through the publication on its website of different types of enforcement notices. These are given to the targets of its enforcement actions at three successive points in the enforcement conveyer belt. The first one, a warning notice, is given at the end of the Authority's investigation, and it describes the action which the Authority is provisionally minded to take, inviting representations from the target.[2] The second, a decision notice, is given after the Authority considers any representations, informing the recipient of their right to refer the matter to the Upper Tribunal (Tax and

1 FSA 2012 Part 5.
2 Section 207 FSMA, and FCA Enforcement Guide 2.15.1.

Chancery).[3] The third, a final notice, is given to the target at the end of the enforcement action, after the decision notice becomes final either because it was not contested or because the Tribunal made a decision supporting the Authority's action.[4] The Authority does not have powers to publish information on specific cases where the investigation was discontinued without suggesting any formal actions, or the cases that were referred for enforcement but were not accepted.

The regulation and expansion of the Authority's powers of disclosure have followed a two-dimensional script. First, publication powers were given to the original Financial Services Authority in Section 391 FSMA, imposing a duty to publish only final notices. Final notices contain statements of the enforcement decision when a case has been concluded, with identifying information on the offender, the type of the sanction, and a report on how the sanction should be executed (e.g. the timeline for payment of a fine, the effects of a prohibition order, etc.). The tight wording of the statutory duty meant that any enforcement decisions that had been challenged through the Tribunal appeal remedy would not be published on the FSA website, thus keeping the process confidential. Only if the Tribunal had confirmed the FSA allegations of misconduct would the decision become a publishable final notice.[5] However, even with the duty to publish final notices, the Authority could consider whether a publication was warranted and exercise discretion not to publish a criticism if this would significantly prejudice the target.

Second, the publication powers were extended through a 'scandal and reform' type of script in the aftermath of scandals and crises. The revisions of Section 391 with the FSA 2010 and FSA 2012 moved the powers to earlier in the enforcement conveyor belt: at the decision notice and at the warning notice, respectively (Figure 5.1). The FCA now has a statutory duty to publish the full wording of decision notices in the same manner and under the same conditions as final notices. While the publication of decision and final notices is compulsory, the publication of warning notices is a distinct FCA discretionary power. This is a particularly powerful enforcement instrument, as it enables the FCA to issue information on targets in the form of a brief summary of the facts[6] before they have had the chance to challenge the regulator's case. Comparatively, this power makes the UK regulatory disclosure regime even more extensive than the one by the much-feared US Securities and Exchange Commission (SEC). A warning notice can be compared to a Wells notice that the SEC may issue to inform persons under investigation that it is considering an enforcement action, the potential violations upon which the enforcement

3 Section 208 FSMA.

4 Section 390 FSMA.

5 If the case was partially successful for the regulator, the final notice would have the phrasing determined by the Tribunal.

6 FCA Enforcement Guide 6.2.1G.

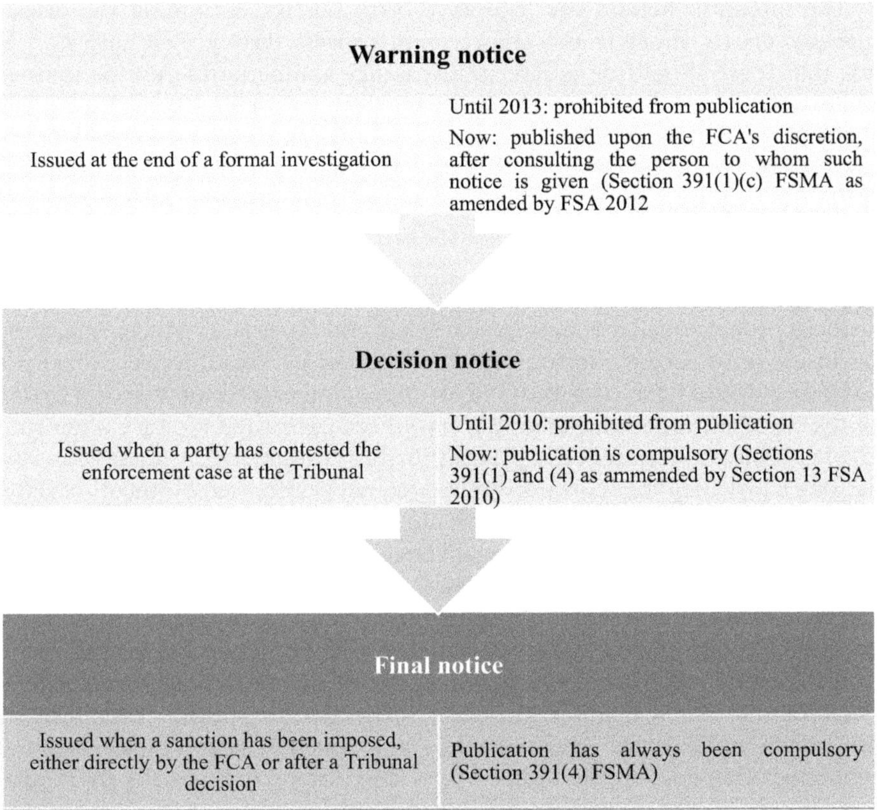

Figure 5.1 Extensions of the FSA/FCA publication powers.

action is based, and that arguments or evidence may be submitted to the SEC. In the SEC regime, a Wells notice is not published, but listed firms may have to disclose it to potential investors on the stock exchange under the market discipline regime (to prevent insider dealing or market manipulation) (Birnbach, 2016).

Both extensions of the publication power mean a gradual erosion of Section 348 FSMA, which is a powerful statutory protection of confidentiality of the agency's decision-making and, by extension, of the City. This provision prohibits the divulging of any identifying information that the agency has gathered in the execution of its powers to third parties. In enforcement matters, Section 348 provides a shield against the revelation of any ongoing regulatory investigations into non-compliance. However, the extensions of the powers have removed confidentiality from the completed investigations, where the FCA is minded to impose an enforcement action but the target has not yet been able to challenge this.

The intention behind the legislative proposals for expanding the disclosure powers to earlier in the enforcement process through warning notices was that there should be greater transparency about the FCA's concerns to protect consumers and prevent detriment from mis-selling scandals, as well as signal to firms what behaviours were considered unacceptable (HM Treasury, 2011a; Joint Committee, 2011a). The payment protection insurance (PPI) mis-selling scandal was used as a particular example of harmfulness, along the lines of the *lost trust in the industry* ground, to extend its use (Joint Committee, 2011a: para. 252). The power was therefore promoted within a contingent of three consumer protection powers: interventions into harmful financial promotions,[7] interventions into harmful financial products,[8] and early disclosure of FCA concerns over misconduct. The justifications were that early disclosure would warn consumers of an impending enforcement action before all the possibilities for challenging it have been exhausted (Joint Committee, 2011a). This could potentially prevent further consumer detriment at an earlier stage, provided that consumers are adequately informed on the disclosure. Research has shown that this is often not the case (Fung et al., 2007; Vogel, 2008), and this concern is raised again later.

The intended use of the power by Parliament supports a growing trend amongst financial regulators, comparatively, on using disclosure to contribute to achieving market efficiency. van Erp (2010), for example, has found that increasing consumer awareness was one of the key legislative considerations for the Dutch financial regulator to be able to publish 'warnings' on non-compliant financial intermediaries. This function goes beyond law and economics thinking on disclosure – as a duty imposed externally by regulators upon market participants to enable informed investment decision-making (Avgouleas, 2009) – in that it appropriates a market function as a regulatory function. The deeper engagement by the FCA in industry product creation and in publicising problematic financial promotions further extends the regulatory interventions in the post-crisis market.

Conceptualised in this way, early disclosure also represents a vehicle to manage regulatory reputational risks since, when regulators use disclosure to publicise risks to society, they also minimise their own reputational risks (Black, 2005; Rothstein et al., 2006; Power, 2009; Gilad & Yogev, 2012). However, the use of the power imposes conflicting regulatory demands that directly impact the regulator's ability to manage reputational risks. Section 391(6) FSMA binds the powers within discretionary considerations of whether the publication would cause unfairness to the target, prejudice against the interests of consumers, or detriment to the stability of the UK financial system. The power needs to be balanced between the publication benefits of protecting consumers and the publication costs of prejudicing consumers through

7 Section 137S FSMA.
8 Section 137D FSMA.

devaluing their investments. Such balancing acts to manage reputational risks are common for regulators. For example, Carpenter (2004) shows that regulators who process pharma applications for new drugs balance reputational risks arising from both delaying applications for robust clinical testing and speeding them up to avoid 'red tape' in authorisations. In the financial markets, the troublesome balancing act is between too much transparency and too little transparency. Both can be equally harmful and lead to reputational damage for the regulator and for market participants.

Disclosure and resistance to disrepute

Disclosure of regulatory risks, especially in the enforcement context, is also a vehicle that influences the reputation and audiences' perceptions of the regulated. The publication of enforcement decisions constructs the targeted financial behaviour as illegal and the targeted individuals and firms as deviant. This may alter the set of symbolic beliefs about the financial institution by the relevant audiences (consumers, investors, regulators) and act as a reputational sanction. It is to no surprise, then, that the legislative shifts towards extending disclosure in the UK financial markets were counteracted with extensive industry resistance. These were conveyed both through responses to consultations on proposed legislative changes by the parliamentary Treasury Select Committee (TSC) (Joint Committee, 2011b) and the HM Treasury (HM Treasury, 2011b, 2012) and through the FSA's own consultations on its proposed policy on publishing decision and warning notices (FSA, 2010; FCA, 2013). The FSA/FCA conducts consultations, inviting responses from the industry, on proposed new rules or new guidance on existing rules. The process is an extension of its substantively principles-based regulatory regime, since the broad and abstract rules at its basis require a 'purposive approach to interpretation worked out through iterated regulatory conversations' (Black, 2008: 439). This gives a central role to the regulatory negotiations between the regulator and the industry as to the meaning, application, and purpose of enforcement powers.

The coding of the submitted consultation responses shows that the narrative employed by the industry towards the extension of the publication powers was one of strong opposition, particularly by large financial organisations, trade bodies, and large law firms. These stakeholders were either fully opposed to the power or called for additional safeguards (HM Treasury, 2012). Conversely, the FSA and consumer associations strongly supported the exercise of the powers. The resistance advocacy employed by the industry commonly challenged the extension of the publication powers due to concerns about suffering reputational damages. Other objections concerned procedural issues, such as challenging the level of safeguards in the FCA's publication decision-making and issues of natural justice, as the target has not had the chance to submit representations, as well as that it will impact the cooperative relationships between firms and the regulator. Alternative proposals were also launched by the industry, for example, that there should be an addition of a compulsory statutory test assessing the necessity of consumer protection, or that only information on unauthorised activities is published. The latter suggestion waters down the publication power mostly to the 'rogue' financial institutions as household financial services providers would not be commonly involved in unauthorised activity.

How the FCA's disclosure power statutorily developed indicates that the opposition resulted in some concessions being given to industry. Different stakeholders according to the divide earlier had opposed views on whether the FCA should have a duty to consult with the target on a proposed publication of a warning notice. The FSA itself was strongly opposed to such duty, arguing that it 'will seriously undermine the effectiveness' of the power as it will likely lead to 'satellite litigation with firms and individuals seeking injunctions through the courts' (Joint Committee, 2011b) to restrain publication. Whilst the Joint Committee (2011a) recommended editing out the duty, government proposals (HM Treasury, 2012) accommodated more the industry perspective, resulting in the imposition of a consultation duty on the FCA. The introduction of the consultation requirement provides scope for corporate resistance over the decision to publish warning notices for reputational management purposes and a more protracted regulatory decision-making.

The publication of enforcement outcomes: functions and audiences

Publication of enforcement outcomes was extensive in practice. The regulatory use of enforcement-related disclosure developed beyond the publication of final notices and decision notices as statutory obligations for the FCA, and the publication of warning notices as a discretionary power. Beyond this, the publicising of enforcement outcomes was also done through official agency publications (speeches, annual reports, annual enforcement performance reports, etc.) and through press releases.[9]

The expansive use of enforcement-related disclosure led to a growing production of regulatory information. Over time, final notices grew in length and detail. For example, whereas in 2010 the average length of final notices was around 10 pages, in 2016 this increased to about 25 pages.[10] Final notices increasingly contained larger amounts of information on the misconduct as they described the breaches, surrounding factors, penalty considerations, and violated regulations. The length and level of details developed from regulatory practice and significantly surpass the minimum statutory requirements:

9 Another publicising tool were informal speeches by enforcement officials at industry events. The same discursive methods and 'credible deterrence' messages were used by Tracey McDermott in her address at the Financial Services Lawyers Association Christmas drinks reception (2013).

10 The longest ones to date are the 50-page notices against Deutsche Bank for the LIBOR fine (FN23/04/15) and against Lloyds Banking Group for mis-selling failures (FN04/06/15).

details and date on the action which is taken, amount of the penalty, method of payment, and recovery of non-payment. This practice was related to the more punitive agenda of 'credible deterrence' for three reasons: the regulator investigating more complex misconduct, the need to send a more elaborate message on the non-compliance, and the need for greater transparency in enforcement decision-making when imposing significant sanctions.

The commitment to a greater transparency was also supported by how the duty to publish final and decision notices was exercised. It was a rare practice that a final notice is not published due to considerations of 'unfairness' towards the offender. Further, the agency's stance was that, save for cases of unfairness, it would always publish decision notices as a general policy and not only in exceptional cases, as advocated by industry responses to its consultation (FSA, 2010). Therefore, final notices (and decision notices) represented a distinct medium through which messages were sent to different audiences and misconduct was constructed. However, despite their length, and perhaps even because of it, final notices were, in practice, constructed through regulatory negotiations between the enforcement parties, as will be seen later.

The issuing of a notice was accompanied by a shorter press release, in which a senior enforcement official, usually a head of a department or – in the case of large institutions, large fines, or otherwise landmark cases – the head of the enforcement division or even the chief executive, commented on the regulatory action. Press releases were often used to reaffirm the overall enforcement strategy. For example, in the case of the record-breaking FX manipulation fines against five banks, Tracey McDermott's statement read: 'Where problems are identified we expect firms to deal with those quickly, decisively and effectively. . . . If they fail to do so they will continue to face significant regulatory and reputational costs' (FCA, 2014).

The information across the different media was aimed at various audiences (the industry, consumers, accountability bodies, and the public at large) and publicised both the enforcement actions and the traits of the misconduct (to a varying degree). Depending on the audience, the publicising of enforcement outcomes was used by the regulator for four interconnected functions: consumer protection, education of the industry, deterrence, and management of the regulator's reputation.

As intended by Parliament, enforcement cases were publicised for the benefit of protecting consumers, in that the decisions provided warnings on identifiable firms, individuals, services, or products designated as problematic: 'In retail cases, if there is possibility of redress, I would make sure to draft [the final notice] with the consumer in mind so a consumer who looked at it can understand it' (LawyerFR20). The final notices would also highlight any negotiated or offered redress packages by the fined firm for consumer compensation, including information on how to access them.

Publicising enforcement outcomes also had the function of sending educational messages to the industry (similar findings on the Dutch financial regulator were reported by van Erp, 2010). Mathiesen (2006) has similarly discussed the educational functions of penalties in the criminal justice context. In the regulatory context, this entailed providing information on what the regulator perceived as *deviant* behaviour, how it interpreted regulatory requirements, and what was expected as a standard of conduct:

> When I drafted a final notice, I always had the reader in mind. For me, the reader was a professional in the same situation as the firm. I'd always make sure to describe in the final notice what went wrong, thinking about what lessons can be learnt from this. I was focusing on making sure that the final notice is coherent, that it is clear what are the failings, what they should have done instead, and how the penalty was calculated. So to make sure that the final notice tells a story.
>
> (LawyerFR20)

The FCA used its regulatory enforcement decisions as messages to the wider regulatory community, as well as a means of disposal of a dispute between two parties (Black et al., 2007). The publication of sanctions aimed to provide guidance to the targeted industry about desired behaviour and the correct interpretation of law. As discussed earlier, compliance officers in the specific financial services sector were one of the main targeted audiences, since regulators intended that they 'would actually learn' (Regulator01) from public enforcement outcomes. Interviewed compliance officers argued that they were, indeed, reading final notices to understand what should not be done and what practices were scorned by the regulator. Further, all compliance officers were aware of the 'credible deterrence' agenda.

The third function of publicising enforcement outcomes was deterrence. Deterrence purposes were achieved through emphasising the level of the penalty and the seriousness of the breach and through sending messages that this type of behaviour would be punished. The conclusions in the FSA/FCA officials' speeches that constructed financial misconduct as a social problem, discussed in Chapter 2, heightened the deterrent effects of the enforcement work (for example, by advertising the increase in enforcement actions' statistics). A further common method of sending deterrence messages through speeches was to use a 'signal case' (Thornton et al., 2005). This meant highlighting recent or high-profile enforcement decisions to warn against the costs of that type of misconduct and to send a message on what behaviour was expected: for example, Barclays[11] as an example of rigging LIBOR (see the speech by McDermott, 2013).

The FCA significantly used adverse publicity as a reputational sanction in achieving general and specific deterrence. It openly relied on this expressive role (Sunstein, 1996) of their enforcement decisions, constantly emphasising the 'need to send clear messages' if standards of compliance were not

11 FN27/06/12.

improving. For example, the former Head of the Enforcement and Financial Crime Department, Margaret Cole (2008), has stated, '[W]e recognise that we need to do enough enforcement cases of the right sort to have "***demonstration effect***" to bring about our strategy of "credible deterrence"' (emphasis added). Cole's successor, Tracey McDermott, justified the Authority's enforcement track in front of the Treasury Committee by stating that 'the impact of enforcement action is not just about the level of the penalty; it is also about what comes out in the public domain and the reputational impact that follows' (Treasury Committee, 2012b: Q1091). The reliance on disclosure for deterrence purposes was also formally reflected in the Authority's Enforcement Guide:[12] '[P]ublishing notices is important to ensure the transparency of FCA decision-making; it informs the public and helps to maximize the deterrent effect of enforcement action'.

The reliance of reputational sanctions is closely interlinked with the regulator's movement towards a more punitive enforcement style after the financial crisis. As the analysis in Chapter 2 shows, one of the most significant traits of 'credible deterrence' was the trend of rising penalties, record fines for a variety of misconduct, and significant fines against the biggest market players. Heavier fines and penalising well-known firms cause more reputational damage, as these are more newsworthy and attract more publicity (Feinberg & Round, 2005; van Erp, 2011b). The rise in penalties and in the profile of penalised corporations carried heightened prospects for effectively using publicity to deter corporate offending:

> The FSA became cognizant that, for an individual, a notice has a quite significant effect on reputation. But the FSA thought that it had a similar impact on firms, to then realise that it had a diminishing, marginal effect over time: 'Oh, just another notice'. This made it move towards bringing up the penalties. They considered that until that point, the penalties had less of an effect; it was just part of doing business.
>
> (LawyerFR20)

Such use of reputational sanctions is in line with the calls for regulators to use a mix of enforcement strategies as advocated by third-generation regulatory regimes: deterrence of financial penalties, other normative and social signals, and importantly, reinforcement by stakeholder pressure and adverse publicity (Gunningham et al., 2004, 2005; Parker & Gilad, 2011). Scholars have indicated that there might be a special merit in using reputational sanctions and 'naming and shaming' as a technique of social control for corporate targets, next to formal penalties (Fisse & Braithwaite, 1983; Braithwaite, 1989; Paternoster & Simpson, 1996; van Erp, 2011a, though see Levi, 2002, 2009; Gobert & Punch, 2003; Klein & Laffler, 1981; Simpson, 2002). The

12 FCA Enforcement Guide 6.2.16.

publication of penalties attracts negative publicity and reputational damages, adding to the formal costs of sanctions. Negative publicity can cause the company to lose the asset of good reputation and associated future business opportunities and to suffer further economic losses, such as loss of share values or the withdrawal of customers (Gunningham et al., 2004; Karpoff et al., 2008). These tangible and intangible losses can have a significant deterrent effect on corporate behaviour, especially in markets that are highly reputation-sensitive. The assumptions on the effects of reputational sanctions are based on rational choice considerations: a higher penalty would attract a higher negative publicity, and this would increase fears of suffering reputational losses. The multiple functions of disclosure strategies and their potential to control corporate behaviour have led to the use of disclosure being heralded as one of the most important third-generation regulatory strategies, after command and control and self-regulation.

Reliance on reputational sanctions encouraged creative thinking about how to amplify their impact through using the media. The media are significant governance actors of corporate crime, though they contribute towards reinforcing its moral ambiguity (Almond & van Erp, 2020). They significantly influence the impact of regulatory sanctions, and the types of media strategies by the regulator (whether proactive or averse) are one of the contributing factors to the effects of publicity as a sanction (van Erp, 2013). The FCA enforcement division was a strategic media player aiming to maximise the exposure and impact from the publication of the enforcement action. The FCA wanted to get good media coverage: 'if you want to achieve a credible deterrent, you need to make sure that the industry [is] aware of what you're doing. The FCA has always aimed to be as media-friendly as possible' (LawyerFR20). This included carefully timing the announcement of significant enforcement actions at 9:30 a.m. to capitalise on the media reporting. The strategy was that the media, including TV, social media, and online news outlets, would pick it up on the day of the announcement, while the newspapers would write about it the following day. Regulators' media strategies also included attempts to make the final notices 'as media-friendly as possible', by including snippets of the case evidence with a perceived scandalising potential. For example, in the final notice to Barclays for the LIBOR manipulation,[13] the FSA had inserted excerpts from the emails and instant messages between the traders that included sensational revelations over the rigging scripts (Jordanoska & Lord, 2020), as well as rewards, such as coffees and a bottle of Bollinger champagne. These snippets were considerably reported and amplified by news outlets on the day of the announcement of the Barclays action (see, for example, BBC, 2012; Guardian, 2012).

Finally, enforcement outputs were publicised as a public relations (PR) mechanism for the work of the regulator itself, especially after the severe

13 Barclays Plc FN27/06/12.

post-crisis criticisms and the FSA becoming 'a bureaucracy in danger' (Chambliss & Seidman, 1971). The advertising of enforcement outcomes was used to justify and legitimise the existence of the agency by sending a message to concerned audiences that actions were taken against corporate crime. This represented a particular type of 'dramatising past harm' (Levi, 2009) to create positive impressions of its activities. Whilst the first three functions of publicising sanctions are common enforcement considerations (Fisse & Braithwaite, 1983; van Erp, 2011a), the reputation management function arose from the FCA's responsiveness to public scrutiny as an accountability mechanism. Regulators were sensitive about getting credit for the work that they were doing:

> We took a case against Jules, an executive at Roses FX.[14] He nicked some money. We batched it up as a regulatory case and fined him loads of money. We went to bed that night thinking, 'We've done a really good job. We've really brought a good case'. The press coverage said: 'Why hasn't this guy gone to prison?' That raises challenges for us.
>
> (Regulator01)

The perception of 'doing something' about a perceived problem was highly important on the scale of regulatory goals. As discussed in Chapter 3, the need to be seen as active and focused on significant outcomes also shaped the FCA's formal enforcement docket as cases were selected for further processing if they had the potential to impair the public image of the FCA. The enforcement power to publish warning notices and early disclosure was also perceived as a vehicle to manage regulatory reputational risks:

> [The FCA] wanted the [warning notice] power because they envisage cases with public interest demands, so that they'd be able to say that 'we have issued a warning notice'. It is a reflection of the FCA's wider movement to more transparency in how they are acting in the public interest. If public issues should demand this, they'd be able to say that 'we are taking an action.'
>
> (LawyerFR20)

The legislative extension of the publication power to warning notices was justified primarily on the grounds of consumer protection. However, in practice, it was significantly used not only for deterrence management but also for presentational management. The FCA published 25 warning notices in the period January 2014–January 2018. Only 2 of these were against a firm, whilst the rest (23) were against individuals. Only 1 of the notices identified the subject – the firm Interactive Brokers (UK) Limited.[15] A closer analysis of the types of

14 The names of the offender and their firm have been changed for anonymity purposes.
15 Warning Notice Statement 17/5.

misconduct shows that the power was more frequently used for misconduct other than one causing direct consumer prejudice – 17 warning notices in total: wholesale markets misconduct (11 for the LIBOR-rigging offences, 4 for market abuse), a false mortgage application (1), and misleading the FCA (1). In comparison, only 6 warning notices were issued for misconduct that concerned treating customers unfairly or providing unauthorised collective investment schemes (UCIS), and 2 for irregularities regarding client assets. The power was therefore more commonly used for managing regulatory blame, for example, to counteract criticisms over the lack of public enforcement cases against the culpable individuals in the highly publicised LIBOR-rigging scandal, especially after the publication of the sanctions against the banks. The FSA was specifically criticised for the lack of enforcement actions against individuals responsible for the LIBOR-rigging corporate crimes by the Parliamentary Commission on Banking Standards (2013). The power also served functions of earlier deterrence against individual financial practitioners across a range of financial misconduct. By providing a public statement on blameworthy individual misconduct, the regulator acted within the 'credible deterrence' priority of targeting insiders of financial institutions.

Such developments of ancillary functions of disclosure, which was principally aimed towards consumer protection, seem expected as an unintended consequence of regulation, though the nature of the ancillary function depends on political and economic contexts and on agencies' enforcement appetites. For example, in a study of how consumer protection disclosure was used by regulators in the Dutch financial markets, van Erp (2010) found that disclosure was used primarily for informing firms about the enforcement policy, reassuring companies that bad apples were being eliminated from the market, and educating the market about the interpretation of open norms. The primary reasons for this were the 'fear of making mistakes and/or of being accused of putting the financial sector in a bad light' (van Erp, 2010: 427). These functions and the reasons behind them should be viewed against their pre-crisis framing by a, comparatively, relatively mild enforcer. The ancillary functions of the FCA publication powers developed to avoid accusations of soft approaches to financial misconduct by an increasingly more punitive enforcer. This is an aspect of the use of presentational strategies for a post-crisis management of external perceptions. In contrast to a denial of a problem and the responsibility for a blameful event (Hood, 2007), it is aimed towards 'owning the problem' and thus the responsibility for suggesting solutions to it. This finding aids knowledge on the little-researched area on how regulatory agencies deploy presentation strategies in the aftermath of crises (see Gilad & Yogev, 2012; Gilad et al., 2013).

In summary, disclosure is an important commodity for financial regulators, and it plays a dual role in a regulatory agency's organisational life. On the one hand, disclosure was used to manage the reputation of industry participants, threaten them with reputational damage, and inflict reputational sanctions. This was an important weapon in the FCA's enforcement armour. Its function was to enable compliance with legal regulation and avoid future harmful behaviour, either through providing an additional informal penalty, through general industry guidance, or ultimately, through education for consumers. On the other hand, disclosure was also a commodity used for the management of the regulator's own reputation and for avoiding regulatory blame (Hood, 2007; Hood & Rothstein, 2001; Hood et al., 2001). These concerns of 'regulation by reputation' (Carpenter, 2010) should also be considered when devising adequate disclosure systems, since they may drive the publication of information that agencies perceive as required or as seen favourably by political and public audiences rather than for consumer protection purposes. The extensive use of non-anonymous sanctions might also indicate that the FCA operated an efficient system of negative publicity through emphasising the (constantly increasing) financial penalties. The effects of this would be a better-managed third-generation regulatory system that relies on a creative mix of penalties. The following section, focusing on the corporate priorities and activities that are launched in response to reputational damage concerns, problematises this notion and explores how both aspects of disclosure interact with each other and against the background of regulatory and corporate reputational concerns.

Corporate management of reputational risks during the settlement of enforcement outcomes

Reputation and image were important commodities also for the subjects of enforcement actions in financial markets. Chapters 3 and 4 touched upon some of the reputational considerations that arose in the self-reporting of information on misconduct to the regulator and in urging a faster conclusion of the settlement process, respectively. There, reputational concerns were examined as factors that contributed towards corporate responses of ***detection avoidance through detection facilitation*** and ***mutual risk mitigation*** practices simultaneously employed by the regulator and the targets. For corporations, concerns over the management of stigma peaked during the process of imposing the penalty, since this was the vantage point where the confidential enforcement process, protected by the cloak of Section 348 FSMA, became public. The disclosure media employed by the regulator brought the misconduct and the attached stigma in the public domain, so significant corporate resources were employed at the sanctioning stage to manage reputational damage.

Such responses were particularly employed during the process of settling enforcement outcomes – a favoured route to complete the process of imposing a financial penalty by both sides of the enforcement process. The pervasiveness of cooperative approaches within the settlement process shows that the adoption of a more punitive enforcement strategy did not result in industry strategies of resistance through invoking the formal mechanisms of the law. Yet concerns over the reputational impacts of the publication of the enforcement decision were constantly present during the settlement procedure. These concerns promoted organisational responses consisting of meddling with the timing of the enforcement decision and *constructing non-compliance* through the settlement discussions.

Game playing over timing

The decision on when to settle the enforcement case could be made for publicity concerns rather than to refute the substantive allegations and the level of the fine. The analysis of notices showed that most targets settled during the first stage of the settlement discussions, receiving 30 per cent discount. However, a smaller pool of targets settled later, at stage 2, with 20 per cent discount. None of the firms settled as late as stage 3. Different informants suggested that the reason behind the late settlement could have been a deliberate non-observation of the deadline to achieve a better publicity outcome. Corporations might calculate and 'fix' the settlement date so that the enforcement decision was published at a more 'convenient' time for the company's business, its share price movements, or the reception from the media and the general public:

> Sometimes our clients want to stretch these things out. The last thing you want to be is coming out just before your year-end results. You might want to stretch this out into the three months afterwards, for example. Sometimes the bank may be facing several different formal investigations all at once on different areas in different parts of the bank. Some of our clients obviously are very large institutions and often are under a lot of investigations. You may want to coordinate those. You don't want them all coming out all together, or maybe you do.
>
> (Lawyer05)

This practice was further illustrated through an example given by a couple of respondents at different law firms: one large financial institution let stage 1 pass and entered into stage 2 for the final notice to be issued immediately before the Christmas holidays in a low-press-attention period. This institution received a significantly higher penalty than a previous institution had received for the same type of misconduct but at a less serious level. Yet the fine of the first institution was discussed more in subsequent commentaries, becoming the public association for the scandal.

Although settling later could bring a higher penalty and/or higher costs for dealing further with the regulator, this was of lesser concern for corporations than attracting greater publicity. Publicity, rather than the level of the fine, appeared to be more of a deterrent factor in the UK financial markets. Such concerns are prevalent across the information-sensitive financial markets, as Williams (2012: 162) found similar timing considerations regarding the publication of settlements in the Canadian securities market. In the corporate crime sphere, rational choice calculations are at play even at the late stage of being punished and not only when the misconduct is committed (Paternoster & Simpson, 1996). This would suggest that it is important to target the 'naming and shaming' at a time that would enable capitalising on reputational losses on the stock market, despite any possible obstacles that may come from the conflicting regulatory demands on the FCA to take into account the impact of the naming upon market confidence.

Settlement discussions and constructing non-compliance: bargaining, but not bluffing?[16]

Corporations worked diligently during the settlement representations and discussions to manage the reputational damage out of the FCA enforcement action. Much of the resistance efforts consisted of organisational behaviour aimed at renegotiating the description of the non-compliance that the FCA established during its investigation. These efforts consisted also of renegotiating, ordering, and removing some of the legal rules that captured such misconduct. The underlying process was one of *constructing non-compliance*, through which the private sector attempted, with varying degrees of success, to craft the description and regulation of the misconduct that ultimately reached public consumption.

The settlement discussions formally begun with the issuing of the warning notice with the FCA's allegations, conclusive findings on the misconduct, the legal basis for the action, and the proposed fine. In the experience of the interviewees, the warning notices frequently conveyed breaches of several principles (or associated rules). The settlement discussions were of different lengths and could go all the way through the night, be staged, or there might be a series of meetings. They reflected what was termed 'a deal-making culture in the city. A very alpha-male thing of staying at midnight and doing a deal' (Regulator01). Despite this, executive settlements were still not commercial settlements in the strict civil out-of-court settlement meaning but were guided by the public interest. For this reason, interviewees commented that sometimes there was a limited amount of 'horse-trading' during the discussions.

In practice, the settlement discussions usually concerned two separate points: the size of the fine and the wording of the final notice. The ability to attempt to negotiate the wording of the final notice was not specifically provided in DEPP or in the Enforcement Guide (the documents on the FCA's enforcement rules and policy). For this reason, the ability to negotiate the wording might be a special concession that was provided in practice to help bring the enforcement process to a faster conclusion. The experiences,

16 The title refers to the famous article by Hawkins (1983) in which he describes the enforcement of environmental regulation as a bargaining and bluffing exercise by regulators.

however, in settlement discussions differed regarding the ability to influence and negotiate the size of the penalty and the wording. Whilst fines were less of a bargaining subject, wordings were more malleable and more open to contribution by targets:

> The FCA is quite reluctant to change the money figure and [is] becoming increasingly reluctant to change it. They tend to be more flexible regarding the wording and charges. I've had cases where the money hasn't changed very much, the nature of the charges hasn't changed very much, but what has changed is the actual wording.
>
> (LawyerFR02)

The FCA's reluctance to negotiate the penalty size should be viewed through the 'credible deterrence' lens, and the regulator's focus on its public image. The ever-increasing penalties of the 'credible deterrence' policy supported the more outcomes-oriented public image of the regulator. For the regulator, the penalty figure was therefore a mostly non-negotiable public outcome and one of the bottom lines in the negotiations. For targets, conversely, the ability to negotiate the wording of the notice was a 'right' that was more important than the ability to negotiate the size of the penalty. For large corporations, the numerical difference between £10 million and £50 million was not that material, though a significant penalty may increase the extent of the publicity and the perceptions of the seriousness of the misconduct. How the misconduct will be portrayed was more important, 'because, naturally, it's what they will be judged on' (LawyerFR03).

The focus on the notice wording was therefore prompted by the corporates' concern over their reputation and the need to manage the description of the misconduct that will become publicly visible. Firms were 'extremely keen to ensure that the wording of the final notice was crafted in a way that presented them in the best possible light' (LawyerFR03). The focus on watering down the content of the final notice was guided by the desire to manage reputational damage since 'even the most lenient of sentences can cause problems' (Lawyer05) if the wording was damning. The concerns extended to the associated press release, as this was what filled up the news. In this respect, although parties could accept the charges and the size of the fine, they contested the wording on the gravity and nature of the charges if the announcement was considered unacceptable. The lawyering up of the enforcement process came to full fruition at this juncture of the settlement proceedings. The discussions were on a without-a-prejudice basis – any negative admissions could not be used in subsequent court proceedings – and they were most commonly with the firm and its legal representatives. Advocacy was a key resistance strategy, since legal representatives would 'argue with every line in the warning notices. It is usually quite a long and quite an intense meeting' (Regulator02). The data revealed that most attempts at (re)claiming 'ownership' of the presentation of the misconduct concerned constructing the non-compliance as:

1. *Not aimed against disadvantaged consumers.* This was a key consideration for retail institutions. Significant efforts were launched at editing out consumer detriment or at least watering down the extent of the misconduct's impact upon the firm's customers. Lawyer05, who worked mostly with big banks, commented that the 'tendentious' words they and their team focused on negotiating were connected to consumer detriment:

   > They'll keep on repeating the fact that you caused widespread customer detriment. Or just a description, without giving context, without an explanation as to why people did things, or they'll just pick the worst examples of the facts and present them that way. Or they'll muck around with statistics. They might be accurate insofar as they go, but they've calculated them in a way that just presents an unfair picture, because they've ignored other statistics or have taken a sample in a skewed way. There's often a lot of work to be done in . . . trying to balance the document.
   >
   > (Lawyer05)

   This quotation exemplifies the opposition by targets to the use of statistics to emphasise the *systemic* and complex nature of the misconduct. Presumably, this is because statistics can be more readily used in newspaper headlines. This negotiating technique is very similar to the ways in which techniques of neutralisation (Sykes & Matza, 1957) are used by offenders in other contexts for 'impression management'. Through a denial of injury, one of the original techniques proposed by Sykes and Matza that neutralises the existence of a victim or harm caused to it, corporations acknowledge the wrongdoing but edit out the extent of the harms caused by the misconduct. In some cases, as seen in what follows, denial of injury impression management edited out the victim completely.

2. *A 'one-off' incident.* It was important to soften and water down the misconduct to represent it as a 'one-off' incident, or even an accident, rather than as a manifestation of a criminogenic corporate culture:

   > You can influence these cases such that when you first receive it, it looks like a business in real trouble which has some significant systems and controls issues, and maybe a cultural problem, and what you can affect that and change into [are] isolated incidents of misconduct which was negligent rather than anything more sinister. That changes completely the complexion of the case. For businesses where reputation is incredibly important, that's something of real value.
   >
   > (LawyerFR02)

   Negligent actions and, in particular, accidents are morally less blameworthy or even morally neutral. The publication of information on such carefully crafted 'incidents' aids towards the long-standing problem of moral ambivalence towards regulatory transgressions, even when these have been sanctioned as regulatory crimes and by criminal penalties. Kadish (1963) has pointed out that these 'moral neutrality' attitudes permeate public perception, but also agency policymaking and the exercise of discretion by officials at the field level, preventing effective deterrence against corporate offences. Practices of watering down the systemic and organisationally infused nature of the transgression contribute to the lack of resentment against organisational offending. The settlement process provides a case in point on how and why regulatory agencies underperform in informing public attitudes about the costs to society of corporate offenses and in cultivating a 'sentiment of moral disapproval' (Kadish, 1963).

3. *A breach involving a principle of perceived lesser 'importance'.* There were significant corporate reputational concerns over the legal labelling of the misconduct in the final notice. Final notices convey a statement on the principle(s) and any rules that were breached, and there has been a movement towards an increased reliance on principles-only enforcement actions. Yet different principles regulate different expectations of appropriate corporate behaviour; thus, the struggles within the settlement discussions are to get a (more) desirable legal labelling reflected in the wording of the enforcement decision.

   In practice, targets perceived different principles to have different levels of strength or importance. For this reason, they attempted to barter the principle(s) for which they will be sanctioned. The struggle was to be penalised for a principle of less perceived importance. For example, Principle 1 (honesty and integrity in conducting business) was generally resisted as that 'calls into question the whole existence of the firm; no one wants that, and it's why you rarely see it' (LawyerFR08). In the retail sector, this concerned avoiding the mention of a breach of Principle 6 (treating customers fairly). Instead, there were attempts to broker a breach of Principle 3 (adequate internal compliance systems and controls), which was considered a more 'favourable' presentation of the misconduct:

> You can sometimes try to get [the essence of the breach] reflected in the final notice, because you get issues around whether or not it's going to be a Principle 6 or a 'systems and controls' breach. You can argue, if you had no regard for the customer's interests, then it should be a Principle 6. Whereas if it's just a failure to properly paper the file, then it's a Principle 3 breach.
>
> (LawyerFR03)

Not having a Principle 6 breach was important to avoid the reputational damages connected to causing harm to consumers. It was not such 'big' news if the firm failed to have adequate systems and controls, and this could be written off as a more technical issue. Firms cared about not being penalised for a Principle 6 breach to the extent that, on occasion, they were willing to challenge the regulator and discontinue the discussions if a favourable wording was not negotiated. The focus on quicker outcomes could result in pressure on the regulator to concede:

> Although it was a breach of Principle 3, the FCA wanted to put in there a statement that the company hadn't treated its customers fairly. This wasn't a Principle 6 case, and so the company felt very strongly against that, ended up walking out of the negotiations, and saying . . . , 'If that's what you're insisting on, then there is no deal'. They then subsequently changed the wording.
>
> (LawyerFR06)

The possibility of a selective attitude towards the principles has not been considered in the PBR literature. In this scholarship, it is presumed that the principles and (non-)compliance with them have the same level of immediacy and importance for the regulated. However, whilst there might be equal attention to different principles during the design and implementation of compliance systems, they appear to have different values during PBR enforcement. Regulatees graded and attached different levels of importance to breaching different principles and most notably to Principles 1 and 6. This does not mean that compliance with them was truly internalised, but that attempts were launched at bartering over the principles and crafting the notice wording in a way that showed that a principle of a lesser *perceived* importance had been breached. The finding has important implications for the FCA's use of reputational sanctions, since research has shown that share prices drop significantly more when the company has been sanctioned for offences involving integrity (e.g. financial misrepresentation) (Karpoff et al., 2005, 2008) or harming parties who trade with the firm (e.g. mis-selling) (Armour et al., 2011), rather than for breaches involving technical regulation.

These empirical insights reveal corporate attempts to shape the final outcome and the misconduct that ultimately reaches the public domain. By succeeding, corporations *construct non-compliance.* Constructing non-compliance is the process through which organisations co-construct the description of the misconduct and the choice of the law that should apply to their behaviour when misconduct has already been established, influencing, or divesting, this prerogative from public regulators. This process is companion to what Lauren Edelman and colleagues (Edelman, 1992; Edelman & Talesh, 2011; Edelman et al., 1999; Edelman, 2016: Ch. 2) have termed the organisational construction of the meaning of the law and compliance: *legal endogeneity.* This is the process through which 'organisations are both responding to and constructing the law that regulates them rendering the law "endogenous": the content and meaning of law is determined within the social field that it is designed to regulate' (Edelman et al., 1999: 407). The concept of legal endogeneity has been applied to explain organisational construction of compliance with regulatory requirements at the initial stages of the regulatory process when implementing these requirements. For example, Edelman and colleagues have shown how organisations construct the compliance with the regulatory demands of equal employment opportunities through reliance on internal advisers (Edelman et al., 1999; Edelman, 2016). Hock and Dávid-Barret (2022) show how proposed 'effective' corporate compliance programs have become endogenous to the meaning and implementation of anti–foreign bribery laws through the negotiations of non-trial resolutions.

Thus, legal endogeneity equally occurs at the final stages of the process, when sanctions are imposed for non-compliance with regulatory requirements. However, here the process concerns the organisational responses to, and construction of, *non-compliance*: organisations are constructing the choice of legal rules or principles that should apply to their misconduct, as well as the description of the misconduct itself that will reach the public. This is then incorporated into the formal outcome of the regulatory decision-making. For this reason, the impression across the board of legal professionals was that some notices were not a representative portrait of what actually happened and the extent of the misconduct but may represent a co-constructed compromise:

> The compromise is around language and around dropping certain aspects of the case to get a deal. There are certainly some notices, some that I've been involved and some that I just read and think, 'That's really weird', where you can tell all it is *is* a compromise. It is just stitch-up kind of face-saving deal. Many others, I think, actually do genuinely reflect what was out there, what the concerns were.
>
> (Lawyer05; emphasis added by interviewee)

Whilst coding the final notices, I also realised that certain factors were highlighted as important in calculating the amount of the penalty in some cases and not in others, though the same factors were also present on the facts. For example, in some cases, there was a particular emphasis on the fact that the breach was not committed deliberately or recklessly as a mitigating factor. In other cases, on a similar set of facts, this was not highlighted, though the misconduct was also not committed deliberately or recklessly. Some aggravating/mitigating factors might be excluded/included based on what the parties subjected to an enforcement action were able to negotiate to be edited in or edited out during the settlement discussions. This selective inclusion or exclusion of content and language during the settling of enforcement outcomes has been found in other empirical research across corporate contexts (Williams, 2012; Hock and Dávid-Barret, 2022).

A key corporate resource in the construction of non-compliance was the expert legal advice provided by contentious regulatory lawyers. Lawyers performed a type of a public relations job in this process since 'it's all about the presentation and the phraseology' (LawyerFR03). Reputation control was one of the crucial objectives for lawyers in the overall enforcement process.

Through negotiating the notice wording, they attempted to re-take 'ownership' of the case and the presentation of the misconduct at the very last stages of the enforcement process, though success in doing so was varied:

> We will obviously look fairly closely at the wording – is it fairly presented? Typically, it isn't. Typically, it's full of kind of tendentious, biased language, and we can do a lot in terms of the drafting. I will typically ask for the language to be changed, to be softened, for new pieces or more context to be put around it, and with varying degrees of success, we will try and change the tone, try and make a more fair and balanced document.
>
> (Lawyer05)

> We'll try and get some more favourable findings, more favourable credit in the notice. 'The firm cooperated fully' – that kind of stuff, so the facts are presented in a more favourable way. The FCA might say, 'The level of fine is non-negotiable, but we are prepared to present the facts more favourably to give you more credit around this or that, etc.'. My experience is that there is always negotiation that can be had with the regulator, but it depends on the degree.
>
> (LawyerFR07)

In contrast, the less powerful and less resourced to afford such legal services were denied access to both advocacy and PR ability. Lawyers, therefore, had a prominent role in the regulation of the financial services industry and in the creation of the meaning of legal rules. This is unlike other, less-technical areas of regulation (e.g. the food industry; Hutter & Jones, 2007), or areas where the maximal penalty is a fixed statutory fine for a strict liability offence (Tombs & Whyte, 2015). Lawyers had a fully visible involvement in the contentious regulatory process, and their presence in regulatory interactions was normalised once the formal investigation started. This has led to a growing specialisation of corporate lawyers in providing advice and advocacy, particularly on issues of regulatory enforcement enquiries. An even more recent trend is the practice to advertise the provision of services of managing reputational damages. For example, one boutique criminal law firm advertised on its website the success in removing a warning notice from the FCA website that stated that a financial services company was involved in providing unauthorised investments to the public. The company claimed that it provided investment bonds to high-net-worth individuals and sophisticated investors. The law firm was able to do this because of the negotiating space provided by the regulation of the warning notice as discretionary and in consultation with the target. The process of constructing non-compliance, therefore, occurred among organisations, legal professionals, and regulators. In the spectre of organisational responses to the law, this was a highly rational behaviour guided by concerns of reputational risks. Corporate lawyers promoted a particular framing of the breach of the regulatory rules, and in view of facilitating a faster conclusion of the enforcement process, the framing may be adopted by regulators and sanctioned in the public enforcement decision.

By focusing mostly on the size of the fine and on constantly increasing it, the FCA was missing out on the potency of the notice wording and its 'scandalising' potential. In the end, the pursuit of a (quick or quicker) resolution of enforcement cases portrayed the regulator as achieving outcomes, but these were not the *right* outcomes, as they did not immediately address the corporate concerns that could lead to deterrence. However, even in this negotiated system of justice, there was a boundary between what could and could not be negotiated. First, the size of the penalty was mostly non-negotiable. Second, the message that the regulator wanted to send with the enforcement action was also non-negotiable, and there were 'some headline messages that, in most cases, the FCA will want to send' (LawyerFR07). For example, the need to raise compliance around the protection and separation of client assets was a prominent message during a certain period, and this part of the notice could not be watered down. The negotiating space was located outside of these boundaries, understood by both sides of the negotiating table. As one interviewee suggested: 'If they are looking to make a point loud and clear, that would be non-negotiable. You may be able to soften the edges of it, you may be able to put some context around it, but that's where they'll be really sticking' (Lawyer05).

Mutual risk mitigation: reconceptualising the management of reputational risks

The process of construction of *non-compliance* raises the problem of 'case ownership': Did the regulator fully own the case, its publicly visible outcome, and the associated shaming? It appears not always, and the reason for this was an underlying process of *mutual risk mitigation* between the regulator and the targets of enforcement. The FCA had a specific regulatory prerogative of achieving outcomes and an outcomes-based style of enforcement. It is understandable that, in the protracted enforcement process that can last up to a few years, the FCA wanted a predictable conclusion which would not be challenged. Such an outcome could be achieved through, and was encouraged by, settlements.

During the settlement process, however, the regulator and the regulatees were guided by different interests and concerns. The regulator was concerned with just outcomes, but also with speed, cost, certainty, and publishable deliverables. By insisting on increasing non-negotiable financial penalties, and through the increasing use of disclosure, regulators hedged the *risk* of being seen as risk-averse, lacking 'teeth', and having insufficiently 'robust' enforcement activities – some of the main criticisms of the pre-crisis FSA.[17] This also

17 See, amongst other, speech by Lord Turner, then-chairman of the FSA (Turner, 2012).

represented mitigation of risks to the regulator's reputation and accusations of 'laziness' in tackling corporate misconduct. For the regulators, therefore, this represented a safety net in view of preserving their public image and giving the appearance of a regulator who was proactive and willing to punish when required. The construction of cases that could impair the regulator's public image as 'egregious' and their prioritisation in the enforcement referral process served the same purpose. Therefore, tweaking the notices' wording may appear to be a minor trade-off in the bigger picture of sending deterrence messages via an unchallenged fine. This underlines a particular way in which weak regulatory reputation factors into agency decision-making.

By agreeing to an unchallenged fine, regulatees and their professional representatives hedged the *risk* of more significant reputational damage through the publication of a non-constructed final notice. They had some leverage in crafting the wording, as they could play against the regulators' fears of the uncertainty of the enforcement outcome. The ability to do so was a trade-off for not employing judicial challenges and adversarialism, and it contributed to the regulator's own ability to manage the risks of the uncertain enforcement process. This was also a device to pre-empt more significant reputational tarnishing through the regulatory sanction. Such risk mitigation practices are a common corporate strategy. In other areas of corporate activism, multinational corporations often design and promulgate unrealistic voluntary corporate codes to pre-empt criticism and state regulation (Sethi, 2002). These actions are also undertaken to craft positive reputations and manage adverse regulatory solutions. In the sphere of enforcement, depending on the political environment and climate, such actions are undertaken to craft enforcement decisions.

For both sides of the regulatory relationship, the sanctioning process as well as the *mutual risk mitigation* was a mechanism for managing perceptions – both mutual and from wider audiences. The concealed world of settlements allowed for the boundaries of reputational damage to be drawn and redrawn by both sides of the process, and this enabled limited reputational damage control. In the original drafting of the FSA's sanctioning decision-making process, concerns were raised on the clandestine nature of the settlement process, with the Joint Committee warning that the procedure 'must avoid any impression of secretive and collusive plea-bargaining' (Joint Committee, 1998). Yet despite the gradual erosion of the confidentiality protections awarded by Section 348 FSMA, the settlement negotiations still occurred in private. Thus, although there could be a common understanding between the parties on what happened and the underlying details, the public representation of the misconduct is constructed and edited. On the one hand, this process was prompted by the regulator's policy of publicising the outcomes and the growth of discursive enforcement notices; on the other, the process was resisted and influenced by the regulated and their business considerations. The importance of keeping the proceedings secret can also be seen in the objections, voiced by the responses to the legislative changes discussed earlier and, separately, by numerous interviewees, to the publication of warning notices – issued before the settlement discussions begin. With an earlier publication, regulatees lose the leeway to negotiate the wording of the proposed warning notice (the regulator's own text) to a final notice (constructed non-compliance). In consequence, not only compliance, but also the publicly revealed non-compliance, was constructed in the contentious regulatory process through the priorities and activities of financial regulators and the responses by parties subjected to enforcement actions.

The issue of constructing the financial misconduct that is publicly revealed and accessible to external audiences (other regulated subjects, social control agents, and the public at large) is closely related to the question of who claims 'ownership' of a social problem and how they claim it. In the financial markets, the accusing voices and actions of defining and treating organisational behaviour as deviant, thus as a 'social problem', were those belonging to the financial regulator. Yet these regulatory organisational claims were met with corporate organisational counterclaims on the appropriate definition of 'deviance'. The channelling of these definitions was done through professional intermediaries, as in other complex areas of business regulation. For example, activities of claiming 'ownership' are undertaken by tax advisers to avoid the costs of enforcing the law in the sphere of tax evasion and tax avoidance (penalties and stigma) on behalf of their organisational clients (McBarnet, 1991; McBarnet & Whelan, 1991; McBarnet & Whelan, 1999). The exchange of claims and counterclaims in the enforcement sphere, played out notably through the process of *mutual risk mitigation*, shaped the definition of 'deviance' and the boundaries of what was allowed.

Social constructivism scholars of deviance have stated that 'whether a perceived departure from social norms comes to be widely labelled and penalised as deviant depends on the power of the accusers to make their label stick' (Ermann & Lundman, 2002: 36). The employment of legal advocacy and counterclaims around the *deviant* label during the settlement of regulatory penalties was one of the many ways through which resourceful private actors attempted to rewrite the rules of the game in times of crisis-inspired reforms. Next to rule interpretation (Pistor, 2013), this is a further way in which power is accumulated in a legally constructed system, such as the financial markets. In the enforcement sphere, corporate actors accumulate and exercise political and economic power through the ability to participate in the interpretation of the coverage of the enforcement notices and the framing of what should be considered misconduct in the market.

Regulating reputation as a two-sided affair: some conclusions

Considerations over reputation as a resource in financial and other markets should take into account that all stakeholders in the markets might be reputation-sensitive, both regulators and the regulated. For both, reputational concerns might give precedence over other enforcement factors. In times of legislative movements towards extending disclosure as well as a greater pressure on enforcement agencies to be more transparent (Hood, 2006), concerns of 'regulation by reputation' may drive the publication of information that agencies perceive as required or as seen favourably by political and public audiences in addition to other objectives, such as deterrence or consumer protection. As the enforcement process is highly subject to political influences (Short, 2021), this politics should be accounted for when defining the aims and audiences of a disclosure policy.

Concepts of regulatory blame should also be extended to account for the concessions that are made in the regulatory game in enforcing regulation. A regulator's reputation management is often viewed as a one-sided undertaking in which public agencies subjected to criticism undertake various activities to avoid 'blame', without a deeper questioning of how such actions may be enacted in a two-sided process that shapes and is shaped by the industry's own reputational concerns. Reputational management must be observed through this two-sided lens. In financial markets, this process is aided by the pervasiveness of a settling culture during the penalties imposition, which frames and enables the mutual management of reputational concerns. As such culture dominates the regulatory sanctioning process in other, highly legally technical regulatory fields, the influence of the context and its outcomes should also be factored into the management of regulatory reputational risks. *Mutual risk mitigation* additionally allows for the reinterpretation of other confidential processes involving the social control of corporations. One example is how large settlements were agreed in the United States after the financial crisis. There is commentary that some of the many lawsuits launched by the SEC after 2008 had little scope for success, but the banks were keen to settle anyway due to the reputational blow that the proceedings were bringing (see Macey, 2013).

The identification of *constructing non-compliance* and *mutual risk mitigation* practices provides a more nuanced understanding also of the risks, audiences, and corporate concerns regarding reputational sanctions and the associated shaming. There have been extensive discussions of the value of publicity as a means of controlling harmful business behaviour (Fisse & Braithwaite, 1983; Makkai & Bratithwaite, 1994; Karpoff et al., 2008; Armour et al., 2011; van Erp, 2011b), and in the financial markets, reputation is something that market players deeply care about. Yet the empirical findings problematise the disclosure system as it appears that there was a misalignment between how negative publicity was used by the regulator and the risks and costs that were relevant for the regulated. Naming and shaming were also important in the UK financial markets; however, whilst shaming might work, there were certain types of shaming that worked better. Corporations did not suffer informal sanctions only for being fined but also for the reasons behind it. The size of the fine was not always the most feared enforcement outcome, as there could be greater concerns about the wording on the misconduct. A fuller distinction between what exactly corporations care about regarding their public image, who are their relevant audiences, and the various risks attached to reputational sanctions will provide a better understanding of how to devise disclosure systems and how to use naming and shaming.

For example, this research shows that retail institutions were concerned about not being seen as acting in consumer detriment and treating customers unfairly. Some empirical research on the wholesale side has found that the involvement of investment banks in environment sustainability programmes was driven by complex corporate reputation risks and considerations of both 'social reputation' and 'client service reputation' (reputation for good business sense) (Bowman, 2013). This complexity of reputational concerns indicates that the perceptions of different relevant audiences can affect corporate behaviour differently and instigate different strategies of managing reputation.

In post-crisis periods, and in any period following an industry scandal, the set of symbolic beliefs by political and public audiences about the history and intentions of regulatees emerge as especially relevant for concerns over reputation: 'Of course, a lot of the distrust came from the financial crisis and the banks' involvement in this. They were quite expedient to blame the bankers and claim that the bankers' behaviour was below the threshold' (FinancialInstitution02). This also promoted cooperative approaches to the more punitive enforcement actions. The post-crisis public backlash (especially against the banking sector) was one of the factors behind the few challenges of the FCA's enforcement actions: 'at the moment, the banks don't push back on anything' (Lawyer05). For example, significant external pressures (political, then FSA, public, consumer websites) were exerted during the judicial review launched by banks over the enforcement actions for the mis-selling of payment protection insurance (*BBA v FSA and FOS* [2011]) ('You know, "bad banks ripping off consumers are now challenging, and they have no conscience"'). In this lawyer's views, when the crisis rescinded and 'the good times [came] back', the banks might perhaps have more freedom to push back, redrawing again the power relations in the industry through contentious means.

On the question of why corporations care about the information on their misconduct reaching the relevant audiences and why targets attempted to construct the wording of the final notice, reputational risks should be further disentangled to account for various additional costs from market and consumer reactions. The fears of public resentment were closely connected to fears of further economic losses that might arise from civil litigation. Perceptions by past consumers were relevant since financial institutions cared about the extent of the redress. This is the case for retail banks and for mis-selling related cases, but also for wholesale misconduct, such as market manipulation, where the firm must restitute the losses of shareholders.[18] The extent of the remedial work and redress might dwarf the penalty amount. In addition, there might be further actions, such as civil suits, class actions, or further customer complaints,

18 Section 384 FSMA.

by claims management companies because of the publication of the notice, 'so if you are a firm, if you're facing the threat of litigation consequent to the level of breaches, you clearly have to have one eye at how those failings are portrayed in any final notice' (LawyerFR07). Global institutions also cared about any US spillover effects from a UK enforcement action. There was a fear of US class action suits, even if the misconduct did not provide basis for a UK action for damages because it was based on a breach of a principle. This was an additional reason that an inclusion of a Principle 6 ('treating customers fairly') breach was so fiercely contested. It enabled consumer-based litigation, on occasion, across jurisdictional bounds.

It is important, therefore, to recognise the multiple levels at which administrative fines may operate in achieving general and specific deterrence and to disaggregate them. The deterrence-associated risks are monetary costs from the fine (which may be negligible for the corporation), monetary costs from further civil actions (which may be significant), reputational costs from the size of the penalty (the larger the fine, the more it attracts public scrutiny), and reputational costs from the wording of the enforcement decision (this might significantly affect public perceptions of the misconduct and could incite further monetary costs if consumers or shareholders decide not to deal with the deviant institution). A fuller distinction between these will provide a better understanding of how to use 'naming and shaming' (Braithwaite, 1989), a popular though not always successful (Levi, 2002, 2009) remedy for corporate crime control. It will also contribute to a more efficient risk-based enforcement and a better employment of scarce regulatory resources.

The existence of *constructing non-compliance* and *mutual risk mitigation* practices, as well as the resultant inadequate shaming, provides a further explanation for the fact that negative publicity disclosures do not evoke strong consumer reactions (Pawson, 2002; Weil et al., 2006; Fung et al., 2007; van Erp, 2010, 2011b). Research has shown that it is unclear, first, to what extent consumers can be empowered or educated enough to rely on such information in making informed decisions on using services and, second, to what extent adverse information causes boycott of deviant firms by consumers. This inability to rely on consumers as a democratic form of corporate governance (Vogel, 2008) seems to be particularly pronounced in the financial markets (Williams, 2007).

However, the question might be whether the information provided is the right information to achieve the desired outcomes. Studies by Karpoff et al. (2008) and Armour et al. (2011) indicate that the content of the information, and not solely its disclosure, is relevant for adverse market reactions – this may also be the case for eliciting retail consumers' reactions. The present study shows how the disclosed information may be moulded, censored, and crafted by corporations using professional resources. The lack of enlisting consumers as a third-party mechanism to control unethical corporate behaviour in finance may be a result of the combined effects of the complexity of the products that are offered, consumer inertia in thinking 'everyone is the same' (Edelman,

2013), and it should be added, because *constructing non-compliance* practices that edit out information showing detriment to consumers.

Appropriate disclosure of the offending behaviour will allow for capitalising on consumer activities, but also on investor reactions, as a further market-based control of corporate behaviour. Research that has estimated reputational losses through measuring the impact of revelation of information about firm misconduct on market values has shown that there is an ambiguous and not fully supported link between the publication of regulatory fines and movements in the offender's share prices. There is no conclusive evidence that shareholders lose trust and punish companies for misconduct. However, one strand of research has suggested that reputational losses are large and significant when the misconduct involved the firm's customers, suppliers, and investors (Karpoff & Lott, 1993; Armour et al., 2011). Conversely, when the misconduct involved third parties, such as other market participants (Armour et al., 2011), the public at large (Feinberg & Round, 2005), or intangible values, such as the environment (Alexander, 1999; Karpoff et al., 2005), the losses were small and insignificant. In the UK, Armour et al. (2011) found that misconduct involving mis-selling to consumers much more significantly impacted the share prices of the firm than did the announcement of misconduct involving breaches of the anti–money laundering or anti-bribery regimes. The publication of not only the amount of the fine but also an appropriate disclosure of the misconduct may contribute to greater impacts on the stock market.

Bibliography

Alexander CR (1999) On the Nature of the Reputational Penalty for Corporate Crime: Evidence. *Journal of Law & Economics* 42: 489–526.

Almond P and van Erp J (2020) Regulation and Governance versus Criminology: Disciplinary Divides, Intersections, and Opportunities. *Regulation & Governance* 14: 167–183.

Armour J, Mayer C and Polo A (2011) Regulatory Sanctions and Reputational Damage in Financial Markets. *Oxford Legal Studies Research Paper No. 62/2010*; *ECGI – Finance Working Paper No. 300/2010*. Available at: https://papers.ssrn.com/sol3/papers.cfm?abstract_id=1678028

Arner AW (2009) The Global Credit Crisis of 2008: Causes and Consequences. *International Lawyer* 43: 101.

Avgouleas E (2009) The Global Financial Crisis and the Disclosure Paradigm in European Financial Regulation: The Case for Reform. *European Company and Financial Law Review* 6.

Baldwin J (1985) *Pre-Trial Justice: A Study of Case Settlements in Magistrates' Courts*. Oxford: Basil Blackwell Ltd.

BBC (2012) *Barclays Trader Talk: 'I'm Opening a Bottle of Bollinger'*. Available at: www.theguardian.com/business/2012/jun/27/barclays-libor-trader-talk

Bennett R and Kottasz R (2012) Public Attitudes towards the UK Banking Industry Following the Global Financial Crisis. *International Journal of Bank Marketing* 30(2): 128–147.

Birnbach D (2016) Do You Have to Disclose a Government Investigation? *Harvard Law School Forum on Corporate Governance*. Available at: https://corpgov.law.harvard.edu/2016/04/09/do-you-have-to-disclose-a-government-investigation/#3b

Black J (2005) The Emergence of Risk-based Regulation and the New Public Management in the UK. *Public Law* (Autumn): 512–549.
Black J (2008) Forms and Paradoxes of Principles-based Regulation. *Capital Markets Law Journal* 3(4): 425–457, 448.
Black J, Hopper M and Band C (2007) Making a Success of Principles-based Regulation. *Law and Financial Markets Review* 1(3): 191–206.
Bowman M (2013) Corporate 'Care' and Climate Change: Implications for Bank Practice and Government Policy in the United States and Australia. *Stanford Journal of Law, Business, and Finance* 19(1): 1–37.
Braithwaite J (1989) *Crime, Shame and Reintegration*. Cambridge: Cambridge University Press.
Braithwaite J (2008) *Regulatory Capitalism: How It Works, Ideas for Making It Work Better*. Northampton, MA: Edward Elgar Publishing.
Carpenter D (2004) Protection without Capture: Product Approval by a Politically Responsive, Learning Regulator. *The American Political Science Review* 98(4): 613–631.
Carpenter D (2010) *Reputation and Power: Organizational Image and Pharmaceutical Regulation at the FDA*. Princeton: Princeton University Press.
Chambliss W and Seidman R (1971) *Law, Order and Power*. Addison-Wesley Publications.
Chartered Insurance Institute (2010) *What We Talk about When We Talk about Trust*. Available at: www.cii.co.uk/media/850551/Trust_CII_2010.pdf
Cole M (2008) *Enforcing Financial Services Regulation: The UK FSA Perspective (Speech)*. Available at: https://webarchive.nationalarchives.gov.uk/ukgwa/20121211011106/http://www.fsa.gov.uk/library/communication/speeches/2008/0404_mc.shtml.
Deakin S (2013) The Legal Theory of Finance: Implications for Methodology and Empirical Research. *Journal of Comparative Economics* 41(2): 338–342.
Edelman (2013) *The Edelman Trust Barometer Executive Summary*. Available at: https://www.edelman.com/trust/2013-trust-barometer.
Edelman LB (1992) Legal Ambiguity and Symbolic Structures: Organizational Mediation of Civil Rights Law. *American Journal of Sociology* 97(6): 1531–1576.
Edelman LB (2016) *Working Law: Courts, Corporations, and Symbolic Civil Rights*. Chicago University Press.
Edelman LB and Talesh SA (2011) To Comply or Not to Comply-That Isn't the Question: How Organizations Construct the Meaning of Compliance. In: Parker C and Nielsen VL (eds) *Explaining Compliance: Business Responses to Regulation*. Cheltenham, UK: Edward Elgar Publishing, 103–122.
Edelman LB, Uggen C and Erlanger HS (1999) The Endogeneity of Legal Regulation: Grievance Procedures as Rational Myth. *American Journal of Sociology* 105(2): 406–454.
Ermann MD and Lundman RJ (2002) Introduction. In: Ermann MD and Lundman RJ (eds) *Corporate and Governmental Deviance: Problems of Organizational Behavior in Contemporary Society* (6th ed.). New York: Oxford University Press.
FCA (2013) *Publishing Information about Enforcement Warning Notices*. Policy Statement PS13/9. Available at: www.fca.org.uk/publication/policy/ps13-9.pdf
FCA (2014) *FCA Fines Five Banks £1.1 Billion for FX Failings and Announces Industry-wide Remediation Programme*. Available at: www.fca.org.uk/news/fca-fines-five-banks-for-fx-failings
Feinberg RM and Round DK (2005) Share-price Responses to Antitrust Enforcement in Australia: Do Investors Care about Price-fixing Cases? *Competition & Consumer Law Journal* 13(1): 23–39.
Fisse B and Braithwaite J (1983) *The Impact of Publicity on Corporate Offenders*. Albany, NY: State University of New York Press.

Froud J, Nilsson A, Moran M and Williams K (2012) Stories and Interests in Finance: Agendas of Governance before and after the Financial Crisis. *Governance* 25(1): 35–59.
FSA (2010) *PS11/3 Decision Procedure and Penalties Manual and Enforcement Guide Review.* Available at: www.fca.org.uk/publication/consultation/cp10_11.pdf
FSA (2012) *FSA Agrees Settlement with Four Banks over Interest Rate Hedging Products.* Available at: https://webarchive.nationalarchives.gov.uk/ukgwa/20121210053412/www.fsa.gov.uk/library/communication/pr/2012/071.shtml
Fung A, Graham M and Weil D (2007) *Full Disclosure: The Perils and Promise of Transparency.* Cambridge: Cambridge University Press.
Gilad S, Maor M and Pazit Ben-Nun B (2013) Organizational Reputation, the Content of Public Allegations, and Regulatory Communication. *Journal of Public Administration Research & Theory* 25(2): 451–478.
Gilad S and Yogev T (2012) How Reputation Regulates Regulators: Illustrations from the Regulation of Retail Finance. In: *Oxford Handbook of Corporate Reputation.* Oxford University Press, 320–340.
Gillespie N. and Hurley R (2013) Trust and the Global Financial Crisis. In: Bachmann R and Zahee A (eds) *Advances in Trust Research.* Edward Elgar Publishing.
Gobert J and Punch M (2003) *Corporate Crime.* London: Butterworths/LexisNexis.
Guardian (2012) *Barclays Fined for Attempts to Manipulate Libor Rates.* Available at: www.bbc.co.uk/news/business-18612279
Guiso L, Sapienza P and Zingales L (2008) Trusting the Stock Market. *The Journal of Finance* 63: 2557–2600.
Gunningham N, Kagan RA and Thornton D (2004) Social License and Environmental Protection: Why Businesses Go beyond Compliance. *Law & Social Inquiry* 29(2): 307–341.
Gunningham N, Thornton D and Kagan R (2005) Motivating Management: Corporate Compliance in Environmental Protection. *Law and Policy* 27(2): 289–316;
Hawkins K (1983) Bargain and Bluff: Compliance Strategy and Deterrence in the Enforcement of Regulation. *Law & Policy* 5(1): 35–73.
HM Treasury (2010) A New Approach to Financial Regulation: Judgement, Focus and Stability (July 2010) CM 7874.
HM Treasury (2011a) A New Approach to Financial Regulation: Building a Stronger System (February 2011) CM 8012.
HM Treasury (2011b) A New Approach to Financial Regulation: The Blueprint for Reform (June 2011) CM 8083.
HM Treasury (2012) A New Approach to Financial Regulation: Securing Stability, Protecting Consumers (January 2012) CM 8268. London: The Stationery Office.
HM Treasury (2016) Treasury Committee's Review of the Reports into the Failure of HBOS: Government Response (October 2016) CM 9340.
Hock B and Dávid-Barret E (2022) The Compliance Game: Legal Endogeneity in Anti-bribery Settlement Negotiations. *International Journal of Law, Crime and Justice* 71: 1–13.
Hood C (2006) A Historical Perspective on Transparency. In: Hood C and Heald DA (eds) *Transparency: The Key to Better Governance?* Oxford: British Academy/Oxford University Press.
Hood C (2007) What Happens When Transparency Meets Blame-avoidance? *Public Management Review* 9(2): 191–210.
Hood C (2010) *The Blame Game: Spin, Bureaucracy, and Self-preservation in Government.* Princeton: Princeton University Press.
Hood C and Rothstein H (2001) Risk Regulation under Pressure: Problem Solving or Blame Shifting. *Administration and Society* 33(1): 21–53.

Hood C, Rothstein H and Baldwin R (2001) *The Government of Risk*. Oxford: Oxford University Press.
Hutter BM and Jones C (2007) From Government to Governance: External Influences on Business Risk Management. *Regulation and Governance* 1(1): 27–45.
Joint Committee in Its Report on the Draft Financial Services Bill, Session 2010–12, HL Paper 236 HC 1447 (2011a).
Joint Committee on Financial Services and Markets (1998) First Report (HL 1998–1999) 50, HC (1998–1999) 328.
Joint Committee on the Draft Financial Services Bill – Evidence (2011b).
Jordanoska A and Lord N (2020) Scripting the Mechanics of the Benchmark Manipulation Corporate Scandals: The 'Guardian' Paradox. *European Journal of Criminology* 17(1): 9–30.
Kadish MS (1963) Some Observations on the Use of Criminal Sanctions in Enforcing Economic Regulations. *The University of Chicago Law Review* 30: 423.
Karpoff JM, Lee DS and Martin GS (2008) The Cost to Firms of Cooking the Books. *Journal of Financial & Quantitative Analysis* 43(3): 581–611.
Karpoff JM and Lott JR (1993) The Reputational Penalty Firms Bear from Committing Criminal Fraud. *Journal of Law & Economics* 36: 757–802.
Karpoff JM, Lott JR, Jr and Wehrly EW (2005) The Reputational Penalties for Environmental Violations: Empirical Evidence. *Journal of Law & Economics* 48(2): 653–675.
Kitchen PJ and Laurence A (2003) Corporate Reputation: An Eight-Country Analysis. *Corporate Reputation Review* 6(2): 103–117.
Klein B and Laffler KB (1981) The Role of Market Forces in Assuring Contractual Performance. *Journal of Political Economy* 89: 615–641.
La Porta R, Lopez-de-Silanes F, Shleifer A and Vishny R (1998) Law and Finance. *Journal of Political Economy* 106(6): 1113–1155.
Levi M (2002) Suite Justice or Sweet Charity? Some Explorations of Shaming and Incapacitating Business Fraudsters. *Punishment & Society* 4(2): 147–163.
Levi M (2009) Suite Revenge? The Shaping of Folk Devils and Moral Panics About White-Collar Crimes. *British Journal of Criminology* 49(1): 48–67, 58.
Levitin AJ (2014) The Politics of Financial Regulation and the Regulation of Financial Politics: A Review Essay. *Harvard Law Review* 127(7): 1991–2068.
Macey J (2013) *The Death of Corporate Reputation: How Integrity Has Been Destroyed on Wall Street*. FT Press.
Makkai T and Braithwaite J (1994) The Dialectics of Corporate Deterrence. *Journal of Research in Crime and Delinquency* 31: 347–373.
Mathiesen T (2006) *Prison on Trial* (3rd ed.). Winchester, UK: Waterside Press.
McBarnet D (1991) Whiter Than White Collar Crime: Tax, Fraud Insurance and the Management of Stigma. *British Journal of Sociology* 42(3): 323–344.
McBarnet D and Whelan C (1991) The Elusive Spirit of the Law: Formalism and the Struggle for Legal Control. *Modern Law Review* 54(6): 848–873;
McBarnet D and Whelan C (1999) *Creative Accounting and the Cross-eyed Javelin Thrower*. Chichester: John Wiley & Sons.
McDermott T (2013) *Financial Services Regulation and Enforcement: Recent Developments and Emerging Issues (Speech)*. Available at: www.fca.org.uk/news/speeches/financial-services-regulation-enforcement.
Myers B (2012) Financial Crisis Caused by Stupidity and Greed: Geithner. *Reuters.com*. Available at: www.reuters.com/article/us-usa-economy-geithner-idUSBRE83P01P20120426
Nienaber AM, Hofeditz M and Searle RH (2014) Do We Bank on Regulation or Reputation? A Meta-analysis and Meta-regression of Organizational Trust in the Financial Services Sector. *International Journal of Bank Marketing* 32(5): 367–407.

Parker C and Gilad S (2011) Internal Corporate Compliance Management Systems: Structure, Culture and Agency. In: Parker C and Nielsen VL (eds) *Explaining Compliance: Business Responses to Regulation*. Cheltenham, UK: Edward Elgar Publishing, 170–195.

Parliamentary Commission on Banking Standards (2013) *Changing Banking for Good: Report, Volume I: Summary, and Conclusions and Recommendations*. HL Paper 27-I HC 175-I.

Paternoster R and Simpson SS (1996) Sanction Threats and Appeals to Morality: Testing a Rational Choice Model of Corporate Crime. *Law and Society Review* 30(3): 549–583.

Pawson R (2002) Evidence and Policy in Naming and Shaming. *Policy Studies* 23: 211–230.

Pistor K (2013) Law in Finance. *Journal of Comparative Economics* 41: 311.

Porter A and Winnett R (2008) Financial Crisis: Gordon Brown Declares 'Age of Irresponsibility' in Banking Is over. *Telegraph.co.uk*. Available at: www.telegraph.co.uk/finance/financialcrisis/3088362/Financial-crisis-Gordon-Brown-declares-age-of-irresponsibility-in-banking-is-over.html.

Power M (2009) The Risk Management of Nothing. *Accounting, Organizations and Society* 34(6–7): 849–855;

Rothstein H, Huber M and Gaskell G (2006) A Theory of Risk Colonisation: The Spiralling Regulatory Logics of Societal and Institutional Risk. *Economy and Society* 35(1): 91–112.

Sethi SP (2002) Standards for Corporate Conduct in the International Arena: Challenges and Opportunities for Multinational Corporations. *Business and Society Review* 107(1): 20–41.

Short JL (2021) The Politics of Regulatory Enforcement and Compliance: Theorizing and Operationalizing Political Influences. *Regulation & Governance* 15: 653–685.

Simpson SS (2002) *Corporate Crime, Law, and Social Control*. New York: Cambridge University Press.

Sunstein CR (1996) On the Expressive Function of Law. *University of Pennsylvania Law Review*144(5): 2021–2053.

Sykes G and Matza D (1957) Techniques of Neutralization: A Theory of Delinquency. *American Sociological Review* 22: 664–670.

Thornton D, Gunningham NA and Kagan RA (2005) General Deterrence and Corporate Environmental Behavior. *Law & Policy* 27(2): 262–288.

Tombs S and Whyte D (2015) *The Corporate Criminal: Why Corporations Must Be Abolished*. Abingdon: Routledge.

Transparency International (2012) *Greed, Reckless Behaviour and the Financial Crisis: A Timeline*. Available at: www.transparency.org/news/feature/greed_reckless_behaviour_and_the_financial_crisis_a_timeline.

Treasury Committee (2012a) *Banking Crisis* (Vol. I, Oral evidence, HC 144-I). London: The Stationery Office.

Treasury Committee (2012b) *Second Report. Fixing LIBOR: Some Preliminary Findings* (Vol. I, Oral evidence, HC 481-II). London: The Stationery Office.

Turner A (2012) *Annual Public Meeting: Chairman's Speech (Speech)*. Available at: https://webarchive.nationalarchives.gov.uk/ukgwa/20120818015156/www.fsa.gov.uk/library/communication/speeches/2012/0703-at.shtml

van Erp JG (2010) Regulatory Disclosure of Offending Companies in the Dutch Financial Market: Consumer Protection or Enforcement Publicity? *Law & Policy* 32(4): 407–433.

van Erp JG (2011a) Naming without Shaming: The Publication of Sanctions in the Dutch Financial Market. *Regulation & Governance* 5(3): 287–308.

van Erp JG (2011b) Naming and Shaming in Regulatory Enforcement. In: Parker C and Nielsen VL (eds) *Explaining Compliance: Business Responses to Regulation*. Cheltenham, UK: Edward Elgar Publishing, 322–343.

van Erp JG (2013) Messy Business: Media Representations of Administrative Sanctions for Corporate Offenders. *Law & Policy* 35: 109–139.
Vogel D (2008) The Private Regulation of Global Corporate Conduct. In: Mattli W and Woods N (eds) *The Politics of Global Regulation*. Princeton, NJ: Princeton University Press, 151–187.
Weil D, Fung A, Graham M and Fagotto E (2006) The Effectiveness of Regulatory Disclosure Policies. *Journal of Policy Analysis and Management* 25: 155–181.
Williams JW (2012) *Policing the Markets: Inside the Black Box of Securities Enforcement*. New York: Routledge.
Williams T (2007) Empowerment of Whom and for What? Financial Literacy Education and the New Regulation of Consumer Financial Services. *Law & Policy* 29(2): 226–256.

Cases

BBA v FSA and FOS [2011] EWHC 999.

6 Corporate managers as 'objects of control'

Senior management became a priority of enforcement within the 'credible deterrence' agenda, in line with the proposition of *lost trust in the markets* discursive mechanism and the shift towards inspecting for the 'root causes of deviance'. This chapter documents the post-crisis movements in the regulator's enforcement priorities and methods towards re-casting managers in financial institutions into an 'object of control' and towards more easily establishing individual responsibility for financial misconduct. This is an important indicator of the FCA's determination, as cases against individuals are more resource-intensive, more contested, and with more uncertain outcomes.

Two distinct enquiries presented in this chapter uncover the process of regulatory transformation towards a more interventionist and punitive engagement with organisational insiders. The first examines the development of a stricter regulatory gatekeeping function during the approval of individuals to senior decision-making roles in financial institutions and the associated endogenous supervisory practices to establish individual accountability more effectively. The second examines the regulatory strategies (and private industry responses) towards the agency's commitment to increased investigations and sanctioning of corporate managers. The focus is on both publicly and privately negotiated outcomes, uncovering the role of regulatory enforcement within and through 'private' regulatory interactions in imposing private warnings and of *constructed non-compliance* in crafting individual accountability. The chapter provides a richer understanding of the reasons behind the discrepancy between official regulatory policies focusing on individual accountability and the relatively few publicly visible outcomes in terms of penalties against senior management, including for crisis-related failures.

Strategies towards stricter gatekeeping functions

The FCA acts as a gatekeeper to the UK financial markets through its powers within the Approved Persons Regime (APER) to vet and approve the appointment of suitable individuals to the most senior decision-making roles in financial institutions. Before we look closely into the post-2008 financial crisis movements towards stricter gatekeeping functions, it is important to

DOI: 10.4324/9781351069328-6

place these in the context of the cyclical development and expansion of the gatekeeping and individual liability regimes in the aftermath of several market and regulatory failures.

Cycles of scandals and reform

Historically, the introduction of tougher requirements for senior managers through the Section 59 FSMA Approved Persons Regime (APER) was a consequence of the financial scandals of the 1980s (Gray & Hamilton, 2006). Notable contribution was also made by the collapse of Barings Bank, where senior managers remained unaware of the serious liquidity risks to which the bank was exposed by the rogue trading of Nick Leeson (*Re Barings plc (No 5)* [2000]):

> How was it possible that you had this guy in the office in Singapore making loads of money and no one in London asking questions where this trading was coming from? The solution for that was the Approved Persons Regime, in which you couldn't say 'It wasn't really me' but you'd know exactly who is responsible for what.
>
> (LawyerFR11)

APER introduced the gatekeeping system of scrutinising designated controlled functions (CF) holders to enter the financial markets. Iterations of Section 59 FSMA have commonly delegated the description of the persons who needed an approval to the regulator's Handbook rules.[1] Broadly, CFs were categorised into two buckets with different levels of seniority and responsibilities for different risk and governance issues: significant influence function holders (SIFs) and customer functions. SIFs clustered together individuals 'closely involved in the running of the firm' (FCA, 2019a), whose role enabled them to exercise a significant influence on the conduct of the firm's regulated affairs.[2] These included managerial (e.g. executive and non-executive directors, general systems and controls and significant management functions, apportionment and oversight managers) and compliance-related positions (e.g. chief compliance officer and money laundering reporting officer).[3] The approval for all APER functions was sought by the firm, not by the individual, so the firm needed to satisfy the regulator of their suitability for the post.[4] This also meant that there was no 'general' approval procedure for a specific CF (e.g. chief executive

1 See, for example, FCA Handbook SUP 10C.4.3R. The exception to this was the intervention of the FSA 2012 that legislated that the CFs consist of significant influence function (SIF) and customer-dealing functions (CDF) holders (CF30) (s. 59 FSMA as amended by the FSA 2012).

2 Previous S. 59[7B] FSMA.

3 See more in the FCA Handbook Chapter SUP 10A FCA Approved Persons, versions until 12.09.2019.

4 Section 59(1) FSMA.

officer), but that these functions were always firm-specific and the justification for seeking their approval had to be tailored to the firm's circumstances. During the approval process, the regulator assessed the individual's suitability against the benchmarks of the 'fit and proper' test. This consisted of evaluating the individual's honesty, integrity, and reputation; competence and capability; and financial soundness.[5] All approved persons were subject to the conduct framework of the Statements of Principle for Approved Persons,[6] mirroring the standard-setting rules of the firm-relevant principles.

APER was significantly revised, and individual liability was yet again enlarged in response to several industry and regulatory failures: the financial crisis, the LIBOR manipulation scandal (Jordanoska & Lord, 2020), and the large-scale mis-selling of financial products (Gilad, 2011). CEOs played a crucial role in the failings of the banks in the 2008 crunch (Engelen et al., 2011), triggering an inquiry led by the Treasury Select Committee into individual accountability. The LIBOR manipulations by large global banks led to an inquiry by the Parliamentary Commission on Banking Standards into the banks' cultural problems. The resulting reports (Treasury Committee, 2012a, 2012b; Parliamentary Commission on Banking Standards, 2013) identified a range of shortcomings in the banks' internal corporate structures, systems, and procedures that enabled a relative lack of accountability by their senior managers.

The aftermath of these regulatory and industry crises showed that the individual accountability frameworks were unable to separate individual action and culpability from the organisational context. Legal standards are, conversely, centred on individualised culpability and the requirement upon regulators to gather evidence on dishonest or reckless personal misconduct or on behaviour below the standard of reasonableness that contributed to corporate misconduct. The difficulties in establishing 'who was in charge' and directly responsible for individual decisions crucially affected the ability of enforcers to satisfy these legal standards (McDermott, oral evidence, Parliamentary Commission on Banking Standards, 2013). First, organisational contexts, particularly those of large financial institutions, have complex structures that make it difficult to establish decision-making hierarchies. Senior management may appear significantly removed from the immediate causes of the regulatory non-compliance (Coffee, 1981; Fisse & Braithwaite, 1993; Katz, 1979b; Black, 2014). This allowed senior individuals to benefit from claiming ignorance of misconduct activities down the line. Second, organisational decision-making may be, to varying degrees, actively structured, either by senior individuals or by the

5 FCA Handbook FIT 2.1–2.3.

6 Acting with integrity (APER 1); acting with due skill, care, and diligence (APER 2); proper market conduct (APER 3); open and cooperative dealing with the FCA and disclosure of information (APER 4). For senior managers also: taking reasonable steps to ensure the effective control of the firm's business (APER 5); exercising due skill, care, and diligence in managing the firm's business (APER 6); taking reasonable steps to ensure that the firm's business complies with regulatory requirements and standards (APER 7).

corporation itself, in a way that evaporates the traces of senior managerial involvement. The FSA/FCA enforcement actions for the manipulation of the LIBOR benchmarks attracted record fines against the involved banks, but actions only against relatively junior individuals. The enforcement decisions and subsequent Tribunal proceedings regarding some of the banks showed that the manipulation practices were sanctioned, and sometimes widely condoned, by senior management.[7] In the Tribunal case *Hussain v FCA [2018]*, Mr Arif Hussain, a relatively junior ex-UBS trader, challenged the FCA's decision to prohibit him due to his involvement in the UBS manipulation of the LIBOR. The issue of why none of his senior managers had been brought to account formed a key aspect of the plaintiff's case. The counsel for the FCA attempted to put forward the lack of direct evidence as justification: 'the documentation that is referred to as fingering senior people is not extensive. As is the way of these things, the senior people somehow manage to keep their fingerprints off the relevant documents sometimes' (*Hussain v FCA [2018*], 288). Additionally, corporations themselves may actively engage in practices that conceal individual accountability of important individuals in the matrix of organisational decision-making. As seen in Chapter 4, during formal investigations, legal advocacy work was undertaken to muddle the decision-making channels and limit the responsibility of senior managers. Such practices permeate the social control of corporate crime. Braithwaite (1984: 138, 308), for example, found that pharmaceutical companies plan carefully in advance how to set internal compliance records for allocating blame for non-compliance. In some cases, responsibilities may be formally attached to a 'scapegoat', whilst the true decision-makers remain in the shadows (Boeker, 1992; Croall, 2009; Hearita and Brown, 2004; Katz, 1979b).

Third, the collectivist nature of decision-making in large organisations through various committees or the board itself clouds the extent of individual participation in the series of decisions that led to or constituted the misconduct. This enabled invoking the 'Murder on the Orient Express' defence in that 'everyone was party to a decision, so that no individual could be held squarely to blame' (Parliamentary Commission on Banking Standards, 2013: 17; Wheatley, 2015). Fourth, establishing 'who was on the watch' was made more difficult in an industry with fluid descriptions of managerial responsibilities. The FSA/FCA had a difficult task in determining the scope and size of the true responsibilities of senior managers in complex organisations, as these changed dynamically in practice (LawyerFR11). APER did not require follow-ups and updating of responsibilities once approval had been given. This led to a mismatch between the regulatory mapping of responsibilities confirmed during the approval process and the actual managerial responsibilities in practice.

7 For example, Arif Hussain FN22/08/18; *Hussain v FCA [2018]*.

In consequence, the PCBS recommended a significant revision of the gatekeeping regime and an expansion of the scope of individual accountability of both senior and mid-level managers in the guise of the Senior Managers and Certification Regime (SMCR). The SMCR was given its legislative footing through the Financial Services (Banking Reform) Act 2013 initially for the banking sector (applied from March 2016) and was then extended through the Bank of England and Financial Services Act 2016 for all FSMA-authorised firms (applied from 2018 for insurers and from 2020 for all other firms).

The SMCR precursors: establishing accountability through endogenous supervisory tools

In the crisis aftermath, and with the development of individual accountability as a key facet of the 'credible deterrence' agenda, the FSA/FCA started employing supervisory tools aimed at ascertaining organisational levels of decision-making and personal responsibilities of senior management. These concerned undertaking significant influence functions (SIF) screening during supervisory visits and asking for attestations. The use of these tools shows how regulatory practice towards more interventionist approaches regarding individual accountability developed in an endogenous manner. The FSA/FCA was able to employ these tools within the extant statutory powers that preceded and paved the way for the legislative interventions with the SMCR.

Through the so-called significant influence functions (SIF) audits (later called SIF reviews), supervisors asked for evidence to help them chart the responsibilities of SIF holders in practice, whether the individuals had been approved for controlled functions appropriate to their roles and whether the firms had appropriately identified and allocated key functions and activities to an accountable SIF (Parliamentary Commission on Banking Standards, 2013: Q2993; FCA, 2013a). The aim was to rely on the review results when determining the extent of senior management liability in a potential firm misconduct. The SIF audits therefore represented an extension of the early intervention attitudes and a method of pre-emptive evidence-gathering for the 'credible deterrence' priority of holding senior management to account. The newly incoming SMCR obligation for approved persons to provide a statement of responsibilities, a map of the managed business areas, and the responsibilities in practice enshrined in legislation an already-ongoing regulatory practice.

Attestations were used by supervisors to obtain a personal commitment from commonly a senior individual in a regulated firm that a specific action has been or will be taken by the firm (Adamson, 2014). Their legal basis is not fully clear, as there are no specific rules on attestations in the Handbook. However, as they represent requests for a written statement confirming particular circumstances regarding the meta-regulatory systems of firms, their legal sources are the general supervisory information-gathering power in Section 165 and the

Principle 11 requirements to be open and cooperative with the FCA. Under an 'accountability model' of corporate wrongdoing, attestations would act as assurances that internal remedial actions will be undertaken within corporations (Fisse & Braithwaite, 1993; Gunningham & Johnstone, 1999). They have the effects of conditions imposed through formal enforcement actions in other contexts, such as conditions of improvement of corporate processes and policies through deferred prosecution agreements or non-prosecution agreements by criminal justice agencies or through the settlement of enforcement actions in the civil context (e.g. by the CFTC [Treasury Committee, 2012b, evidence by Lord Turner]). Attestations enabled regulators to receive assurances that the meta-regulatory systems were compliant without having to use regulatory resources for formal investigative powers.

As a regulatory innovation, their use developed in the immediate aftermath of the crisis and grew out of the FSA/FCA's focus on individual accountability. In a 2013 interview for the *Financial Times*, Clive Adamson, then FCA director of supervision, stated that 'attestations evolved from our greater emphasis on personal accountability. We find that when we ask for them it focuses the mind not only of the individuals but of the firm' (Masters, 2013a, also Masters, 2013b).

Attestations were prominently used in the LIBOR manipulation enforcement cases. In 2011, the Authority requested attestations from all LIBOR-contributing panel banks regarding the adequacy of their systems and controls in the LIBOR submissions process. This was done due to wide-ranging concerns over the integrity of the process.[8] The fact that senior management signed attestations which were deliberately false (e.g. Deutsche Bank claimed the systems were adequate when no systems were in place) or recklessly inaccurate (e.g. Rabobank and Lloyds group affirmed an incorrect assessment of the mitigated risks) led to additional liability of the banks penalised for LIBOR systems failures.[9] The additional penalties were imposed for breaches of Principle 11 for not being open and cooperative with the Authority in the case of Deutsche Bank; breaches of Principle 2 for lack of due skill, care, and diligence for Rabobank; and breaches of Principle 3 for systems and controls failings for Lloyds group. However, while the deliberately or recklessly false attestations increased the liability of the corporations, they were not used to pursue the individuals who gave them. Thus, attestations have not yet been used for enforcement actions against individuals, and their function remains more of a signalling one in terms of raised expectations from, and commitments by, senior management.

8 Deutsche Bank FN23/04/15.

9 Coöperatieve Centrale Raiffeisen – Boerenleenbank B. A. ('Rabobank') FN29/10/13; Lloyds Bank Plc, Bank of Scotland Plc FN28/07/14.

The expanding legislative framework: the Senior Managers and Certification Regime

The Senior Managers and Certification Regime (SMCR) encompasses a vast post-crisis legislative undertaking to increase individual accountability in the UK financial markets. Its introduction aimed to amend the perceived causes of financial misconduct through encouraging staff to take personal responsibility for their actions, improving conduct, and making sure 'firms and staff clearly understand and can show who does what' (FCA, 2023; see further, PRA and FCA, 2014; FCA, 2015a, 2015b, 2017a; PRA, 2015a, 2015b). The SMCR introduced three key regulatory interventions to the approval process: the provision of a statement of responsibilities, the certification of a range of managerial staff, and the application of the conduct rules to a wider staff population.[10] These are reflected in its three building blocks: the Senior Managers Regime, the Certification Regime, and the conduct rules.

The Senior Managers Regime regulates the approval procedure and responsibilities for the most senior managers. Earlier SIF designations are now divided into senior manager and certified positions, with only the most senior managers being subject to regulatory approval sought by the employing firm. These include key governing and compliance functions, largely mirroring the previous APER SIF holders: the CEO, chair of the board, chairs of key governance committees (e.g. remuneration, nominations, etc.), chief finance officer, chief risk officer, chief compliance officer, money laundering reporting officer, etc.[11] There is a complex division of responsibilities between the PRA and the FCA when it comes to the approval process of dual-regulated firms, in which the PRA manages the approval process for some liquidity and risk-related functions with the FCA providing consent, whereas the FCA solely manages the approval process for other key executive and compliance functions.[12]

A key legislative intervention of the Senior Managers Regime was the introduction of a new obligation for senior managers to provide a statement of responsibilities during the approval process, mapping out the areas of the business they would manage in practice.[13] The statement of responsibilities form is a detailed document with requirements to also show how the manager's employment responsibilities fall within key managerial and compliance posts and activities deemed essential for proper corporate governance (the so-called 'prescribed responsibilities').[14] For the dual-regulated firms by the PRA and the FCA and the largest solo-regulated firms by the FCA, the statement of

10 Section 36 of the Financial Services (Banking Reform) Act 2013 also created a criminal offence relating to a decision which causes a financial institution to fail. For a critique, see Black and Kershaw (2013).

11 See further FCA Handbook SUP 10C.4.3.

12 FCA Handbook SUP 10C.9.

13 Section 60(2A) FSMA.

14 See further FCA Handbook SYSC 24.2.

responsibilities operates concomitantly with an additional 'management responsibilities map' – a comprehensive and up-to-date document describing the firm's management and governance arrangements, its reporting and responsibility lines, and the relevant persons and their responsibilities.[15]

The rest of the relevant decision-making individuals are not approved directly by the regulator but are subject to the Certification Regime (the second SMCR building block). This was conceptualised as a type of 'licensing' regime (Parliamentary Commission on Banking Standards, 2013) in which the firm has regulatory obligations to assess the fitness and propriety of a range of individuals below the most senior managers but whose role could cause *significant harm* to the firm or its customers (e.g. heads of banking and lending units, proprietary and algorithmic traders, retail investment advisers, etc.).[16] The certified individuals are assessed against the same 'fit and proper' test as the approved individuals. The same criteria for access to financial institutions roles are now considered by both public and private gatekeeping stakeholders (the PRA, FCA, and authorised firms). The firm issues the certificates and notifies the regulator of the list of its certified and assessed staff. The fitness and propriety of the certified staff are then reassessed by the firm once per year.[17] The Certification Regime enables a greater, albeit indirect, regulatory reach into corporate meta-regulatory systems as firms are made responsible for the conduct of a wider range of their staff (FCA, 2013b). The two-pronged effects of the responsibilisation of a broader contingent of corporate insiders and the responsibilisation of firms to facilitate this process significantly enables the regulatory project of 'governing at a distance'.

Finally, the SMCR extended the application of the conduct rules to a greater population of corporate employees in finance. The conduct rules do not differ greatly in content from the previous APER; they are drafted as standard-setting principles akin to the previous Statements of Principles and equally operate at two tiers. The first tier of duties applies to both senior managers and certified staff: acting with integrity (Rule 1); acting with due skill, care, and diligence (Rule 2); being open and cooperative with the FCA, the PRA, and other regulators (Rule 3); treating customers fairly (Rule 4); observing proper standards of market conduct (Rule 5); and from 2023, acting to deliver good outcomes for retail customers (Rule 6).[18] The second tier of duties applies to senior managers only: taking reasonable steps to ensure that the business of the firm within their responsibility is controlled effectively (SC1) and complies with regulatory requirements (SC2); taking reasonable steps for appropriate delegation and oversight of the delegation of responsibilities (SC3); and disclosing any information of which the FCA or PRA would

15 FCA Handbook SYSC 25.2.
16 Section 63E(5) FSMA. The full list is set out in FCA Handbook SYSC 5.2.
17 Sections 63(E)-63(F) FSMA.
18 FCA Handbook COCON 2.1.

reasonably expect notice (SC4).[19] The regulator provides considerable guidance on the reasonable steps a senior manager must take in complying with the conduct rules,[20] but as in a substantive, principles-based regime (Black, 2008), managers still have broader discretion as to what to do in their responsibility towards implementing the spirit of the conduct rules standards.

Completing the individual accountability rules for senior managers was the introduction of liability for regulatory misconduct under a new 'duty of responsibility'.[21] This enables the FCA to take enforcement action where a regulated firm has breached a regulatory requirement and the responsible senior manager had failed to take reasonable steps to prevent the firm's non-compliance. The provision expands the statutory framework on individual liability for corporate misconduct with a 'failure to prevent' type of liability, next to the liability from being knowingly concerned in the firm's breach.[22] In consequence, the FCA (and PRA) gained multiple bases for taking disciplinary actions against senior individuals for organisational non-compliance: for being knowingly concerned in the firm's non-compliance, for breaching the duty of responsibility, for breaching the conduct rules, or a combination.

There was much consternation in the industry over the introduction of the duty of responsibility, especially since it was initially drafted as 'presumption of responsibility' enacted with the Financial Services (Banking Reform) Act 2013 (PRA and FCA, 2014). Under the initial statement, the individual manager was presumed to be guilty of personal misconduct, unless they could show that they had taken 'reasonable steps' to avoid the firm's misconduct in their area of responsibility. Though this 'reverse burden of proof' created a strict liability offence for industry insiders (Chiu, 2016), it represented a key recommendation of the Parliamentary Commission on Banking Standards meant to directly address the challenges of the 'accountability firewall' of complex organisational structures (Parliamentary Commission on Banking Standards, 2013: 9–10). Even before the provision came in power, it was amended to a 'duty of responsibility', which shifted the burden of proof whether the steps taken were reasonable to the regulators. The government justified the change as introducing 'a fairer system' (HM Treasury, 2015); however, some of the debates on the Bank of England and Financial Services Bill in the House of Lords put forward accusations that the reversal was due to 'industry lobbying' and unsubstantiated claims of senior management losing focus on banking issues or leaving the UK industry due to the compliance burden (House of Lords Debate, 2015).

19 FCA Handbook COCON 2.2.

20 FCA Decisions Procedure and Penalties Manual 6.2. Deciding whether to take action: DEPP 6.2.4, DEPP 6.2.9-F.

21 Section 66A FSMA as amended by the Bank of England and Financial Services Act 2016. The duty became in force in May 2016.

22 Section 66 FSMA.

The SMCR has the potential of decreasing the ability of senior managers to hide behind collective accountability (Clarke, 2018), increasing professionalisation across the industry (FCA, 2017a; McGrath and Walker, 2022), and driving cultural change in banking (Hickman, 2022; Keller & Kokkinis, 2022). However, it is not straightforward that the SMRC framework eases the enforcement process against individuals. What must be accounted for are the limits of what is possible in law and the limits of what is possible in practice due to the influence of corporate priorities in enforcement proceedings. As to the legal framework itself, the revamped senior managements conduct provisions are not vastly different from the previous principles of conduct (also MacNeil, 2018), in particular, the wording of former APER 7 that established a personal liability of senior managers for the firm's regulatory breach if they had not taken 'reasonable steps' to ensure the firm is compliant.[23] This provision has been largely replicated in Senior Manager Conduct Rule 2. Inspecting senior managers for corporate non-compliance failures was therefore always a possibility under the law and, as will be argued later, a growing enforcement practice with the onset of the 'credible deterrence' agenda. But so long as enforcers were unable to evidence that the senior manager had not taken 'reasonable steps' adequate to the role and responsibilities of the senior manager, individual liability could not be established.[24] Additionally, the reversal of the 'reversed burden of proof' rendered the wording of the 'duty of responsibility' to mirror Conduct Rule 2, thus not adding a new basis in substance for managerial liability. The reversal also possibly softened the duty 'so much as to make it ineffective' (Hickman, 2022: 1448).

Yet the SMCR adds two substantive contributions to enforcement against organisational insiders. First, the responsibilities statements and maps enable regulators to identify the extent of responsibilities and adequate 'reasonable steps' for the role more easily in practice (see FCA, 2017a, 2019b). Embedding this requirement into the approval process provides ex ante investigative evidence of the scope of managerial responsibilities should things go wrong. It also overcomes past deficiencies in corporate compliance with the systems and controls rules in the Handbook that required firms to record its apportionment and allocation of significant responsibilities among its managers so that it was clear who had those responsibilities, and to take reasonable care to keep that record up to date.[25] These firm-level requirements are very similar to those of the SMCR statement of responsibilities, yet corporate compliance had shortcomings: 'Firms should have had those [statements of responsibilities, *n.b.*] previously. Those were a requirement of apportionment and oversight. But they tended not to do it very well' (LawyerFR06). The ability to 'muddle' the decision-making channels and the changing responsibilities in practice

23 FCA Handbook APER 2.1A.3P.
24 See *Pottage v FSA* [2010].
25 FCA Handbook SYSC 2.2R, SYSC 2.1.1R and SYSC 2.1.3R.

significantly affected regulatory efforts to establish individual liability for the failures of the financial crisis and more generally. The duty to provide a statement of responsibilities crucially alleviates the problem of tracing the complex lines of decision-making within firms and establishing where 'the buck stops' (Coffee, 1981).

The second major contribution of the SMCR, paradoxically, concerns the liability of middle rather than senior managers. From an enforcement perspective, the Certification Regime provides a new legal basis to take action against middle-level managers for corporate non-compliance. Middle managers represent important conduits of ethical behaviour in corporations and may promote organisational changes consistent with regulatory demands (Gray & Silbey, 2014). At the same time, corporate crime may be facilitated where middle managers succumb to pressures by top management towards non-compliance (Clinard, 1983). Middle-level managers were often found to be involved in the corporate non-compliance decision-making but against whom the FCA could not exercise enforcement powers for managerial failures:

> The problem was always with tracing the individual responsibility of people at different levels, so the people at the bottom will say that they just followed procedures, and in any way, these are not the individuals that the FCA would be particularly interested in. The problem would be with the guy in the middle, and then it would happen that he wasn't approved, so you can't do anything to them. Now that is no longer the case.
>
> (LawyerFR20)

The Certification Regime now imposes new regulatory duties upon middle managers. An important requirement in the context of contributing to corporate compliance is Conduct Rule 2 on the duty to act with due skill, care, and diligence. With the introduction of the SMCR, the guidance to the rule was changed and split into two sections with examples of non-compliant behaviour: for all staff and for managers.[26] The guidance on managers is not qualified to mean that it applies only to *senior* managers but instead includes examples of duties on managerial roles more broadly, such as that their area of business is managed effectively and that it abides by regulatory requirements and standards: 'it's effectively saying, if you are a manager, albeit not a senior manager, you still have very onerous managerial responsibilities to make sure that risks are being managed effectively in the area you're responsible for' (LawyerFR06). This was considered to be the most onerous demand, as it required taking significant proactive steps to be compliant.

26 FCA Handbook COCON 4.1.2G – 4.1.8G.

Transforming the 'fit and proper' assessments

The pre-crisis period was also characterised by insufficient FSA probing (Black, 2011) of senior managers appointments and a deference to corporate business prerogatives during the approval process. This concerned a lack of questioning over certain managers' risk-taking appetite and competence during the approval stage, even in systemically important financial institutions, leading to significant (and embarrassing for the FSA) failures in the performance of its gatekeeping functions.

A poignant example is the appointment of Johnny Cameron, ex-chairman of the Global Banking and Markets (GBM) at the Royal Bank of Scotland. Johnny Cameron headed the GBM division from 2001 until the bank's near collapse in 2008. He also joined the RBS board in 2006 in recognition of the significant rise in GBM profits from its investment activities in wholesale markets products. Losses incurred by the GBM division played a significant contribution to the bank's demise, eroding its capital base once the market conditions turned sour and the unviability of the structured products became apparent (FSA, 2011: 33). The scale of the losses reflected a poor strategic decision to expand the business and a flawed response to emerging problems, including through a 'bias to optimism'; flawed risk management, control, and reporting processes; and senior management occasionally displaying 'flawed understanding of key aspects of the risks being taken' (FSA, 2011: 32). The control failings within the GBM division led to enforcement investigations into both Mr Cameron's personal culpability as well as into any appointment and delegation omissions made by the then-CEO Fred Goodwin (FSA, 2011). The investigation questioned Mr Cameron's competence and appointment to the role, since his principal experience was in credit and corporate banking rather than in traded markets. This caused concern that there was an unreasonable risk that 'traded markets issues were not adequately managed and reported to the Board' (FSA, 2011: 369). Ultimately, the FSA found that the delegation was not unreasonable as Mr Cameron was assisted by staff with relevant expertise, so it did not find that he was not competent judged by the prevailing standards at that time (FSA, 2011: 406). However, the FSA's report into the failure of the RBS also acknowledged its own shortcomings in assessing managerial competence through its approval process, concluding that Mr Cameron would not have met its 'current standards for a new approval' (FSA, 2011: 406). The report signalled a regulatory movement towards a more robust approach to the approval of senior managers, with a greater focus on assessing their competence and expertise for the post rather than only their integrity (FSA, 2011: 30).

While these changes may have been underway, further high-profile examples in the immediate crisis aftermath uncover continuing problems in the approval discretionary decision-making. Such was the approval of Reverend Paul Flowers as chair of the Co-Operative Bank (Co-Op) in 2010. His appointment came under scrutiny after the collapse of the Co-Op Bank acquisition of 632 branches by Lloyds Banking Group in April 2013 (known as 'Project Verde'). This acquisition was meant to cement the Co-Op as a major challenger bank (Treasury Committee, 2014a: para. 34). Yet the deal collapsed only six weeks before it took place as a £1.5 billion capital shortfall was uncovered at the Co-Op, showing ambitious expansion plans amid a precarious prudential health. The Treasury Committee Report from the inquiry into the collapsed sale identified serious governance failures in the running of the bank, including lack of financial services experience by several board members (Treasury Committee, 2014a: para. 203). The report stated that Mr Flowers 'embodied' the 'deficient composition of Co-op Bank's governance' and 'lacked both the desirable experience and the minimum essential skills' (para. 205). The Committee particularly criticised the regulator for not adopting a more scrutinising approach regarding the approval of Mr Flowers, with accusations that the interview consisted of an 'hour and a half of general chit-chat' (Treasury Committee, 2014b: Ev 222), and for ultimately permitting his appointment. The inquiry labelled the failings of the Co-Op Bank's board an 'indictment of the discredited Approved Persons Regime' (Treasury Committee, 2014c: Chairman's Comments).

Finally, the PCBS inquiry into the LIBOR scandal revealed inadequacies within the FSA's approval of Mr Bob Diamond to the post of CEO of Barclays – the first penalised bank for the LIBOR misconduct.[27] The FSA was inadequately communicating to firms the concerns it had regarding the senior managers it was minded to approve, including its concerns on their risk appetite and what it required of the firm to put in place as remedial steps. Until his promotion, Mr Diamond held various other senior positions at Barclays, and to be able progress to the most senior role in 2005, he required a new CF1 (CEO) approval. The then CEO of the FSA, Mr Hector Sants, expressed concerns about Bob Diamond's 'attitude to risk and a tendency to "push the limits"' (Parliamentary Commission on Banking Standards, 2013: para. 124) in the areas of business where he was directly involved. In addition, in its approval letter to Barclays, the FSA set out four issues that they expected the board to address in its ongoing governance and oversight of Bob Diamond, including expectations of increased level of engagement by Bob Diamond with regulators. The FSA concerns were 'not, however, serious enough to prevent the regulator from approving his appointment', rendering 'Barclays to regard the points raised by Mr Sants as "issues" rather than "concerns"' (Parliamentary Commission on Banking Standards, 2013: para. 124). The PCBS concluded that 'on the basis of the evidence it is unclear whether Barclays "got the message"' (Parliamentary Commission on Banking Standards, 2013: para. 124). The serious misconduct of Barclays in the rigging of the LIBOR benchmark rendered Mr Diamond to resign from the position under a serious pressure in July 2012.

27 Barclays Bank Plc FN27/06/2012.

The mistakes by the predecessor FSA and the lessons learnt led to the strengthening of the approval process regarding the gatekeeping philosophies and the approval procedure. The key benchmark of the approval regime, the 'fit and proper' test, did not undergo changes in legal drafting; what changed was the implementation policy and its application 'on the ground'. These changes started emerging in 2008–2009 and hence preceded the legislative interventions with the introduction of the landmark Senior Managers and Certification Regime (SMCR). Policy-wise, the approval process was re-conceptualised as one of the FCA's 'early intervention' mechanisms, enabling it to 'address risks before they emerge and intervene early to protect consumers' (FCA, 2013c: 15). The 'fit and proper' test also aimed to support the incoming FCA's growing interventionism in corporate cultures by enabling an ex ante screening and judgements on the applicants' skills, capabilities, and outlook towards the regulatory requirements, and towards promoting a consumer-minded culture, risk management, and product design (FCA, 2013c: 15).

In practice, the application of the three prongs of the 'fit and proper' test shifted towards an increased scrutiny of managers' competence, next to their integrity (Black, 2011). Previous considerations of an individual's suitability for a managerial post predominately concerned assessments of integrity through, for example, any evidence of previous regulatory or disciplinary contraventions, criminal convictions, involvement in insolvent firms, and similar.[28] Post-crisis, the 'fit and proper' considerations expanded, with a greater focus on assessing the individual's competence, relevant skills, and experience for the roles. These were the areas where the regulator had failed to exercise a more probing approach in the past, as seen in the examples of Johnny Cameron and Paul Flowers:

> There was then this decisive change after the financial crisis, when the regulator did a lot of internal soul searching. This is also what led to the strengthening of the Approved Persons Regime. Now they are looking into: 'Do you have the right background? Do you understand the business? Do you understand the company?'
>
> (LawyerFR11)

The broadening of the 'fit and proper' assessments also included a deeper regulatory engagement with individuals' risk appetite and understanding of the risks behind the business model of their firm. For example, an individual was refused approval as they were 'blasé about the risks' behind the complex business model of the firm, showing an inadequate understanding of the company's business activities (LawyerFR20).

The shift towards assessing competence and relevant experience is in line with the adoption of the 'judgement-based' (Ferran, 2011) regulation policy

28 See further, FCA Handbook FIT 2.1.

approach. It strengthened the role of the approval process as an intervention mechanism to prevent the crystallisation of regulatory risks through reaching deeper into the corporate governance of financial firms. The shifts also represented part of the broader regulatory objectives to raise the expectations and standards regarding individual accountability, as embedded in the Senior Managers Regime at the legislative level. For example, in their oral evidence to the Project Verde inquiry, the then chief regulators, Clive Adamson and Andrew Bailey, confirmed that an individual with as little financial experience as Mr Flowers would 'not be appointed as Chairman of a bank today' (Treasury Committee, 2014c). The changed interpretation of the 'fit and proper' criteria and, as will be seen next, the changed procedural aspects of the approval process also had the potential to signal to regulated firms that there were now heightened regulatory expectations of hiring quality managers at top positions in financial institutions.

Strengthened procedural aspects of the approval process

The approval procedure was itself strengthened due to the previous gatekeeping shortcomings. One safeguard was the introduction of an interview with the applicant, next to the written approval application, at the discretion of the FCA approvals team. The practice of interviewing senior managers started in 2007–2008 (Lawyer02), a timeline that correlates with the FSA's movement towards a more stringent approval process (see FSA, 2011; also, Black, 2011). During these interviews, a practice developed to seek attestations from senior managers on the scope of their responsibilities as SIF holders through signing written statements as well as to capture this on the interview recording:

> It is a statement that the FSA gives to you to sign, as a part of the SIF approval procedure, in which your signature says that you are responsible for x, y, z, as part of your SIF position. It is a complicated process, and I have coached people through it. This attestation means that you agreed you'd be responsible for x, y, z. And you've said this on tape. This blocks possible exit routes. Afterwards, when something happens, it is difficult to argue, 'I wasn't responsible for that', when it's on tape and the FSA has it.
>
> (LawyerFR11)

Much like the attestations requested from firms to assure that certain compliance processes were in place, the approval-related attestations also preceded the legislative interventions of the SMCR. These attestations had a comparable effect to the incoming statement of responsibilities under the SMCR. Again, this regulatory practice developed endogenously, showing that the preventative tracing of decision-making lines to hold managers accountable if things go wrong was possible within the existing gatekeeping powers of the regulator. What pushed towards the use of these powers was the resolve towards establishing individual accountability as an enforcement priority. The introduction of the statement of responsibilities gave this endogenous practice a top-down sanction and a wider footing in terms of its signalling effects as an obligation enshrined in legislation.

A further safeguard was the greater involvement of more senior regulatory staff in the interviewing of senior appointments at major institutions (Treasury Committee, 2014b, evidence by Andrew Bailey). For example, in the oral evidence to the Project Verde inquiry, Andrew Bailey, the then CEO of the Prudential Regulation Authority, stated that he does 'the interviewing with a very senior adviser, typically, and that is a very big contrast to the arrangements that were in place when the Reverend Flowers was approved' (Treasury Committee, 2014b). In interviews, applicants could be questioned on their risk appetite, skills, and to validate their fitness: for example, 'Why they have left an institution? What was the reason for resigning?' (Lawyer02). This line of questioning was important to ascertain whether individuals have left due to being subjected to the private justice systems (Parker, 2002) of the firm.

Still, these procedural safeguards were of note only for a very small subset of applicants due to the discretionary and risk-based nature of the approval process. According to FOI disclosures, in the years 2016 to 2020, the FCA conducted an average number of 173 interviews per year (FCA, 2020).[29] Further, out of 19,238 persons who were approved in 2016, only 77 (0.4 per cent) were approved after an interview, whereas only 0.9 per cent of the applicants were approved after an interview in both 2017 and 2018 (respectively, 169 out of 18,963 and 145 out of 16,799) (FCA, 2018).[30] Whether an applicant was invited to an interview depended on several factors: the size of the firm, the seniority and level of risk of the post (high-risk roles were commonly subject to interviews), how routine the approval was, and how experienced the applicant firm was in submitting approval applications (interview data). High-risk roles were interpreted not only with reference to their responsibilities and where the individual sat in the corporate structure but also with reference to the sector of the market. Here again, risk-based supervisory considerations shaped the interviewees selection. The highest number of interviews were conducted with applicants from typical systemic risk sectors, such as retail banks and wholesale firms (including banks) (FCA, 2020), but the FCA also led on interviews with candidates from niche sectors that topped its supervisory priorities at a given point in time. For example, the FCA considered the contracts for differences (CFD) sector as high-risk (FCA, 2017b). An applicant for a top compliance role in a CFD firm was scrutinised by two interview panels regarding their competence for the role. The vetting concerned whether they had a detailed understanding of the financial crime risks specific to the firm's business model and a proactive risk approach. Procedurally, risk assessment considerations led

29 The data for 2020 is until 3 November 2020.
30 The data for 2018 is until 29 November 2018.

to varying decision-making times. Routine cases could be decided in as little as a week, whereas firms and roles that were high-risk, moving to a new line of business or getting a new CEO, could take up to several weeks and two interviews, both by the FCA and the PRA (LawyerFR20).[31]

Experienced financial institutions commonly hired external lawyers to draft the application and prepare the individual for the interview, especially if there was a difficulty with the application. Contentious regulatory lawyers also commonly got involved where the FCA was minded to refuse or had already refused the approval. The 'mind to refuse' decision could be first challenged in front of the internal Regulatory Transactions Committee (RTC), composed of heads of the enforcement and supervision divisions. The RTC acted as a vetting committee for an independent and additional level of scrutiny of regulatory decisions that prevented regulated access to the financial markets (approvals of individuals, authorisations of firms, and variations of the permission to conduct regulated activities [Lawyer02]). Failure to reach a positive decision at the RTC allowed a second review mechanism at the Regulatory Decisions Committee.

The 'quasi-enforcement' function of the approval process

The substantive and procedural changes to the approval process initiated in the post-crisis period led to stricter approval requirements, but also to a subtle development of a 'quasi-enforcement' function of the gatekeeping process. This happened where the FSA/FCA would refuse an approval due to concerns over the individual's past behaviour at their previous financial institution but where it had not undertaken an enforcement action for those past failings (e.g. to impose a prohibition order or withdraw their approval) – due to a lack of either evidence or resources. Even where the regulator had only indicated its intentions to refuse the approval, there was a similar outcome as the applicant would then withdraw their application. This meant that the practical effects of prohibition orders to prevent access to the financial markets could be equally achieved through the approval route in a way that was less contentious and less evidence- and resources-demanding for the regulator. The approval process could be used as an alternate means of achieving an enforcement-like goal 'but without having to go through all the rigmarole of enforcement' (Lawyer12).

The 'quasi-enforcement' nature of the approval process developed to address the accountability deficit regarding senior managers in the failed banks. Hector Sants, the ex-CEO of the FSA, stated in oral evidence to the Treasury Committee's independent review of the RBS failure that as far as he was concerned, if any of the RBS individuals submitted a future application to work at an FCA-regulated firm, he 'would not consider them to be competent on the basis of the track record demonstrated' (Treasury Committee, 2012c).

31 According to s. 61(3A) FSMA, the FCA needs to deliver a decision on the approval application within three months from receiving it.

Individuals in senior management posts at crisis-associated failing institutions were unlikely to be approved, even if no public action was taken against them for decision-making or control failures. Supporting these outcomes was the reluctance of firms to engage in contentious regulatory conversations over problematic managers:

> I was preparing a director of one of the big banks that failed who was applying to be a non-executive of one of my clients. The FCA just looked at my client and said, 'Are you really satisfied that you want to employ someone who was a non-executive director at [name of failed bank]? Have you really satisfied yourselves [they are] fit and proper?' We didn't proceed. The regulator was, in effect, saying – you know the English expression 'give a dog a bad name'? 'We think you, the firm, have got a very high hurdle to satisfy us that this person is fit and proper because they were associated with one of the banks that has failed.' Who wants to have a fight over that?
>
> (Lawyer02)

A high-profile example of the use of the gatekeeping regime as a mechanism to achieve post-crisis individual accountability where an enforcement action was not feasible was the case of Johnny Cameron. The investigation into his culpability for the demise of RBS did not result in a formal enforcement action. Though the regulator labelled his decisions as poor, in retrospect, it could not establish that they were 'outside of the bounds of reasonableness at the time' (FSA, 2011: 32). Instead, Cameron's case was concluded with an informal settlement in May 2010 in which he undertook not to take up any managerial positions in an authorised firm or any further full-time employment in the financial services industry, and the FSA agreed not to take any enforcement action against him (FSA, 2011: 354). The settlement was reached without the FSA making any regulatory findings against him and without an admission of guilt. Yet even before the settlement was reached, news reports indicated that Cameron had been blocked in the first quarter of 2009 in efforts to take on a role with independent investment bank Greenhill (Kleinman, 2009). The talks to join Greenhill were discontinued after the FSA indicated that it would not push through the approval for his appointment, despite not indicating that it was moving towards imposing a prohibition order against Mr Cameron.

The use of the gatekeeping regime for enforcement functions should be accounted for when attaching blame upon regulators for the relative lack of public enforcement outcomes or more serious public enforcement outcomes against senior managers. With it as a risk mitigation strategy, regulators could still ensure individual accountability for past mistakes and recklessness short of liability for fines or prohibition orders, albeit only if the individual wished to apply for another regulated role in financial services. These practices exemplify public regulation 'in private', and while achieving a certain regulatory outcome, the confidential nature of the approval regime lacks the general deterrence, symbolic, and reputational functions of formal enforcement outcomes.

As argued in what follows, enforcement actions against individual actors have a strong potential for deterrence and reputational benefits for regulatory interventions, capturing the attention of both the financial markets and the general public.

The more intense social control of corporate managers through investigations and penalties

In the aftermath of the crisis, the FCA developed an enforcement philosophy and accompanying investigative practices toward inspecting individuals, alongside their firms, for regulatory breaches, thus individualising responsibility for non-compliance (Jordanoska, 2021). This marked a stark difference from the pre–'credible deterrence' era, in which most of the enforcement actions targeted corporate responsibility. According to one participant, there was sometimes a sense that firms were sacrificed for particular individuals (LawyerFR01). The enforcement docket against senior individuals predominately consisted of prohibition orders against dishonest individuals in smaller firms, where the individual's and the firm's liability were significantly entangled, or of fines for market abuse-type activities which only centre on individual liability.

Actions against senior management became a key enforcement priority of the post-crisis regulatory activism and the 'credible deterrence' agenda: 'We do believe that one of the key elements of credible deterrence and what we care about is actions against individuals' (Regulator01). The focus on senior management was closely tied to the original concern of the 'credible deterrence' policymaking to improve individual liability for market abuse and insider dealing (Jordanoska, 2021). By late 2008, one of the FSA's 'strategic priorities' was an increased focus on bringing actions against individuals at higher levels of corporate decision-making (Green, 2015).

However, the early post-crisis years were marked by a mismatch between the regulatory enforcement philosophy and the 'regulatory craft' (Sparrow, 2000) that was needed to enliven it. The Green Report (Green, 2015) revealed a 'materially flawed' decision-making process in the enforcement referral and the opening of formal investigations against senior managers. The report reviewed the FSA's dealing with the crisis-related failings at the bailed-out HBOS bank and the enforcement considerations over the bank's senior managers in the period 2008–2012. It revealed that Peter Cummings, then CEO of the Corporate Division, was the only investigated (and then sanctioned) former HBOS senior manager. The FSA had not considered investigating any other former board members (e.g. the group CEO or chairman) or individuals at the bank's other troubled divisions. The main criticism was on the FSA's reliance on the 'probability of success' and 'importance' as tests for opening a formal investigation with the 'probability of success' concerning the likelihood of the case resulting in a public outcome (Green, 2015: 15–16). The probabilistic calculations of success included needing to be satisfied of 'getting a good result' before an investigation was opened and taking on cases that had 'a good chance of winning' (interview with Mr Jones [Green, 2015: 16]). In HBOS, the non-compliance of others was perceived difficult to prove, and potential cases too fraught with challenges: '[T]he ethos was that these would be difficult to bring, so in a sense, why bother? The responsibility of individuals was sort of gleaned over, as in a sort of accepted defeat that this wouldn't lead to success anyway' (LawyerFR20).

The enforcement ethos, policies, and procedures started shifting around 2012–2013, precipitated by regulatory blame and deterrence-related considerations. There were already significant public criticisms following the HBOS enforcement actions and their limited scope (the final notices against Peter Cummings and the bank were published in 2012), prompting the Green Review in 2014. Enforcement staff were already anticipating that the report coming out of the review would be critical. This was coupled with the influence of the inquiries undertaken by the parliamentary accountability bodies, the Treasury Select Committee, and the Parliamentary Commission on Banking Standards.

A second factor was the realisation that fining firms was an insufficient deterrent, and that actions against individuals had great deterrent and transformative values.[32] In its Enforcement Guide, the FCA emphasised that deterrence would most effectively be achieved by making the senior managers that have failed to meet the FCA standards 'realise the consequences of their actions'.[33] Furthermore, enforcement actions against high-profile senior executives served a 'signal case' (Thornton et al., 2005) function as they attracted significant interest not only from the industry but also from the media and the general public: 'actions against individuals are the best news the FSA ever produces' (Lawyer03).

The 'regulatory craft' was built up through multipronged actions of organisational restructuring, policy changes, and building up the investigative skills of staff. An internal expert committee was established to improve the success of actions against individuals and increase the rigour of the process. Staff were trained in how to acquire the evidence that shows individual culpability, for example, that it was necessary to request the individual notebooks of board meetings attendees and not only the minutes. These were commonly 'very anodyne' (LawyerFr20), not revealing much on who said what and who knew what. Internal policymaking resulted in more stringent decision-making procedures and requirements of investigators to more thoroughly justify their discretionary decision-making that excluded pursuing culpable individuals (McDermott, 2013; Symington, 2017; Jordanoska, 2021):

> When the case team would reach stage 1 and set the papers to be shown to more senior members of staff, they could expect questions around

32 FCA Enforcement Guide 2.11.2.
33 FCA Enforcement Guide 2.11.1.

> why individuals were not included in the investigations. The thinking was that this would focus minds on individual culpability and who to hold responsible. Same with the case referral processes and document: 'Why were individuals not referred?' The aim was to show evidence of rigour in arriving to a decision on why individuals were not investigated or suggested for a penalty.
>
> (LawyerFR20)

In practice, this meant a reinterpretation of the thresholds for opening formal investigations, leading to an increased trend of investigating individuals alongside their firms (Jordanoska, 2021) as well as an increased focus on penalising individuals for corporate crime issues. In response to the recommendations made by the Parliamentary Commission on Banking Standards (Parliamentary Commission on Banking Standards, 2013), the FCA stated that it was considering 'actions against individuals throughout all enforcement investigations' (FCA, 2013b: 10). The trend of inspecting individuals became a common enforcement practice, confirmed by all interviewees, and this also meant inspections high up the corporate hierarchy: '[N]ow enforcement has a mandate . . . that in whatever case it has, to also look whether there are any individuals that can be held responsible' (LawyerFR11).

At the micro-level, and behind the veil of confidential investigation practices, the 'credible deterrence' priority of inspecting individuals was very much alive. The FCA's practice of immediately tracing the lines of decision-making and probing senior managers could serve a powerful deterrence function on its own. Research in other areas has shown that compliance increases after inspections (e.g. Gunningham et al., 2005; Short & Toffel, 2008). The FCA's determination to inspect individuals could have removed any perceptions of immunity or ability to hide behind the corporate shield – 'to the extent that senior management within firms feel that they are potentially in the firing line every time something goes wrong; they're much more motivated to avoid problems from occurring in the first place' (LawyerFR03).

The docket of published cases in the period 2008–2017 confirms the increased enforcement focus on individuals, matching the 'credible deterrence' discourse. There were more regulatory actions against individuals than against firms in most of the years during this period (except for a close second in 2013 and 2014). In some years, actions against individuals represented the bulk of the docket; for example, 77.5 per cent of all substantive cases in 2016 were against individuals, 74 per cent in 2010, and 73 per cent in 2011.[34] The

34 These percentages were calculated by coding data on fines and public censures against firms and individuals, redress against firms, and prohibition orders, withdrawal of approvals, and combinations of these against individuals in the period 2008–2017. The numbers, therefore, exclude refusal of approvals for individuals and cancellation orders for firms. Penalties that had

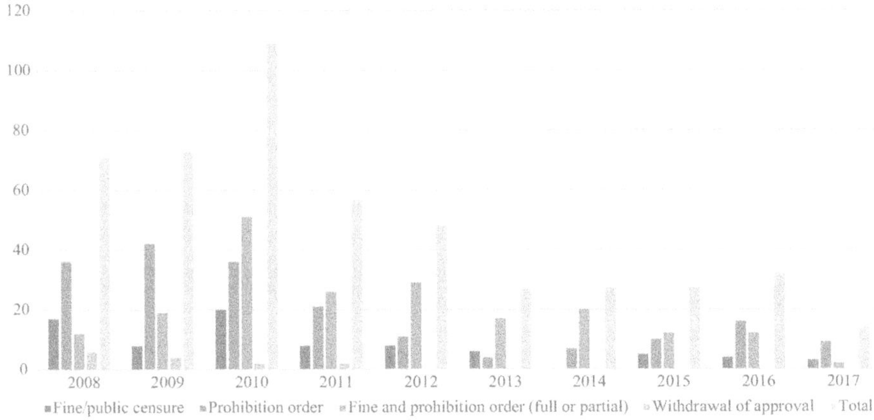

Figure 6.1 Types of sanctions against individuals (2008–2017).

calendar year of 2010 represents the peak of FSA/FCA enforcement activity against individuals in real numbers (n = 107).

Figure 6.1 provides a breakdown of the different sanctions against individuals in the calendar years 2008–2017, organised around fines/public censures, prohibition orders (full and from a specific controlled function, such as, for example, from performing a significant influence function or compliance function), combined fines/public censures and prohibition orders (full and partial), and withdrawal of approvals. The figure clusters together fines and public censures since public censures were not imposed frequently in practice. They also did not feature prominently as an independent tool of enforcement (to punish less-serious deviance) but as a substitute, when the FCA was initially minded to impose a monetary penalty (the FCA would even indicate a specific amount or state that the behaviour would have attracted 'a significant penalty'), but it realised that the money could not be collected when the individual produced verifiable evidence of financial hardship. Individuals were punished only by a censure because of a combination of mitigating factors: they had left the industry; they had taken 'immediate and proactive remedial steps', including training; they made no profit; they had no recidivism history; or they had lesser *mens rea*. The discussion in the next section shows that, in similar circumstances, individuals were only warned in private. This indicates that, in practice, other investigators' considerations, such as equity, policy, or resources could shift the response from private to public.

Several trends indicating a more punitive outlook towards (certain categories) of individuals can be observed from the data. First, there was an

been appealed at the Tribunal or at the Court of Appeal were allocated to the year of the issuing of the decision notice rather than to when the Tribunal made the decision and the issuing of the final notice.

increasing number of prohibition orders. The numbers were highest in the years 2008–2011 (49, 57, 85, and 48, respectively), and these reflect the increased enforcement actions against fraudulent mortgage brokers. Second, there was also an increased practice of combining different enforcement powers against individuals, such as a fine and a full or partial prohibition order or a withdrawal of an approval. Third, the data show a drastic decrease in imposing only withdrawals of approval as a penalty; in fact, withdrawals were not awarded as a single penalty since 2011. The more serious penalties are an indicator of the more punitive outlook, but also of an enforcement practice that targeted more serious misconduct, which could attract a partial or full prohibition order.

The crafting of managers as 'objects of control' was evidenced also in enforcement actions, in which the FCA showed its determination to test the limits to which senior individuals could be held responsible for systems and controls failings. A landmark case in this respect is *Pottage v FSA FS/2010/33*, where the FSA unsuccessfully attempted to fine John Pottage, the CEO of the of UBS's UK Wealth Management business, for supervisory failings over unauthorised trading at the branch. The FSA had already fined UBS bank for allowing the unauthorised trading. *Pottage* was the first time that the FSA had tried to fine a senior manager for inadequate supervision and responsibility for the firm's systems and controls failings rather than their own wrongdoing. The FSA/FCA alleged that Mr Pottage had breached APER Statement of Principle 7 (failing to take reasonable steps to ensure that the business of the firm in his responsibility complied with the regulatory requirements and standards) in failing to undertake systematic review of risk management and governance upon his appointment.

The precedent-setting nature of the case meant that a successful outcome for the FSA/FCA would lead to a new and more interventionist interpretation of the rules on supervisory procedures. The FSA stated in its opening submissions that it viewed 'these proceedings as being of particular importance in establishing a benchmark by which senior managers who carry out SIF controlled functions in medium-high and high-impact financial services firms will be judged' (Berwin Leighton Paisner, 2011: 2). Ultimately, however, the Tribunal concluded that Mr Pottage's steps were reasonable, so APER fault could not be established. Yet the action against John Pottage served as a 'signal case' (Thornton et al., 2005) for the industry, inciting talks on the FSA's appetite for senior management accountability and the 'lessons learned'. In many respects, this case anticipated the subsequent legislative changes through the instalment of the duty of responsibility of managers to prevent non-compliance by their supervisees.

The emphasis on senior management responsibility conveyed the changes in the regulatory perceptions of the causes of corporate crime in the financial markets (or, again, the underlying 'theories of deviance'). Underpinning these shifts was 'moral entrepreneurship': constructing individuals as enforcement targets and 'objects of control' in every case of organisational non-compliance.

These signalled a deeper regulatory reach into the culture and organisational decision-making of individual corporations.

The discrepancy between regulatory goals and public outcomes

Despite the organisational statements of increasing scrutiny of senior managers and industry perceptions of these threats, the extent to which the FCA's focus on individual culpability corresponded to public enforcement outcomes is questionable. On aggregate, there were more enforcement actions against individuals than firms. However, it is necessary to disentangle these data and analyse the types of misconduct for which individuals were pursued. To do this, I coded the final notices against individuals for the nature of the breaches and for any links with a comparable enforcement action against their firms.

Figure 6.2 shows the percentage of enforcement actions against individuals for the period 2008–2017 according to the nature of their misconduct: personal or organisational. Personal misconduct includes non-compliance that occurred in an organisational setting but did not involve breaches by the employing firm and where any benefits accrued solely to the breaching individual. This includes, for example, personal non-compliance with the 'fit and proper' regulatory requirements (such as other legal proceedings affecting the individual's integrity), market abuse infringements (such as disclosing confidential information to clients), or acting against the internal compliance rules

Figure 6.2 Percentage of cases against individuals for personal and organisational-type misconduct.

of the firm for personal benefit (such as through providing false information to the firm's compliance office). Organisational-type misconduct includes the cases where an individual was sanctioned for being involved in the regulatory breach by the firm. These cases occurred in an organisational setting, using the structures of the firm for the benefit of the firm – though it is often very difficult to disaggregate corporate from personal benefit in cases of complex corporate crime (Jordanoska & Lord, 2020). Compiling the enforcement docket on organisational-type misconduct was a complex task, and it included two stages. I included all the cases where the firm was also formally sanctioned for the same breach either with a financial penalty or a censure. Additionally, there was a set of cases where the FSA/FCA sanctioned a manager but where the firm was not fined for a regulatory breach because it either went into liquidation (this includes the four individuals whose financial institutions failed for crisis-associated reasons), its regulatory permissions were cancelled, or its funds were reserved for redress. In a final set of cases, the firm had not been fined for the individual's regulatory breach but it had received a supervisory notice conveying regulatory concerns on the same misconduct, its compliance failings were referred to in findings by a skilled persons report, or the final notice on the individual stated that they were fined for being ***knowingly concerned*** in the firm's contraventions or for failing to take reasonable steps (under APER 7), thus causing the firm to be non-compliant. These sets of cases were also included in the organisational-type misconduct bracket, as there was a statement with a regulatory reprimand for the firm in the individual's final notice or the misconduct fulfilled the organisational nature criteria discussed earlier.

The data show that cases of organisational-type misconduct dominated the enforcement actions against individuals across most of the period, with the exceptions of 2009, 2016, and 2017. The percentage of cases where individuals were sanctioned for organisational non-compliance moves between the lowest 29 per cent (2017) and the highest 74 per cent of all cases in 2013, with an average of 53 per cent. These numbers indicate that, on aggregate, most enforcement resources spent for pursuing culpable individuals were expanded on tackling individual liability for organisational non-compliance. This is in line with the 'credible deterrence' enforcement priorities of pursuing culpable individuals in the organisational context and establishing individual accountability.

However, it is necessary to dig deeper into the statistics to understand the nuances of enforcement actions for organisational-type non-compliance. I was interested to measure the instances in which both a firm and associated individuals were sanctioned for the same regulatory breach. This provides some insights into how the enforcement philosophy of spinning off an investigation into a firm into associated individuals was transposed into public enforcement outcomes. These data are presented in Figure 6.3. In the first column, I calculated the ratio between the cases where firms and associated individuals were sanctioned and the total number of cases where firms were sanctioned. There were additional challenges in compiling these data, as the corporate

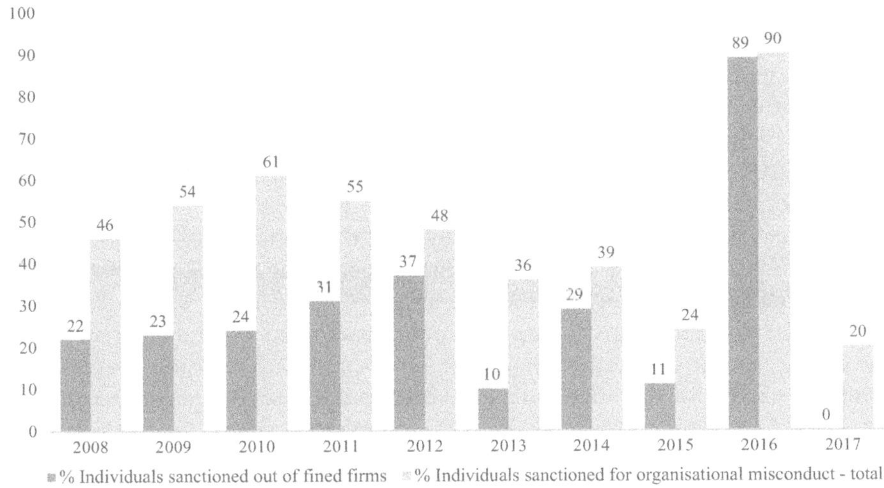

Figure 6.3 Percentage of actions against individuals within actions for firms.

and individual cases were commonly not resolved at the same time due to the differential stances of more common cooperation and settlement by firms and more common adversarialism by individuals. To mitigate against this, I traced all individuals associated with a specific breach by a firm over time, so the year in the figure corresponds to the year the firm was fined rather than the year when the individual was sanctioned. I counted instances rather than the number of persons, which means that even if, for example, four individuals were pursued for the same corporate breach, I only counted this as one instance.

The data are uneven throughout the period; 2016 is the outlier year, where most actions against firms were accompanied by actions against individuals associated with those firms (89 per cent of all cases on firms). In other years, actions against individuals were undertaken in a relatively much smaller percentage of the cases taken against firms, ranging from no such cases in 2017 to 31 per cent of cases where both the firm and related individual(s) were sanctioned in 2011 and 2012. The average percentage of cases across the years where both the firm and related individuals were sanctioned was 28 per cent of all cases against firms. This means that there was a public enforcement outcome on associated culpable individuals in only a very small number of enforcement cases taken against firms for corporate misconduct. The resolve to spin off an ongoing investigation into corporate non-compliance into associated individuals did not have the expected effects in an increased number of formal outcomes (i.e. fines and prohibition orders).

The second column in Figure 6.3 expands these data. It includes also instances where an individual was sanctioned but where an enforcement action could not or was not taken against the firm (because of bankruptcy, cancellation, redress, etc.), though where there was a regulatory reprimand on the firm's non-compliance. These instances were added both to the tally of firms with associated reprimanded individuals and to the total number of firms. The average percentage of cases where both the firm and related individuals suffered adverse consequences now raises to 47 per cent which still represents a much smaller portion of the cases where corporates were found at fault. The year 2016 remains to be the outlier year, but now these actions represent the bulk of cases in 2009–2011.

The qualitative and quantitative analysis of the notices also did not show a more significant increase of fines against managers at the bigger institutions in conjunction with their firms across all years. Most cases where the FSA/FCA had enforced against a large firm and associated individuals concerned lower-level employees rather than high-level corporate decision-makers. For example, except for the fines and partial prohibition orders against David Caplin, then CEO, and Jeremy Kraft, then compliance officer, at the relatively smaller interdealer broker Martins for failings related to the manipulation of LIBOR,[35] in none of the involved banks were senior executives pursued, only traders. This was also replicated in the cases where there was enforcement against individuals and no fine against the firm but a regulatory reprimand. For example, the peak of actions against individuals in 2009 and 2010 can be explained through the significant enforcement against fraudulent mortgage brokers with both prohibition orders and fines (also Figure 6.1). In these cases, the FSA had fined and/or prohibited directors or other approved persons of relatively smaller intermediary firms.

The exception to this is a very modest sample of enforcement actions against high-profile market participants, for example, Peter Cummings, the then director of HBOS Corporate Division, for being *knowingly concerned* in the contravention by HBOS of Principle 3 (£500,000 and a prohibition order);[36] Tidjane Thiam, CEO of Prudential, for being *knowingly concerned* in the contravention of Prudential of Principle 11 (public censure);[37] Achilles Macris, then Head of CIO International for JPMorgan Chase Bank, whose failings to be open and cooperative with the Authority (in breach of APER Statement of Principle 4) contributed to JPMorgan being fined for breaches of Principle 11, among other breaches (£792,900);[38] and Stewart Owen, then CEO of Keydata, found by the Tribunal to have had a primary responsibility for the now-defunct Keydata mis-selling complex financial products (£76 million).[39]

The relatively low number of cases where an enforcement action was taken against both the firm and associated individuals, and in particular

35 David Caplin FN22/01/15; Jeremy Kraft FN22/01/15; Martin Brokers (UK) Ltd (Martins) FN22/01/15.

36 FN12/09/12.

37 FN27/03/13.

38 FN09/02/16.

39 *Stewart Owen Ford and Mark John Owen v The Financial Conduct Authority* [2018].

senior managers, can be explained by several interrelated factors: evidentiary, policy-related, and interactionist. First, it may be the case that, on the facts, no evidence was found on individual culpability for the firm's failures. However, as discussed earlier, financial regulators commonly faced significant evidentiary difficulties to build cases on the culpability of senior managers. In the first period after the crisis, this was aggravated by the apprehensive and public success–oriented referral policies (Green, 2015), as well as the inadequate staff experience that impeded collecting evidence on culpable individuals.

Further challenges emerge from the tripartite interactions between the individual and firm, the individual and regulator, and the firm and regulator (Jordanoska, 2021) in regulatory enforcement that increase the uncertainty of outcomes. During joint investigations into corporate and individual accountability, firms may attempt to 'corporatise' the enforcement proceedings against the individual, launching corporate strategies to deflect the claims of individual responsibility or binding more closely the corporate and the individual case together (Jordanoska, 2021). Some of these strategies exacerbate the evidentiary challenges for enforcers by controlling the flow of information to the regulator. This can be done through providing carefully managed reports from internal investigations that obscure senior management involvement, scapegoating tactics, or maintaining tight oversight and control over the individual's disclosures to regulators (Jordanoska, 2021: 309–311). How corporate responses further mediated the construction of individual accountability for regulatory non-compliance through their private justice systems and the practices of *constructing non-compliance* is discussed later in this chapter. At the same time, at the individual–regulator level of interactions, actions against individual targets were also more uncertain due to their more common adversarial stance, challenging the enforcement action internally or at the Tribunal. Gava (2022) has similarly found that regulatory actions targeting individuals were at a higher risk of appeal in court in a cross-country analysis covering 18 other financial regulators and 13 national jurisdictions.

Regulatory enforcement within and through 'private' regulatory interactions

Interactionist notions, and how they might have contributed to the stated discrepancy between official regulatory policies on individual accountability and the relatively few publicly visible outcomes, are employed again here to explore the process of issuing private warnings to resolve an enforcement case. Private warnings are a non-statutory enforcement tool in the guise of a letter that sets out the problematic issue and the regulatory concerns over the conduct of the target, but with no conclusive findings on whether a breach has taken place, despite possible evidence.[40] In terms of their punitiveness, private

40 FCA Enforcement Guide 7.6.

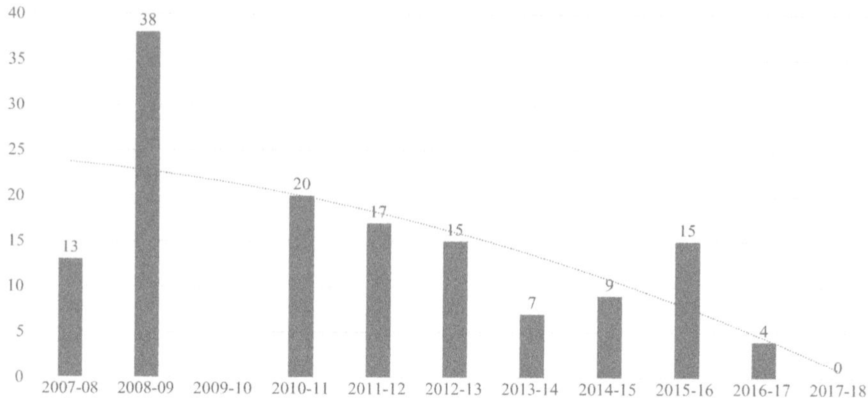

Figure 6.4 Private warnings distribution.

warnings are located at the lower end of the enforcement pyramid, as they attract no immediate adverse effects as a penalty or in adverse publicity. The process of issuing private warnings is confidential, and the letter is not made public. It encompasses performing regulatory enforcement functions within and through 'private' regulatory interactions.

Because of their confidential nature, private warning cases remain relatively unknown. Figure 6.1 provides some quantitative information on the distribution of private warnings issued by the enforcement team in the period 2007–2008 to 2017–2018.[41] The figure shows that, over the years, private warnings were imposed with varying frequency, with a significant peak in 2008–2009 (data are missing for 2009–2010). The FCA does not publish any information on the identity of the person or the condemned activities. The interviewees, both with experience as regulators and in private practice, observed that enforcement private warnings were more commonly issued against individuals than firms.

According to the official policy, private warnings were issued when the misconduct was considered *minor* in 'nature or degree, or where the person has taken full and immediate remedial action'.[42] This would indicate that they were imposed for behaviour that was considered less deviant but still warranted a reaction in which 'something will be kept on file'. The interview data, however, showed that private warnings were not used solely for sanctioning a *minor* misconduct but also for *evidentiary* and *resources* reasons in cases in which

41 The data for this figure were compiled from the FSA/FCA annual enforcement performance accounts, with two caveats: data for 2009–2010 and 2016–2017 were missing. Data for 2016–2017 were extracted from a freedom of information request (FOI6897, November 2019) on overall private warnings across 2016, so the actual number of enforcement private warnings in 2016–2017 may be even less.

42 FCA Enforcement Guide 7.6.3.

the enforcement division was either unable to fully prove the misconduct or unwilling to dispense further resources to achieve a public outcome.

In cases *of minor* violations, the regulator had evidence of a rule breach but deemed that it was not 'justified to take [public] action' (Lawyer02). Non-compliance was assessed as minor against the same 'seriousness' factors discussed in Chapter 3 on whether an issue is significant enough to merit self-reporting or whether a certain sample (of, for example, non-compliant files) crossed the 'normal deviancy' threshold to be considered 'serious' in supervisory activities. This confirms the 'shared interpretative community' (Black, 1997) established around serious or significant misconduct: though regulatees may not have always been able to assess whether they were acting according to regulatory standards, it might have been easier to assess whether they had committed serious misconduct.

For firms, *minor* violations were established when the detected misconduct fell below the standards of being widespread or systemic but had been committed in an area in which the FCA wanted to re-enforce a regulatory message. *Minor* violations were also established when the FCA assessed the misconduct as a risk to greater breaches if left untreated by any kind of enforcement action. For example, in one case, a firm was found in non-compliance with the CASS requirements since 'it had got a number of accounts and it had not recognised them as client money accounts. They had ten or twenty thousand pounds in them. This firm has billions, trillions all the time' (Lawyer02). Here, even though the firm had several non-compliant accounts, this misconduct was below the 'systemic' threshold and below the criteria for a formal penalty due to the small amount of money on them. Though the EFCD had evidence that the firm had not segregated its accounts and a breach had been committed, they opted for a private warning, stating only that the FCA believed 'there may be grounds to indicate you have breached CASS 7, a client money rule, and Principle 10 (the client assets principle, *n.b.*)'. Yet the firm was issued with an enforcement private warning rather than just being dealt with through supervisory means both because CASS breaches represented an important enforcement theme and because the size of the firm meant that significant amounts of clients' assets could have been exposed to risk if the firm was not made to 'stand up and listen' by the private warning.

For individuals, *minor* violations involved non-compliance that posed a lesser risk to the FCA's statutory objectives due to a perceived lesser *mens rea* (negligent, incompetent, or inattentive behaviour). This was consistent with the FCA's policy on fining in which negligent, inadvertent, or behaviour due to an error in law was weighed as having a lesser seriousness level than a deliberate one. For example, a lawyer described the circumstances in which their team successfully persuaded the enforcement staff that their client's misconduct of market manipulation should be penalised with only a private warning despite the ample evidence of various communications showing that the client was pushing up share prices. The defence argument was that the client's behaviour was not deliberate but rather a consequence of the fact that they 'didn't have a clue that what [they were] doing was wrong' (LawyerFR06), as they were young, had recently moved from the United States, and lacked proper training. The FCA had sufficient evidence to impose a fine and was initially minded to do so, but the negotiations ultimately resulted in a private warning.

The regulator's focus on a particularly important theme, such as the requirement to cooperate with the regulator, could also be the decisive factor for an individual's inattentive behaviour to escalate from a supervisory reprimand or no action at all to a private warning. In another case, an investment banker was censured for not being cooperative with the regulator, though it was the banker's client who was originally under a regulatory investigation. The banker was reckless in supplying six emails on a transaction requested by the FSA and found themselves under both a criminal investigation for knowingly misleading the FSA[43] and a regulatory investigation with a threat of a fine for breaching Principle 11. The outcome was a private warning despite the defence's legal advocacy disputing the banker's *mens rea* and arguing that they had been inattentive rather than outright non-cooperative.

Evidentiary considerations could form a reason for issuing a private warning (again, mostly to individuals) in cases where the FCA suspected serious misconduct but was unable to prove it to the standards required for a formal penalty (e.g. due to the established difficulties of tracing the decision-making tree or the higher *mens rea* requirements). Evidence of a lesser misconduct would then form the basis of the private warning decision: 'there were a number of individuals, some of them maybe didn't reach the threshold, but there was a reason to consider that a breach had happened' (LawyerFR20).

This reason behind issuing a private warning was a preventative one and in line with the FCA's focus on individual accountability. When the FCA was unable to impose a formal sanction, private warnings could be employed to indirectly monitor and control the individual's movements within the industry. First, this could be done through notifying the individual's employer of the decision, as this was something that the FCA could decide to do as a discretionary measure.[44] This could set in motion the firm's 'private justice' mechanisms, resulting in dismissal. Second, the fact that private warnings had to be disclosed to a new employer to obtain a new approval, or to an existing employer when promoted to a higher SIF, was used as leverage to closely monitor or even prevent the individual's movements, since 'most people with private warnings continue at their firms, but they would find it possibly difficult to move. Who wants to employ someone with a private warning?' (Lawyer02).

Resources considerations could lead to a private warning in cases where the seriousness of the misconduct merited a formal outcome (a fine or a prohibition order) but the enforcement staff were no longer pursuing the targeted

43 Section 177 FSMA.
44 FCA Enforcement Guide 7.14.

individual because they were leaving the industry either voluntarily or due to pressures 'never to work again'. These were issued for symbolic but also preventative reasons, since the FCA were 'not prepared to drop it entirely; they want something in the file, so if this person ever comes back, almost invariably, this person won't work again in the industry' (LawyerFR17). The private warning, therefore, represented a special concession for leaving the market, especially when the regulator was minded to issue a prohibition order.

These regulatory enforcement actions, performed within and through private interactions, were beneficial for both sides of the regulatory relationship. For the individual, such an outcome allowed an untarnished reputation. The private warning had an essentially symbolic rather than punitive function, confirming a decision already made by the individual. For the regulator, it allowed a more economically efficient enforcement whilst achieving the same outcome of removing problematic individuals from roles in financial institutions. Social control was achieved without expending resources on a formal action and without the uncertainties from possible challenges to the decision to issue a public sanction. Some interviewees commented that their experience with such private warnings was connected to the financial crisis and the banking collapses:

> We have had lots of private warnings in relation to the banking collapse with individuals who will fight because there is nothing that they are going to lose. The FSA just doesn't want the time and effort but also the adverse publicity, because there's going to be criticism of the quality of its supervision at the time. If these individuals fight, they are going to call every single supervisor and cross-examine them. The FSA just basically wants these guys to go away, and so it's a compromise position, very often even when the conduct clearly should have been going to enforcement.
>
> (LawyerFR10)

This practice might explain the spike in private warnings in the financial years 2008–2009 and 2010–2011 (data are missing for 2009–2010). It might also explain the lack of more visible formal enforcement actions against senior managers connected to the failings in the financial crisis, a point that has led to much criticism of the FSA. Coupled with the evidentiary difficulties discussed earlier, resource considerations might have led the FSA to deal with these executives through informal rather than formal sanctions yet to consider that the social control function has been achieved.

In the cases in which private warnings had been issued due to *resources considerations*, the FCA exchanged the evidence on the misconduct for an uncontested private warning. This is similar to what Baldwin (1985: 79–80) found in the magistrates' courts during plea bargaining, when the prosecution decides not to bring any evidence in exchange for a bind over order (a restraint order, and failure to keep it results in forfeiture of an agreed sum of money).

This also means that, in the enforcement pyramid, the severity of the penalty could also depend on issues of resources constraints and the need for more efficient rather than equitable treatment of non-compliance.

The ambiguous nature of private warnings

Despite their lower level of punitiveness, private warnings were an ambiguous enforcement outcome and were described by one informant as a 'strategy black hole' (LawyerFR17). On the one hand, they represented an attractive outcome as they remained confidential and prevented reputational damages. 'Most firms will take the regulator's hand off!' (LawyerFR18) – if they were offered a private warning. Lawyers for firms frequently attempted to persuade the regulator throughout the investigation that there was a case for a private warning instead of a formal sanction. Regulatory negotiations occurred even as late in the formal enforcement process as the stage of imposing a regulatory sanction over whether the outcome should be (in)formal.

On the other hand, some lawyers criticised private warnings as 'insidious' (LawyerFR02; Lawyer03), for two main reasons: there was no effective recourse to challenging them, and in practice, private warnings were only semi-private. Private warnings could not be contested through the RDC process as there was no legal decision but merely a letter. A private warning could only be challenged either by a complaint to the Financial Regulators Complaints Commissioner or by judicial review through the Tribunal regime. This was considered 'unreal', as the decision would then become public.

The semi-private nature of private warnings meant that, on certain occasions, they had to be disclosed. The severity of the consequences of disclosure depended on whether the sanctioned target was a firm or an individual. For firms, save for forming part of the firm's compliance history, previous private warnings were not particularly important penalties, as often there were no requirements to disclose them to third parties. An exception might be when a firm was applying for requests for proposals (RFPs) or tenders and was asked to disclose regulatory criticisms as part of the tendering process. Even here, private warnings might not be disclosed, depending on the 'precise tendering wording'. The involvement of lawyers might lead to situations of 'creative compliance' (McBarnet & Whelan, 1999), raising questions about the effectiveness of private warnings as remedies for firms' misconduct:

> Sometimes I say no [to disclosing a private warning] because the wording is not right. You are being asked, 'Have you ever received regulatory criticism central findings?' and the private warning says this is not a finding of fact, so you can deal with it that way.
>
> (Lawyer02)

The effects of private warnings were more onerous for individuals. The warnings remained private, as long as the person did not move within the same firm to a position that required a different type of FCA authorisation or to a regulated position within a different firm. The first requirement could prevent a censored individual moving to a more senior position; the second acted as a disincentive for movements within the market, as the private warning might then become semi-private. The target was permanently labelled as deviant despite the lack of a formal social control outcome, as there was 'always the potential for [it] to be used against them at some point in the future' (LawyerFR04). This semi-private nature led to what one lawyer termed the practice of 'two bites of the cherry' (Lawyer05), where the FCA could refuse an approval to a new SIF, where there had been a private warning, or even where there had been an investigation that had been discontinued. For these reasons, the lawyers who represented individuals most cogently expressed negative views on private warnings. In the cases they described, they had not been actively advocating for a private warning but had made representations that the case should be dropped. The lawyers had little leeway in proposing this measure or, indeed, had any chance to ward it off, potentially appearing as less-helpful advisers or less legitimate in the eyes of clients (on this, see Feeley, 1982).

To summarise, although private warnings could be conceptualised as the most benign enforcement outcome in the FCA's enforcement pyramid, they had more complex functions. First, due to resources constraints, they were, on occasion, used to privately signify more serious rather than only minor misconduct, and second, through the 'two bites at a cherry' practice, they could be used as a more punitive enforcement tool to control the movement of individuals within the market.

No private warnings were imposed in 2017–2018, and a follow-up analysis shows that no private warnings have been issued in subsequent years. The declining use of private warnings is part of a general regulatory trend towards more transparency in enforcement decision-making. The focus on more formal enforcement outcomes, spurred by the 'credible deterrence' agenda and the increasing legalistic demands on the process, led to demands for increased disclosure and transparency (Baldwin et al., 1998), and a reduced use of private methods of dispute resolution. The FCA first consulted on whether private warnings were consistent with its desire to be more transparent in 2016 (FCA, 2016), receiving a variety of views. Despite strong support by firms for their continued use (FCA, 2017c), the FCA had decided not to issue private warnings since the consultation feedback, intending to consult more fully on their use (FCA, 2019b). Thus, while the tool remained available 'in the books', it was effectively abolished in practice.

Corporate responses to constructing individual accountability

The regulatory project to establish individual accountability for non-compliance was differentially aided and resisted by the individual's corporate employer. Companies also engaged in risk mitigation strategies, motivated by calculated considerations of cooperating with the enforcement investigation, of a social license in view of the regulator, and of public image management, as high-profile cases against senior management were widely publicised. Corporate prerogatives classified individuals into 'disposable' and 'non-disposable', or into 'assets' and 'liabilities', attracting differential corporate responses. Managers were considered an 'asset' during joint investigations into corporate and individual accountability, where their case was closely tied with the firm's case, to maintain informational control over the assistance they might award the regulator against the firm or because of reputational concerns of a precedent case against the individual (Jordanoska, 2021). These individuals were supplied with corporate resources, given access to organisational documents to aid their defence, and supported through adverse enquiries into their personal culpability.

Individuals labelled 'liabilities' were those whose involvement in the organisational misconduct did not gravely affect the firm's liability, too reputation-tarnished individuals, and previous management. 'Liabilities' were also considered individuals under scrutiny for individualised misconduct, such as insider dealing (even where the employing company was not affected by the individual's transgression). Conversely, individuals considered 'liabilities' were not awarded such corporate support throughout the regulatory investigation. The classification into 'assets' and 'liabilities' also set in motion corporate responses of processing individuals through corporate private justice systems and of tactics of *constructed non-compliance*.

Private justice systems

Individuals suspected of involvement in non-compliance were processed through corporate social control methods and private 'managerial justice' systems (Henry, 1983; Clarke, 1990; Parker, 2002). Dealing with culpable individuals represented part of the remedial work the firm undertook to limit or discontinue formal enforcement investigations into its misconduct. This process included enhanced monitoring, disciplinary proceedings, suspensions, or firing 'bad people within the organisation' (Lawyer05). Such corporate responses were often also expected by regulators once the enforcement investigation was underway:

> The company will be expected to start the disciplinarily process. They say to the company, 'Why is it you haven't sacked them? How do you defend your decision? What is the evidence that you have that they are "fit and proper"?' So companies are effectively trying to sweep it under the carpet and not find themselves under that sort of pressure.
>
> (LawyerFR17)

Individuals could be subject to private justice processes when they were considered to have a damaged reputation that could also mar the corporate reputation. Individuals could also be considered a 'liability' with a tarnished reputation because of concerns expressed by the regulator:

> We are responding to the criticisms we have had. You have read about us in the papers. A lot of the senior management has changed. We have a new chief financial officer, a new head of compliance – the board has changed completely! If the regulator is not happy with a person, which board would support it?
>
> (FinancialInstitution01)

The processing through disciplinary proceedings negatively impacted the individual's access to organisational documents useful for their defence. The protective functions of corporate legal privilege would also not be engaged for 'disposable' individuals. Such individuals could be invited to an internal investigations interview at the firm, questioned to establish misconduct, and then this information passed on to the regulator (LawyerFR28). If applicable, the privilege over the products of internal investigations interviews (reports, interview notes, transcripts) lies with the employing firm and not the employee, so the firm could easily decide to waive it to the employee's detriment.[45] Employees cannot be compelled to attend such interviews, but failing to attend or cooperate may put them in breach of their employment contract obligations. There is then an impossible choice between appearing at the interview and risking that the interview notes are passed on to the FCA without the safeguards when the FCA is using its public powers of interviewing or not appearing at the interview and likely being fired due to gross misconduct.

Recent enforcement developments across areas of corporate deviance indicate that passing on the underlying witness interviews notes or transcripts, next to the reports from internal investigations, is increasingly considered a sign of good cooperation with the investigation (Day & Hodges, 2023). For example, the deferred prosecution agreement between the Serious Fraud Office and Güralp Systems Limited in 2019 over making corrupt payments and failure to prevent bribery recognised Güralp's extensive cooperation through providing materials from interviews.[46] The DPA with Airbus SE over serious bribery referenced Airbus's 'exemplary cooperation' through, amongst other things, providing the first accounts from internal interviews of all relevant individuals and the disclosure of interview transcripts under a limited waiver of privilege.[47] A handful of FCA final notices also single out practices of handing over interview notes or transcripts as 'good cooperation' and mitigating factors in calculating the fine.[48] Across all enforcement areas, cooperation

45 See, for example, *R (on the Application of AL) v SFO* [2018].
46 *R (SFO) v Guralp Systems Limited* (Statement of Facts) [2019], p. 5.
47 *R (SFO) v Airbus SE* (Statement of Facts) [2020], p. 11.
48 See, for example, Santander UK Plc FN19/12/18 and JLT Specialty Limited FN16/06/22.

with the enforcement investigation delivers a reduction (on occasion, hefty) in the financial penalty. These developments may further input into the firm's calculations over receiving cooperation credit by providing accounts that help construct the liability of 'dispensable' individuals.

Dispensations through companies' 'private justice systems' (Parker, 2002) aid regulatory enforcement objectives. The closer regulatory governance of the firm by 'meddling' with employment decisions represents a mechanism of social control of culpable individuals through informal means rather than through the formal process of fining or imposing prohibition orders. From a governance perspective, this is a cheaper method of achieving 'credible deterrence' policy goals of holding senior management or other individuals to account, since it is notoriously difficult, contentious, and costly to bring formal enforcement against individuals. Though the individuals were only dismissed and not prohibited from the markets, how the approval system operates meant that in the case of a future hiring to a regulated senior position at another firm, they would need to disclose their dismissal and might not get re-approved over concerns of integrity in the 'fitness and propriety' assessments. The social control functions achieved by private justice systems are similar to those of the regulatory justice actions against individuals that remain private, such as the imposition of private warnings or the use of the approval system for 'quasi-enforcement.'

The impact of **constructed non-compliance** *on individual accountability*

The negotiation of the wording of enforcement decisions was identified as a key process of *constructing non-compliance* that occurs at the final stages of the enforcement process. Corporate attempts to (re)claim 'ownership' of the presentation of the misconduct could also be launched regarding jointly negotiating the outcome of a double enforcement action when the FCA was minded to impose penalties on both the firm and a senior individual within the firm. These 'saving the CEO' tactics concerned negotiating both the wording and the penalty outcome for the senior manager considered an 'asset'. The tactics represented the most adversarial responses by firms to diminish or reduce the liability of key managers (Jordanoska, 2021). The overall cooperative context of the confidential settlement room could become fraught when the firm was unwilling to settle the case, unless the manager also received a good outcome. Large firms could significantly rely on their 'regulatory authority' (Reichman, 1992) and position of power (Jordanoska, 2021) to withhold settlement of the firm's case as a bargaining chip for negotiating the extent of non-compliance of its senior manager.

In one example of a double enforcement action, the FCA was minded to fine the firm and also take an action against a senior manager involved in the firm's misconduct. The investigative case into the senior manager's liability had transformed from allegations regarding their 'fitness and propriety' (with a possible outcome of a full or partial prohibition order or a withdrawal of approval) to finding personal culpability for the firm's misconduct that merited a fine. The firm was happy to settle its own case but was refusing to do so unless negotiating a more favourable outcome for the senior manager. The enforcement outcome was crafted in tripartite negotiations between the regulators, the individual's representatives, and the firm's representatives:

> The firm's position was, 'We are quite happy to settle. We are happy to pay this ridiculously extortionate fine that you are demanding from us, but we will not settle without the [senior manager] also having a good result'. . . . We deliberately delayed the procedure. We went to the RDC, had representations there, we fought it, and still got a settlement after the RDC. It was a case where the firm and the [senior manager] were refusing the outcome, so enforcement came across this passionate [person] who was willing to fight [their] case.
>
> (Lawyer14)

The originally proposed fine for the individual was contested and reduced after the RDC representations, but this was still resisted as an unfavourable outcome. The tripartite negotiations continued until reaching an agreement on a penalty and associated description of the seriousness of the individual's misconduct that was deemed acceptable also to settle the corporate case. As with corporate penalty settlements, these negotiations concerned the construction of non-compliance, which was then incorporated into the formal and publicly visible outcome of the regulatory decision-making. The employing organisations were constructing the level of condemnation, as communicated via the type of penalty and its size, that should apply to the individual's misconduct, as well as the description of the seriousness of the misconduct itself. The regulatory process was affected by these attempts to *construct non-compliance* in double enforcement actions as the proceedings became prolonged, more costly, and with an uncertain outcome. Regulators could feel pressured to provide concessions on individual accountability to not undermine the larger enforcement outcome. Questions are also raised over the educational messages sent to the industry (a key function of the publication of enforcement outcomes) regarding what represents (serious) individual misconduct of senior managers.

These insights give possible explanations for the differential treatment of senior managers after the financial crisis, in which some individuals[49] were publicly penalised for their management failings and others were not. One line of evidence shows that a number of individuals were given private warnings, effectively prohibiting them from leaving their positions or re-entering the financial markets altogether. These individuals were dealt with through social control means, but in private. A second line of evidence shows that, depending on the firm's relational distance from the manger, firms can use

49 Notably, Peter Cummings.

their regulatory authority as a bargaining chip for important senior managers, and such individuals may never have been penalised. If the firm considered such individuals to be dispensable, part of previous management, or too reputation-tarred, it would be unwilling to use this regulatory authority to achieve a better outcome for the individual. The fact that firms were prepared to fight for some managers further impaired the FCA's ability to bring successful actions against senior managers (Jordanoska, 2021).

Individuals without organisational support in double enforcement actions could equally be prejudiced by the process of settlement, construction, and publication of corporate enforcement notices. Settling early is a prime corporate consideration while individual targets tend to engage in adversarialism (Jordanoska, 2021), leading to separate enforcement timelines for firms and 'dispensable' individuals. If the firm and the individual had diametrically opposite interests in the case outcome (the firm wanted to settle, the individual to fight), this could result in the facts of the misconduct being agreed between regulators and corporations without considering the impact upon the individual's position. Final notices have the effect of admission of guilt[50] and an implied acceptance of the facts as alleged by the regulator. UK-based companies also do not have a practice of subsequently using PR instruments to question the regulatory findings.[51] Once the firm had negotiated the wording, the enforcement decision against the corporate could be published with prejudicial and not yet defended admissions on individual liability. Early corporate settlements and admissions of the facts, therefore, frustrated the trail of cases against individuals (industry event, 2017) since the litigation for the individuals could proceed for years after the firm's case:

> We acted for one of the FX brokers. [They] were under an investigation and won't work in finance again. The banks just wanted the matter resolved, and in a way to avoid any potential litigation, the banks agreed to pay the fine and the cases were hurried through. But they threw the individuals under the bus. The outcome is that the final notice against the institution is now seen as evidence of wrongdoing by individuals, and there was no challenge to this, not by the banks, nor the individuals.
> (LawyerFR19)

The 'London Whale' case, concerning JPMorgan Chase and the litigation against Achilles Macris, aptly exemplifies the negative impact of corporate priorities to settle upon the individual's case.[52] In 2012, JPMorgan suffered

50 FCA Handbook PRIN 1.5.

51 Similar practices exist in the United States, for example, because of the so-called 'muzzle-clauses' requirements written in DPAs and NPAs that prohibit the corporate defendant from publicly contesting its admission of wrongdoing (Koehler, 2015).

52 JPMorgan Chase Bank, N.A. FN18/09/13.

losses of $6.2 billion in the so-called synthetic credit portfolio run by the bank's Chief Investment Office (CIO). JPMorgan's misconduct consisted of operating a high-risk trading strategy, championed by the trader Bruno Iksil – dubbed the 'London Whale' because of the size of the positions he was taking. JPMorgan's misconduct was aggravated by traders trying to conceal the losses through mismarking their positions. JPMorgan was also found in breach of Principle 11 for misleading the FCA on the extent of the losses and the misconduct. Achilles Macris was, at that time, the head of the CIO International, a division of CIO, and Bruno Iksil's manager. JPMorgan settled the case and admitted in the final notice published in September 2013 that it had 'deliberately misled' the FCA 'by virtue of the conduct of CIO London Management'.[53] Though the notice did not identify Achilles Macris, the reference to the CIO London Management could, in effect, amount to a statement that Macris had *deliberately* misled the FCA. This left the individual in a 'strange position to try to show that he hadn't done this deliberately, while it was accepted that the firm had done so' (Lawyer14).

The divergent corporate/individual interests and the differential timing of the proceedings eventually led to inconsistent public outcomes and legal liabilities: Mr Macris was ultimately fined for *negligently* misleading the FCA in February 2016, almost three years after the JPMorgan settlement.[54] In the period between the publication of the two enforcement decisions, Achilles Macris judicially challenged the FCA's publication of the JPMorgan's final notice identifying him as the person responsible, 'without giving him the chance to make representations' (*Financial Conduct Authority (Appellant) v Macris (Respondent)* [2017], para. 1) to the wording in his own defence. The Supreme Court, however, confirmed that the designation 'CIO London Management' was not a sufficiently identifiable synonym for Macris on the facts (para. 11).

Procedural justice for individuals may be thwarted when there are tensions between them and their employers, or when there is no interest by the employing firm to defend the case against its employee. Paradoxically, the early settlement of the case aided both corporate and regulatory interests. Corporations could settle enforcement cases quickly without consideration of their employees' interests or the need to adopt common defence strategies. Regulators could pursue their focus on publicising outcomes through a quicker route without having to wait for the resolution of the commonly protracted adversarial individual liability proceedings. Yet for the individuals caught up in the corporate action, corporate admissions constructed 'legal truths' that may differ from the 'factual truths' (Bankowski, 1981) on their liability.

53 For example, paragraph 4.135.
54 Achilles Macris FN09/02/16.

Conclusion

In the aftermath of the financial crisis, public accountability bodies called for a greater focus on the role of individuals in the failings of their financial institutions (Treasury Committee, 2012a, 2012b; Parliamentary Commission on Banking Standards, 2013). This is unsurprising, as experience shows that in the aftermath of any regulatory disaster, there are normally calls from politicians and the public for individual liability to be imposed, for there to be some 'heads to roll' (Black, 2014). In the UK financial markets, such calls spurred on, enmeshed with, and supported the growing resolve by the financial regulator to craft senior managers as important 'objects of control' and as personally accountable for organisational misconduct. More intrusive regulatory strategies emerged towards achieving this objective: a stricter gatekeeping process through the legislative changes in the Senior Managers and Certification Regime and the more demanding substantive and procedural requirements of the approval regime, an expansion of tools for tracing decision-making lines across complex corporate hierarchies, and the inception of an overarching enforcement priority of joint investigations against firms and relevant individuals for corporate misconduct.

The resolve to spin off an ongoing investigation into corporate non-compliance into associated individuals, however, did not have the expected effects in increased formal outcomes (i.e. fines and prohibition orders). Cases against individuals were fraught with evidentiary difficulties and were hence harder to investigate and prove (Jordanoska, 2021). But the discrepancy between the public resolve towards achieving individual accountability and the public enforcement outputs can also be attributed to the operation of several non-exhaustive, parallel, constructivist strategies on both sides of the regulatory relationship. What also seemed to happen in practice was the operation of a system of social control of individuals through confidential means which achieved governance effects but avoided putting in motion the uncertain formal control apparatus. Regulators employed risk mitigation strategies through the preventative functions of the approval gatekeeping regime and its 'quasi-enforcement' nature when considering individuals associated with failing financial institutions. Similar risk mitigation and preventative functions were achieved through issuing private warnings to individuals. Regulatory enforcement within and through 'private' regulatory interactions conferred benefits for both sides of the regulatory relationship as individuals could maintain a publicly untarnished reputation while regulators could impose regulatory criticism with career-stifling effects but without engaging the uncertain formal enforcement process. Any criticism of the FCA's failures to achieve greater success against individuals for crises failings should be viewed in light of these findings.

Corporate strategies also mediated the construction of individual accountability for regulatory non-compliance. Informal outcomes against individuals with prejudicial effect upon their future approvals to posts in finance, or upon potential regulatory investigations against them, were produced through the corporate private justice systems of firing or (threatened) disciplinary proceedings. Public outcomes against culpable individuals may equally be a product of *constructed non-compliance* strategies as much as is corporate deviance. Firms could withhold the settling of their case unless the liability of valuable senior managers, that would eventually reach the public domain, was constructed in a favourable manner. While these constructivist strategies hindered the regulatory process, in cases of 'dispensable' individuals, the corporate prerogative of settling the case early conversely assisted the regulatory prerogative of quicker public outcomes.

Bibliography

Adamson C (2014) *Letter of Clive Adamson, FCA Director of Supervision to Graham Beale, Chairman of the FCA Practitioner Panel Clarifying the FCA's Use of Attestations.* Available at: www.fca.org.uk/publication/correspondence/attestations-clive-adamson.pdf

Baldwin J (1985) *Pre-Trial Justice: A Study of Case Settlements in Magistrates' Courts.* Oxford: Basil Blackwell Ltd.

Baldwin R, Scott CD and Hood C (1998) *A Reader on Regulation.* Oxford: Oxford University Press.

Bankowski Z (1981) The Value of Truth: Fact Scepticism Revisited. *Legal Studies* 1: 257–266.

Berwin Leighton Paisner (2011) *Tackling the Increased Regulatory Exposure of Senior Approved Persons.* Financial Regulation: Project Zepelin. Available at: www.blplaw.com/media/BLP_Project_Zeppelin_overview.pdf

Binham C (2012) SFO Opted Out against LIBOR Probe. *Financial Times.* (29.06.2012) Available at: www.ft.com/cms/s/0/b8900f3e-c1d8-11e1-8e7c-00144feabdc0.html#axzz3itWuDjYH

Black J (1997) *Rules and Regulators* (Oxford Socio-legal Studies). Oxford: Oxford University Press.

Black J (2008) Forms and Paradoxes of Principles-based Regulation. *Capital Markets Law Journal* 3(4): 425–457.

Black J (2011) The Rise, Fall and Fate of Principles-Based Regulation. In: Kern A and Moloney N (eds) *Law Reform and Financial Markets* (Elgar Financial Law Series). Cheltenham, UK: Edward Elgar Publishing, 3–34.

Black J (2014) Learning from Regulatory Disasters. *LSE Law, Society and Economy Working Papers 24/2014.* Available at: http://eprints.lse.ac.uk/60569/1/WPS2014-24_Black.pdf

Black J and Kershaw D (2013) *Criminalising Bank Managers. Law and Financial Markets Project Briefing 1/13.* Available at: www.lse.ac.uk/collections/law/projects/lfm/LFMP%201%20%E2%80%93%20Criminalising%20Bank%20Managers%20[final].pdf

Boeker W (1992) Power and Managerial Dismissal: Scapegoating at the Top. *Administrative Science Quarterly* 37: 400–421.

Braithwaite J (1984) *Corporate Crime in the Pharmaceutical Industry.* London: Routledge Kegan & Paul.

Chiu H (2016) Regulatory Duties for Directors in the Financial Services Sector and Directors' Duties in Company Law: Bifurcation and Interfaces. *Journal of Business Law* 6: 465–490.

Clarke B (2018) Individual Accountability in Irish Credit Institutions – Lessons to Be Learned from the United Kingdom's Senior Managers' Regime. *Common Law World Review* 47(1): 35–52.

Clarke M (1990) *Business Crime: Its Nature and Control.* Cambridge: Polity Press.
Clinard M (1983) *Corporate Ethics and Crime: The Role of Middle Management.* Thousand Oaks: SAGE Publications.
Coffee JC, Jr (1981) No Soul to Damn: No Body to Kick: An Unscandalized Inquiry into the Problem of Corporate Punishment. *Michigan Law Review* 79(3): 386–459.
Croall H (2009) Corporate Crime: Issues of Definition, Construction and Research. In: Croall H (ed) *Corporate Crime* (Vol. 2). Los Angeles: SAGE Publications, xx–xli.
Day C and Hodges L (2023) Witness Interviews in Internal Investigations: The UK Perspective. *Global Investigations Review.* Available at: https://globalinvestigationsreview.com/guide/the-practitioners-guide-global-investigations/2023/article/witness-interviews-in-internal-investigations-the-uk-perspective#footnote-059.
Engelen E, Ertürk I, Froud J, Johal S, Leaver A, Moran M, Nilsson A and Williams K (2011) *After the Great Complacence: Financial Crisis and the Politics of Reform.* Oxford: Oxford University Press.
FCA (2013a) *Enhancing Accountability within the Financial Services Sector, Banking Standards: Written Evidence from the Financial Conduct Authority.* Available at: https://publications.parliament.uk/pa/jt201314/jtselect/jtpcbs/27/27v_we76.htm
FCA (2013b) *The FCA's Response to the Parliamentary Commission on Banking Standards.* Available at: www.fca.org.uk/publication/corporate/pcbs-response.pdf
FCA (2013c) *The FCA's Approach to Advancing Its Objectives.* Available at: www.fca.org.uk/static/documents/fca-approach-advancing-objectives.pdf.
FCA (2015a) *CP15/9 Strengthening Accountability in Banking: A New Regulatory Framework for Individuals – Feedback on FCA CP14/13/PRA CP14/14 and Consultation on Additional Guidance.* Available at: www.fca.org.uk/publication/consultation/cp15-09.pdf
FCA (2015b) *CP15/22 Strengthening Accountability in Banking: Final Rules (Including Feedback on CP14/31 and CP15/5) and Consultation on Extending the Certification Regime to Wholesale Market Activities.* www.fca.org.uk/publication/consultation/cp15-22.pdf
FCA (2016) *Our Future Mission.* Available at: https://webarchive.nationalarchives.gov.uk/ukgwa/20230902005300/www.fca.org.uk/publications/corporate-documents/our-mission
FCA (2017a) *CP17/25 and CP17/26 Individual Accountability: Extending the Senior Managers and Certification Regime: Cost-Benefit Analysis.* Available at: www.fca.org.uk/publication/research/cba-extension-senior-managers-certification-regime.pdf
FCA (2017b) *Contracts for Differences.* Available at: www.fca.org.uk/firms/contract-for-differences#revisions
FCA (2017c) *FS17/1 Our Mission 2017 Feedback Statement.* Available at: www.fca.org.uk/publications/corporate-documents/our-mission
FCA (2018) *Freedom of Information: Right to Know Request FOI6090.* Available at: www.fca.org.uk/publication/foi/foi6090-response.pdf.
FCA (2019a) *Controlled Functions.* Available at: https://webarchive.nationalarchives.gov.uk/ukgwa/20190902220308/https://www.fca.org.uk/firms/approved-persons/controlled-functions.
FCA (2019b) *Freedom of Information: Right to Know Request FOI6897.* Available at: www.fca.org.uk/publication/foi/foi6897-response.pdf
FCA (2020) *Freedom of Information: Right to Know Request FOI7714.* Available at: www.fca.org.uk/freedom-information/search-results?f_search_term=
FCA (2023) *Senior Managers and Certification Regime.* Available at: www.fca.org.uk/firms/senior-managers-certification-regime
Feeley MM (1982) Plea Bargaining and the Structure of the Criminal Process. *The Justice System Journal* 7(3): 338–354.

Ferran E (2011) Break-up of the Financial Services Authority. *Oxford Journal of Legal Studies* 31(3): 455–480.
Fisse B and Braithwaite J (1993) *Corporations, Crime and Accountability*. Cambridge: Cambridge University Press.
FSA (2011) *The Failure of the Royal Bank of Scotland (FSA Board Report)*. Available at: www.fca.org.uk/publication/corporate/fsa-rbs.pdf.
Gava R (2022) Challenging the Regulators: Enforcement and Appeals in Financial Regulation. *Regulation & Governance* 16: 1265–1282.
Gilad S (2011) Institutionalizing Fairness in Financial Markets: Mission Impossible? *Regulation & Governance* 5(3): 309–332.
Gray G and Silbey S (2014) Governing Inside the Organization: Interpreting Regulation and Compliance. *American Journal of Sociology* 120(1) (July 2014): 96–145.
Gray J and Hamilton J (2006) *Implementing Financial Regulation*. Chichester: John Wiley & Sons Ltd.
Green (2015) *Report into the FSA's Enforcement Actions Following the Failure of HBOS*. London: Bank of England Prudential Regulation Authority and Financial Conduct Authority.
Gunningham N and Johnstone R (1999) *Regulating Workplace Safety: Systems and Sanctions*. Oxford: Oxford University Press.
Gunningham N, Thornton D and Kagan R (2005) Motivating Management: Corporate Compliance in Environmental Protection. *Law and Policy* 27(2): 289–316.
Hearita KM and Brown J (2004) Merrill Lynch: Corporate Apologia and Business Fraud. *Public Relations Review* 30: 459–466.
Henry S (1983) *Private Justice: Towards Integrated Theorising in the Sociology of Law* (1st ed.). Routledge.
Hickman E (2022) Is the Senior Managers and Certification Regime Changing Banking for Good? *The Modern Law Review* 85(6): 1440–1462.
HM Treasury (2015) *Chancellor Announces Bank of England and Financial Services Bill*. Available at: https://www.gov.uk/government/news/chancellor-announces-bank-of-england-and-financial-services-bill.
House of Lords Debate (2015) *Bank of England and Financial Services Bill, 26 October, Vol. 765*. Available at: https://hansard.parliament.uk/Lords/2015-10-26/debates/15102629001685/details
Jordanoska A (2021) Regulatory Enforcement against Organizational Insiders: Interactions in the Pursuit of Individual Accountability. *Regulation & Governance* 15: 298–316.
Jordanoska A and Lord N (2020) Scripting the Mechanics of the Benchmark Manipulation Corporate Scandals: The 'Guardian' Paradox. *European Journal of Criminology* 17(1): 9–30.
Katz J (1979b) Concerted Ignorance: The Social Construction of Cover-Up. *Urban Life* 8: 295–316.
Keller A and Kokkinis A (2022) The Senior Managers and Certification Regime in Financial Firms: An Organisational Culture Analysis. *Journal of Corporate Law Studies* 22(1): 299–334.
Kleinman M (2009) Former RBS Investment Bank Chief Johnny Cameron Banned from City. *Telegraph*. Available at: www.telegraph.co.uk/finance/newsbysector/banksandfinance/5179069/Ex-RBS-banker-blocked-by-FSA.html.
Koehler M (2015) Measuring the Impact of Non-Prosecution and Deferred Prosecution Agreements on Foreign Corrupt Practices Act Enforcement. *UC Davis Law Review* 49: 497, 522.
MacNeil I (2018) Regulating Instead of Punishing: The Senior Managers Regime in the UK. In: Ligetti K and Tosza S (eds) *White Collar Crime: a Comparative Perspective*. Oxford: Hart Publishing, 225–252.

Masters B (2013a) UK Regulators Tell Executives to Sign on the Dotted Line. *Financial Times.* Available at: www.ft.com/content/49758c74-c22b-11e2-8992-00144feab7de

Masters B (2013b) Watchdogs Keep Up Pressure on Responsibility. *Financial Times.* Available at: www.ft.com/content/60e3d152-c2e6-11e2-9bcb-00144feab7de

McBarnet D and Whelan C (1999) *Creative Accounting and the Cross-eyed Javelin Thrower.* Chichester: John Wiley & Sons.

McDermott T (2013) *Enforcement and Credible Deterrence in the FCA (Speech).* Available at: www.fca.org.uk/news/speeches/enforcement-and-credible-deterrence-in-the-fca.

McGrath J and Walker C (2022) *New Accountability in Financial Services Changing Individual Behaviour and Culture.* Palgrave Macmillan.

Parker C (2002) *The Open Corporation.* Cambridge: Cambridge University Press.

Parliamentary Commission on Banking Standards (2013) *Changing Banking for Good: Report, Volume I: Summary, and Conclusions and Recommendations.* HL Paper 27-I HC 175-I.

PRA (2015a) *PS3/15 Strengthening Individual Accountability in Banking and Insurance – Responses to CP14/14 and CP26/14.* Available at: www.bankofengland.co.uk/-/media/boe/files/prudential-regulation/policy-statement/2015/ps315.pdf

PRA (2015b) *PS16/15 Strengthening Individual Accountability in Banking – Responses to CP14/14, CP28/14 and CP7/15.* Available at: www.bankofengland.co.uk/-/media/boe/files/prudential-regulation/policy-statement/2015/ps1615.pdf

PRA and FCA (2014) *CP14/14/CP14/13 Strengthening Accountability in Banking: A New Regulatory Framework for Individuals.* Available at: www.fca.org.uk/publication/consultation/cp14-13.pdf

Reichman N (1992) Moving Backstage: Uncovering the Role of Compliance Practices in Shaping Regulatory Policy. In: Schlegel K and Weisburd D (eds) *White-collar Crime Reconsidered.* Boston, MA: Northeastern University Press, 244–268.

Short JL and Toffel MW (2008) Coerced Confessions: Self-policing in the Shadow of the Regulator. *Journal of Law, Economics, & Organization* 24(1): 45–71.

Sparrow M (2000) *The Regulatory Craft: Controlling Risks, Solving Problems, and Managing Compliance.* Washington, DC: The Brookings Institute.

Symington J (2017) *Our Investigations – The Evolving Approach (Speech).* Available at: www.fca.org.uk/news/speeches/investigations-evolving-approach.

Thornton D, Gunningham NA and Kagan RA (2005) General Deterrence and Corporate Environmental Behavior. *Law & Policy* 27(2): 262–288.

Treasury Committee (2012a) *Banking Crisis* (Vol. I, Oral evidence, HC 144-I). London: The Stationery Office.

Treasury Committee (2012b) *Second Report. Fixing LIBOR: Some Preliminary Findings* (Vol. I, Oral evidence, HC 481-II). London: The Stationery Office.

Treasury Committee (2012c) *The FSA's Report into the Failure of RBS: Report, Together with Formal Minutes, Oral and Written Evidence* (HC 640). London: Stationary Office.

Treasury Committee (2014a) *Project Verde: Sixth Report of Session 2014–15* (Vol. I, Report, together with formal minutes, HC 728–I). London: The Stationary Office.

Treasury Committee (2014b) *Project Verde: Sixth Report of Session 2014–15* (Vol. II, Oral evidence, HC 728–II). London: The Stationary Office.

Treasury Committee (2014c) *Treasury Committee Publishes Project Verde Report.* Available at: https://committees.parliament.uk/work/5136/project-verde/news/184141/treasury-committee-publishes-project-verde-report/

Wheatley M (2015) *Nothing to Fear from High Standards (Speech).* Available at: www.fca.org.uk/news/speeches/nothing-fear-high-standards

Cases

Financial Conduct Authority (Appellant) v Macris (Respondent) [2017] UKSC 19.
Pottage v FSA FS/2010/33.
Pottage v FSA FS/2010/33.
R (on the Application of AL) v. SFO [2018] EWHC 856 (Admin).
R (SFO) v Airbus SE (Statement of Facts).
R (SFO) v Guralp Systems Limited (Statement of Facts).
Re Barings plc (No 5) [2000] 1 BCLC 523.
Stewart Owen Ford and Mark John Owen v The Financial Conduct Authority [2018] UKUT 0358 (TCC).

7 Conclusion

The 2008 financial crisis exposed the financial markets as being complex, volatile, and difficult to regulate yet as indispensable for all developed economies, including that of the UK. The debates about the role of regulators in the post-crisis period inspired this book, and the research set out to move beyond the narrow focus of contemporary debates on regulatory failures to investigate the reform of regulatory enforcement in their aftermath. The theoretical underpinnings of social constructivism in social theory, regulatory conversations, and regulatory enforcement style were used to make sense of the empirical data on the regulatory interactions in the post-crisis enforcement of financial regulation.

The study revealed that the enforcement process is intricate, dynamic, at some points predictable, yet at others less so. Despite statutory regulation, extensive implementation guidance, and policy documents, the limits of the law and the boundaries between compliance and deviance were fully shaped only in social dynamics. Three broader conclusions can be drawn from this work. First, in the post-financial crisis period, the enforcement of financial regulation in the UK markets became more intrusive, intense, and punitive. This was evidenced in the rhetoric of the 'credible deterrence' policy, increased use of information-gathering powers, increased legal and extra-legal penalties, and heightened focus on the liability of corporate managers. Second, regulated organisations and their legal representatives responded to the more punitive approach with strategies of adaptation and resisting a deviant label through 'creative compliance', *detection avoidance through detection facilitation*, and *constructing non-compliance*, notably through the careful management of the self-reporting process, the negotiation of the wording of final notices, and techniques for softening the liability of senior managers. Paradoxically, the effect of the regulator's more punitive approach was to promote strong cooperative relationships managed through regulatory conversations tightly controlled on both sides by regulatory lawyers. The theoretical construct of *mutual risk mitigation* allows for the focus on negotiation and cooperation to be understood in the context of a highly reputation-sensitive environment in which the regulator and regulated benefited from a process where credibility and trust were fostered on both sides. Lastly, the research showed that legal

DOI: 10.4324/9781351069328-7

actors were key in this process since the strategies were promoted through the active involvement of lawyers and the ways in which they deployed their expertise and networks.

These findings relating to the particular context of the post-financial crisis period also have relevance for broader concerns regarding regulatory control, the limits of regulatory enforcement, and the nature of regulatory relationships. The following sections discuss what the analysis in this book suggests for conceptual understandings of regulatory activism and its outcomes, the nature of regulatory interactions and the role of regulatory intermediaries in the enforcement process, and the design of regulatory architectures.

Regulatory activism in enforcing regulation

Regulatory reform processes in post-crisis periods and the resulting change in governance are of critical interest to regulation scholars (Levi-Faur, 2005; Jordana & Levi-Faur, 2004; Moschella & Tsingou, 2013; Haines, 2011; Hutter & Lloyd-Bostock, 2017). The analysis presented here argues for a multi-dimensional approach towards understanding regulatory activism in enforcing regulation in crises aftermaths by linking the claims-making process through regulatory policymaking, indicators on organisational resourcing, and the use of enforcement tools in micro-level interactions.

The expansion of the 'credible deterrence' enforcement policy rested on communicational tools, a simultaneous claims-making process, and a range of supporting internal and external factors. Speeches of senior enforcement officials introducing and expanding on the facets of 'credible deterrence' signified financial misconduct as a social problem that needed to be tackled through enforcement means. This also involved a process of claims-making in which, based on the grounds of *unresponsiveness* by the industry to previous actions (the unchanged business behaviour) and the *lost trust in the industry*, the FCA proposed more deterrence-oriented enforcement as a response. Through the process of proposing solutions to the unchanged behaviour in the financial markets, the FCA claimed ownership of the problem of financial misconduct. This finding, however, cannot be viewed solely through the prism of the 'scandal and reform' literature that has shown that regulators commonly adopt pro-regulation stances after sharing responsibility for regulatory failures (Braithwaite, 2008). 'Credible deterrence' was initially formulated before the financial crisis regarding market abuse only. Post-crisis, it gained legitimacy and was expanded across the range of misconduct over which the FCA has jurisdiction.

A range of factors can be identified which explain regulatory policymaking; some are organisational (internal moral entrepreneurs, staff skills and resources, and occupational cultures), while others are external (political context, accountability bodies, and crises). The hiring of skilled and litigation-minded enforcement staff in the pre–'credible deterrence' period and during its development acted as an internal catalyst toward more formalistic enforcement approaches. The internal organisational shifts towards creating a more risk-taking and litigious enforcement culture were aided post-crisis by external pressures from various political and public accountability mechanisms. This political climate enabled (and pushed) the FCA to move more deliberately towards the deterrence end of the regulatory styles continuum, increasing the role of its response in attaching deviance labels to business behaviour. Regulatory enforcement in finance is highly politicised (Froud et al., 2012; Levitin, 2014), and the politics happens both in high-level debates on the objectives and scope of regulatory regimes and in agencies' policymaking.

At the micro-level of interactions, the perceived past regulatory failures incentivised the use of discretionary powers towards addressing those failings. The increase in the use of information-gathering powers (information requests, information provision, and skilled persons' reports) indicated a change in the regulator's attitude to using its considerable statutory and Handbook powers 'on the ground'. The FCA turned into an 'information-hungry regulator'. This identity, achieved through enforcement activities involving Principle 11, also led to an increase in the awareness and extent of self-reporting by regulatees of their own misconduct. The increased outsourcing of enforcement functions to external experts via skilled persons' reports created a more formalistic approach to enforcement, as the involvement of third parties in carrying out regulatory functions is a factor of more intense regulatory scrutiny (May & Winter, 1999). The hiring of skilled persons also shifted the power balance in terms of owning proprietary knowledge and technical expertise towards the regulator. The informational public–private imbalances commonly arise because financial institutions have access to expertise, analysis, and interpretations of their risks and hazards, making regulators 'captives of experts'. The hiring of third-party experts that ultimately reported to the regulator alleviated some of these concerns. The greater regulatory resolve towards crafting managers as 'objects of control' also addressed criticisms of past regulatory failures, reinforcing the notions of an enforcement-minded regulator. This was evidenced through the organisational priorities to screen more vigorously and take more actions against certain culpable individuals (predominately senior management) which were harder to investigate, prove, and resource.

Finally, the tools (May & Burby, 1998) of 'credible deterrence' were the increased use of substantive enforcement powers against firms and individuals, increased size of penalties, and the use of adverse publicity. The FCA awarded record-breaking financial penalties for a range of complex financial misconduct and against some of biggest players in the industry. The decisions around fines frequently concerned considerations of a just desert (Schlegel, 1990). Although the determination to impose bigger penalties led the regulator to introduce an improved and more transparent system of sentencing, notions of the 'right' or just size of the penalty still took precedence, in line with the 'credible deterrence' agenda. The FCA also relied significantly on reputational sanctions and negative publicity to manage the reputation of corporate actors, publicising enforcement outcomes to send deterrence, educational, and consumer protection messages, as well as to manage its own reputation. All these activities led to identifying more business behaviour as non-compliance (through the increased substantive caseload) or identifying it as more serious non-compliance (through the increased levels of fines and reputational damages).

The 'regulatory precedents' of post-crisis periods

Post-crises periods are commonly busy in legislative reform to fix past regulatory failures. Sequences of legislative interventions expanded the FCA's enforcement remit through adding new statutory obligations upon the regulated and new enforcement powers. The major intervention of the SMCR gave the regulator new tools to establish individual liability through the required statement of responsibilities and the Certification Regime. The FCA gained new powers to intervene in financial products and financial promotions and new disclosure powers through the publication of decision and warning notices, moving the transparency behind the confidential enforcement proceedings earlier in the process. The latter complimented the regulator's existing focus on publicising enforcement outcomes.

During post-crises periods of regulatory activism, regulators also gain a mandate to experiment with introducing new policies of heightened control over segments of the markets or with using old powers in new ways. The FCA experimented with using its existing powers in new ways: the power to fine was used to impose record-breaking penalties, thus shifting the industry expectations on the size of monetary fines. The existing information-gathering powers were used with greater intensity and variety in the types of information requested to understand the 'root causes of non-compliance'. Existing supervisory powers of inspection were engaged for the first time to trace and increase individual accountability through SIF audits and attestations. These practices developed in an endogenous (bottom-up) manner, preceding the statutory (top-down) interventions of the Senior Managers and Certification Regime and its key new obligation for senior managers to provide statements of responsibilities during the regulatory approval process.

These experimentations represent 'regulatory precedents' of the more punitive period. A 'regulatory precedent' marks the initial use of a legal power in a new way that then becomes every day or common tool in the regulatory toolkit. The concept helps trace the historical inception of an enforcement practice, and the influencing macro-level political factors, micro-level regulatory dynamics, and actors of change. 'Regulatory precedents' have the potential to grow into established enforcement practices, carrying through the legacy of the post-crisis dynamic period of change. These are companions to what Hutter and Lloyd-Bostock (2017) have termed the 'long shadow of regulatory crisis'.

The extent to which these changes have continued beyond the post-crisis period should be the subject of future studies. There are, however, some indicators of the longer-term incorporation of some 'regulatory precedents' into the FCA toolkit. For example, a review of FCA fines in the years beyond the research period shows a continuing trend of imposing nine-figure financial penalties for the more egregious financial misconduct, as well as an established practice of PR techniques in publishing those actions. Attestations remain to be used as supervisory tools with a varying frequency across subsequent financial years (FCA, 2024a). Additionally, very recent regulatory proposals (FCA, 2024b), at the time of writing under consultation, to remove the confidentiality cloak over regulatory investigations indicate further embracing of increased disclosure and potential reputational damages as a regulatory tool.

Mutual risk mitigation through the regulatory interactions: the swinging pendulum

Despite the increased focus on enforcement, it is not necessarily the case that the power has tilted more towards the regulator, as the scandal and reform literature would suggest (Braithwaite, 2008). The findings of this study caution that enforcement practice in post-crisis periods is much more complex than simple cyclical movements along the regulatory spectrum away from deregulation and self-regulation to a more interventionist and punitive role for regulators (Lodge & Wegrich, 2010; Moschella & Tsingou, 2013). A more accurate interpretation is that the power transfers between regulators and the regulated at different points in the enforcement process, making the 'regulatory game' more complex but not one-sided.

Against the background of increasingly punitive enforcement, this research finds that, paradoxically, the process of interaction fostered strong cooperative relationships between the regulator and regulatees. Cooperative approaches rather than adversarialism and legal challenge were present throughout the entire enforcement process. At the stage of detecting a potential problem, self-reporting was extensive and consisted of organisations offering to conduct their own investigations and remedial plans. At the investigation stage, cooperation was evidenced in the few challenges to the reasonableness of evidence-gathering powers and in targets providing an open and cooperative attitude within the investigation. Most formal enforcement outcomes were settled and negotiated rather than subjected to the more formalistic and legalistic process of challenging them before the internal FCA body (the Regulatory Decisions Committee) or, externally, before the Tribunal or the High Court. The FCA awarded significant financial penalties, and with the LIBOR and FX trading scandal fines, it remains the regulator with by far the highest overall and single fines in the UK (as Macrory found as early as 2006 [Macrory, 2006]). Yet it was able to impose these sanctions without significant opposition from the industry either in public, through the judicial system, or in private, within the settlement discussions.

The theoretical construct of *mutual risk mitigation* allows for the cooperation to be understood in the context of a highly reputation-sensitive environment against which the regulator and regulated mutually hedged various risks. By demanding more information and emphasising the importance of Principle 11, regulators hedged the *risk* of being seen as risk-averse, not asking enough questions, and probing regulatees. By insisting on increasing non-negotiable financial penalties and through the increasing use of disclosure, regulators hedged the *risk* of being seen as risk-averse, lacking 'teeth', and having insufficiently 'robust' enforcement activities. These were some of the main criticisms of the pre-crisis FSA, including by different accountability bodies, to which the regulator was highly sensitive. The strategies also represented mitigation of risks to the regulator's reputation and accusations of 'fault' or 'laziness' in cases of regulatory failure. For the regulators, therefore, this represented a means to preserve their public image and give the appearance of a regulator who was proactive and willing to intervene or punish when required.

By providing more information, regulatees hedged the risk of ending up in enforcement – either for the original breach and/or for Principle 11 breaches. (Over-)reporting served the function of shifting the responsibility for a regulatory failure back to the regulator. For regulatees, this also represented a means to preserve their standing with the regulator (a social motive for compliance) and avoid enforcement (a calculated motive for compliance). By agreeing to a fine without challenge, regulatees and their professional representatives hedged the *risk* of more significant reputational damage through the publication of a non-constructed final notice. This negotiated system of justice regarding case settlement was largely guided by reputational considerations. Regulatees settled cases to avoid restatement of the misconduct facts in a subsequent and public complaints process. During the negotiation of the wording of the enforcement notice, corporations accepted the liability and the size of the fine but contested the presentation of the misconduct for reputational concerns. For both sides of the regulatory relationship, the reporting and settlement processes and the *mutual risk mitigation* embedded in them were mechanisms of managing perceptions – each other's and that of wider audiences.

Both sides trusted that they had achieved better outcomes through cooperation. For the regulator, cooperative approaches made the enforcement process more efficient, less resource-intensive (saving costs of the formal legal process of challenge) and provided quicker outcomes that could be advertised faster. For regulatees, cooperation also made the enforcement process more efficient, less resource-intensive (it could contribute towards faster conclusion, lower costs on senior management time and legal advice, and a lesser penalty) and allowed for credibility and trust to be established and maintained throughout the process. The interests of the two sides merged, labelling the contentious process as ultimately cooperative.

Deterrence approaches to regulation and regulatory enforcement as part of command-and-control regulation (Snider, 2009; Tombs & Whyte, 2013) or as a sequence of the enforcement pyramid (Ayres & Braithwaite, 1992; Braithwaite, 2017) should be reconceptualised to include this aspect of regulatory enforcement reality: even if the process is contentious and oriented towards rule enforcement rather than informal rule negotiation, the process might still be cooperative, accommodating, and accompanied by bargaining and concessions. Strategies of dialogue and persuasion, though perhaps of a different kind than persuading the virtuous regulatees to comply, are commonly employed even at the 'tough deterrent peak' of the enforcement pyramid and not only at its 'dialogic base', as suggested by the responsive regulation framework (Braithwaite, 2017: 433). Even when the formal apparatus of the law is employed against organisations with a punitive outlook (on its own a much rarer occurrence than the social control of disempowered subjects), the system is not entirely punitive or adversarial. Corporations may not always be successful in avoiding the imposition of a deviant label, regardless of the resources at their disposal. This inability, in turn, promotes creative ways to adapt and soften the deviant label effects.

What does this mean for regulatory activism and the regulatory project more broadly? There are differing views on the 'more regulation' agenda, ranging from calls for more 'heavy-handed oversight', calls for professionalising the industry of regulators, considerable scepticism of 'more regulation' as it should be weighed against potential 'government failure' and limited to reducing blatant failings only, and considerable scepticism of 'more regulation' because of the 'inherent counterlearning, creative compliance, and evasion' by the regulated (Lodge & Wegrich, 2010: 338). My view is somewhere in between the first and last of these approaches. I am not sceptical of the 'more regulation' approach, as the crisis has shown that regulatory failures through light oversight, and insufficient challenges of financial practices and of senior management appointments contributed to industry failures. 'More regulation' initiatives also contribute to experimentations with existing powers that push towards creating 'regulatory precedents', testing the full capacity of regulatory tools, and an internal building of an 'interventionist' institutional memory. Interventionist regulation can also shift the understanding in the regulatory community over the interpretation of regulatory requirements, such as on self-reporting and individual accountability.

However, we need to also understand and recognise the potential limitations of regulatory enforcement activism in post-crisis periods. First, shifts in regulatory policies can create unwanted consequences for the regulatory project if coupled with limited organisational resources and understanding of their effects. For example, increased self-reporting could contribute to informational overburden, preventing critical insights. Regulatory enforcement philosophies committed to increasing individual accountability may deliver unsatisfactory outcomes if not coupled with matching 'regulatory craft' (Sparrow, 2000) by way of adequate internal organisational structures, discretionary decision-making policies, and investigative skills needed to enliven them.

Second, the emphasis on *mutual risk mitigation* uncovers the 'game playing' in the markets in post-crisis periods, an issue of regulatory enforcement and compliance practice that is beyond the deterrence/compliance debate, and broader theorising on regulatory systems design and has been insufficiently addressed in the literature. Though after the 2008 crisis, the pendulum swung to a more intense and punitive regime, changing the playing field conditions, the regulatory game adapted and became more complicated, but it did not drastically change the power balance between the same key players or their overarching symbiotic cooperative relationships. The pre-crisis power relations were deconstructed, with some leverage added to the regulatory side by the legitimisation of using significant financial penalties and the expansion of the disclosure powers. And then, they were reconstructed with a degree of leverage reclaimed by the industry side in concessions around text and wording. The rules of the game might have changed, but the actors and the power relations between them remained much the same. The simultaneous exploration of the different relationships between the same players shows that both sides fully understood the tactics of the other.

Third, the findings in this study show that regulators were able to achieve changes towards a more interventionist and punitive regime only with the tacit 'support' and lack of challenge by the industry. In the post-crisis period, the industry could not and did not want to push back, as might happen during regular times, but instead adapted to the new world and developed different kinds of responses and engagement to manage the enforcement outcome. These nuances are critical in understanding what punitive turns can achieve and how. The existence of *mutual risk mitigation* and negotiated practice implies that a regulator can tackle the 'belly of the beast' only through a recognition of where the give and take lie in the regulatory game. Yet this is not a simple story of regulatory capture, where agencies act solely as mouthpieces to the industry (Rex, 2020). Regulators were still trying to do their job, but within the reality of scarce resources, imperfect knowledge, and policy deficiencies, leading to *mutual risk mitigation* practices in which the trade-offs between regulatory and regulatees' interests were, in fact, made to pursue the public interest. The background of cooperative and negotiation-based relationships between the parties allowed for such practices and ultimately led to situations where the public interest was visibly satisfied yet where the ultimate definition of non compliance was constructed with inputs from the industry. In some ways, therefore, the regulatory relationships that develop in a post-crisis or a post-failure period are necessary for the markets to function and to reproduce themselves as 'stable'. Studies of enforcement and compliance practice must understand the pockets in the regulatory relationship where the balance of power shifts, and the *mutual risk mitigation* practices; what kinds of interests and formal and informal rules underpin them, and what kinds of social networks and institutional resources support them.

The role of lawyers as regulatory intermediaries

Intermediaries play a significant role in regulatory processes as third parties that act on behalf of the regulators, or together with them, to achieve regulatory goals. They do so through a range of activities, such as providing expertise, facilitating regulatory implementation, monitoring, and enforcement (Abbott et al., 2017). Research on the role of regulatory intermediaries or third parties in regulation is in line with work which has shifted the focus from the concept of 'government' (implying the state) towards 'governance' (implying a wider range of actors and tools that perform governing functions) (Levi-Faur, 2011; Black, 2008; Scott, 2004). What light is shed on the role of regulatory intermediaries by the analysis presented here?

Lawyers are key actors who engage in regulation and have a prominent role within the regulatory conversations. Most of the enforcement team involved in investigating and negotiating the sanctions for misconduct in this empirical study were lawyers. Many of these enforcement staff lawyers had left the regulator for private practice, mostly in global and international law firms. Indeed, around 60 per cent of lawyers interviewed had, at a certain point, worked at the FSA/FCA. The pool of contentious regulatory lawyers who represented enforcement targets then mostly consisted of former FCA staff. Contentious regulatory lawyers themselves were a small and well-interconnected 'repeat players' group. This created a socially small and closed market in which lawyers on both sides knew each other and preserved professional acquaintances. On occasion, lawyers representing targets were able to elicit a 'reasonable attitude' from enforcement or supervisory staff over the exercise of investigation powers based on these ex-colleague connections. However, though these micro-level interactions facilitated a more cooperative environment, staff still enforced regulation with the public interest at the centre of their decision-making.

Legal actors were key intermediaries in the process of constructing (non-) compliance since the constructivist strategies were mediated and promoted through, and on occasion, relied on, the active involvement of regulatory lawyers and how they deployed their professional power, expertise, and social networks. With the move towards a more punitive regime, the reliance on legal expertise also grew. Regulatory lawyers became increasingly present throughout the contentious regulatory relationship, from the process of detection through to the sanctioning stage. In fact, if lawyers were frowned upon by supervisors and were acting 'more behind the scenes' in supervisory matters, their presence became normalised after the enforcement referral.

The implication of the increased involvement of lawyers was not only that they served as an exertion of corporations' professional capital but that they also contributed to the interpretation of legal regulations, thus influencing the development of regulatory law (by, for example, encouraging a wider view of the Principle 11 demands). As a professional group with an expert authority (Parker, 1999; Picciotto, 2007; Schmidt, 2005), contentious regulatory lawyers shared and re-enforced the regulatory expectations from targets and contributed to the interpretation of regulatory requirements (e.g. the meaning of a 'significant' breach and when and what to report). At first glance, the heavier involvement of lawyers might mean that the outside counsel took up the role of gatekeeper (Coffee, 2006; Kraakman, 1986). This is especially the case as lawyers were frequently approached to give advice on resolving dissonant internal opinions on whether the regulator should know about an internal issue. The lawyer's judgement and advice often represented a decisive factor in constructing certain conduct by the firm as a rule breach that warrants reporting to the regulator. However, their involvement in the creative compliance with the reporting requirements to avoid further detection questions their role of gatekeepers in discovering misconduct.

The more punitive turn increased the reliance on legal expertise also for the regulator. Legal actors were employed for regulatory objectives as barristers from private chambers to represent the regulator's case in contentious Tribunal proceedings and as skilled persons to detect and provide expert evidence on non-compliance. The increased outsourcing of regulatory functions to skilled persons, including law firms, provided capacity and expertise for a more interventionist and punitive agenda while being strapped for resources. However, as with any outsourcing of regulatory functions to intermediaries, the use of this method raises questions on the skilled persons' accountability and their adequate oversight, especially when law firms that also specialise in defence work are hired.

The legal profession performs dual and conflicting roles in regulatory governance: as a high-quality resource in implementing regulation (when hired by regulators and when acting as gatekeepers) and as a high-quality resource in implementing corporations' professional embeddedness and regulatory authority (when professional networks and knowledge are used to dismay an enforcement action). From an interactionist perspective, lawyers on both sides of the regulatory relationship sustain the creation of dialogue and trust, facilitating the enforcement of regulation with lesser costs than adversarial approaches, and contribute towards creating shared understandings in the regulatory community regarding the meaning of the broad standards of principles-based frameworks. Lawyers provide leadership in these regulatory processes as they produce the life of the law. In consequence, lawyers may act indirectly 'in conjunction' with a regulator or the regulatory regime as theorised by the regulator-intermediary-target (RIT) model (Abbott et al., 2017). Yet this allegiance is based on shaky foundations so long as the private and public interests merge. It quickly disintegrates when the need arises to develop strategies of resisting a deviant label against regulatory enforcement objectives. The scholarship on regulatory intermediaries, therefore, needs a more nuanced understanding of the conflicting roles of legal actors as regulatory intermediaries and what are the 'brighter' and 'darker' sides of their involvement (van der Heijden, 2017). Fruitful ways forward would be studies designed to investigate the role of private barristers' chambers in enforcing public financial regulation, and the role and functions of law firms with the status of skilled persons. Further research should address the potential of skilled persons to be enrolled as a regulatory actor (Black, 2003), along with deeper considerations of their accountability and legitimacy to do so.

Regulatory architectures

Much research discusses the optimal design of regulatory regimes in terms of choosing the appropriate level of rules indeterminacy (Black, 1997, Black et al., 2007; Braithwaite, 2002; Picciotto, 2007). The choice is between detailed prescriptive rules and standard-level setting principles as regulation building blocks. Scholars have argued that principles are more capable of preventing creative compliance (Black, 2008; Black et al., 2007; Ford, 2008; McBarnet, 1991; McBarnet & Whelan, 1999). The findings of this study contribute to, and challenge, this long-standing debate.

Principles-based enforcement operated in ambiguous ways in practice by aiding or detracting from enforcement outcomes. The principles allowed for more misconduct to be inspected and enforced along the lines of the perceived *root causes of deviance*, which represented a key enforcement priority within the 'credible deterrence' agenda. The standard-setting level of the principles could be used to capture a wider range of misconduct and grey areas of business behaviour than detailed rules. Legal advocacy by targets was also more difficult, as cases brought on the back of breaches of the principles allowed less space for organisations to contest and negotiate the meaning of compliance, contrary to some arguments in the scholarship (c.f. Edelman & Talesh, 2011; Hutter, 2011). Certain principles could act as 'vehicles' of more efficient enforcement themselves. In particular, the broad standards of Principle 11 represented a key enforcement tool. Its self-reporting demands led to greater scope for detection, whilst its cooperation demands represented an important leverage in the supervisory and investigation process.

However, though principles impose broader standards of regulatory demands, compliance could still be motivated by more perverse reasons. This first concerns how Principle 11 requirements of notifying the FCA of anything that the regulator would reasonably require notice of were interpreted in practice. Firms were aware of, and showed compliance with, their reporting obligations and the requirements of Principle 11. Yet self-reporting could be undertaken to ensure that case ownership was retained and not subjected to further proactive detection by the regulator. The occurrence of *constructed non-compliance* and *detection avoidance through detection facilitation* obfuscates the argument that principles have the benefit of minimising the scope for 'creative compliance', enabling 'supervisors and enforcers to police the spirit of the rules as well as the letter' (Black et al., 2007: 192). How firms constructed compliance with the 'reasonable expectation' standard meant that principles can also be a subject of 'creative compliance', just as much as prescriptive and detailed rules can be.

A second problematic issue with enforcement in a principles-based regime was the identified process of bartering over the principles when negotiating the wording of the final notice. Parties subjected to enforcement actions perceived different levels of importance of compliance with different principles (most notably Principle 6 – treating customers fairly). However, this did not mean that compliance was truly internalised but rather that the principles were evaluated and graded according to their perceived impact upon the target's reputation once the breach was made public. Attempts were launched at crafting the final notice wording in a way that showed that the parties had not breached a principle of a more perceived importance. This also entailed a process of attempting to *construct the non-compliance* that would be made visible for public consumption.

These findings uncover the challenges and limits of principles-based regulation in controlling corporate behaviour, minimising creative compliance and achieving higher standards of conduct. Principles-based regulation may not always fare any better than detailed rules in achieving these objectives. The promises of principles-based regulation need to be revised in view of recognising the impact of supervision and enforcement procedures and regulatory interactions that weaken its operation. Beyond debates on adequate regulatory structures, there is the need to recognise the reality of corporate power, interests, and resources than can influence *any* type of rule structure and indeterminacy. This should also include a recognition of the role played by regulatory intermediaries in standards or rules interpretation and implementation. Lawyers may resist principles-based regulation due to its inherent reliance on purposive rule interpretation (Black, 2008: 439–440). However, the regulatory lawyers in this study still represented a crucial professional group for the functioning of the principles-based enforcement regime and the interpretation and implementation of the standard-setting principles. As Braithwaite (2002) predicted, a principles-based regime has advantages over detailed rules if there is no involvement by lawyers. The heavy involvement of the small and well-connected group of contentious regulatory lawyers, especially the ones representing larger institutions, challenges the capacity of principles-based enforcement frameworks to stem creative compliance.

Policy implications

The contributions of this study are mainly towards the scholarship, but the discussion presented here also has policy implications. The study shows that regulators are key proprietors of information: vast amounts of information flow towards regulators through information-gathering powers and self-reporting obligations (input) and out of regulators through regulatory transparency obligations and the use of disclosure on enforcement actions (output). This study has shown that post-crisis periods with more punitive and interventionist enforcement policies augment these flows through calls for enforcement agencies to be more transparent in their actions, including their sanctioning decisions, and to use disclosure powers more efficiently.

Policy responses should centre on addressing the limits of the informational input/output processes in view of the findings in this study. There are hazards behinds informational overload. Regulators need caution in designing and implementing regulatory frameworks based on significant demands for information. Though these may contribute towards overcoming informational asymmetries (Manning, 1989), paradoxically, they also contribute towards 'blinding' effects in the sense that informational overload may shade the 'real' extent of misconduct or the existence of misconduct altogether. The imbalance between the resources of public regulators and the industry is a well-established challenge for policymaking, but the growth of informational input further exacerbates this problem. Though regulators must rely on the industry for significant amounts of information to craft effective and efficient regulatory policies, any (in)capacities for proper assessment and follow-up on information that indicates non-compliance seriously affect the legitimacy of the regulatory regime. The risks are that regulators miss signals of systemic non-compliance issues, hidden across numerous inputs and within carefully crafted self-reporting submissions. Insights from other areas of regulation, both of business (e.g. the system of suspicious activities reporting) and of crime (e.g. the system of terrorism-related information gathering), show similar patterns in the extent of reporting and managing information. Therefore, in an age of increasing informational demands from regulators across regulatory fields, frameworks based on the gathering of significant amounts of information need careful planning and building in awareness of the potential for the reporting lines to be abused for creative compliance and detection avoidance through detection facilitation. The discussion is topical as there are live policy debates over the adoption of principles to self-report (and be open and cooperative) akin to Principle 11. For example, Ofgem, the UK energy regulator, has introduced a requirement that regulated energy suppliers must be 'open and cooperative', which includes a requirement to tell Ofgem, as soon as the supplier is aware of it, of any circumstance that Ofgem would reasonably expect notice of in order to perform its own functions, in particular where acts or omissions give rise to a likelihood of detriment to domestic customers.[1]

Further, movements towards greater transparency in regulatory decision-making are welcome, though the findings of this study require some recommendations to be made on devising quality disclosure systems. Reputational sanctions may be more effective and disclosure may result in better compliance if not just shaming but also 'appropriate' shaming is employed, enforcers are sensitive to the processes of *non-compliance construction*, and the responsiveness of enforcers to political and public demands when guiding disclosure is recognised and clearly distinguished. Whilst shaming might work (Braithwaite, 1989; van Erp, 2011), certain types of shaming might work better, and these require distinguishing between monetary costs and reputational costs from penalties and disclosure and a fuller understanding of the reputational concerns of corporations and the targeted audiences. The finding that corporations were more concerned about the wording of the

1 Ofgem Standard License Conditions 5A of the gas and electricity supply licences – Principle to be Open and Cooperative.

decision (where concessions could be made) rather than the monetary penalty (which was difficult to negotiate) has important implications for ascertaining the deterrence effects of disclosure. Deterrence might be more efficient if equal attention is placed on preserving the facts of the true extent and nature of the misconduct as on the size of the penalty. This will enable regulators to capitalise on the scandalising potential of wordings of enforcement notices more fully. Enforcement decision-making should be made sensitive to the pockets in the proceedings where the extent and effects of negative publicity can be diluted by the launching of corporate responses, especially through the 'professional embeddedness, resources and activities' (Reichman, 1992) of law firms. Moving the stage of publicity of enforcement decision-making earlier in the process (at the stage of investigations) represents a commendable way forward in providing an important deterrent mechanism and in preventing the ability of corporations to construct non-compliance. This interrupts the possibility of *mutual risk mitigation* practices and can defy the reputation-guided responses of resistance employed by the industry.

Bibliography

Abbott KW, Levi-Faur D and Snidal D (2017) Theorizing Regulatory Intermediaries: The RIT Model. *The ANNALS of the American Academy of Political and Social Science* 670(1): 14–35.

Ayres I and Braithwaite J (1992) *Responsive Regulation: Transcending the Deregulation Debate*. Oxford: Oxford University Press.

Black J (1997) *Rules and Regulators* (Oxford Socio-legal Studies). Oxford: Oxford University Press.

Black J (2003) Enrolling Actors in Regulatory Processes: Examples from UK Financial Services Regulation. *Public Law* 47: 62–90.

Black J (2008) Forms and Paradoxes of Principles-based Regulation. *Capital Markets Law Journal* 3(4): 425–457.

Black J, Hopper M and Band C (2007) Making a Success of Principles-based Regulation. *Law and Financial Markets Review* 1(3): 191–206.

Braithwaite J (1989) *Crime, Shame and Reintegration*. Cambridge: Cambridge University Press.

Braithwaite J (2002) Rules and Principles: A Theory of Legal Certainty. *Australian Journal of Legal Philosophy* 27: 47–82.

Braithwaite J (2008) *Regulatory Capitalism: How It Works, Ideas for Making It Work Better*. Northampton, MA: Edward Elgar Publishing.

Braithwaite J (2017) Types of Responsiveness. In: Drahos P (ed) *Regulatory Theory: Foundations and Applications*. Canberra: ANU Press.

Coffee JC, Jr (2006) *Gatekeepers: The Professions and Corporate Governance*. Oxford: Oxford University Press.

David L-F (2005) The Global Diffusion of Regulatory Capitalism. *The Annals of the American Academy of Political and Social Science* 598(1): 12–32.

David L-F (2011) Regulation and Regulatory Governance. In: David L-F (ed) *Handbook on the Politics of Regulation*. Cheltenham, UK: Edward Elgar Publishing, 3–21.

Edelman LB and Talesh SA (2011) To Comply or Not to Comply-That Isn't the Question: How Organizations Construct the Meaning of Compliance. In: Parker C and Nielsen VL (eds) *Explaining Compliance: Business Responses to Regulation*. Cheltenham, UK: Edward Elgar Publishing, 103–122.

FCA (2024a) *Attestations.* Available at: www.fca.org.uk/publications/consultation-papers/cp24-2-enforcement-guide-publicising-enforcement-investigations-new-approach

FCA (2024b) *CP24/2: Our Enforcement Guide and Publicising Enforcement Investigations – A New Approach.* Available at: www.fca.org.uk/publication/consultation/cp24-2.pdf

Ford CL (2008) New Governance, Compliance, and Principles-Based Securities Regulation. *American Business Law Journal* 45(1): 1–60.

Froud J, Nilsson A, Moran M and Williams K (2012) Stories and Interests in Finance: Agendas of Governance before and after the Financial Crisis. *Governance* 25(1): 35–59.

Haines F (2011) *The Paradox of Regulation: What Regulation Can Achieve and What It Cannot.* Cheltenham, UK: Edward Elgar Publishing.

Hutter BM (1997) *Compliance: Regulation and Environment: Oxford Socio-legal Studies.* Oxford, UK: Oxford University Press.

Hutter BM (2011) Negotiating Social, Economic and Political Environments: Compliance with Regulation within and beyond the State. In: Parker C and Nielsen VL (eds) *Explaining Compliance: Business Responses to Regulation.* Cheltenham, UK: Edward Elgar Publishing, 305–321.

Hutter BM and Lloyd-Bostock S (2017) *Regulatory Crises.* Cambridge University Press.

Jordana J and Levi-Faur D (eds) (2004) *The Politics of Regulation: Examining Regulatory Institutions and Instruments in the Governance Age.* Cheltenham, UK and Northampton, MA: Edward Elgar Publishing.

Kraakman R (1986) Gatekeepers: The Anatomy of Third-party Enforcement Strategy. *Journal of Law, Economics and Organisation* 2(1): 53–104.

Levi M (2009) Suite Revenge? The Shaping of Folk Devils and Moral Panics about White-Collar Crimes. *British Journal of Criminology* 49(1): 48–67.

Levitin AJ (2014) The Politics of Financial Regulation and the Regulation of Financial Politics: A Review Essay. *Harvard Law Review* 127(7): 1991–2068.

Lodge M and Wegrich K (2010) Letter to the Editor of Public Administration Review in Response to a Recent Symposium on Financial Regulatory Reform. *Public Administration Review* 70(2): 336–341.

Macrory R (2006) *Regulatory Justice: Making Sanctions Effective.* London: Better Regulation Executive.

Manning KP (1989) The Limits of Knowledge: A Note on the Role of Information in the Regulation of Complex Systems with Special Reference to Nuclear Power Generation. In: Hawkins K and Thomas J (eds) *Regulatory Policy-Making.* Pittsburgh: University of Pittsburgh Press, 49–87.

May PJ and Burby RJ (1998) Making Sense Out of Regulatory Enforcement. *Law & Policy* 20(2): 157–182.

May PJ and Winter S (1999) Regulatory Enforcement and Compliance: Examining Danish Agro-Environmental Policy. *Journal of Policy Analysis and Management* 18(4): 625–651.

McBarnet D (1991) Whiter Than White Collar Crime: Tax, Fraud Insurance and the Management of Stigma. *British Journal of Sociology* 42(3): 323–344.

McBarnet D and Whelan C (1999) *Creative Accounting and the Cross-eyed Javelin Thrower.* Chichester: John Wiley & Sons.

Moschella M and Tsingou E (2013) Regulating Finance after the Crisis: Unveiling the Different Dynamics of the Regulatory Process. *Regulation & Governance* 7(4): 407–416.

Parker C (1999) *Just Lawyers: Regulation and Access to Justice.* Oxford: Oxford University Press.

Picciotto S (2007) Constructing Compliance: Game-Playing, Tax Law and the Regulatory State. *Law and Policy* 29(1): 11–30.
Reichman N (1992) Moving Backstage: Uncovering the Role of Compliance Practices in Shaping Regulatory Policy. In: Schlegel K and Weisburd D (eds) *White-collar Crime Reconsidered*. Boston, MA: Northeastern University Press, 244–268.
Rex J (2020) Anatomy of Agency Capture: An Organizational Typology for Diagnosing and Remedying Capture. *Regulation & Governance* 14: 271–294.
Schlegel K (1990) *Just Deserts for Corporate Criminals*. Boston: Northeastern University Press.
Schmidt PD (2005) *Lawyers and Regulation: The Politics of the Administrative Process*. New York: Cambridge University Press.
Scott C (2004) Regulation in the Age of Governance: The Rise of the Post-regulatory State. In: Jordana J and David L-F (eds) *The Politics of Regulation: Institutions and Regulatory Reforms for the Age of Governance*. Cheltenham, UK: Edward Elgar Publishing, 145–174.
Snider L (2009) Accommodating Power: The 'Common Sense' of Regulators. *Social & Legal Studies* 18(2): 179.
Sparrow M (2000) *The Regulatory Craft: Controlling Risks, Solving Problems, and Managing Compliance*. Washington, DC: The Brookings Institute.
Tombs S and Whyte D (2013) The Myths and Realities of Deterrence in Workplace Safety Regulation. *British Journal of Criminology* 53(5): 746–763.
van der Heijden J (2017) Brighter and Darker Sides of Intermediation. *Annals of the American Academy of Political and Social Science* 670: 207–224.
van Erp JG (2011) Naming Without Shaming: The Publication of Sanctions in the Dutch Financial Market. *Regulation & Governance* 5(3): 287–308.

Index

Note: Please note that the numbers followed by 'fn' represents the footnotes.

For Product Safety Concerns and Information please contact our EU
representative GPSR@taylorandfrancis.com
Taylor & Francis Verlag GmbH, Kaufingerstraße 24, 80331 München, Germany

www.ingramcontent.com/pod-product-compliance
Ingram Content Group UK Ltd.
Pitfield, Milton Keynes, MK11 3LW, UK
UKHW020149200926
475702UK00016B/2622
9781032944265